POSITIVE PSYCHOTHERAPY

CLINICIAN MANUAL

D1711626

Tayyab Rashid

and

Martin Seligman

OXFORD
UNIVERSITY PRESS

Oxford University Press is a department of the University of Oxford. It furthers
the University's objective of excellence in research, scholarship, and education
by publishing worldwide. Oxford is a registered trade mark of Oxford University
Press in the UK and certain other countries.

Published in the United States of America by Oxford University Press
198 Madison Avenue, New York, NY 10016, United States of America.

© Oxford University Press 2018

CIP data is on file at the Library of Congress
ISBN 978–0–19–532538–6

9 8 7 6 5

Printed by Sheridan Books, Inc., United States of America

T.R: *To Zain, Zaid, & Afroze, the light of my eyes*

M.S: *To John Abela, Susan Nolen-Hoeksema, and Christopher Peterson, three superb students who died before they could know the full fruits of their work.*

CONTENTS

PART I
INTRODUCTION AND THEORETICAL FOUNDATIONS

PART II
SESSION-BY-SESSION PRACTICE

PREFACE

THE APPLICATION OF POSITIVE PSYCHOLOGY
IN CLINICAL SETTINGS

An unspoken and untested premise of psychotherapy-as-usual is that when a client is encouraged to talk at length about what is wrong, this client will somehow recover. Positive psychotherapy (PPT) takes the opposite approach. It encourages clients to recognize fully what is right and strong and good in their lives and to deploy what is best about them in order to buffer against mental disorders. Consider the following examples:

- *Emma, a young female obsessed with memories of trauma, musters the courage to discover that forgiveness helps as well as hurts.*
- *Alejandro, a middle-aged man with depression and suicidal ideation, sits in the psychiatric emergency room. He comes to notice that almost everyone else sitting there appears worse off than he is, and he realizes that he has enough internal resources to cope well with his troubles.*
- *Myriam, a female graduate student in her late 20s, experiences visual and auditory hallucinations that do not neatly fit into any diagnostic category. She goes back into therapy, having been referred to numerous specialists who cannot agree on a diagnosis.*

Over the past 15 years, these individuals, and hundreds of others, have come to positive psychotherapy (PPT) because this approach does not view them merely as wounded souls, fatigued bodies, and listless spirits. PPT assesses, appreciates, and amplifies what is good about clients—without minimizing their distress—and uses these strengths as the levers of healing.

- When Emma was ready to look at her trauma, PPT became a process of understanding the nuances of forgiveness—where it can help or hurt. She discovered that her strength of forgiveness defines her as a kind and empathic person.
- During PPT, Alejandro discovered that perspective is one of his signature strengths. He was able to determine that others are worse off than he is, and this understanding gave him the strength to look at and use the positives in his life.
- When asked what brought her back to therapy (despite the fact that our clinic doesn't have specialized services for her), Myriam found that PPT is the only place in the world that sees her beyond her symptoms and appreciates how her creativity and perseverance will allow her to finish her degree.

Psychotherapy has largely evolved as a remedial discipline mostly concerned with fixing and repairing weaknesses. In the pages that follow, you will learn that psychotherapy can be centered on exploring and cultivating genuine positive emotions, character strengths, meaning and purpose. The vignettes (cases) appearing in this manual show that despite being sad, stressed, anxious, ambivalent, or angry, clients are able to uncover and deploy their kindness, gratitude, zest, self-regulation, and, above all, hope and optimism. This manual tells these stories and frames a systematic structure for using positive skills to buffer against disorders. We believe that this manual describes a transformative process whereby cultivation of positive emotions, amplification of character strengths, pursuit of meaning, fostering positive relationships, and striving toward intrinsically motivating goals are central to the way clients, as well as clinicians, heal and grow.

Mental health professionals can use this manual with a number of clinical conditions that require flexibility and cultural considerations. Part I lays the theoretical foundations, while Part II guides clinicians step-by-step in the practices of PPT. Relevant clinical resources are listed at the end of each session as well as in the appendices at the end of this manual. There is also an online appendix (available at www.oup.com/ppt) that contains a large number of additional PPT-related resources.

PPT is new, a work in progress, still lacking large-scale definitive outcome studies. It is our highest hope that this book will lead to thorough evaluation of its promise.

ACKNOWLEDGMENTS

Numerous helping hands and kind hearts have contributed in curating this manual. We are thankful to Sarah Harrington of Oxford University Press for spearheading this project with the thoughtfulness and care it needed. Kate Scheinman's editorial acumen polished the manuscript immensely. The following individuals have helped in their own unique ways: Our heartfelt thanks go to Robert and Diane Ostermann, Jane Gillham, John Abela, Karen Reivich, Judy Saltzberg, Peter Schulman, James Pawelski, Angela Duckworth, Acacia Parks, H'Sien Hayward, Linda Newstead, Barbara Fredrickson, Denise Quinlan, Neal Mayerson, Ryan Neimeic, Robert McGrath, Dan Tamasulo, Juan Humberto Young, Hamid Peseschkian, Ruth Louden, Alexandra Love, Curtis Cole, Miriam Shuchman, Desmond Pouyat, George Vaillant, Rick Summers, Carol Kaufmann, Carolyn Lennox, Ruth Baumal, Judith Kaufmann, Amanda Uliaszek, Ryan Howes, Danielle Uy, Aryel Maharaj, Karen Young, Shafik Kamani, Gjylena Nexhipi, Noman Siddque, Wenbin Cai, Steve Holtje, Louisa Jewell, Tanya De Mello, John Hendry, Mike Slade, Beate Schrank, Simon Riches, Carol Yew, Samuel Ho, Michael Alexander, Sarah Spinks, Neil Docherty, Abdul Rauf, Faisal Nisar, Asif Saeed, Eman Bente Syed, Mehreen Raza, Timothy Gianotti, Robert Fazio, and our clients, who taught us how to heal amidst hurts.

Tayyab Rashid
Martin Seligman

POSITIVE PSYCHOTHERAPY

INTRODUCTION AND THEORETICAL FOUNDATIONS

I

POSITIVE PSYCHOTHERAPY

WHAT IS IT AND WHY DO WE NEED IT?

FOR MORE THAN A CENTURY, PSYCHOTHERAPY HAS been a place where clients discuss their troubles. Thousands of people each year attend motivational lectures, workshops, retreats, and courses, and more purchase self-help books and digital applications. The focus of these therapeutic ventures is based on the assumption that uncovering childhood trauma, untwisting faulty thinking, or restoring dysfunctional relationships is curative. This focus on the *negatives* makes intuitive sense, but as the authors of this manual, we believe that clinicians have lost sight of the importance of the *positives*. Psychotherapy does a good job of making clients feel less depressed and less anxious, but the well-being of clients is not an explicit goal of the therapy. Positive psychotherapy (PPT), on the other hand, is a therapeutic endeavor within positive psychology (PP) that aims to alleviate symptomatic stress by way of enhancing well-being.

This clinician's manual is divided into two parts:

- Part I provides the theoretical framework for PPT; explores character strengths; and concludes with practices, processes, and mechanisms of change.
- Part II contains 15 PPT sessions, including core concepts, guidelines, skills, and worksheets for practicing these skills. Each session includes a fit and flexibility section that presents various ways that PPT practices can work (without losing their core elements) given clients' specific situations. Each session includes at least one vignette as well as cross-cultural implications.

WHAT IS POSITIVE PSYCHOTHERAPY?

PPT is an emerging therapeutic approach that is broadly based on the principles of PP. PP studies the conditions and processes that enable individuals, communities, and institutions to flourish. It explores what works, what is right, and what can be nurtured (Rashid, Summers, & Seligman, 2015). PP's impact on areas of psychology can be ascertained from the results of an extensive systematic review (Donaldson, Dollwet, & Rao, 2015), which identifies 1,336 articles published between 1999 and 2013. Of these articles, more than 750 include empirical tests of PP theories, principles, and interventions.

PPT is the clinical or therapeutic arm of PP. PPT integrates symptoms with strengths, risks with resources, weaknesses with values, and regrets with hopes, in order to understand the inherent complexities of human experience in a balanced way. Without dismissing or minimizing the client's concerns, the PPT clinician empathically understands and attends to pain associated with trauma and simultaneously explores the potential for growth. We do not consider PPT to be a new genre of psychotherapy; rather, we see it as a therapeutic reorientation—a "build-what's-strong" model—that *supplements* the traditional "fix-what's-wrong" approach (Duckworth, Steen, & Seligman, 2005).

PPT is about more than positives. As PPT clinicians, we are not suggesting that other psychotherapies are negative, and, in fact, PPT is not meant to replace existing psychotherapies. Rather, PPT is an incremental change to balance therapeutic focus on weaknesses. Psychologically distressed clients can be better understood and served if they are taught to use their highest resources—both personal and interpersonal—to meet life's challenges. Knowing our personal strengths; learning the skills necessary to cultivate positive emotions; strengthening positive relationships; and imbuing our lives with meaning and purpose can be tremendously motivating, empowering, and therapeutic. The ultimate goal of PPT is to help clients learn concrete, applicable, personally relevant skills that best use their strengths to strive for engaged, satisfying, and meaningful lives. In achieving this goal, PPT expands the role of the clinician from one with a prescriptive authority to diagnose deficits to one who also actively facilitates growth, resilience, and well-being.

WHY DO WE NEED POSITIVE PSYCHOTHERAPY?

Psychotherapy is the central activity of mental health professionals (such as psychologists, psychiatrists, social workers, and counselors), and it draws on a wide spectrum of theoretical methods (Watkins, 2010). Across methods, psychotherapy has been shown to effectively ameliorate psychological distress (e.g., Castonguay, 2013; Seligman, 1995). It significantly outperforms placebo, and, in many cases, psychotherapy fares better in the long run than medication alone (e.g., Leykin & DeRubeis, 2009; Siddique et al., 2012). In fact, psychotherapy has been shown to be as effective as many empirically validated medical treatments, including almost all interventions in cardiology (e.g., beta-blocker, angioplasty, and statins), geriatric medicine, and asthma (Wampold, 2007). Empirically validated psychotherapies are available for dozens of psychological disorders, such as depression, schizophrenia, posttraumatic stress disorder, obsessive-compulsive disorder, phobias, panic disorder, and eating disorders (Barlow, 2008; Seligman, 1995). The Substance Abuse and Mental Health Services Administration's (SAMHSA) web site lists 145 manualized treatments for 84 of the more than 365 mental disorders (SAMSHA, 2015). Finer aspects of psychotherapy such as the therapeutic alliance, nuances of therapeutic communication, nonverbal language, therapist effects, treatment process, and the feedback process to and from the client have all been studied (Wampold, 2001; Watkins, 2010).

The focus in traditional psychotherapy on what has gone wrong has resulted in treatments that reduce symptoms for many disorders. However, we believe that psychotherapists' intensive focus on negatives has reached an impasse: Between 20% and 30% of clients experience little change during therapy, with a further 5% to 10% of clients actually deteriorating during treatment (Hansen, Lambert, & Forman, 2002; Lambert, 2013). Psychotherapy, in our view, therefore faces a significant barrier, what we call the "65% barrier," which means that approximately 65% of clients in psychotherapy see any benefit from the treatment. We believe that a strengths-based approach such as PPT can improve the effectiveness of psychotherapy by

- expanding the scope of psychotherapy,
- broadening beyond the medical model,
- expanding the outcome of psychotherapy, and
- attenuating the impact on the clinician.

Expanding the Scope of Psychotherapy

The tendency for clinicians to skew focus toward the negatives in psychotherapy is understandable. Evolution has endowed us with brains that are oriented toward and more strongly responsive to negative experiences than to positive ones (e.g., Baumeister, Bratslavsky, Finkenauer, & Vohs, 2001; Rozin & Royzman, 2001). This innate propensity for negativity helped us secure shelter, food, and mates in the evolutionary past. The human mind spends a disproportionate amount of time thinking about what goes wrong and not nearly enough time thinking about what goes right in our lives. In essence, negatives largely define the function of psychotherapy. While negatives serve an important function in psychotherapy, they also limit its scope.

As human beings, we want lives that are imbued with purpose and meaning (Duckworth, Steen, & Seligman, 2005). With increasing awareness of mental health concerns, people with mental illness are becoming more vocal in describing what their lives are like and what would help them move beyond the role of a patient with a psychiatric disorder (Secker, Membrey, Grove, & Seebohm, 2002). Such clients want a full recovery, which includes hope, positive relationships, and meaningful pursuits (Secker, Membrey, Grove, & Seebohm, 2002; Slade, 2010). Psychotherapy presents an unparalleled opportunity to scaffold the personal development of clients through the cultivation of their strengths, and this process should not be squandered by exclusive attention to bettering symptoms or deficits. Recovery is not ameliorating or eliminating problems; it is assessing and enhancing strengths, skills, abilities, talents, and aptitudes (Crits-Christoph et al., 2008; Le Boutillier et al., 2011; Rapp & Goscha, 2006).

Broadening Beyond the Medical Model

Psychotherapy continues to operate on a medical model in which mental disorders are brain diseases caused by neurotransmitter dysregulation, genetic anomalies, and defects in brain structure and function (Deacon, 2013; Maddux, 2008). David Elkin (2009) and many others have noted that superimposition of the medical model in psychotherapy is a problem. In the medical model, a physician diagnoses an illness on the basis of symptoms and administers treatment designed to cure the illness. In psychotherapy, both illness and treatment often depend on interpersonal contextual features—which have little to do with medicine—yet the medical model remains the dominant descriptive framework because it lends psychotherapy a level of cultural respectability and economic advantages that other descriptive systems do not (Elkins, 2009). However, unlike medical disorders, psychiatric disorders cannot be traced to simple etiologic agents.

James Maddux (2008) has noted that the influence of the medical model on psychotherapy can be ascertained by the terms that are most commonly associated with psychotherapy, including symptoms, dysfunction, diagnoses, disorder, and treatment. This influence disproportionately dictates clinical focus on disorders and dysfunctions and not on health. Rather than abandoning the medical model of psychotherapy, which is thoroughly ingrained in training, research, and professional organizations, we suggest incorporating a strengths-based approach to make psychotherapy more balanced. Evidence shows that strengths can become active ingredients in treatment for serious afflictions such as psychosis (Schrank et al., 2016), suicidal ideation (Johnson et al., 2010), and borderline personality disorder (Uliaszek et al., 2016). By infusing and integrating strengths, the field of psychotherapy can enrich the experience of both clients and clinicians. Slade (2010) argues that such an expansion can also offer clinicians the opportunity to challenge stigma and discrimination and to promote societal well-being. However, expanding the model of psychotherapy from deficit to strengths will require changes in both assessment and treatment. This shift in the role of the clinician could become the norm rather than the exception in the 21st century. Alex Wood and Nicholas Tarrier (2010) have suggested that the understanding and treatment of clinical levels of distress ought to be balanced with an equally weighted focus on the positives because

- Strengths can buffer against the effect of negative life events on distress, potentially preventing the development of psychological disorder (Huta & Hawley, 2008; Marques, Pais-Ribeiro, & Lopez, 2011).
- Strengths have been linked to several indicators of well-being, such as quality of life (Proctor et al., 2011), psychological well-being, and subjective well-being (Govindji & Linley, 2007), and almost all character strengths are related to academic satisfaction, grade point average (Lounsbury et al., 2009), and mental health (Littman-Ovadia & Steger, 2010; for a review see Quinlan et al., 2012).
- Strengths-based interventions yield a number of benefits. Strengths predict psychological disorder above and beyond the predictive power of the presence of negative characteristics or symptoms (Wood et al., 2009). Strengths-based interventions confer a number of benefits (for a review see Quinlan et al., 2012).

- Enhancement of strengths may be more efficient and acceptable for clients from diverse cultural backgrounds (Harris, Thoresen, & Lopez, 2007; Pedrotti, 2011).
- Character strengths of social intelligence and kindness are indicative of less stigma toward people with mental health concerns. Open-minded people do not hold individuals diagnosed with mental health disorders personally responsible for acquiring the disorders (Vertilo & Gibson, 2014).

Expanding the Outcome of Psychotherapy

Psychotherapy-outcome researchers have emphasized that indicators of quality of life and psychological well-being should be incorporated into the definition of recovery (Fava & Ruini, 2003). Larry Davidson and his colleagues have used the term "recovery-oriented care" to describe treatment that cultivates the positive elements of a person's life—such as assets, aspirations, hopes, and interests—at least as much as it attempts to ameliorate and decrease symptoms (Davidson, Shahar, Lawless, Sells, & Tondora, 2006).

A thematic analysis of 30 international documents offering recovery-oriented practice guidance recommends that the notion of recovery be expanded beyond symptom remission to include well-being. The analysis recommends that recovery include assessing and using strengths and natural supports to inform assessment, reviews, care plans, and goals and that care and treatment make active use of these strengths (Le Boutillier et al., 2011). Defining and expanding recovery also expands the role of the mental health professional, with greater emphasis on partnership with the client (Slade, 2010). Schrank and Slade (2007) conceptualize recovery as a deeply personal, unique process in which one's attitude, values, feelings, goals, skills, and roles change. Full recovery means that, despite limitations caused by psychological distress, one is able to live a fulfilling and satisfying life. Full recovery also involves developing new meaning and purpose in one's life as one grows beyond the catastrophic effects of mental illness.

Attenuating the Impact on the Clinician

The very nature of psychotherapy requires mental health clinicians to listen to graphically detailed descriptions of sometimes horrific events and to bear witness to the psychological (and sometimes physical) aftermath of acts of intense cruelty and/or violence. If psychotherapy largely entails confronting negative memories and adverse experiences—subtle and severe—the cumulative experience of such an empathic engagement can have negative effects on clinicians. Evidence has shown that these effects manifest through emotional exhaustion, depersonalization, and a lack of personal accomplishment—causing burnout and compassion fatigue (Berzoff & Kita, 2010; Deighton, Gurris, & Traue, 2007; Hart, 2014). Exploring what sustains the well-being of clinicians and what makes them exemplary, Harrison and Westwood (2009) find an overarching positive orientation conveyed through an ability to maintain trust in three attributes: (a) the self as good enough—that is, the clinician has confidence in her expertise; (b) the therapeutic change process; and (c) the world as a place of beauty and potential (despite and in addition to pain and suffering). These three attributes are essential to PPT's theoretical orientation and are promoted throughout in practices.

THE 65% BARRIER

As noted earlier in this chapter, some clients do not receive any benefit from psychotherapy and others (between 5% and 10%) actually deteriorate during therapy (Lambert, 2007). Let's discuss this barrier as it applies to the most common form of psychopathology: depression—a disorder sometimes called "the common cold of mental illness." Consider two treatments that we know are effective: cognitive behavioral therapy and the use of selective serotonin reuptake inhibitors such as Prozac, Zoloft, and Lexapro. Each treatment produces about a 65% response rate, and we know that this response incorporates a placebo effect that ranges from 45% to 55% (e.g., Rief et al., 2011); the more realistic the placebo, the greater the placebo response. These numbers crop up over and over. A recent 30-year meta-analytic review of randomized, placebo-controlled trials of antidepressants documents that a high percentage of treatment effect can be attributed to the placebo response (Kirsch et al., 2002; Undurraga & Baldessarini, 2017).

Why is there a 65% barrier, and why are the specific effects of therapy so small? We believe this is because behavioral change is difficult for people in general, and it is especially difficult for clients who are seeking therapy, who may lack motivation, who have comorbid issues, or who live in unhealthy environments that are not amenable to change. As a result, many clients continue to behave in entrenched and maladaptive ways, and the notion of change can be perceived as threatening and impossible to achieve.

In fact many clinicians have given up on the notion of cure. Managed care and limited treatment budgets have sometimes resulted in situations in which mental health professionals devote their time and talents to firefighting rather than to fire prevention. Their focus is almost entirely on crisis management and providing cosmetic treatments. The fact that treatment is often only cosmetic partly explains the 65% barrier (Seligman, 2006).

In traditional, deficit-oriented psychotherapy, many clinicians believe that one way to minimize negative emotions, especially bottled-up anger, is to express them, with the assumption that if anger is not expressed, it will manifest itself through other symptoms. The therapeutic literature is filled with phrases such as, "hit a pillow," "blow off steam," and "let it out" that illustrate this kind of hydraulic thinking (Seligman, 2002a). However, this approach leaves current psychotherapy as largely a science of *victimology* that portrays clients as passive responders to circumstances. Drive, instinct, and need create inevitable conflicts that can only partially be relieved through venting. In our view, venting is at best a cosmetic remedy and at worse a treatment that may trigger amplified anger, resentment, and heart disease (Chida & Steptoe, 2009).

ALTERNATIVES TO TRADITIONAL PSYCHOTHERAPEUTIC APPROACHES

Learning to function well in the face of psychological distress is an alternative approach that is embraced by PPT. Depression, anxiety, and anger often result from heritable personality traits that can be improved but not eliminated. All negative emotions and negative personality traits have strong biological boundaries, and it is unrealistic to expect that psychotherapy can overcome these limits. The best that traditional psychotherapy can do with its palliative approach is to help clients live in the uppermost part of these set ranges of depression, anxiety, or anger. Consider Abraham Lincoln and Winston Churchill, two historical figures who suffered from serious mental illness (Pediaditakis, 2014). They were both enormously high-functioning human beings who functioned well despite experiencing significant mental health issues. Perhaps they functioned well because they utilized their strengths. Psychotherapy needs to develop interventions that teach clients to utilize their strengths to function well in the presence of symptoms. We are convinced that PPT can help clients function well and possibly break the 65% barrier.

There is another critical reason to challenge and change traditional approaches to psychotherapy. A good life, the ultimate goal of psychotherapy, cannot be fully achieved through the traditional deficit-oriented framework. For example, in a study that controlled for these negative characteristics, researchers found that people who had few positive characteristics (e.g., hope and optimism, self-efficacy, and gratitude) had twice the risk of developing depression (Wood & Joseph, 2010). Likewise, the presence of character strengths (e.g., hope, appreciation of beauty and excellence, and spirituality) has been shown to make a significant contribution toward recovery from depression (Huta & Hawley, 2008). Hope and optimism (Carver, Scheier, & Segerstrom, 2010) as well as gratitude (Flinchbaugh, Moore, Chang, & May, 2012) have all been shown to lead to lower levels of stress and depression.

POSITIVE INTERVENTIONS AND THEORETICAL ASSUMPTIONS

PSYCHOLOGICAL INTERVENTIONS THAT ATTEND TO POSITIVES ARE few and far between. We begin this chapter by briefly reviewing early interventions and related treatments, which serve as precursors to contemporary positive psychology interventions (PPIs) and positive psychotherapy (PPT).

A HISTORICAL VIEW OF POSITIVE PSYCHOLOGICAL INTERVENTIONS

Scientists, philosophers, and sages have tried to describe happiness, well-being, and flourishing from many perspectives. For example, Confucius believed that the meaning of life lies in ordinary human existence combined with discipline, education, and harmonious social relationships. To achieve happiness, the pursuit of a virtuous life is the necessary condition according to Socrates, Plato, and Aristotle. Prior to the Second World War, psychology had three clear missions: curing psychopathology, making the lives of all people more productive and fulfilling, and identifying and nurturing high talent (Seligman & Csikszentmihalyi, 2000). William James noted in *Varieties of Religious Experiences* (1902) that courage, hope, and trust can conquer doubt, fear, and worry. John Dewey (1934) underscored the need of artistic-aesthetic exchanges between people and environment. Henry Murray (1938) posited that the study of positive, joyful, and fruitful experiences is essential to the understanding of human beings.

Immediately after the Second World War, largely because of economic and political exigencies, the assessment and treatment of psychopathology became the more narrow main focus of psychology. However, humanistic psychologists such as Carl Rogers, Abraham Maslow, Henry Murray, Gordon Allport, and Rollo May continued to advocate for positive approaches to psychotherapy. They tried to describe the good life and to identify ways our inherent tendency toward growth can facilitate this life. Maslow (1970) pointed out:

> The science of psychology has been far more successful on the negative than on the positive side. It has revealed to us much about man's shortcomings, his illness, his sins, but little about his potentiates, his virtues, his achievable aspirations, or his full psychological height. It is as if psychology has voluntarily restricted itself to only half its rightful jurisdiction, and that, the darker, meaner half. (p. 354)

Marie Jahoda discussed the concept of positive mental health in the 1950s (Jahoda, 1958). Michael Fordyce turned these notions into a few positive interventions and tested them with college students (Fordyce, 1983). Solution-focused therapy, developed in the 1980s by Steve de Shazer and Ing Kim Berg (De Shazer et al., 1986; Hawkes, 2011), focuses on generating solutions and goals from changeable options. Well-being therapy integrates cognitive behavioral therapy with elements of well-being and has been shown to be effective in treating affective and anxiety disorders (Ruini & Fava, 2009). Similarly, Frisch's quality of-life therapy integrates cognitive therapy with positive psychology ideas and has been shown to be efficacious with depressed clients (Frisch, 2013). However, given that there have been so few positive-focused interventions compared to the overwhelming number of deficit-oriented treatments, psychotherapists have learned a lot about damage, deficits, and dysfunction and very little about the ingredients for a good life and how these can be nurtured.

POSITIVE PSYCHOLOGY INTERVENTIONS AND POSITIVE PSYCHOTHERAPY

PPT is a therapeutic approach based broadly on the principles of positive psychology. In other words, PPT is the clinical and therapeutic work within positive psychology. PPT is made up of 14 specific practices which were empirically validated as PPIs, either on their own or in sets of two or three practices (Seligman et al., 2005). After empirical validation, these practices were organized into a cohesive protocol and called positive psychotherapy (PPT). In this section we evaluate the empirical standing of the PPIs before describing PPT in detail.

Often delivered online, PPIs are relatively simple strategies to increase well-being. Martin Seligman and colleagues empirically validated three PPIs (*Three good things*, also known as *Blessings Journal, Using Signature Strengths in a New Way*, and *Gratitude Visit*; Seligman et al., 2005). Independent lines of research have replicated these findings (Gander et al., 2013; Mitchell et al., 2009; Mongrain, Anselmo-Mathews, 2012; Odou & Vella-Brodrick, 2013; Schueller & Parks, 2012; Duan et al., 2014; Schotanus-Dijkstra et al., 2015; Vella-Brodrick, Park, & Peterson, 2009).

Ever since their initial validation, PPIs have been applied widely (e.g., Parks et al., 2012; Proyer et al., 2013; Quinlan et al., 2015; Winslow et al., 2016). They have provided a new impetus to somewhat parallel ongoing theoretical and clinical attempts to foster well-being and positive attributes such as gratitude (Emmons & McCullough, 2003), forgiveness (Worthington, & Drinkard, 2000), savoring (Bryant, 1989), strengths (Buckingham & Clifton, 2001; Saleebey, 1997), psychological well-being (Ryff & Singer, 1996; Ryff, Singer, & Davidson, 2004), and empathy (Long et al., 1999).

Both the theoretical framework and the applied implications of PPIs are attracting scholarship in the form of edited volumes. *The Handbook of Positive Psychology Interventions* (Parks & Schueller, 2014) provides a comprehensive view of established, new, and emerging PPIs. Alex Wood and Judith Johnson have recently published a comprehensive edited volume, *The Handbook of Positive Clinical Psychology* (Wood & Johnson, 2016). It offers an integrated perspective of well-being as it relates to personality, psychopathology, and psychological treatments by examining clinical conditions such as depression, emotional dysregulation, anxiety, posttraumatic stress, suicidality, and psychosis. The *Handbook* also discusses positive psychology-based clinical treatments such as PPT (Rashid & Howes, 2016), well-being therapy (Fava, 2016), and quality of life therapy (Frisch, 2016) and reinterprets traditional treatments such as acceptance commitment therapy, client-centered therapy, and schema therapy from the vantage point of positive psychology.

How PPIs have contributed to the development and refinement of PPT protocol can be seen in Table 2.1: Selected Positive Psychology Interventions in Clinical Settings. This table lists 20 PPIs, applied in a variety of clinical and health care settings with adults. These PPIs focus on core clinical issues such as depression, anxiety, eating disorders, suicidality, and conduct problems. These independent lines of research clearly demonstrate that PPIs are effective in reducing symptoms. Notably, it appears that through the use of focused constructs (such as gratitude, hope, kindness, forgiveness, and character strengths), PPIs can be used in active or adjunct treatment of a wide range of health concerns, such as cardiac problems and rehabilitation, rehabilitation following stroke, brain injury, Type II diabetes, and breast cancer. The PPIs were applied cross-culturally, including in Hong Kong, Indonesia, Iran, Korea, Australia, Germany, and Spain.

The relevant PPT practice used with each study is also listed in Table 2.1. This information is particularly important for clinicians because it demonstrates that although PPT is a new and evolving treatment modality, such practices have an evidence base.

Table 2.1

SELECTED POSITIVE PSYCHOLOGY INTERVENTIONS IN CLINICAL SETTINGS[a]

No.	Source	Clinical Focus and Relevant PPT Practice	Description (Sample, Methodology)	Outcome
1	Huffman et al., 2011	Cardiac Concerns Gratitude Expressions Gratitude Letter Best Possible Self Three Acts of Kindness	An eight-week PP telemedicine intervention for cardiac patients was piloted.	PPI intervention appeared to be feasible and was well accepted in a cohort of patients with acute cardiac illness
2	Fung et al., 2011	Caregiving Stress Character Strengths, Counting Blessings Gratitude Visit Using Strengths to Resolve Problems	Parents and caregivers of children with cerebral palsy, at an orthopedic and traumatology department of a hospital in Hong Kong, completed four weekly sessions	Participants exhibited a significantly lower level of parental stress and higher hope level both after the four intervention sessions and at the booster session. Their perceived social support increased when the group was ongoing but not after it ended.
3	Cheavens et al., 2006	Depression Character Strengths	Thirty-four adults meeting criteria for MDD were randomized to 16 weeks of treatment, with one group focusing on strengths and one group on deficits or compensation, in addition to CBT.	Results showed that the client in group that focused on strengths of clients, showed a faster rate of symptom change compared to the deficit or compensation approach
4	Flückiger et al., 2008	Anxiety Client's sources, such as individual strengths, abilities, and readiness are incorporated in the treatment	The study, conducted in Germany, explored weather focusing on patient's resources (competencies), especially in the initial phases of therapy, had an impact on treatment outcome	Results showed that focusing on competencies was associated with a positive treatment outcome, irrespective of pretreatment distress, rapid response of well-being and symptom reduction, as well as the therapists' professional experience and treatment duration.
5	Ho, Yeung, & Kwok, 2014	Depression Story of Happiness, Noticing gratitude in everyday life, Identifying optimistic way of thinking, Savoring, Curiosity	Seventy-four participants from community and nursing homes in Hong Kong, aged 63 to 105 years, completed PPIs in nine-week group settings	Results showed a reduction in depressive symptoms and increased the levels of life satisfaction, gratitude, and happiness.

Table 2.1

CONTINUED

No.	Source	Clinical Focus and Relevant PPT Practice	Description (Sample, Methodology)	Outcome
6	Andrewes, Walker, & O'Neill, 2014	Brain Injury Three Good Things Signature Strengths	Ten patients with brain injury were randomly assigned to intervention or control group.	After 12 weeks, intervention group showed increase in happiness and improved self-concept
7	Huffman et al., 2014	Suicidality Gratitude Visit Character Strengths Best Possible Self Counting Blessing Meaningful Activities	The study assessed the feasibility and acceptability of nine PP exercises delivered to patients hospitalized for suicidal thoughts or behaviors and to secondarily explore the relative impact of the exercises	Results showed overall effects of PPIs, accounting for age, order, and skipped exercises. Both gratitude and personal strengths showed effectiveness
8	Kerr, O'Donovan, & Pepping, 2015	Psychiatric concerns including depression, anxiety, substance abuse, and such Gratitude and Kindness	Participants were 48 adults at one of seven outpatient psychology clinics in Queensland, Australia, who were on a waiting-list for individual psychological treatment. They were assigned to two-week self-administered interventions	Results demonstrated that a brief PPI can reliably cultivate the emotional experiences of gratitude but not kindness in this brief period. However, both the gratitude and kindness interventions built a sense of connectedness, enhanced satisfaction with daily life and optimism, and reduced anxiety compared to a placebo condition.
9	Huffman et al., 2015	Type-2 Diabetes Gratitude for Positive Events Personal Strengths Gratitude Letter Acts of kindness	In this proof-of-concept study, 15 patients (mean age 60.1 ± 8.8 years) with Type II diabetes and cardiovascular risks completed PP exercises.	Results suggest that higher levels of positive affect, optimism, and well-being was associated with improved health behavior adherence (and outcomes) in patients with chronic illnesses like Type II diabetes.
10	Huynh et al., 2015	Conduct problems resulting in incarceration Activities and assignments based on PERMA incorporated in Good Lives Model	This PPI, the Positive Re-Entry in Corrections Program, offered through weekly lectures, discussions, and homework, focused on teaching offenders skills that facilitate re-entry into the community.	Results indicated significant differences on pre- and postintervention scores on measures of gratitude, hope, and life satisfaction.

(continued)

Table 2.1
CONTINUED

No.	Source	Clinical Focus and Relevant PPT Practice	Description (Sample, Methodology)	Outcome
11	Ko & Hyun, 2015	Depression Writing about Good Things, Positive Feedback, Letter of Gratitude	Fifty-three adults diagnosed with the MDD, received eight-week PPIs or no treatment control, in a hospital setting in Korea.	Group receiving PPIs reported significant decline on scores on measure of depression and significant increase on scores on measures of hope and self-esteem.
12	Lambert D'raven, Moliver, & Thompson, 2015	Depression Writing Gratitude Letters Engaging in good deeds	In a six-week pilot program, 76 patients in a primary health care setting with symptoms of depression participated in an intervention which included engaging in good deeds and writing gratitude letters.	Results showed scores improved from baseline to six-month follow-up for health, vitality, mental health, and the effects of mental and physical health on daily activities.
13	Retnowati et al., 2015	Depression following a natural disaster Hope Intervention Goal identification, Planning, Keeping the Motivation	Intervention group was 31 adults, affected directly by eruptions of Mount Merapi, Indonesia, who received four two-hour sessions on Hope Intervention. They were compared to an untreated control group ($n = 31$)	The intervention group at the posttreatment showed a significant decrease in depression.
14	Chaves et al., 2017	Depression Gratitude Savoring Character Strengths Kindness	In this randomized and controlled trial, followed by structured diagnosis, clients with MDD were assigned to either a group CBT ($n = 49$) or Group PPI ($n = 47$)	Clients in both groups showed significant pre-to-postinterventions changes on all major outcomes but no significant differences were found between two treatments.
15	Nikrahan et al., 2016	Coronary bypass Gratitude and Forgiveness Signature Strengths Best Possible Selves Positive Social Interactions Reframe Past	Sixty-nine patients with recent coronary artery bypass graft surgery or percutaneous intervention were randomized to a PPI or a wait-list control group. Risk biomarkers were assessed at baseline, post-intervention (7 weeks) and at 15-week follow-up.	The PPI group had significantly lower high sensitivity and significantly lower cortisol awakening response at seven weeks when compared with control participants.
16	Sanjuan et al., 2016	Cardiac Rehabilitation Noticing Good Things, Signature Strengths Best Possible Self Expressing Gratitude Acts of Kindness	Cardiac patients ($n = 108$) in Spain, were randomly assigned to a control group (regular rehabilitation program) or the well-being program and rehabilitation program.	After controlling for functional capacity, the well-being program and rehabilitation group reported a significantly less negative affect than the rehabilitation group alone.

Table 2.1

CONTINUED

No.	Source	Clinical Focus and Relevant PPT Practice	Description (Sample, Methodology)	Outcome
17	Wong et al., 2018	Psychiatric Distress Gratitude Letters	Adults ($n = 293$) seeking psychotherapy were randomly assigned to (a) control (psychotherapy only), (b) a psychotherapy plus expressive writing, and (c) a psychotherapy plus gratitude writing.	Participants in the gratitude condition wrote letters expressing gratitude to others. Participants in the gratitude condition reported significantly better mental health than those in the expressive and control conditions.
18	Harrison, Khairulla, & Kikoler, 2016	Eating Disorder Cultivation of Positive Emotions Character Strengths	Eight female inpatients aged 11 to 18 years, completed a positivity group and were assessed before, after and at six-month follow-up	Meaningful improvement was reported by 75% of patients in subjective happiness and 87.5% in life satisfaction
19	Terrill et al., 2016	Rehabilitation following stroke Expressing Gratitude Practicing Kindness	Participants were couples consisting of one partner who had a stroke >6 months ago and a cohabiting partner/caregiver. One or both partner(s) reported depressive symptoms. Intervention was an eight-week self-administered behavioral PPI, completing two activities alone and two together each week	Five couples completed the program (83% retention). Participants engaged in activities for at least six out of eight weeks and reported being were "very satisfied" with the intervention (M = 3.5 out of 4)
20	Muller et al., 2016	Chronic pain and a physical disability Expressing Gratitude Acts of kindness Forgiveness Flow Taking care of body	Individuals with spinal cord injury, multiple sclerosis, neuromuscular disease, or post-polio syndrome and chronic pain were randomly assigned to a PP or a control condition. Participants in the PP group completed a personalized PPI while the participants in the control group write about life for eight weeks.	The PP group reported significant pre- to postintervention improvements in pain intensity, pain control, pain catastrophizing, pain interference, life satisfaction, positive affect, and depression. Improvements in life satisfaction, depression, pain intensity, pain interference, and pain control were maintained to the 2.5-month follow-up.

Note: PP = positive psychology; PPI = positive psychology intervention; CBT = cognitive behavioral therapy; MDD = major depressive disorder.
[a] Listed chronologically by year of publication.

Further, reviewing this table will help clinicians to adapt the PPT model to address the specific clinical needs of their clients. For example, based on emerging evidence, clinicians can decide which practice is more effective for clients with eating concerns, how the *Gratitude Letter* or *Gratitude Visit* can be executed cross-culturally, or which practice may not be appropriate for clients dealing with trauma.

The theoretical underpinnings of PPIs, their potential mechanism of change, and their role in explaining clinical conditions have also been explored. These include gratitude as a counter to the pernicious effects of depression (Wood, Maltby, Gillett, Linley, & Joseph, 2008), hope as a change mechanism in the treatment of posttraumatic stress disorder (Gilman, Schumm, & Chard, 2012), the therapeutic role of spirituality and meaning in psychotherapy (Steger & Shin, 2010; Worthington, Hook, Davis, & McDaniel, 2011), and forgiveness as a gradual process of exercising one's right to take revenge or to let go of anger (Harris et al., 2006; Worthington, 2005). Other studies have documented the relationship between creativity and bipolar disorder (Murray & Johnson, 2010), positive emotions and social anxiety (Kashdan et al., 2006), and social relationships and depression (Oksanen et al., 2010). Fitzpatrick and Stalikas (2008) suggest that positive emotions powerfully predict therapeutic change. Other converging scientific evidence shows that positive emotions do not simply reflect success and health; they also produce success and health by adaptively changing attitudes and mindsets (Fredrickson, 2009).

Overall effectiveness and relevance of PPIs have also been explored through several reviews. These reviews synthesize theoretical strands and offer important clinical implications regarding the application of PPIs. Twelve of these reviews are presented in Table 2.2: Review of Positive Interventions with Clinical Implications. These include two meta-analyses published on the overall effectiveness of PPIs. The first meta-analysis conducted by Sin and Lyubomirsky (2009) of 51 positive interventions including both clinical and nonclinical samples found that positive interventions are effective, with moderate effect sizes in significantly decreasing symptoms of depression (mean $r = 0.31$) and enhancing well-being (mean $r = 0.29$). The second meta-analysis, by Bolier and her colleagues (2013), involved 6,139 participants (including 19 studies from Sin and Lyubomirsky). It reported that PPIs reduced depression with small effect sizes (mean $r = 0.23$) but enhanced well-being with moderate effect sizes ($r = 0.34$). Exploring the effectiveness of 40 PPIs, Hone, Jarden, and Schofield (2015) used a standardized framework: RE-AIM, evaluating an intervention's **R**each, **E**fficacy, **A**doption, **I**mplementation, and **M**aintenance (Glasgow, Vogt, & Boles, 1999; National Collaborating Centre for Methods and Tools, 2008). RE-AIM evaluates the representativeness of study samples and settings, costs, and endurance of effects at individual and institutional levels. According to RE-AIM, PPI scores varied substantially: with Reach 64%, Efficacy 73%, Adoption 84%, Implementation 58%, and Maintenance 16%. Two meta-analyses using positive emotions—one with behavioral activation (Mazzucchelli, Kane, & Rees, 2009) and another with mindfulness-based approaches (Casellas-Grau & Vives, 2014)—demonstrated that strengths-based approaches can enhance well-being.

Other reviews have explored the effectiveness of specific positive attributes such as positive emotions in emotional regulation (Quoidbach, Mikolajczak, & Gross, 2015) and the effectiveness of specific strengths (gratitude and kindness) in symptom reduction and in enhancing well-being (D'raven & Pasha-Zaidi, 2014; Drvaric et al., 2015). Other reviews have looked at how positive attributes affect the management of physical health problems (Macaskill, 2016), breast cancer and gratitude (Ruini, & Vescovelli, 2013), and the identification of robust outcome measures (Stoner, Orrell, & Spector, 2015). The relevance of PPIs in complex situations such as trauma and war has also been explored (Al-Krenawi et al., 2011), as well as their relevance to neuroscience (Kapur et al., 2013).

Louise Lambert D'raven and Pasha-Zaidi (2016) have reviewed the relevance of positive interventions utilizing character strengths such as gratitude, savoring, self-compassion,

Table 2.2

REVIEW OF POSITIVE INTERVENTIONS WITH CLINICAL IMPLICATIONS[a]

	Source	Review Description	Salient Findings
1	Sin & Lyubomirsky, 2009	**Meta-Analysis:** Includes 51 PPIs with 4,266 individuals, exploring PPI effectiveness and to provide practical guidance to clinicians.	Results indicated that PP interventions significantly enhanced well-being (mean $r = 0.5$) and decreased depressive symptoms (mean $r = 0.31$).
2	Mazzucchelli, Kane, & Rees, 2010	**Meta-Analysis:** The study examined the effect of BA on well-being. Twenty studies with a total of 1,353 participants were included.	The pooled effect size (Hedges' g) indicated that the difference in well-being between BA and control conditions at posttest was 0.52. BA would seem to provide a ready and attractive intervention for promoting the well-being of a range of populations in both clinical and nonclinical settings.
3	Quinlan, Swain, & Vella-Brodrick, 2012	**Review:** A review of eight studies that explicitly sought to teach or use a strengths classification to enhance well-being and used pre- and postintervention measures and a comparison group.	Review found that interventions work better when they ask participants to plan, to visualize a different future, and implicitly or explicitly, to set goals. Goals related to one's motivation, relationships, and autonomy are more likely to be accomplished. Longer interventions are more effective than shorter ones.
4	Bolier et al., 2013	**Meta-analysis:** A review of 39 randomized published studies, including 7 clinical, involving 6,139 participants.	The meta-analysis found a standardized mean difference of 0.34 for subjective well-being, 0.20 for psychological well-being, and 0.23 for depression, indicating small effects for PPIs.
5	Casellas-Grau & Vives, 2014	**Systematic Review:** Focused on 16 studies including mindfulness-based approaches, expression of positive emotions, spiritual interventions, hope therapy, and meaning-making interventions.	PPIs applied to patients and survivors of breast cancer were found to be able to promote positive aspects.
6	D'raven & Pasha-Zaidi, 2014	**Review:** Geared toward counseling practitioners, this review explores a sampling of PPIs such as savoring, gratitude, and self-compassion to describe why, how, and under what conditions these PPIs are effective and for whom they work optimally.	The review concluded that PPIs can contribute to greater well-being. However, important considerations such as fit, timing, and culture are to be considered and more is not always better.
7	Drvaric et al., 2015	**Critical Review:** This review of 11 studies explored the relevance and effectiveness of strengths-based therapeutic approaches in treating those at clinical risk for developing psychosis.	Positive coping skills and resilience emerged as the protective factors that may mitigate against high levels of psychological stress, suggesting that resilience-boosting may be efficacious in enhancing well-being and promoting adaptive mental health for clinical high risk for psychosis.

(continued)

Table 2.2
CONTINUED

	Source	Review Description	Salient Findings
8	Hone, Jarden, & Schofield, 2015	**Effectiveness Review:** Focusing on the effectiveness of 40 PPIs involving 10,664 participants, this review explored the effectiveness on five dimensions of intervention utility including: Reach, Efficacy, Adoption, Implementation, and Maintenance (REACH)	Reporting levels on RE-AIM scores varied substantially: with Reach 64%, Efficacy 73%, Adoption 84%, Implementation 58%, and Maintenance 16%.
9	Quoidbach, Mikolajczak, & Gross, 2015	**Review:** Using a process model of emotional regulation, a review of more than 125 studies was conducted. It included PPIs such as Acts of Kindness, Best Possible Selves, Counting Blessings, Gratitude Visit, Goal Settings, Hope, and Savoring.	Authors propose that positive emotions can be cultivated through five short- and long-term strategies, including situation selection, situation modification, attentional deployment, cognitive change, and response modulation. This reviews offer a comprehensive framework and a detailed roadmap to help clinicians to increase their clients' happiness.
10	Roepke, 2015	**Meta-Analysis:** This review explored whether people grow after adversity, through diverse treatment approaches. It included 12 randomized controlled studies, with a valid or reliable measure of PTG (or closely related construct).	Although none of these interventions was designed to foster PTG as the primary outcome, growth (medium to large effect sizes) was found on PTG.
11	Stoner, Orrell, & Spector, 2015	**Systematic Review:** The review assessed PP outcome measures using standardized criteria in populations that were identified as having shared characteristics. It aimed to identify robust measures that were suitable for potential adaption or use within a dementia population.	The review identified 16 PP outcome measures within the constructs of resilience, self-efficacy, religiousness/ spirituality, life valuation, sense of coherence, autonomy, and resourcefulness. The review highlighted the importance of reporting appropriate psychometric analyses in PPIs.
12	Macaskill, 2016	**Review:** This review examined application of PPIs to clinical populations with physical health problems.	PPIs are beginning to be applied to clinical populations with physical health problem. This study surveys application of PPIs for cancer, coronary heart disease, and diabetes. PPIs show promising initial results.

Note: PP = positive psychology; BA = behavioral activation; PPI = positive psychology intervention; PTG = posttraumatic growth.

[a] *Listed chronologically by year of publication.*

and positive relationships in the counseling context. They conclude that PPIs are effective in generating positive affect and experience and in alleviating depression. More importantly, PPIs used in a clinical context can mobilize inherent abilities in helping to motivate clients to make desirable changes. Furthermore, PPIs offer strategies for clinical practices in general to maintain and improve positive emotions and well-being.

PPIs applied in diverse clinical settings, tackling complex clinical issues, are advancing the knowledge base of psychotherapy and health outcomes. Strong empirical evidence and emerging work in PPIs has been essential in establishing a foundation for the development and refinement of PPT.

POSITIVE PSYCHOTHERAPY AND THE THEORY OF WELL-BEING

PPT is based primarily on two major theories: Seligman's PERMA conceptualization of well-being (Seligman, 2002a, 2012) and character strengths (Peterson & Seligman, 2004). We begin by explaining PERMA, which is a model that sorts well-being into five scientifically measurable and manageable components, as outlined in Table 2.3: Theory of Well-being (PERMA): (a) positive emotions, (b) engagement, (c) relationships, (d) meaning, and (e) accomplishment (Seligman, 2012). Research has shown that fulfillment in three dimensions of PERMA (positive emotions, engagement, and meaning) is associated with lower rates of depression and higher life satisfaction (Asebedo & Seay, 2014; Bertisch et al., 2014; Headey, Schupp, Tucci, & Wagner, 2010; Kern et al., 2015; Lambert D'raven & Pasha-Zaidi, 2016; Lamont, 2011; Schueller, & Seligman, 2010; Sirgy & Wu, 2009).

Positive Emotions

Positive emotions represent the hedonic dimension of happiness. This dimension consists of experiencing positive emotions about the past, present, and future and learning skills to amplify the intensity and duration of these emotions.

- Positive emotions about the past include satisfaction, contentment, fulfillment, pride, and serenity.
- Positive emotions about the future include hope and optimism, faith, trust, and confidence.
- Positive emotions about the present are complex experiences, such as savoring and mindfulness (Seligman, 2002a).

- -

Table 2.3

THEORY OF WELL-BEING: PERMA[a]

Elements	Brief Description
Positive Emotions	Experiencing positive emotions such as happiness, contentment, pride, serenity, hope, optimism, trust, confidence, and gratitude.
Engagement	Immersing oneself deeply in activities that utilize one's strengths to experience flow, an optimal state marked with razor sharp concentration, intense focus, and intrinsic motivation to further develop.
Relationship	Having positive, secure, and trusting relationships.
Meaning	Belonging to and serving something with a sense of purpose and belief that it is larger than the self.
Accomplishment	Pursuing success, mastery, competence, and achievement for its own sake.

[a] *Seligman, 2012.*

Compared to negative emotions, positive emotions tend to be transitory, yet they play a key role in making thought processes more flexible, creative, and efficient (Fredrickson, 2009). Research has also shown that positive emotions build resilience by "undoing" the effects of negative emotions (Fredrickson, Tugade, Waugh, & Larkin, 2003; Johnson et al., 2009) and are robustly associated with longevity, marital satisfaction, friendship, income, and resilience (for reviews see Fredrickson & Branigan, 2005; Lyubomirsky, King, & Diener, 2005). Barry Schwartz and colleagues (2002) found that depressed clients seeking psychotherapy tend to experience a lower than 0.5 to 1 ratio of positive to negative emotion. It appears, then, that lack of positive emotions is central to psychopathology.

Positive emotions also impact physical health. For example, public health officials maintain records of heart disease as the underlying cause of death. They also collect data about possible risk factors, such as rates of smoking, obesity, hypertension, and lack of exercise. These data are available on a county-by-county level in the United States. A research team from the University of Pennsylvania aimed to correlate this physical epidemiology with their digital Twitter version. Drawing on a set of public tweets made between 2009 and 2010, these researchers used established emotional dictionaries to analyze a random sample of tweets from individuals who had made their locations available. With enough tweets and health data from about 1,300 US counties, which contain 88% of the country's population, they found that after controlling for income and educational level, the expressions of negative emotions such as anger, stress, and fatigue in the tweets from people in a given county were associated with higher heart disease risk in that county. On the other hand, expressions of positive emotions like excitement and optimism were associated with lower risk (Eichstaedt et al., 2015).

Engagement

Engagement is the dimension of well-being that relates to the pursuit of engagement, involvement, and absorption in work, intimate relations, and leisure. The notion of engagement stems from Csikszentmihalyi's (1990) work on flow, which is the psychological state brought about by intense concentration that typically results in a lost sense of time while engaged in an activity, as in feeling "one with the music." Provided a person's skill levels are sufficient to meet the challenge of the task, individuals are likely to become deeply absorbed or "at one" with the experience and to lose their sense of time passing. Seligman (2002a) proposed that one way to enhance engagement is to identify clients' "signature" strengths (discussed later in this manual—see Chapter 8, Session 2) and then help them to find opportunities to use them more often. PPIs that encourage individuals to intentionally use their signature strengths in new ways have been identified as being particularly effective (Azañedo et al., 2014; Berthold & Ruch, 2014; Buschor et al., 2013; Forest et al., 2012; Güsewell & Ruch, 2012; Khumalo et al., 2008; Littman-Ovadia & Lavy, 2012; Martinez-Marti & Ruch, 2014; Peterson et al., 2007; Proyer et al., 2013; Ruch et al., 2007).

In PPT, clients learn to undertake activities that use their signature strengths to create engagement. These activities are relatively time-intensive and might include rock climbing; chess; basketball; dancing; creating or experiencing art, music, or literature; spiritual activities; social interactions; and other creative pursuits such as baking, gardening, and playing with a child. Compared with sensory pleasures, which fade quickly, these engagement activities last longer, involve more thinking and interpretation, and are not habituated too easily. Engagement can be an important antidote to boredom, anxiety, and depression.

Anhedonia, apathy, boredom, multitasking, and restlessness—hallmarks of many psychological disorders—are largely manifestations of disrupted attention (Donaldson, Csikszentmihalyi, & Nakamura, 2011; McCormick et al., 2005). Intense engagement typically eliminates boredom and rumination—in trying to successfully complete a challenging task, attentional resources must be activated and directed toward the task at hand, thereby leaving less capacity for processing self-relevant, threat-related information. Additionally, a sense of accomplishment after engaged activity often leaves us reminiscing and basking, which are two forms of positive rumination (Feldman, Joormann & Johnson, 2008). These features of engagement have been successfully applied to therapeutic interventions (Grafanaki et al., 2007; Nakamura & Csikszentmihalyi, 2002).

Relationships

It has been argued that all humans have a fundamental "need to belong" that has been shaped by natural selection over the course of human evolution (Baumeister & Leary, 1995). Positive and secure relationships strongly correlate with a sense of well-being (Wallace, 2013). According to the American Time Use Survey, we spend the majority of our waking hours interacting in one form or another, actively or passively, which can include discussing, collaborating, and exchanging goods with others (Bureau of Labor Statistics, 2015). The quality of our relationships is more important than quantitative features, such as the number of friends we have or the length of time we spend together. For example, children with broad social support, including parents, peers, and teachers, experience less psychopathology (i.e., depression and anxiety) and more well-being (life satisfaction) than peers without such supports, independent of academic achievement (Demir, 2010; Stewart & Suldo, 2011). In addition, positive relationships not only buffer us from psychopathology; they also add to our longevity. Across 148 studies involving 308,849 participants, those who had stronger social relationships had a 50% increased likelihood of survival. This finding remained consistent across age, sex, initial health status, cause of death, and follow-up period (Holt-Lunstad & Timothy, 2010). Almost all PPT practices involved in-person or recalled reflections that involve others. In a randomized trial, researchers found that individuals who completed relationship-focused positive activities reported increased relationship satisfaction (O'Connell, O'Shea, & Gallagher, 2016).

Meaning

Meaning consists of using signature strengths to belong to and serve something that is bigger than oneself. Victor Frankl (1963), a pioneer in the study of meaning, emphasized that happiness cannot be attained by desiring happiness. Rather, it must come as the unintended consequence of working for a goal greater than oneself. People who successfully pursue activities that connect them to such larger goals achieve a "meaningful life." There are a number of ways that this can be achieved: close interpersonal relationships; pursuing artistic, intellectual, or scientific innovations; philosophical or religious contemplation; social or environmental activism; careers experienced as callings; and spirituality or other potentially solitary pursuits such as meditation (e.g., Stillman & Baumeister, 2009; Wrzesniewski, McCauley, Rozin, & Schwartz, 1997). Regardless of the way in which a person establishes a meaningful life, doing so produces a sense of satisfaction and the belief that one has lived well (Ackerman, Zuroff, & Moskowitz, 2000; Hicks & King, 2009).

Adults with higher levels of purpose in life show more rapid recovery from brain injury (Ryff et al., 2016). Therapy can be a useful venture to help clients define and set concrete goals, and clarify the overarching meaning associated with such goals, in ways that increase the likelihood of goal attainment (McKnight & Kashdan, 2009). There is good evidence that having a sense of meaning and purpose helps us recover or rebound quickly from adversity and buffers against feelings of hopelessness and uncontrollability (Graham, Lobel, Glass, & Lokshina, 2008; Lightsey, 2006). Clients whose lives are imbued with meaning are more likely to persist rather than quit in the face of a difficult situation (McKnight & Kasdhan, 2009). PPT can help clients forge connections to deal with psychological problems.

Accomplishment

Accomplishment can denote objective, concrete achievements; promotions; medals; or awards. However, the essence of accomplishment lies in its subjective quest to progress, advance, and ultimately grow personally and interpersonally. In the PERMA model of well-being, accomplishment is defined as harnessing our strengths, abilities, talents, and skills to achieve something that gives us a deep sense of satisfaction and fulfillment.

Accomplishment requires active and strategic use of strengths (i.e., which strengths to use and when) and close monitoring of situational fluctuations to make timely changes. Along with changes, accomplishment requires consistency of specific behaviors or habits. Finally, accomplishment may have external rewards, but it boosts well-being when we pursue and accomplish an intrinsically motivating and meaningful goal.

POSITIVE PSYCHOTHERAPY: THEORETICAL ASSUMPTIONS

PPT was developed on the empirical foundations of positive intervention studies and the theoretical foundations of the PERMA model and character strengths. However, PPT also operates on three assumptions regarding the nature, cause, course, and treatment of specific behavioral patterns, as discussed next.

Inherent Capacity for Growth

Consistent with humanistic psychology, PPT posits that psychopathology ensues when clients' inherent capacities for growth, fulfillment, and well-being are thwarted by prolonged psychosocial distress. Psychotherapy offers a unique opportunity to initiate or restore human potential through the transformative power of human connection. It presents an unparalleled human interaction in which an empathic and nonjudgmental clinician is privy to a client's deepest emotions, desires, aspirations, thoughts, beliefs, actions, and habits. If this exclusive access is used mostly to process the negatives—something that comes naturally to us—and repair the worst, the opportunity to nurture growth is either overshadowed or often completely lost.

Focusing on strengths enables clients to learn specific skills to be more spontaneous, playful, creative, and grateful, rather than merely learning how not to be rigid, boring, conventional, and complaining. Evidence shows that strengths can play a key role in growth—even in dire life circumstances. Character strengths predict resilience, over and above demographics, social support, self-esteem, life satisfaction, positive affect, self-efficacy, and optimism (Martínez-Martí & Ruch, 2016). Growing evidence is supporting this assumption about the importance of strengths. For example, Linley and colleagues (2010) have shown that people who use their strengths are more likely to achieve their goals. Further, use of strengths buffers the impact of negative experiences (Johnson, Gooding, Wood, & Tarrier, 2010). The depressive symptoms among older adults were reduced when they focused on their strengths, such as optimism, gratitude, savoring, curiosity, courage, altruism, and purpose in life (Ho, Yeung, & Kwok, 2014). Taken together, PPT assumes that clients are capable of growth and emphasizes the growth process, which in turn helps to reduce symptoms.

Strengths Are as Authentic as Symptoms

PPT values strengths in their own right. PPT considers positive emotions and strengths to be authentic and as real as negative symptoms and disorders. Strengths are not defenses, illusions, or by-products of symptom relief that sit idly on the clinical periphery. If resentment, deception, competition, jealousy, greed, worry, and stress are real, so are such attributes as honesty, cooperation, contentment, gratitude, compassion, and serenity. Research has demonstrated that the mere absence of symptoms is not the presence of mental well-being (Bartels et al., 2013; Keyes & Eduardo, 2012; Suldo & Shaffer, 2008). Incorporating strengths with symptoms expands the self-perception of clients and offers the clinician additional routes of intervening. Cheavens and colleagues (2012) have shown that focusing on the relative strengths of clients in psychotherapy, rather than on their weaknesses, leads to a superior outcome. Likewise, Flückiger and Grosse Holtforth (2008) found that focusing on client strengths before each therapy session improved therapy outcomes. When a clinician actively works to restore and nurture courage, kindness, modesty, perseverance, and social intelligence, the lives of clients are likely to become more fulfilling. In contrast, when a clinician focuses on amelioration of symptoms, clients' lives may become less miserable.

Therapeutic Relationship

The third and final assumption of PPT is that effective therapeutic relationships can be built on exploration and analysis of positive personal characteristics and experiences (e.g., positive emotions, strengths, and virtues), and not just on talking about troubles. The establishment of a therapeutic alliance is a core common factor to therapeutic change (Horvath et al., 2011; Kazdin, 2009). Scheel, Davis, and Henderson (2012) found that focusing on strengths helped clinicians build trusting relationships with clients and motivate them by instilling hope. Another study, based on interviews with 26 Brazilian psychotherapists, found that when clinicians derive positive emotions from a client's input in the therapy, this positive input from the client offers the clinician greater awareness of the client's resourcefulness. Furthermore, positive emotions strengthen the therapeutic relationship as the client's resources are given equal importance, compared to their deficits (Vandenberghe & Silvestre, 2013). Thus the therapeutic alliance can be fostered through a relationship that incorporates strengths.

This process is in contrast to the traditional approach of psychotherapy, in which a clinician analyzes and explains a constellation of symptoms and troubles to a client in the form of a diagnosis. This role of the clinician is further reinforced by the portrayal of psychotherapy in the popular media, which shows therapeutic relationships marked by talking about troubles, disclosing bottled-up emotions, and recovering lost or tattered self-esteem with the help of a clinician.

3

PSYCHOPATHOLOGY

SYMPTOMS AND STRENGTHS

THE CORE CONCEPT OF PSYCHOPATHOLOGY IN POSITIVE psychotherapy (PPT) rests on the notion that positives (e.g., character strengths, positive emotions, meaning, positive relationships, and accomplishments) are as central as symptoms in assessing and treating psychopathology. This is a significant departure from the traditional view of psychopathology, in which symptoms occupy the central position. A purely symptom-based classification system is inadequate to understand the rich and complex lives of clients. Before we present our arguments, we want to clarify that we understand the reasons behind exclusive focus on symptoms. Indeed, troubling symptoms stand out and are more readily approached and assessed in a clinical setting than are positive ones. Negative experiences often invite more complex and deeper clinical discourse—for clients and clinicians. Therefore, it is not surprising that clients seeking clinical services easily recall negative events, setbacks, and failures, or that clinicians readily assess, elaborate, and interpret stories of conflict, ambivalence, deceit, and personal or interpersonal deficits. Because of their apparent greater informational value, clinicians pay more attention to negatives and engage in complex cognitive processing (e.g., Peeters & Czapinski, 1990). Thus clinical assessment is typically conducted to explore symptoms and disorders. However, an almost exclusive focus on symptoms limits clinical assessment in important ways, as discussed next.

SYMPTOMS
The Central Ingredients
Symptoms are assessed with an underlying assumption that they are the central ingredients of clinical discourse. Therefore, symptoms warrant serious exploration, whereas positives are considered to be by-products of symptomatic relief that do not need to be assessed. So entrenched is this assumption that traditionally positive attributes are often considered to be defenses. For example, anxiety has been theorized as a driving force behind a work ethic that characterized the Protestant Reformation (Weber, 2002). It has been theorized that depression develops as a defense mechanism to ward off feelings of guilt, and compassion results as compensation for such feelings (McWilliams, 1994). In PPT, human strengths are just as real as human weaknesses, as old as time, and valued in every culture (Peterson & Seligman, 2004). Strengths are as critical in evaluating and treating psychopathology as are symptoms. Strengths are not considered to be defenses, by-products, or compensations. They are valued in their own right and are weighed independently of weaknesses in the assessment procedure. For example, humility is not necessarily a trait deployed to elicit cooperation of others by holding oneself back. Being helpful is not necessarily an attempt to diffuse or neutralize a stressful situation, and creativity is not only harnessing anxiety to innovation.

Skewed Profiles and Framing
The traditional deficit-oriented assessment and therapeutic approach labels clients within the artificial categories of the *Diagnostic and Statistical Manual of Mental Disorders* (*DSM*; American Psychiatric Association, 2013). Labeling in and of itself is not undesirable; labels

categorize and organize the world (Maddux, 2008). However, reducing or objectifying clients to a label in psychopathology may strip clients of their rich complexity (Boisvert & Faust, 2002; Szasz, 1961). When this excessive focus on diagnosis occurs, *DSM*-based diagnoses produce a personality profile of a client, which predominately outlines deficits, dysfunctions, and disorders. Clinical assessment of personality ought to be a hybrid process that explores strengths as well as weaknesses (Suldo & Shaffer, 2008). Once the clinical assessment frames the presenting issue as a problem, reducing the presenting issue is seen as a measure of the success of the intervention. However, psychological issues are complex and multidimensional and often have idiosyncratic presentation (Harris & Thoresen, 2006). Further, the amelioration of psychiatric symptoms will not ensure that clients have attained well-being. Clinical real estate, in terms of time and resources allocation, is finite. If most of this real estate is taken up by symptom amelioration, not much time and effort will be left for amplification of strengths, meaning, or purpose.

Stigma

Current clinical practice is largely geared toward uncovering childhood traumas, evaluating distorted thoughts, and assessing interpersonal difficulties and emotional chaos. People avoid seeking clinical services because they fear being stigmatized if their challenges are formulated into a psychiatric diagnosis (Corrigan, 2004). Portrayals of individuals with mental illnesses in the popular media maintain the stigma against mental health (Bearse, McMinn, Seegobin, & Free, 2013). Moreover, increasingly diverse and cosmopolitan individuals do not always subscribe to Eurocentric diagnostic labels (Zalaquett et al., 2008).

PSYCHOPATHOLOGY AS DYSREGULATION OF STRENGTHS

Judith Johnson and Alex Wood (2017) have argued that most of the constructs studied by both positive and clinical psychology exist on continua ranging from positive to negative (e.g., gratitude to ingratitude, calmness to anxiety), and so it is meaningless to speak of one or other field studying the "positive" or the "negative." Traditional deficit-based psychology would benefit by integrating positive psychology because

- Positive psychology constructs, such as character strengths and positive emotions, can independently predict well-being when accounting for traditional clinical factors, both cross-sectionally and prospectively.
- Key foci of positive psychologists, such as strengths and positively valanced emotions, interact with risk factors to predict outcomes, thereby conferring resilience.
- Positive psychology interventions (such as PPT) typically used to enhance well-being can also be used to alleviate symptoms.
- The largely Eurocentric clinical psychology research can be adapted for cross-cultural applications by incorporating positive psychology constructs.

In light of these arguments, we invite clinicians to reconceptualize *DSM*-based psychological disorders. More than two decades ago, Evans (1993) postulated that negative behaviors or symptoms have alternative positive forms. To some extent, this reciprocity is a matter of semantics. Symptoms are defined in everyday language that can always be translated into simple opposites, although not all symptoms or disorders lend themselves naturally to this reciprocity. For example, courage could be conceptualized as the antithesis of anxiety, yet not all anxious individuals lack courage. Evans has argued that most constructs in psychopathology can be scaled into two parallel dimensions. First, the pathological or undesirable attribute moving from severe deviance through some neutral point to its positive nonoccurrence. Second, the antithetical attribute moving from nonoccurrence through some neutral point to its desirable form.

Along the same lines, Peterson (2006) proposed that psychological disorders could be considered as an *Absence* of strength, the *Opposite* of strength, or the *Excess* (AOE) of strength. Peterson argues that absence of character strengths is a hallmark of real psychopathology. However, like Evans (1993), Peterson acknowledges that absence of character strengths may not necessarily apply to disorders such as schizophrenia and bipolar disorder, which have clear biological markers. Many psychologically based disorders (e.g., depression, anxiety, attention and conduct problems, and personality disorders) may be more holistically understood both in terms of the presence of symptoms and as the absence, opposite, or excess of character strengths. Using Peterson's AOE approach, conformity is due to the absence of originality, especially when an entire group adheres to conformity. The absence of curiosity would be disinterest. Disinterest that imposes limits on what a person can know is undesirable. The opposite of curiosity would be boredom. Exaggerated curiosity could be equally harmful, especially if someone is curious about violence, sex, or illicit drugs. Considering clinical sensitivities and subtleties, applying an AOE approach in a clinical setting might be challenging. Conceptualizing clients with a total absence of a strength (e.g., courage, optimism, or kindness), having opposites of strengths (e.g., triteness for creativity, deceit for honesty, or prejudice for fairness), or exaggeration of strengths (emotional promiscuity for emotional intelligence, chauvinism for citizenship, or buffoonery for humor) could be demoralizing both for clinicians and clients and may not even be theoretically plausible. It is hard to imagine that someone does not have an iota of kindness or that bravery is completely missing. Therefore, we propose a slightly modified version of AOE of strengths.

We propose that *DSM*-based disorders be reviewed in terms of lack or excess of strengths. For example, focusing on *lacks*, depression can result, in part, because of a lack of hope, optimism, or zest, among other variables; likewise, a lack of grit and patience can explain some aspects of anxiety; and a lack of fairness, equity, or justice might underscore conduct disorders. A number of psychological disorders could plausibly be conceptualized as an *excess* of specific strengths. For example, depression could be, in part, an excess of humility (reluctance to show one's needs), an excess of kindness (toward others, at the cost of self-care), an excess of perspective (narrowly constructed view of reality), and an excess of meaning (which leads to hyperfocusing and unrelenting commitment). Table 3.1, Major Psychological Disorders as Dysregulation of Strengths lists symptoms of major psychological disorders in terms of lack or excess of strengths.

Lack of strengths alone is insufficient to warrant a diagnosis. Nonetheless, emerging lines of research by Alex Wood at the University of Sterling, United Kingdom, are showing that absence or lack of positives, poses a risk for a clinical condition. In a longitudinal study of 5,500 participants, Wood and Joseph (2010) found that individuals low on positive characteristics—such as self-acceptance, autonomy, purpose in life, positive relationships with others, environmental mastery, and personal growth—were up to seven times more likely to experience depressive symptoms in the clinical range. Absence of positive characteristics independently constituted a risk factor for psychological disorder over and above the presence of numerous negative aspects, including current and previous depression, neuroticism, and physical ill-health. Furthermore, people high on positive characteristics are buffered from the impact of negative life events including clinical distress (Johnson et al., 2010; Johnson, Gooding, Wood, & Tarrier, 2010).

How, exactly, can a lack or excess of strengths work from a PPT perspective? Consider a clinical example. The Center for Epidemiologic Studies-Depression scale (CES-D; Radloff, 1977) is one of the five most frequently used measures of depressive symptoms. With 16 negative and 4 positive items, it was widely believed that this measure looks at two separate factors—depression and happiness (Shafer, 2006). Analyzing the data from 6,125 adults, Alex Wood and his colleagues demonstrated that a two-dimensional structure of the CES-D is most likely a statistical artifact: Depression and happiness may largely be synonymous, and the existing measure may tap different ends of the same continuum (Wood, Taylor, & Joseph, 2010). That is, depression and happiness are part of the same continuum, and studying them separately unnecessarily duplicates the research effort. Likewise, the State-Trait Anxiety Inventory (Spielberger et al., 1983) can be conceptualized on an anxiety-to-relaxation continuum.

Individual Differences

In PPT, our selection of traits to describe a lack or excess of strengths is a blend of defined and well-researched strengths (such as gratitude, curiosity, and forgiveness) and traits that are expressed in everyday life experiences (such as carefreeness, composure, reflection, and flexibility). One way to reconceptualize symptoms is to consider their opposites—that is, their strengths—as lacking or in excess in everyday experiences. Although the everyday terms we use to describe lack or excess of strengths may have discernable and measurable individual differences, a number of them have not been the focus of empirical examination.

Lack and Excess of Strengths

We realize that numerous terms used to describe a lack or excess of strengths may imply that the lack or excess is undesirable, rendering strengths prescriptive. For example, lack of perspective, moderation, and courage are generally considered to be undesired states, whereas excessive passion, self-preservation, and risk-taking are generally considered to be desired states. Our approach and effort are to provide a less subjective and more scientific understanding. Evidence shows that more gratitude, kindness, curiosity, love, and hope is strongly related with life satisfaction (Park, Peterson, & Seligman, 2004), whereas a lack of social intelligence, moderation, self-regulation, and perseverance is associated with psychological problems (Aldao, Nolen-Hoeksema, & Schweizer, 2010; Bron et al., 2012).

Situational Dynamics

Psychological disorders and related symptoms can be better grasped by understanding complex situations and cultural milieus in which clients are embedded and in which they often have very little control to change these dynamics. Here are two examples:

One of our clients, Michel, had symptoms of social anxiety. He avoided social situations because he was excessively cautious about saying something wrong or inappropriate because English was not his first language. Michel became socially anxious when he inadvertently said something inappropriate, which offended one of his friends who accused him of discrimination. Looking at symptoms in terms of a lack or excess of strengths also requires understanding contextual features. Michel showed no signs of social anxiety when he was interacting with friends speaking his native language; in that situation he felt confident, made jokes, and showed empathy. A symptom-driven approach would likely describe the situation as, "the client does not exhibit symptoms of social anxiety when interacting in his native language." A strengths-based approach is likely to describe the same situation as, "the client is playful, socially comfortable, and empathic when interacting in his native language."

Another client, Sharon, had two part-time jobs—one at a high-end retail store and the other at a psychiatric facility working with children with developmental disabilities. At the retail store, Sharon was expected to be very professional and vigilant in taking care of minute details at the time of a sale. She stated that she was quite cautious at her retail job and gradually found herself preoccupied about making mistakes or forgetting something. On the other job, despite having the challenging task of engaging children in therapeutic activities, Sharon found herself relaxed, playful, and social. A symptom-driven approach would likely describe the situation as, "the client experiences moderate levels of anticipatory anxiety at her retail job. She doesn't experience a similar level of anxiety at her job in the psychiatric facility." A strengths-based approach is likely to describe the same situation as, "the client in the retail position is cautious and vigilant—at times more than she ought to be. Therefore, she is not able to use some of her other strengths, such as creativity and playfulness. At the psychiatric facility, on the other hand, she is better able to use her strengths. She is playful, relaxed, and connects genuinely with others."

It is important to consider situational dynamics and how strengths play a nuanced role in understanding the complex and rich lives of clients.

Having versus Developing Strengths

Having a specific constellation of symptoms that cause marked distress and functional impairment generally yields a clinical diagnosis. This was the case with one of our clients, Yasmin, who came to therapy after being diagnosed with borderline personality disorder by several mental health professionals.

In the first 10 minutes of our time together, Yasmin narrated her symptoms almost verbatim as listed in the DSM. All she saw in herself was emotional dysregulation, relationship difficulties, and self-damaging impulsivity. After she completed a comprehensive strengths assessment (described in Chapter 8 of this manual), without dismissing her symptoms, we described her as someone who basically is a loving person who lacks skills to express love appropriately, and as someone who could benefit from understanding and then acquiring the skills of building empathy, kindness, and prudence. Although Yasmin was able to identify many domains in which she tended to demonstrate poor judgment, she was also able to share times when she exercised good judgment. She shared an incident when her spontaneous, timely reaction saved the life of a friend. A strengths assessment made her realize that she has specific strengths and that, although these qualities are indeed strengths, an overuse of them often landed her in trouble. At the same time, she lacks specific strengths, such as prudence, self-regulation, and adaptive use of zest that she could use to solve her problems.

Mere knowledge of symptoms or strengths, in our view, is insufficient to foster change. Therapeutic change can occur when the clinician helps the client to develop an adaptive and nuanced use of strengths. Change happens when the clinician highlights the client's past successes to address present concerns, when the clinician is sufficiently proficient to spot even a small or brief instance of using or displaying strengths, when the clinician communicates the client's self-worth through concrete examples of strengths, and when the clinician does not give up searching for strengths.

Degree or Extent

The clinician should ascertain if a client possesses a sufficient amount of a particular strength to be able to apply it effectively (Ajzen & Sheikh, 2013). For example, Julia, a middle-aged client, was experiencing symptoms of generalized anxiety disorder marked by worrying excessively, feeling restless, and having concentration difficulties. If her symptoms could be treated by developing strengths, then to what extent would Julia need to have, for example, critical thinking, perspective, and savoring? Is there a specific pairing or constellations of strengths that might be therapeutically effective? Research has shown that working on our signature strengths or working on lesser strengths is equally effective in increasing life-satisfaction (Gelso, Nutt Williams, Fretz, 2014; Rashid, 2004; Rust, Diessner, & Reade, 2009).

Table 3.1

MAJOR PSYCHOLOGICAL DISORDERS AS DYSREGULATION OF STRENGTHS[a]

Presence of Symptoms	Dysregulation of Strengths Lack or Excess
Major Depressive Disorder	
Depressed mood, feeling sad, hopeless (observed by others, e.g., appears tearful), helpless, slow, fidgety, boredom	Lack of joy, delight, hope and optimism, playfulness, spontaneity, goal orientation Excess: prudence, modesty
Diminished pleasure	Lack of savoring, zest, curiosity Excess: self-regulation, contentment
Fatigued, slow	Lack of zest, alertness Excess: relaxation, slacking
Diminished ability to think or concentrate and indecisiveness, brooding	Lack of determination and resolution winnowing, divergent thinking Excess: overanalytical
Suicidal ideation/plan	Lack of meaning, hope, social connectivity, resolution winnowing, divergent thinking, resourcefulness Excess: carefreeness (defensive pessimism)
Disruptive Mood Dysregulation Disorder	
Sever temper outbursts (verbal and physical)	Lack of self-regulation, prudence
Persistent irritability and anger	Excess: enthusiasm
Unspecified Depressive Disorder With Anxious Distress	
Feeling keyed up or tense, feeling unusually restless	Lack of contentment (distress tolerance), gratitude, relaxation, prudence Lack of openness to new and novel ideas (curiosity) Excess: zest, gusto, eagerness
Bipolar Disorder	
Elevated, expansive, irritable mood	Lack of equanimity, even-temperedness, and level headedness Excess: composure, passion
Inflated self-esteem or grandiosity	Lack of humility, self and social intelligence Excess: will power, introspection
More talkative than usual	Lack of reflection and contemplation Excess: zest, passion
Excessive involvement in pleasurable activities (e.g., unrestrained buying sprees, sexual indiscretions, thoughtless business/career choices)	Lack of moderation, prudence, simplicity Excess: passion (obsession), self-indulgence
Excessive involvement in activities that have a high potential for painful consequences (e.g., unrestrained buying sprees, sexual indiscretions, or foolish business investments)	Lack of self-regulation, perspective, balance, humility, emotional regulation Excess: self-care (self-indulgence), zeal, gratification
Generalized Anxiety Disorder	
Worrying excessively about real or perceived danger	Lack of perspective, wisdom, critical thinking Excess: caution, attentiveness
Feeling restless, fatigued, fidgety, jittery, edgy, difficulty concentrating and sleeping	Lack of equanimity, mindfulness, spontaneity Excess: farsightedness, composure

(continued)

Table 3.1
CONTINUED

Presence of Symptoms	Dysregulation of Strengths Lack or Excess
Separation Anxiety Disorder	
Persistent and excessive worry about losing major attachment figures	Lack of love, capacity to love and be loved, social trust, optimism, bonding Excess: affection, self-regulation
Selective Mutism	
Failure to speak in specific social situations in which there is an expectation to speak	Lack of initiative, personal and social intelligence, social skills Excess: prudence, self-scrutiny
Specific Phobia	
Marked anxiety about a specific object or situation	Lack of courage, creativity Excess: sensitivity, cautious reactivity
Active avoidance or endured with intense fear or anxiety; out-of-proportion fear	Lack of relaxation, mindfulness, courage to withstand social judgment, rational self-talk (reflection and introspection) Excess: observance, awareness, caution
Feeling restless, fidgety, jittery, edgy	Lack of equanimity, self-intelligence, self-evaluation, monitoring, relaxation, mindfulness, level-headedness, self-composure Excess: caution, sensitivity, reactivity, critical evaluation
Social Phobia	
Fear of social or performance situation	Lack of courage, extemporaneity, trust in others Excess: social intelligence (self seen as audience, rather than part of the social picture), critical appraisal and evaluation
Agoraphobia	
Marked fear or anxiety using public transportation, parking lots, bridges, shops, theatres, standing or being in a crowd Being outside of the home alone	Lack of courage, extemporaneity, open-mindedness, flexibility Excess: sensitivity, caution about a situation, caution
Panic Disorder	
Intense fear of "going crazy" marked by heart pounding, feeling dizzy, unsteady, or light-headed Derealization and depersonalization Persistent concerns about future attacks	Lack of composure, social and personal intelligence, creativity and curiosity to explore the environment/ situation beyond the surface, optimism (expecting unexpected adverse outcomes) Excess: sensitivity, reactivity to environmental cues, awareness
Obsessive-Compulsive Disorder	
Recurrent, persistent, intrusive, unwanted thoughts, urges, or images	Lack of mindfulness and letting go, curiosity, perspective Excess: reflection and introspection, morality or fairness
Repetitive behaviors or mental acts individual feels compelled to do to prevent anxiety	Lack of contentment with less than perfect objects and performance, creativity, flexibility, ability to restrain Excess: reflection and introspection, planning

INTRODUCTION AND THEORETICAL FOUNDATIONS

Table 3.1
CONTINUED

Presence of Symptoms	Dysregulation of Strengths Lack or Excess
Body Dysmorphic Disorder	
Preoccupation with perceived defects in physical appearance that are not observable or slight to others	Lack of contentment with less than perfect self-image, acknowledgement of personal character strengths, modesty Excess: personal intelligence, self-care, self-worth
Hoarding Disorders	
Persistent difficulty discarding or parting with possessions, regardless of actual values	Lack of perspective regarding what is important and meaningful, distinct self-image (identity melded with objects), relationship with object and artifacts than with people and experiences, inability to override one's perceived needs (lack of compassion) Excess: optimism, caution
Posttraumatic Stress Disorder	
Recurrent, involuntary, and intrusive distressing memories of a traumatic event	Lack of resilience, ability to bounce back, personal intelligence to process emotions or to seek support to process emotions, ability to take risks/creativity to explore various coping mechanism, persistence, optimism, hope, social support, making meaning of the traumatic event, or putting things in perspective Excess: reflection (rumination), viewing or perceiving the event only through negative lens or perspective, adherence (to the traumatic experience)
Intense or prolonged psychological distress and fear of external cues that symbolize the traumatic event	Lack of ability to self-sooth, relax, or regain composure; creativity and courage to experience the distressing objection or situation in a different or adaptive manner, self-determination Excess: composure, caution, keeping the status quo
Avoidance of distressing memories (people, places, conversational activities, objects, situations)	Lack of resolve to handle distressing memories head-on (emotional bravery) Excess: self-preservation at the cost of not yielding to spontaneous experiences, or taking necessary risks
Attention Deficit Hyperactivity Disorder	
Failing to give close attention to details, not seeming to listen when spoken to directly	Lack of vigilance and social intelligence Excess: watchfulness
Difficulty organizing tasks and activities	Lack of discipline and managing Excess: gusto, eagerness
Avoiding or disliking tasks requiring sustained attention or mental effort	Lack of grit and patience Excess: hedonic pleasures
Excessive fidgeting, motor activity, running, pacing	Lack of calmness and composure Excess: agility, fervor
Talking excessively, interrupting or intruding on others, difficulty awaiting turn	Lack of social intelligence, self-awareness Excess: zest, initiative, and curiosity
Oppositional Defiant Disorder	
Annoying people deliberately	Lack of kindness, empathy, and fairness Excess: clemency

(continued)

Table 3.1
CONTINUED

Presence of Symptoms	Dysregulation of Strengths Lack or Excess
Often being angry, resentful, spiteful, or vindictive	Lack of forgiveness, gratitude, and level-headedness Excess: fairness, equality
Disruptive, Impulse-Control, Conduct Disorder	
Bullying, threatening, intimidating others	Lack of kindness and citizenship Excess: leadership, control, governance
Stealing, destroying other's property	Lack of honesty, fairness, and justice Excess: courage, fairness
Personality Disorders	
Paranoid Personality Disorder	
Suspicion without sufficient basis that others are exploiting, harming, or deceiving	Lack of social intelligence, trust in others, open-mindedness, curiosity Excess: caution, diligence
Doubts loyalty or trustworthiness of others, reluctant to confide in others, reading hidden demeaning or threatening meaning into benign remarks or events	Lack of personal intelligence, giving or receiving love, lack of deep and secure attachment Excess: social intelligence, open-mindedness
Borderline Personality Disorder	
Pervasive relationship instability; imagined or real abandonment	Lack of capacity to love and be loved in deep and sustained relationship one-to-one, secure attachment, emotional intimacy and reciprocity in relationships, relational prudence and kindness, empathy Excess: curiosity and zest which phases out quickly, attachment, emotional intelligence
Idealization and devaluation	Lack of authenticity and trust in close relationships, moderation, prudence, and open-mindedness (being swayed by a single event), reality orientation, perspective Excess: judgment, spontaneity
Self-damaging impulsivity (e.g., spending, reckless driving, binge eating) and anger outburst	Lack of self-regulation (tolerance), moderation, prudence Excess: bravery without prudence (actions without prudence), risk-taking
Narcissistic Personality Disorder	
Pattern of grandiosity, arrogance, need for admiration, sense of self-importance	Lack of authenticity, humility Excess: self-deprecation, criticism
Lack of empathy	Lack of social intelligence, kindness (being genuinely interested in others) Excess: personal intelligence (personal needs or wants are prioritized)
Fantasies of unlimited success, power, brilliance, beauty, or ideal love	Lack of humility, perspective, and personal intelligence Excess: creativity (fantasizing), rationalizing, intellectualizing
Sense of entitlement, expectations of unreasonably favorable treatment, requires excessive admiration	Lack of humility, citizenship, and fairness Excess: leadership, need for appreciation

Table 3.1
CONTINUED

Presence of Symptoms	Dysregulation of Strengths Lack or Excess
Interpersonal exploitation	Lack of fairness, equity, and justice Excess: righteousness, despotism, bossiness
Envious of others	Lack of generosity and appreciation Excess: self-preservation
Histrionic Personality Disorder	
Excessive emotionality and attention seeking	Lack of equanimity and modesty Excess: personal and emotional intelligence
Easily suggestible (i.e., easily influenced by others or circumstances)	Lack of persistence, determination, goal orientation, Excess: of efficiency of concentration
Inappropriate sexual seduction, overemphasis on physical appearance	Lack of discretion and self-regulation Excess: emotional disinhibition
Shallow and hasty emotional expression	Lack of mindfulness and social intelligence Excess: spontaneity
Self-dramatization, theatricality, and exaggerated and shallow expression of emotion	Lack of authenticity; authentically expressing one's needs, emotions, and interests; moderation, mindfulness Excess: emotional intelligence, enthusiasm
Overvaluing relationships	Lack of social intelligence Excess: tending and befriending
Obsessive-Compulsive Personality Disorder	
Preoccupation with details, orderliness, and perfectionism	Lack of perspective as what is more important, spontaneity Excess: persistence, orderliness
Interpersonal control at the expense of flexibility, openness, and efficiency	Lack of kindness, empathy, and ability to follow Excess: submission and leniency
Preoccupation with details, rules, lists, organizations, or schedules to the extent that primary aim of the activity is overshadowed	Lack of flexibility, creativity in thinking of novel and productive ways to do things Excess: perfection, organization
Excessively devoted to work at the expense of leisure and friendships	Lack of balance, savoring, appreciation for relationships Excess: self-indulgence
Rigidity and stubbornness	Lack of adaptability, flexibility, creative problem-solving Excess: discipline, prudence
Overconscientious, scrupulous, and inflexible about morality, ethics, or values	Lack of perspective, consideration of implication of decision, adaptability, flexibility, creative problem-solving Excess: self-righteousness
Avoidant Personality Disorder	
Avoiding activities with others due to fear of criticism, disapproval, or rejection	Lack of interpersonal courage to take risks, critical reasoning to put criticism or disapproval of others in perspective, courage Excess: self-awareness, caution
Social isolation, avoiding people, inhibition in new interpersonal situation because of feelings of inadequacy	Lack of interpersonal strengths, melding one's identity with others/group Excess: prudence, critical thinking

(continued)

Table 3.1
CONTINUED

Presence of Symptoms	Dysregulation of Strengths Lack or Excess
Views self as socially inept, personally unappealing, and inferior to others	Lack of self-assurance, self-efficacy, hope, and optimism Excess: humility, authenticity
Reluctance to take risks to engage in any new activities	Lack of bravery and curiosity Excess: self-regulation, compliance
Dependent Personality Disorder	
Excessive need to be taken care of, fear of being left alone	Lack of independence, initiative, and leadership Excess: seclusion
Difficulty making everyday decisions, lack of perspective	Lack of determination, perspective Excess: critical analysis, focusing on details
Difficulty expressing disagreements with others	Lack of bravery, not being able to speak up for what is right, judgment Excess: uncompromising
Difficulty initiating	Lack of self-efficacy, optimism, curiosity Excess: organization, autonomy
Antisocial Personality Disorder	
Failure to conform to social norms or laws	Lack of citizenship, communal purpose, respect for authority, kindness, mercy, forgiveness Excess: courage (risk-taking), vitality
Deceitfulness, repeated lying, conning others for personal profits	Lack of honesty, integrity, fairness, moral compass, empathy Excess: self-centered personal intelligence
Irritability, impulsivity, aggressiveness as indicated by physical fights or assaults	Lack of equanimity, mindfulness, tolerance, kindness and consideration, knowledge of others, self-control, perspective (inability to anticipate consequences) Excess: mental and physical vigor, passion, ambition, courage, too ready to go out of zone of comfort

Lack = diminished capacity to exercise/use a character strength; Excess = excess of strength, not to be considered as excess of symptoms.

[a] Based on Diagnostic and Statistical Manual of Mental Disorders (5th ed.).

## 4

THE CENTRALITY OF CHARACTER STRENGTHS AND HOW TO USE THEM IN POSITIVE PSYCHOTHERAPY

CHARACTER STRENGTHS—AS CENTRAL AS SYMPTOMS

Peterson and Seligman's (2004) *Character Strengths and Virtues* (CVS) was the first comprehensive, coherent, and systematic effort in psychology to classify core human strengths (see Table 4.1: Values in Action: Classification of Strengths). Character strengths are defined as universal traits that are valued in their own right and do not necessarily lead to instrumental outcomes. For the most part, character strengths do not diminish; rather, individuals with such strengths elevate those who witness the strength, producing admiration rather than jealousy. There are tremendous variations in the patterns of strengths that we possess. Societal institutions attempt to cultivate these character strengths through rituals. However, the CVS classification is descriptive rather than prescriptive, and character strengths can be studied like other behavioral variables.

Character Strengths, Values, and Talents

What distinguishes strengths (descriptions of desired behavior) from values (prescriptions of desired behavior)? Character strengths and values are both morally desirable, but they differ on a few points:

First, compared to a broader set of core values, character strengths are more fine-grained and subtle attributes of our selves. For example, the value of getting along with others is extrapolated from more specific attributes (character strengths) such as the ability to love and be loved, kindness, social intelligence, teamwork, and gratitude.

Second, compared to character strengths, values are often actively cultivated by institutions, through parenting practices, education, and an intricate system of reward and recognition. We are deemed to be good citizens if we uphold or demonstrate these values. In other words, values are used as criteria to evaluate us as individuals.

Values and strengths are close cousins with a number of similarities. One or more core values may be operating underneath various character strengths, and numerous character strengths may intersect with one or more core value. Both values and character strengths guide our behavior. Both values and character strengths offer us an opportunity to reflect on who we are and the principles that guide our actions and decisions. Both values and character strengths are strongly associated with higher life satisfaction and well-being.

Values tend to be more prescriptive than character strengths. For example, the value of being successful is not only desired for the sake of being successful—there is more to it. Institutions such as schools, business, work, politics, arts, and sports have set up specific rules and requirements to measure and master our success. Some of these rules include the values of getting along with others, maintaining good hygiene, staying organized, and being meticulous. These values are nearly required attributes for personal and professional accomplishment. Comparatively, character strengths are considered to be

Table 4.1

VALUES IN ACTION CLASSIFICATION OF STRENGTHS[a]

Virtue: Wisdom & Knowledge—strengths which involve acquiring and using knowledge

a.   **Creativity:** Thinking of novel and productive ways to do things

b.   **Curiosity:** Openness to experience: Taking an interest in all of ongoing experience

c.   **Open-mindedness:** Thinking things through and examining them from all sides

d.   **Love of learning:** Mastering new skills, topics, and bodies of knowledge

e.   **Perspective:** Being able to provide wise counsel to others

Virtue: Courage—emotional strengths which involve exercise of will to accomplish goals in the face of opposition, external or internal

a.   **Bravery:** Not shrinking from threat, challenge, or pain

b.   **Persistence:** Finishing what one starts; persisting in a course of action in spite of obstacles

c.   **Integrity:** Speaking the truth and presenting oneself in a genuine way

d.   **Vitality & Zest:** Approaching life with excitement and energy; not doing things half-way or halfheartedly; living life as an adventure; feeling alive and activated

Virtue: Humanity—interpersonal strengths that involve tending and befriending others

a.   **Love:** Valuing close relations with others, in particular those in which sharing and caring are reciprocated; being close to people

b.   **Kindness:** Doing favors and good deeds for others; helping them; taking care of them

c.   **Social intelligence:** Being aware of the motives and feelings of self and others; knowing what to do to fit into different social situations; knowing what makes other people tick

Virtue: Justice—strengths that underlie healthy community life

a.   **Citizenship & Teamwork:** Working well as member of a group or team; being loyal to the group; doing one's share

b.   **Fairness:** Treating all people the same according to notions of fairness and justice; not letting personal feelings bias decisions about others; giving everyone a fair chance

c.   **Leadership:** Encouraging a group of which one is a member to get things done and at the same time maintain good relations within the group; organizing group activities and seeing that they happen

Virtue: Temperance—strengths that protect against excess

a.   **Forgiveness & Mercy:** Forgiving those who have done wrong; accepting the shortcomings of others; giving people a second chance; not being vengeful

b.   **Humility & Modesty:** Letting one's accomplishments speak for themselves; not seeking the spotlight; not regarding oneself as more special than one is

c.   **Prudence:** Being careful about one's choices; not taking undue risks; not saying or doing things that might later be regretted

d.   **Self-regulation [Self-control]:** Regulating what one feels and does; being disciplined; controlling one's appetites and emotions

Virtue: Transcendence—strengths that forge connections to the larger universe and provide meaning

a.   **Appreciation of beauty and excellence:** Noticing and appreciating beauty, excellence, and/or skilled performance in all domains of life, from nature to arts to mathematics to science

b.   **Gratitude:** Being aware of and thankful for the good things; taking time to express thanks

c.   **Hope & Optimism:** Expecting the best in the future and working to achieve it; believing that a good future is something that can be brought about

d.   **Humor & Playfulness:** Liking to laugh and tease; bringing smiles to other people, seeing the light side; making (not necessarily telling) jokes

e.   **Spirituality:** Knowing where one fits within the larger scheme; having coherent beliefs about the higher purpose and meaning of life that shape conduct and provide comfort

[a] From Peterson & Seligman, 2004. ©VIA Institute; reprinted with permission.

more personalized attributes. For example, Person A can be equally successful and accomplished (values) with the character strengths of creativity, courage, authenticity, prudence, and playfulness compared to Person B with the character strengths of curiosity, fairness, social intelligence, self-regulation, and spirituality.

Character strengths are also distinct from talents. Talents such as musical ability, athletic agility, or manual dexterity are more inborn and fixed, whereas strengths are acquired, built individually, and often nurtured by larger societal institutions. Talents tend to be more automatic, while strengths can be exercised deliberately (e.g., understanding when kindness versus fairness is appropriate to use). As noted, talents are more innate (e.g., musical, athletic, manual dexterity) and are sometimes squandered. Individuals whose salient strengths are kindness, curiosity, gratitude, or optimism often find ways to use, not waste, their talents. Talents tend to be morally neutral, whereas strengths and values have a moral undercurrent. Evidence shows that individuals who are grateful, curious, loving, optimistic, and zestful are more likely to be satisfied with their lives. In other words, character strengths improve well-being (Peterson, Park, & Seligman, 2005).

Talents tend to be more independent than strengths or values. A person's athletic agility has less bearing on his intellectual functioning, and someone's artistic ability is less likely related to her day-to-day practical intelligence. Strengths, compared to talents, are more interrelated and often work in constellation. Someone high on curiosity is also likely to be high on creativity; self-regulation and prudence go hand in hand, as do leadership and citizenship.

Third, character strengths are expressed in combinations (rather than singularly) and viewed within the context in which they are used. For example, strengths such as kindness and forgiveness can cement social bonds but, if used in excess, can be taken for granted. In this classification scheme, character strengths (e.g., kindness, teamwork, zest) are distinct from talents and abilities. Athletic prowess, photographic memory, perfect pitch, manual dexterity, and physical agility are examples of talents and abilities that are often valued because they lead to other outcomes. Strengths have moral features, whereas talents and abilities do not.

INCORPORATING STRENGTHS IN POSITIVE PSYCHOTHERAPY

Throughout the course of positive psychotherapy (PPT), the clinician actively looks for events, experiences, and expressions of strengths in the lives of their clients. These may manifest through abilities, skills, talents, capacities, and aptitudes that can be nurtured in order to cope with and potentially buffer against psychological disorders. Positive psychologists are often criticized for either minimizing weaknesses or focusing exclusively on strengths and positives. We reiterate, as we are doing throughout this manual, that exploration of character strengths does not come at the cost of ignoring symptoms. We believe that clients can move from ill-being to well-being if their symptoms are integrated with strengths, risk with resources, and vulnerability with resilience to offer them a complex yet realistic portrait of self-awareness. However, thoughtful integration of strengths in the overall psychological profile of clients is not something usually done in traditional psychotherapy. We therefore recommend utilizing three considerations to bring out client strengths:

- Using valid and reliable measures of strengths.
- Developing a nuanced and contextualized understanding of strengths.
- Framing strengths into meaningful goals.

Using Valid and Reliable Measures of Strengths

Strengths in most positive interventions are commonly assessed using the free online measure, Values in Action–Inventory of Strengths (https://www.viacharacter.org/) (VIA-IS; Peterson & Seligman, 2004). Some alternative measures of character strengths have also be developed and empirically validated including Strength Finder (Buckingham & Clifton, 2001), Realise 2 (Linley, 2008), Adult Needs and Strengths Assessment (Nelson & Johnston, 2008), and Quality of Life Inventory (Frisch, 2013). Typically, clinicians follow a straightforward "identify and use your strengths" strategy, where the top five scores (out of 24 total) are regarded as signature strengths. Clients are then asked to find new ways to use their signature strengths. This approach, although useful and effective in nonclinical settings, may not meet critical clinical needs. Exclusive focus on top-ranked strength scores could lead clients to think that their top five strengths carry the most therapeutic potential when this may not be the case for every client. For example: A middle-aged, well-accomplished male client in our practice stated, "After every accomplishment, my instinctive reaction is that someone else has done better." A client such as this may not benefit from working on his top strengths, which include persistence, leadership, and love of learning. Some of his lower strengths, such as gratitude, spirituality, and playfulness, may carry greater therapeutic benefit for him. It is important to keep in mind that not all 24 strengths carry the same therapeutic potential in every case.

Developing a Nuanced and Contextualized Understanding of Strengths

The most critical aspect of a strengths-based therapeutic approach is a contextualized use of strengths, which keeps presenting problems and symptoms front and center. The clinical setting often requires a more nuanced and theoretically driven approach of using strengths (Biswas-Diener, Kashdan, & Minhas, 2011). To overcome this shortcoming, we suggest utilizing a comprehensive strengths assessment approach (Rashid & Seligman, 2013; see the worksheets in Chapter 8, Session 2). In this approach, the clinician gives the clients a brief description of each core strength (approximately 20 to 25 words per strength—based on the CVS) and asks the client to identify (not rank) up to five strengths that best illustrate his personality. In addition, the client collects collateral data from a friend or family member to share with the clinician. The clinician then synthesizes all of this information and provides the client with descriptions of the selected strengths with titles—to identify each strength with a name and specific context. Next, the clinician encourages the client to share memories, experiences, real-life stories, anecdotes, accomplishments, and skills that illustrate the use of these strengths in specific situations. The client then completes a self-report measure of strengths (e.g., VIA-IS). Collaboratively with the clinician, clients set specific, attainable, and measurable goals that target their presenting concerns and identify adaptive uses of their signature strengths. In a recent clinical study, among clients diagnosed with depression and anxiety, the strengths of curiosity, humor, and authenticity were the most likely to be identified by other people, whereas humility, fairness, and perspective were least likely to be endorsed by others (Rashid et al., 2013).

Framing Strengths into Meaningful Goals

It is important that goals be personally meaningful as well as adaptive in the interpersonal context of clients. For example, if the client's goal is to use curiosity more, the client and clinician discuss what an optimal balance of curiosity through concrete actions is, so that the use of curiosity does not lead to intrusiveness (excess/overuse) or boredom (lack/underuse). Clients are also taught to use their strengths in a calibrated and flexible way in setting goals to adaptively meet situational challenges (Biswas-Diener, Kashdan, & Minhas, 2011; Schwartz & Sharpe, 2010). See Table 4.2: Using Strengths to Overcome 15 Common Challenges.

Table 4.2

USING STRENGTHS TO OVERCOME 15 COMMON CHALLENGES

Challenges (Symptoms)	Potential Character Strength(s)	Strengths-based Considerations
1. Client does not show interest in socializing (e.g., does not talk much, share or participate much in social activities, has few friends).	Vitality & Zest, Enthusiasm, Self-regulation	Encourage client to initiate and maintain at least one outdoor activity weekly such as hiking, biking, mountain biking, mountain climbing, brisk walking, or jogging.
2. Client gives up easily, has difficulty finishing tasks, and makes careless mistakes.	Persistence, Industry, Diligence, Perseverance	Help client to identify factors that diminish interest in daily activities; set small and attainable goals that can be monitored or shared with someone client trusts.
3. Client behaves impulsively, struggles to regulate emotions, experiences mood swings.	Self-regulation, Personal intelligence	Explore triggers of emotional outburst (personal and emotional intelligence); reassure client that instead of reacting to perceived threats, client can devise concrete and strengths-based substitute behaviors that could serve the same function or goals. For example, instead of screaming to draw attention or express frustration, client can exercise curiosity and open-mindedness to ask questions about things that annoy him. If problems persist, client can use perspective, for example, is this a solvable problem, and, if not, what parts are solvable? Then the client can look for creative ways to solve the problem by working with others (teamwork) while keeping a realistic but hopeful outlook (optimism).
4. Client holds grudges, exaggerates minor offenses by others, and does not accept sincere apologies.	Forgiveness & Mercy	Discuss the emotional impact of holding on to grudges and negative memories. Help client to use kindness to empathize with the offender, where appropriate, and normalize the experience by helping client to recall times when she offended someone and was forgiven.
5. Client doesn't respond to friendly and light-hearted gestures of others and appears emotionally stifled.	Humor & Playfulness, Social & Emotional Intelligence	Encourage client to engage in light-hearted gestures and playful activities with a good-natured attitude. Show clients some relevant and engaging videos, real-life visual anecdotes, or contemporary exemplars.
6. Client wants but struggles to initiate meaningful social interactions, avoids social situation, and feels isolated and listless.	Social Intelligence, Courage, Persistence	Encourage client to start by attending social events in which she feels safe and which don't require a lot of one-on-one interaction, such as attending a class on a creative endeavor (e.g., photography, painting, graphic design, cooking, or knitting). Encourage client to pay close attention to social interactions and find ways to offer her observations and share her views without fearing evaluations.

(continued)

Table 4.2

CONTINUED

Challenges (Symptoms)	Potential Character Strength(s)	Strengths-based Considerations
7. Client is preoccupied with her failures and shortcomings and is overly negative.	Hope & Optimism	Work actively with client to build a list of things that are currently working or are at least good enough and elicit client's views about their causation; elicit past success, even small ones, to build mastery and optimism.
8. Client is competitive and high-achieving and spends a lot of time and energy on being the best; he resents or regrets when others outperform him.	Citizenship & Teamwork, Perspective, Humility & Modesty	Educate client about scientific findings that material gains have diminishing returns. Help him to experience savoring, slowness, and gratitude through experiential activities so that he can feel the benefits. Teach client about psychological benefits of humility, allowing one to do great work without need of external approval or reward.
9. Client has rigid, inflexible thinking; does not adjust well to changes, such as new settings, colleagues, and situations.	Curiosity, Open-mindedness	Systematically cultivate curiosity and open-mindedness by encouraging client to try new experiences, especially *around people, places, and processes*. Encourage client to deliberately play devil's advocate to build her open-mindedness, by deliberately examining all sides; read and discuss contrary points of views to better inform herself.
10. Client takes good things in life and well-intentioned acts of others for granted.	Gratitude, Social intelligence, Kindness	Discuss with client some of the things he is genuinely grateful for but has not explicitly articulated. Encourage client to reflect on how he would feel if things he takes for granted were not present in his life. Help client to notice and record (in writing or visually through a smartphone) positive acts done by others throughout the day.
11. Client lacks modesty, draws attention unnecessarily, and overrates her qualities and achievements.	Humility & Modesty, Authenticity	Lead client to an accurate, realistic estimate of her abilities and achievements and help her to visualize/recall the experience by feeling authentic, genuine, and without any external pretense. Have client write statements acknowledging her imperfections and how these make her human.
12. Client does not learn from mistakes and often repeats them. Client lacks a deeper understanding of moral and ethical issues and is unable to apply knowledge to practical problems.	Perspective, Practical Wisdom, Prudence	Using a recent decision made by client that had an unfavorable outcome, engage client in sharpening practical wisdom by discussing: (a) What is the impact of this decision on client and others? (b) Has the client optimally used or considered relevant contextual features of the situation? (c) Are there alternative strengths that can be used to achieve a better outcome, such as social intelligence and kindness instead of rigid application of rules (perceived fairness)? (d) Does the client's behavior convey underlying strengths? (e) Has the client sought wise counsel from a peer or a trusted, well-informed source?

Table 4.2
CONTINUED

Challenges (Symptoms)	Potential Character Strength(s)	Strengths-based Considerations
13. Client withdraws by self-isolating or appearing uninterested.	Capacity to Love and Be Loved, Social Intelligence	Client shows genuine love and affection through everyday gestures and actions. Help client communicate care in small ways to those who are interested in her and to be honest and transparent with her friends
14. Client behaves inappropriately in specific situations and does not demonstrate sensitivity or care toward those who are different.	Fairness, Equity & Justice	Without shaming or blaming, encourage client to become aware of positive attributes of people who are different. Gradually encourage client to interact and engage with them. Client stands up for others when they are treated unfairly, bullied, or ridiculed.
15. Client feels stuck at work, is unable to find opportunities for growth, feels listless, bored.	Creativity, Courage, Persistence	Encourage client to approach routine tasks at work in a novel but adaptive manner, without fear of failure. If he tries this and is not successful, coach client to find ways to explore and express his creativity by starting an activity outside of work, something he has always wanted to do but has not been able to do so far. If this activity isn't fulfilling, encourage client to try another until he finds one that is fulfilling.

Consider the following case of our young female client, Emma, who sought psychotherapy to deal with divorce after a short-lived marriage.

Like many clients, Emma entered therapy feeling hurt, harmed, and betrayed. She felt embarrassed that she had chosen to marry at a relatively young age, against the will of her conservative parents who wanted her to continue with her education. She reported experiencing intrusive negative thoughts. Our initial therapeutic focus was on processing the trauma, simply by mutually creating a space where Emma was able to share her feelings of hurt, anger, and betrayal, and where she could feel empathy and validation—by being heard. In these conversations, the clinician focused on the details of trauma as well as gently pointing out some of the healthy behaviors the client demonstrated (such as healthy coping and resilience). The clinician also showed appreciation for Emma's commitment to coming to therapy (recognizing), as well as that she shared her embarrassment, regrets, and fears (courage), and her effort and persistence. This support helped the client to express a desire for change. The strengths-based clinician mindfully seized the moment and encouraged Emma to discuss the possibility of change by gently sharing her strengths noted in therapy thus far. Although initially hesitant to acknowledge her strengths, just hearing about them from a clinician, in a genuine way, increased Emma's self-efficacy.

INCORPORATING STRENGTHS IN POSITIVE PSYCHOTHERAPY: SKILLS AND STRATEGIES

Assessing a client's strengths offers a unique clinical opening to collaboratively devise goals. Clinicians can discuss with clients the goal of the treatment. For example, "Do you want to get rid of all your worries, fears, stressors, and doubts or are you also interested in being happy, confident, and content?" Almost every client in our experience endorses the later, in addition to the former. However, it is critical for clinicians to be cognizant that the goal of PPT is to help clients understand that the absence of weaknesses is not the only clinical goal and that the presence of well-being is equally important for treatment and further prevention of psychological disorders (Keyes, 2013). The following are strategies for incorporating strengths in PPT.

Ways of Assessing Character Strengths

Most measures of psychopathology are expensive and require completion in clinical settings. Valid and reliable strengths measures, developed by practitioners and researchers of positive psychology, are readily available online free of charge. For example, the Authentic Happiness website (www.authentichappiness.org; affiliated with the University of Pennsylvania) and the Values in Action website (www.viacharacter.org) offer such measures. Clients can complete these measures at home and can bring printouts of results to therapy. As previously mentioned, one of the most widely used measures to assess strengths is the VIA-IS (Peterson & Seligman, 2004; www.viacharacter.org). Based on the CVS model of strengths, the VIA-IS is available in two versions—in 240 and 120 items. Also based on the CVS model, a 72-item brief version with feedback mechanism is available (Rashid et al., 2013; www.tayyabrashid.com). All three of these websites provide measures free of charge and provide instant feedback about strengths and other positive attributes.

In addition to self-report measures, interviews guided by research can be used to assess strengths. If clinicians prefer not to use formal assessment, they can use questions during intake or ongoing therapy to elicit strengths, positive emotions, and meaning. Sample questions include, "What gives your life a sense of meaning? Let's pause here and talk about what you are good at. What are your initial thoughts and feelings when you see someone doing an act of kindness or courage?" Flückiger and colleagues (2009) have used a clinical interview to elicit client strengths in the therapeutic process. Following are several of their "resource activation questions" that can be readily incorporated into a life history questionnaire or clinical interview in routine practice:

- What do you enjoy most? Please describe your most enjoyable experiences.
- What are you good at? Please describe experiences that brought out the best in you.
- What are your aspirations for the future?
- What makes a satisfying day for you?
- What experiences give you a sense of authenticity?
- Please describe a time when you felt "the real you."

In their study of psychotherapists, Michael Scheel and his colleagues (2012) identified five themes that can guide clinicians conducting PPT or any strengths-based therapy to assess strengths of clients through interviews. These five themes are described next, with examples from our clinical practice:

AMPLIFICATION OF STRENGTHS

This theme helps clients to see their strengths in the past, notice positives in what is being presented, and tease out successes, even if only small.

> ***Examples:*** *A male client who presented with symptoms of social anxiety shared a story of overcoming the fear of playing his sport in front of the "piercing eyes" of the crowd, by stepping on the field and playing for three minutes during the*

entire season and scoring three points—but this was enough to take his team to the playoffs. A female client with symptoms of posttraumatic stress disorder (PTSD) and depression was able to recall her courage in standing up to someone who was bullying her friend. These stories offer clinicians opportunities to amplify past client strengths.

CONTEXTUAL CONSIDERATIONS

For situations that require more of a problem focus, the clinician needs to understand the limitation of strengths. Working from the theme of contextual considerations postulates that pushing too quickly can prevent a client's future acceptance of strengths.

> ***Examples:*** *Clients with acute symptoms of panic disorder or obsessive-compulsive disorder need specific, well-established treatment protocols. Suggesting that a client who has severe symptoms of social anxiety spontaneously hone her social skills or asking a client to consider posttraumatic growth without processing his trauma first might push such clients away from a strengths-based approach in the future.*

STRENGTHS-ORIENTED PROCESSES

This theme looks at finding ways to define identity from a place of strengths, helping clients to overcome their selective attention on problems and deficits, and taking advantage of good times to discuss strengths.

> ***Example:*** *During an early phase of therapy, a client remarked that "despite taking meditation classes, I feel a sense of restlessness. . . . I feel as if my mind is always in the express lane." The clinician guided this client to mindfully recall the past three days, one day at time, and asked her to look for at least one positive experience—no matter how small. She was able to recall and then write down these three experiences. The clinician complemented the client on her strength of savoring (reminiscence) as well as on appreciation of beauty (one remembered experience included enjoyment of a five-minute walk, exactly when the sun peeked through the clouds). The experience of writing about positive events served as a visual cue to go back to positive moments. The client agreed to begin a gratitude journal, and eventually she found her meditation practice to be helpful.*

STRENGTHS-ORIENTED OUTCOMES

This theme helps clients increase ownership of changes, form goals using their strengths, and learn to set goals of finding or harnessing a specific strength.

> ***Example:*** *A client had established a successful financial consultancy firm, but she went into therapy because she felt a lack of purpose and meaning. In compiling her strengths profile, the client was able to realize that the process of starting a company from scratch and making it successful in a competitive market might not have been possible without her persistence and an abiding sense of optimism and resilience. Along the way, she suffered many setbacks, but she endured. Naming strengths helped the client to acknowledge them deeply, as she had never taken the time to own and celebrate her accomplishments. There was always another target to achieve before moving on to the next. Moreover, this client was able to see that her firm supported many employees and their families—a realization that increased her sense of purpose. To further develop her sense of meaning, the client decided to start an educational scholarship for a student from an economically disadvantaged background.*

POSITIVE MEANING-MAKING

The clinician utilizes the theme of positive meaning making when helping clients to see that strengths develop through increased understanding of their problems, when helping clients to balance their negative and positive traits through realistic perspective, and by helping clients to understand the context in which a challenge or a problem can be a strength.

> *Example:* A male client experienced traumas throughout his life, including surviving multiple air strikes on his homeland, enduring civil war, and struggling to obtain refugee status. In his new country, this client had to work more than 60 hours a week and attend high school and then college. At the beginning of therapy, he saw himself as nothing more than a collection of PTSD, attention deficit hyperactivity disorder, anxiety, and depression symptoms. Identifying strengths and contextualizing them through real-life challenges helped alter his self-perception. Strengths facilitated and helped this client to see his transformation from victim to survivor. Now he is helping other victims of torture and trauma as a counselor—one of the few who can speak their language and understand their cultural nuances.

Spotting Strengths in the Environment

Some clients will be more aware of their strengths than others. Clinicians can encourage their clients to seek collateral information from family members, colleagues, and friends about client strengths, as well as about the strengths of concerned individuals as they relate to the client. This is particularly helpful in assessing and identifying social and communal buffers. For example, in addition to inquiring about problems with family members, clinicians may assess attachment, love, and nurturance from the primary support group, institutions (associations, societies, clubs, fraternities, sororities), and social networks. Clients' problems at work or in the community ought to be explored, as well as benefits and supports embedded in social institutions (Wright & Lopez, 2009).

Strength Exemplars

To help clients discern and identify their own strengths, clinicians can refer to paragons (also called exemplars or icons) of certain strengths. Examples include Malala Yusuf Zai representing bravery; Mahatma Gandhi representing leadership and self-regulation; Mother Theresa representing kindness and humanity; Nelson Mandela representing leadership and persistence; Martin Luther King Jr. representing courage, self-regulation, and fairness; Albert Einstein representing curiosity; Charlie Chaplin representing humor and playfulness; Bill Gates representing altruism; and Meryl Streep representing creativity. Appendix D: Building Your Strengths (which also appears in the client workbook and online at www.oup.com/ppt contains descriptions, behaviors, ways of using strengths, salient research findings, scholarly books, contemporary examples, and relevant websites related to each of 24 strengths.

Using specific icons and film characters to discuss strengths allows for concretized discussions of the application of strengths within the context of real-life conflicts and scaffolds strength development by providing an exemplar to learn from. Clinicians can explore the ways a client does and does not identify with the relevant strength-specific icons and can make reference to these icons when working to resolve dilemmas in the client's life. Clinicians can provide concrete illustrations of strengths by using resources like *Positive Psychology at the Movies* (Niemiec & Wedding, 2013), which lists movies, their themes, and their characters linked with each of the 24 VIA strengths. Appendix D also contains an extensive list of ideas for using strengths with names of movies and exemplars.

Assessing Strengths at the Onset of Therapy

Strengths can be assessed early in the therapeutic process. As rapport is being built through empathic listening, the clinician can start noticing strengths as clients unfold their stories. We recommend discussing strengths as early as possible in therapy for several reasons. First, knowledge and acknowledgment of strengths can be particularly beneficial if a crisis ensues. This understanding equips clinicians with a valuable additional resource that can potentially be activated, especially when resilience is needed to ride the rough waves. At the Health & Wellness Centre, University of Toronto Scarborough, where one of the manual authors is a clinical psychologist and researcher, online assessment of character strengths is part of the standard intake assessment. Upon completing a strengths measure, clients receive feedback about their salient character strengths. Following are three examples.

Example 1: A young female who experienced an automobile accident presented at the intake with severe symptoms of depression, including cognitive and motor slowness. The clinician drew attention to one of her strengths—gratitude—and asked how it represents her. The client reluctantly smiled and after a long pause said, "I am grateful to be alive. . . . I took many good things in my life for granted. I never take anything for granted now."

Example 2: A third-year male student started individual therapy after having just received a college suspension letter, which was due to his academic struggles. During the first session, he appeared dejected and stated that college was not for him. The clinician attended empathically to his concerns and then asked him to share an anecdote that might demonstrate his strength of social intelligence. Despite struggling academically, he always excelled at work as a sales representative at a large retail store. "I could connect with almost everyone and convince them that they needed this specific product. At the end of my first year, to my utter surprise, I was told by my manager that I was number three in the country, in terms of products sold and revenue generated."

Example 3: A middle-age woman had been diagnosed with borderline personality disorder and sought individual therapy after having completed a dialectical behavior therapy group in an outpatient setting. At the intake, when the client and clinician discussed the client's top character strengths, she remarked, "I have been through a lot of treatments, psychotherapies, support groups, and what not, but this is the first time a treatment has started with telling me what I am capable of, in a positive way. . . . I always heard about my weaknesses. This is very generous of you."

Systematic assessment of character strengths, in addition to symptoms, will enrich clinical understanding of your client. If there is a trail of distress behind every symptom, there is also a tale of resilience, connection, and fulfillment for every strength. Naming strengths gives you the opportunity to connect with you client in ways that will instill hope, optimism, courage, and creativity.

5 POSITIVE PSYCHOTHERAPY

PRACTICE, PROCESS, AND MECHANISMS OF CHANGE

PRACTICE AND PROCESS

There are three broad phases of positive psychotherapy (PPT).[1] Table 5.1: Positive Psychotherapy: Session-by-Session Description presents the outline of PPT.

1. At the start of Phase One, the client creates a personal narrative, recalling and writing a story that brought out the client's best, especially in overcoming a challenge. The bulk of therapeutic work in this phase focuses on assessing and assembling a signature strengths profile and acquiring the skills needed to integrate strengths with psychological stressors.
2. Phase Two helps clients learn to reappraise intra- and interpersonal experiences, especially shifting negative ones toward the positive to promote a balanced perspective.
3. Phase Three helps clients pursue meaning and purpose through their strengths.

In this chapter we outline each phase, and, within each phase, we describe the process and the practices used in session and between sessions. Although we describe PPT in a concrete, sequential manner, clinicians need to use their clinical judgment to adaptively apply this process to each client. PPT can be a stand-alone treatment, or its practices can be incorporated into other treatment approaches.

Throughout the entire course of therapy, clinicians encourage clients to keep a *Gratitude Journal* to describe three good things that happened to them during the course of each day. (For more on the *Gratitude Journal*, see Chapter 7, Session 1.) Most clients find it helpful to direct their attention deliberately toward good experiences, which are often otherwise missed in the hustle and bustle of daily life. By the end of therapy, clients have learned to journal their everyday positive experiences in written (handwritten, scribbles, or digital scripts), visual (taking pictures with their mobile devices), or interpersonal (discussion, appreciation, and/or expression in person) formats. This process helps them to sustain the broader experiential awareness they learn to cultivate in session and continue to resist the natural human penchant for the negativity bias. Clients learn that they have a unique set of strengths and that they can use these strengths in different ways. With this in mind we continue to explore PPT's methods.

---

[1] Another treatment approach, also known as positive psychotherapy, was developed by Nosrat Peseschkian in Germany. Peseschkian and his colleagues have worked on their positive psychotherapy for more than 20 years. Although both treatments accidently share the same name, they are distinct from one another. The PPT discussed in this volume is rooted in the more recent and contemporary movement of positive psychology, whereas positive psychotherapy as practiced by Peseschkian and his colleagues is a systematic integrative approach that incorporates cross-cultural and intertheoretic perspectives (Peseschkian, 2000; Peseschkian & Tritt, 1998).

Table 5.1

POSITIVE PSYCHOTHERAPY: SESSION-BY-SESSION DESCRIPTION

Session Number and Title	Content	Main Practices
Phase One		
1: Positive Introduction and Gratitude Journal	This session orients clients to the clinical milieu and clarifies client and clinician roles and responsibilities. This session also teaches how to start the ongoing practice of cultivating gratitude through journaling positive experiences and appreciating the impact of gratitude on well-being.	*Positive Introduction:* Client recalls, reflects, and writes a one-page *Positive Introduction* sharing a story with a beginning, middle, and positive end, in concrete terms that called for the best in the client. *Gratitude Journal:* Client starts an ongoing journal to record three good things every night (big or small) and also writes what made these happen.
2: Character Strengths and Signature Strengths	This is the first of three sessions focusing on Character Strengths and Signature Strengths, which are positive traits that can be developed through practice and can contribute to personal growth and wellness.	*Character Strengths:* Client compiles his signature strengths profile by collecting information from multiple resources including self-report, an online measure, a family member, and a friend.
3: Practical Wisdom	This session presents the skills of practical wisdom. These skills teach us how to adaptively apply our signature strengths in a balanced way to solve problems.	*Know-How of Strengths:* Client applies four practical wisdom strategies (specificity, relevance, conflict, reflection and calibration) to resolve three specific scenarios.
4: A Better Version of Me	This session looks at articulating and implementing a written plan of positive, pragmatic, and persistent self-development.	*A Better Version of Me:* Client writes a self-development plan called *A Better Version of Me*, that uses her strengths adaptively through specific, measurable, and achievable goals.
Phase Two		
5: Open and Closed Memories	In this session, clients recall, write, and process memories, and they learn to develop skills for dealing with open or negative memories.	*Positive Appraisal:* After practicing relaxation, client writes bitter memories and explores four ways to deal with them adaptively.
6: Forgiveness	This session teaches that forgiveness is a process for change, rather than an event. This session explains what forgiveness is and what it is not.	*REACH:* Client learns about REACH—a process of forgiveness; and/or *Forgiveness Letter:* Client writes a letter of forgiveness but does not necessarily deliver it.
7: Maximizing versus Satisficing	This session presents the concepts of maximizing (aiming to make the best possible choice) and satisficing (making a "good enough" choice).	*Toward Satisficing:* Client explores in which domains of life he maximizes or satisfices. Client drafts a plan to increase satisficing.

(continued)

Table 5.1
CONTINUED

Session Number and Title	Content	Main Practices
8: Gratitude	This session expands the concept of gratitude by having the client recall and write to someone who is alive now and who in the past did something positive but who the client has never fully thanked.	*Gratitude Letter:* Client reflects and writes a letter of gratitude to someone who helped at a time of need and who has not been thanked properly. *Gratitude Visit:* Client invites the person for whom she wrote the *Gratitude Letter* for a one-on-one meeting. Without explaining in advance, client reads the letter in person.
Phase Three		
9: Hope and Optimism	In this session, clients learn to see the best possible, realistic outcomes. They learn that challenges are temporary and how to develop a sense of hope.	*One Door Closes, Another Door Opens:* Client reflects and writes about three doors that closed and three doors that opened.
10: Posttraumatic Growth	This session invites clients to explore their deep feelings and thoughts about a traumatic experience that continues to bother them.	*Expressive Writing:* Client can complete an optional exercise of transporting troubling and traumatic experiences to a piece of paper, with the assurance that this writing is only for the client's eyes, to be kept in a secure place. The practice is completed after the client develops healthy coping skills and is not overwhelmed by current stressors.
11: Slowness and Savoring	In this session, clients learn how to deliberately slow down and develop an awareness of how to savor. In so doing, they learn to attend mindfully to the positives.	*Slow and Savor:* Client selects one slowness technique and one savoring technique that fit her personality and life circumstances.
12. Positive Relationships	In this session, clients learn the significance of recognizing the strengths of their loved ones.	*Tree of Positive Relationships:* The client, along with his loved ones, assesses his strengths; everyone plots them on a large "tree"—drawn on paper. Client discusses with his loved ones ways of enriching relationships by celebrating one another's strengths
13: Positive Communication	In this session, clients learn about four styles of responding to good news and which of these predicts relationship satisfaction.	*Active Constructive Responding:* Client explores the strengths of her significant other and also practices active-constructive responding.
14: Altruism	In this session, clients learn how being altruistic helps both themselves and others.	*Gift of Time:* Client plans to give the gift of time by doing something that also uses client's signature strengths.
15. Meaning and Purpose	This session focuses on the search and pursuit of meaningful endeavors for the greater good.	*Positive Legacy:* Client writes how she would like to be remembered, especially in terms of her positive footprints.

Phase One

PROCESS

Phase One of PPT occurs in the first four sessions. Starting with the first session, clinicians encourage clients to reflect upon their personal narrative, which is centered on a specific experience or event that brought out a client's best. The clinician encourages clients to share anecdotes, accounts, and stories that show their strengths in tandem with their struggles—that is, to express how clients have successfully coped with or overcome challenges—big or small.

The clinician empathically listens to the presenting concerns of clients to establish and maintain a trusting therapeutic relationship. The discussion of symptomatic distress is deepened with a conversation about simple acts of goodness in everyday life, such as the client making and enjoying a specific meal, savoring the nice weather, or successfully completing everyday chores. These discussions allow clients to bring their attention to small but positive aspects of their lives, aspects that may be obscured by an excessive focus on diagnostic distress.

Clients then assess their strengths through multiple resources (see Chapter 8, Session 2) and set realistic goals that are relevant to their presenting problems and their well-being. The core of Phase One of PPT is broadening clients' perspectives by introducing them to their own strengths, past and present, through self-appraisal and by incorporating input from significant others. This process is achieved primarily through writing a narrative of resilience and identifying strengths that enabled this resilience. The clinician actively looks for opportunities to help clients deepen their understanding of how strengths can be used adaptively to handle a challenging situation. Evidence shows that recall of positive experience plays an important role in mood regulation (Joormann, Dkane, & Gotlib, 2006). Such recall allows individuals to "savor" these positive emotions (Bryant, Smart, & King, 2005). Fitzpatrick and Stalikas (2008) have suggested that positive emotions, especially in the early phase of the therapeutic process, serve as a generator of change—enabling clients to consider new ideas and perspectives—and can build long-term cumulative resources.

The last step in the assessment of strengths is for the clinician to encourage clients to develop practical wisdom (see Chapter 9, Session 3). In terms of using strengths, practical wisdom is considered a master strength (Schwartz & Sharpe, 2010). It is the *Know-How of Strengths*. Practical wisdom entails the ability to adapt fluctuating situational demands by reconfiguring mental resources including strengths; shifting perspective; and balancing competing desires, needs, and life domains (Kashdan & Rottenberg, 2010; Young, Kashdan, & Macatee, 2015).

PPT helps clients to regulate emotions and enhance self-evaluation in various contexts by teaching them nuanced, calibrated, and contextualized use of both positives and negatives. For example, clients may be motivated to experience or even reinforce negative emotions because these may be more useful to them than positive ones:

- Anger, frustration, or disappointment in a close relationship may signal wrongdoing by the other person.
- Confidence about completing an important task, without an optimal level of anxiety, may turn into procrastination.
- Avoiding the acknowledgment of loss and grief and resorting to unhealthy coping means (e.g., drugs, sex, or shopping) may prevent clients from comprehending the meaning of loss and contemplating a revised personal narrative that may be necessary for adaptive coping.

PPT does not necessarily ask clients to use specific strengths more; rather, PPT encourages clients to engage in deeper reflection of when and how using specific strengths could be adaptive or maladaptive and how this use can impact others (Biswas-Diener, Kashdan, & Minhas, 2011; Freidlin, Littman-Ovadia, & Niemiec, 2017; Kashdan & Rottenberg, 2010). Table 4.2 (in Chapter 4) presents potential connections between psychological challenges and ways specific strengths-based strategies can be used to overcome them.

PRACTICES

Clients begin PPT by creating a *Positive Introduction*, which provides the opportunity to be introduced through a story that depicts them when they believe they are at their best, especially in overcoming a challenge (see Chapter 7, Session 1). For homework, clients reflect further and concretize this introduction into an approximately 300-word written story. For the remainder of Phase One, the focus is on strengths practices, which begin with a comprehensive strengths assessment (see Chapter 8, Session 2). PPT recommends using two valid and reliable measures, the 120-item Values in Action–Inventory of Strengths (VIA-IS; Peterson & Seligman, 2004) and the Signature Strengths Questionnaire (Rashid et al., 2013). Both of these measures are derived from the Classification of Strengths & Virtues (Peterson & Seligman, 2004). The strengths assessment also incorporates other self-report measures (identifying strengths based on descriptions and based on associated photos) and collateral reports from significant others identifying (*not ranking*) client signature strengths. (The collateral reports are acquired by the client between sessions.) The clinician then aggregates data from all sources to determine the client's signature strengths. This comprehensive assessment process enables clients to identify, comprehend, and contextualize their strengths in concrete terms. A comprehensive list of behaviors and actions which are meant to display 24 character strengths is available at the end of this manual in Appendix D: Building Your Strengths (which also appears in the client workbook and online at www.oup.com/ppt). This resource translates abstract notion of strengths into manageable concrete actions.

Throughout the course of therapy, to keep signature strengths equally prominent with symptoms, clinicians gently nudge clients to share memories, experiences, real-life stories, anecdotes, accomplishments, and skills that illustrate the use and development of their signature strengths. However, in discussing strengths, the clinician should not undermine or minimize negative characteristics; context is important in determining when to use strengths. For example, as noted, clients may be motivated to act upon or even reinforce negative emotions because these may be more useful than positive emotions in a given context. PPT does not necessarily ask clients to use a specific strength more but rather engages clients to consider when and how expressing specific strengths could be adaptive or maladaptive. This approach is consistent with strategies advanced by Kashdan and Rottenberg (2010) and Biswas-Diener, Kashdan, and Minhas (2011).

Phase One of PPT ends with clients setting specific and attainable behavioral goals that adaptively use their signature strengths to address their presenting concerns. These goals are central to the practice, *A Better Version of Me* (see Chapter 10, Session 4). This practice is a modification of the original positive psychology intervention *Our Best Selves* (Sheldon & Lyubomirsky, 2006) and encourages clients to become their more attainable "better selves." With increased understanding about their deepest assets and signature strengths, clients are guided to visualize and then write, in concrete terms, a personal goal related to their presenting concerns. The aim is to improve self-regulation toward restructuring the client's priorities and to increase the client's motivation and emotions. The writing portion of this practice is important. Research shows that making a written plan of self-improvement increases chances of success by 42% (Fadla, 2014).

Phase Two

PROCESS

Phase Two of PPT is made up of Sessions Five through Eight. This phase focuses on helping clients apply strengths adaptively through discussions of the nuances of effectively navigating day-to-day hassles and resolving or otherwise constructively addressing more significant adversities, like grudges, negative memories, or traumas. Clients are further taught to use their strengths in a calibrated and flexible way that could adaptively meet situational challenges (Biswas-Diener, Kashdan, & Minhas, 2011). In doing so, the clinician highlights specific client actions or habits that may explain symptoms or troubles as either a lack of or an excess of strengths (as discussed previously), rather than in terms of deficits.

The core of Phase Two of PPT is to help clients learn specific positive and meaning-based coping strategies to reinterpret open (unresolved) and negative memories that continue to trouble clients (Folkman & Moskowtiz, 2000). Consider the following example from one of our clinical practices:

Sam, a psychologically minded young male, spent the first three sessions of his individual therapy sharing what appeared to be a well-rehearsed narrative. It was filled with recent and past memories of feeling insecure about his current romantic relationship, feeling angry at his father who left the family when Sam was barely nine, dissatisfaction with his appearance, and feeling awkward in social situations. The need to share these details, with a rationale, was so strong that his clinician did not feel compelled to intervene until this client shared one positive memory about his father. Sam stated that although his father was rarely present in Sam's life due to drug issues, the father participated in one ritual with Sam, almost religiously. This was an opening, and the clinician did not hesitate to ask for details. Sam explained that every December, his father would take him to a local Christmas fair, and they would wait for a long time to ride the Ferris wheel. Bundled up, with hot chocolate in their hands, Sam described the 10- to 12-minute ride as the best thing of the year. While discussing the details of this memory, Sam's affect changed. Although his views about his father did not change much, describing a specific positive memory created a soft, small niche of positivity in his heart. Sam also realized that he had spent a lot of time brooding on negative memories of his father, events from the past that could not be changed. Sam, nevertheless, had the option now to change his reactions toward these memories.

Throughout Phase Two of PPT, clients become aware of the amount of attention and other resources they have been using on open and negative memories, and they learn ways to redeploy this attention toward genuine and authentic positive events in their lives. (See Chapter 11, Session 5.) After learning what forgiveness is and is not (see Chapter 12, Session 6), clients are presented with the option of utilizing forgiveness to halt the cycle of resentment-based emotion. They may experience an enduring sense of thankfulness by reflecting on past positive memories. Writing about and reflecting on deeply personal experiences helps clients make sense of their emotions, which in turn, offers them a greater sense of control—an essential ingredient of personal growth (Deci & Ryan, 2008).

PRACTICES

In Phase Two of PPT, after establishing therapeutic rapport and helping clients identify their strengths, clinicians encourage clients to write about their grudges, bitter memories, or resentments and then discuss the effects of holding onto these negatives. PPT does not discourage expression of negative emotions; rather, PPT encourages clients to access a full range of emotions—positive and negative. However, as noted previously, negative emotions (often in the form of grudges or bitter memories) linger and stick with us much longer than their positive counterparts. There are a number of PPT practices that help clients to deal with negative memories adaptively. For example, *Positive Appraisal* (Rashid & Seligman, 2013) helps clients unpack their grudges and resentments (see Chapter 11, Session 5), and reappraise them through four strategies:

- *Creating psychological space:* Clients write about a bitter memory from a third-person perspective, which is less personal and more neutral. This practice helps clients dispense less effort and time on recounting emotionally evocative details of negative memories (Kross, Ayduk, & Mischel, 2005). As a result, more cognitive and attentional resources are available for clients to reconstitute their feelings and the meaning of the negative memory, rather than rehashing what happened and what they felt.

- *Reconsolidation:* Clients recall finer and subtle aspects of a bitter memory in a relaxed state. The purpose is to recollect, refile, and reconsolidate positive or adaptive aspects of the bitter memory that might have been overlooked due to the mind's tendency toward negativity.
- *Mindful self-focus*: Clients are encouraged to *observe* negative memories rather than *react* to them. This practice is about stepping back and letting the open and negative memories unfold in front of a client's eyes, like watching a film. Clients are taught to be observers of these memories rather than participants, with a deliberate effort to loosen the emotional strings attached to the memory.
- *Diversion:* Clients are encouraged to recognize cues that activate the recall of a bitter memory and are helped to immediately engage in an alternative physical or cognitive activity (diversion) to stop the full rehearsing of the bitter memory. Densely interconnected, the bitter memories of psychologically distressed clients are often triggered by external cues. Engaging clients in an adaptive alternative activity helps to halt the cyclical slide into negative memories. If done effectively, clients learn to deal with negative memories rather than be consumed by them.

In Chapter 12, Session 6, the clinician explores scenarios with clients to help them understand what forgiveness is and what it is not. Forgiveness in PPT is conceptualized as a process of change—to willingly forsake one's right (perceived or real) to take revenge (Harris et al., 2007; Wade, Worthington, & Haake, 2009). Clients are taught that forgiveness is not condoning or pardoning the offender, undermining socially acceptable justice, forgetting the wrong, or ignoring the consequences of the offense. They learn that forgiveness is also not simply replacing the negative thoughts or emotions with neutral or positive ones (Enright & Fitzgibbons, 2015). Using this understanding, clients write about one of their own negative experiences with the intention of resolving it through forgiveness.

Another practice in the middle part of PPT, *Toward Satisficing* (Schwartz et al., 2002), helps clients understand how to be aware of energy and time spent on tasks and to manage this expenditure for appropriate and beneficial ends. (See Chapter 13, Session 7.) The intent of this practice is to raise client awareness that we often spend a lot of time shopping, which distracts us from encountering negatives head-on and doesn't add much to our well-being.

A related and equally central construct in PPT is gratitude, which is a state of being thankful for recognized positives in one's life. Gratitude has been reliably found to have strong associations with well-being (Davis et al., 2016; Kerr, O'Donovan, & Pepping, 2015; Wood, Froh, & Geraghty, 2010). Two related practices, as described in Chapter 14, Session 8, are essential to cultivating gratitude in this phase of PPT. The first is the *Gratitude Letter*, in which the client recalls a person who did something kind for her and for which the client never thanked that person. In session, clients write a first draft of a letter that clearly and authentically expresses their gratitude, describing the specifics of the person's act of kindness and its positive consequences. For homework, clients write another two drafts of the letter and then organize a *Gratitude Visit*. In this second practice, clients are encouraged to read the letter to the recipient in-person or over the phone. When done in-person, this practice can generate powerful positive emotions on both sides and is often described by clients as a deeply moving experience that they were initially reluctant to engage in.

Phase Three
PROCESS
Phase Three of PPT, which spans Sessions Nine to Fifteen, focuses on restoring or fostering positive relationships (both intimate and communal). Frankl's *Man's Search for Meaning* (1963) and *The Doctor and the Soul: From Psychotherapy to Logotherapy* (1986)—two seminal texts on meaning and purpose—emphasize that happiness cannot be attained by desiring it alone. Rather, happiness must "ensue" as the unintended consequence of working for a goal greater than oneself. People who are able to pursue activities that connect them

to such larger goals experience greater well-being (McKnight & Kashdan, 2009; McLean & Pratt, 2006; Schnell, 2009). Therefore, in Phase Three of PPT, clients are likely ready to pursue meaning and purpose; strengths have broadened clients' self-concepts, and clients have been able to deal with troubling memories and to learn about forgiveness, and have started to see the benefits of gratitude. Research strongly supports that a sense of meaning and purpose helps clients to deal with psychological distress effectively, and the presence of a sense of purpose helps clients to recover or rebound from adversity as well as buffers against feelings of hopelessness and lack of control (Bonanno & Mancini, 2012; Calhoun & Tedeshi, 2006; Graham, Lobel, Glass & Lokshina, 2008; Skaggs & Barron, 2006). Phase Three of PPT encourages clients to cultivate meaning by engaging in a number of processes, such as strengthening close interpersonal and communal relationships; pursuing artistic, intellectual, or scientific innovations; or engaging in philosophical or religious contemplation (Stillman & Baumeister, 2009; Wrzesniewski, McCauley, Rozin, & Schwartz, 1997). Practices in this phase, such as *One Door Closes, Another Door Opens; Expressive Writing;* and *Gift of Time,* help clients to search for and pursue meaning and purpose. During the process, clients often share painful and sometimes traumatic experiences. The clinician empathetically attends to these client experiences and, whenever appropriate, also explores themes of growth from such experiences. The following are two clinical illustrations of this exploration:

> One of our female clients, a student named Nafissa, was being emotionally abused by her partner and was raising a developmentally challenged child. This client felt that no one cared about her. After establishing a solid therapeutic relationship through empathy and appreciating her resilience, the clinician asked how, despite all of these challenges, she was able to continue her studies? Nafissa paused and then described details of tremendous support she receives from her older sister. Barely 10 minutes prior, she felt alone and helpless, but after discussing the details of support from the sister, Nafissa's affect within session changed; discussing the details of her support helped this client appreciate the strengths of others and assuaged her anger—somewhat.

> Nyugen, a female client with emotional dysregulation symptoms and drug addiction issues, was seeing one of us for individual therapy. Toward the end of one session, this client stated that she was troubled by the thought that some months before she had had an abortion—something she had not discussed in previous sessions. She had already completed her Signature Strengths Profile, and kindness was one of her strengths. Incidentally, prior to this last-minute comment, the clinician and Nyugen had discussed her kindness. A week later, in the next session, this client said, "you know I mentioned how bothered I was by that thought. . . . I thought about it because we were discussing kindness. . . . I suddenly wondered what would be a kind thing to do in this situation. . . . I searched and have decided to donate one of my eggs to a couple who would benefit from it." She further elaborated that, in order to donate, she has to remain drug-free for a year. She felt that her decision would support others as well as herself.

PRACTICES

The practices in Phase Three of PPT continue to use the client's strengths and focus on using these strengths to belong to and serve something bigger than oneself. Several practices in Phase Three focus on improving interpersonal relationships by noticing, acknowledging, and celebrating the strengths of others or by deploying one's strengths to connect with others (Ryan, Huta, & Deci, 2008). Clients also learn to spot strengths of their loved ones and plan interpersonal events around shared or relevant strengths through the practice called *Tree of Positive Relationships.* Another practice, *Active Constructive Responding,* teaches clients ways to validate and capitalize on precious moments when their partners share good news with them (Gable, Reis, Impett, & Asher, 2004). The final two practices of this phase (*Gift of Time* and *Positive Legacy*), help clients to share their strengths in serving others through meaningful endeavors and to articulate a vision as how they would like to be remembered.

Mindfulness can promote meaning by making us aware of pleasurable moments that would have slipped by unfulfilled if we did not explicitly draw our attention to them. Clinical experience suggests that most clients seek therapy to manage stressors associated with living in fast-paced and highly complex environments. The *Slow and Savor* practice (Bryant & Veroff, 2007) requires clients to pay close attention to the sensations associated with performing a simple task, such as eating a raison, touching a feather, or smelling a fragrance. Clients tend to find that by simply paying attention to such activities, they become more pleasurable and interesting. The clinician should work to help clients implement this mindful savoring into varying aspects of their lives. Another practice, the *Gift of Time*, helps clients experience the importance and impact that explicitly making time for significant others has on their relationships and the individuals within the relationships.

The final practice of PPT, *Positive Legacy*, asks clients to write a brief (maximum one page) piece focused on how they themselves would like to be remembered. The process is intended to teach clients the ability to select and streamline specific strengths to achieve long-term goals, as well as to anticipate or adjust to any obstacles they may face along the way (Schmid, Phelp, & Lerner, 2011). This final practice ties in with the opening practice in terms of gaining mastery from the past (*Positive Introduction*) and calibrating strengths and motivation for the future (*Positive Legacy*). The following is an illustration:

> *Malika, a client in her 40s, returned to school to complete her graduate degree after her children became independent. She started individual psychotherapy feeling cynical and bitter, mostly toward her ex-partner. But as she worked actively and created a healthy distance from toxic memories of the past, Malika became increasingly future oriented, and the Positive Legacy practice helped her articulate what she really wants from life:*
>
> *"I don't want to be remembered as an angry and bitter person. . . . Sure, I want to be remembered as authentic but not too authentic in the sense that I am always wrapped in bitterness. I want to be remembered as happy and perhaps more importantly as a caring and committed person—someone who worked hard, and did not give in to the harsh bellows of life. I want to be remembered as a mother who taught her three children that the real test of life is not to collect wealth and resources but to share them. I don't want to be remembered as a person who couldn't forgive those who harmed her. I know I didn't receive the most cheerful genes, but whatever I received, I made it better, not worse."*

Clinician Note

The three phases and processes described here may not always unfold as intended and may not work equally well with all clients. Consider these phases to be interweaving paths toward recovery and well-being. A client may not fully comprehend the meaning in her story until meaning and purpose are discussed in the later phases of therapy. Similarly, the Positive Appraisal practice may open a lot more than can be contained within 15 sessions. Situational or other factors, such as a limited number of therapy sessions, an emerging crisis or trauma that requires immediate and ongoing attention, or client preference not to focus on strengths may prohibit some clients from fully expressing their strengths. Change is hard. Years spent focusing on negativity may need more than 15 sessions to cultivate and cement strengths like hope, zest, and gratitude.

INTRODUCTION AND THEORETICAL FOUNDATIONS

MECHANISMS OF CHANGE

In a systematic review of PPT, Walsh, Cassidy, and Priebe (2016) have identified some mechanisms of change, as shown in Figure 5.1. These mechanisms are discussed in five broad categories. The parenthetical descriptors following each heading broadly correspond with variables described in Figure 5.1.

Cultivation of Positive Emotions (Reeducation of Attention)

Several PPT practices explicitly cultivate positive emotions, which open our attentional resources. Barbara Fredrickson's seminal work on positive emotions has shown that positive emotions, although fleeting in nature, broaden our cognitive and behavioral repertoire (Fredrickson, 2001, 2009). PPT practices such as the *Gratitude Journal, Gratitude Letter, Gratitude Visit*, and *Slow and Savor* specifically facilitate cultivation of positive emotions. In the *Gratitude Journal* practice, before going to bed, clients write three good things—small or large—that happened during the course of the day. Most clients find this practice to be helpful not only in coping with negative experiences but also in cementing relationships through explicitly noticing kind acts and gestures of friends and family. Thus a new sense of appreciation develops for existing relationships. Explicitly expressing gratitude for a kind act—preferably in person, although not easy—almost always produces positive emotions because this expression comes with a genuine and focused sense of enduring thankfulness, which engenders positive emotions on all sides. For example, after completing this practice, one of our clients, a middle-aged male manager, remarked:

> *At work, I used to only see gaps, mistakes of my supervisees. Ever since I started my journal, I am deliberate to find something good my employees did . . . and there are plenty of things I missed. . . . I can now see.*

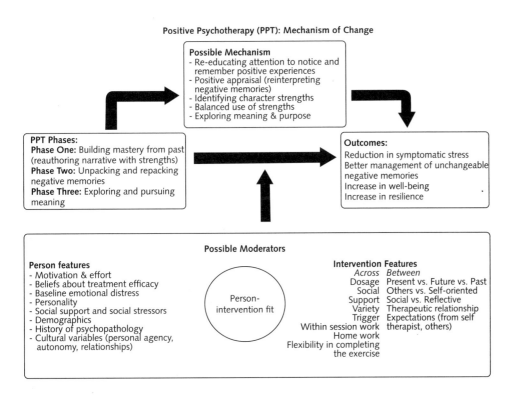

FIGURE 5.1 **Mechanisms of Change in PPT**

Likewise, the *Gratitude Letter* and *Gratitude Visit* often produce deeply felt positive emotions, as shown in the following illustration of our client, Lawrence, who described the *Gratitude Visit* experience:

> *It took me seven drafts to write what I exactly wanted to say, for I didn't want to rush.*
>
> *Mark and I used to have dinner or lunch once a week, at a particular diner. I choose the same one when I recently invited Mark for a dinner on a weekend. We were sitting in the middle of the busy diner. While we were waiting for the food, which we were told would take at least 25 minutes to arrive, I told Mark, "I have a note for you that I want to read."*
>
> *He looked at me and asked in a worried tone, "Are you all right, Lawrence? Is everything okay with your health? You don't look well—"*
>
> *"No, no, I am fine. I need to read this to you out loud," I tried to explain.*
>
> *"Okay, go ahead," he said, somewhat ambivalently.*
>
> *I read the letter, and to my utter surprise, I saw tears in his eyes—something I have never seen. We have been friends for 33 years. He was speechless, and so was I. But this was one of the times we both were salient and connected like never before.*

This example illustrates that positive emotions can produce transformative moments. Toepfer and Walker (2009) have found that the quality, expressive words, and tone of the *Gratitude Letter* can contribute to well-being. In addition, by identifying their own character strengths and that of others, clients are likely to feel valued and to recognize the value of others. Clients develop awareness about savoring and relating to others in a positive manner. The letter and visit had a positive impact on the previous client's well-being as it revived an important relationship that was perhaps adversely impacted by his ongoing depression. Underscoring the importance of positive emotions as potential generators of therapeutic change, Fitzpatrick and Stalikas (2008) posit that broadening has heuristic value to psychotherapy, enlarging the scope as to what contributes to change and how change can be achieved. For example, in PPT, one can argue that practices not only generate positive emotions but also prepare clients to be more open. When clients experience positive emotions, they are more likely to think of novel ideas, develop alternative solutions to their problems, reinterpret their current challenges, and initiate fresh solutions and new courses of action. Positive emotions broaden thinking, making it flexible and inclusive. This expansion, coupled with the knowledge of their strengths, encourages clients to reframe their problems. Week-by-week PPT practices enable clients to condition and harness their attention and awareness to spot, label, and describe positive experiences. Thus PPT practices serve as "mini change events" that accumulate over time to create a larger outcome.

Positive Appraisal (Rewriting of Memories)

Phase Two of PPT focuses on helping clients encounter negative memories (referred to as "open memories" in PPT) in a systematic way. In a relaxed and safe therapeutic environment, after clients have established therapeutic alliance, explored their strengths, and acquired practical wisdom strategies, they attempt to reinterpret negative experiences, events, or situation in a realistically positive way (Watkins et al., 2008). The emphasis is on helping clients see the adverse impact of carrying negative memories and the positive implications for developing a richer, deeper, and more nuanced emotional and cognitive vocabulary. Clients also learn specific strategies to shift their attention from negative moods—which keep them trapped—to more neutral moods. In conjunction with these skills, clients acquire other skills to help them use their strengths. For instance, *Positive Appraisal* skills helped one of our clients, Gina, who was embittered by her open and negative memories of an acrimonious divorce:

While she undertook this practice, Gina also kept a Gratitude Journal (an ongoing practice), which reinforced her skills of recognizing both the adaptive and maladaptive dimensions of her strengths. For this client, the change was not due to one or two practices or skills but was due to contemplating her strengths (Signature Strengths Profile), reinterpreting the past (Positive Appraisal), initiating and maintaining a positive frame of mind to overcome her negativity bias (attending therapy regularly), and keeping a Gratitude Journal). Together, these processes helped Gina understand that emotional reactions can be dynamic3 and awareness of strengths helps us to explore the positive or adaptive aspects of these dynamics.

Emotions associated with memories are malleable because of their inherent reconstructive property. Negative memories can be re-written, reducing their adverse impact (Redondo et al., 2014). Through *Positive Appraisal*, clients learn to associate negative experiences with positive ones.

Therapeutic Writing (Identification of Character Strengths)

A number of PPT practices that facilitate *Positive Appraisal* involve reflection and writing. Writing—following reflection (individual) and discussion (with the clinician) about a significant experience, to make sense of it—is another potential mechanism of change. This approach is considered to be a powerful therapeutic avenue (Frattaroli, 2006). It appears that writing about both positive (*Positive Introduction, Gratitude Letter, Positive Legacy*) and negative events (open memories) allows clients to make sense of the events. The benefits of writing about traumatic events are well documented (Pennebaker, 1997). Writing about both negative and positive events helps clients to explore deeper dimensions of the experiences. How exactly might the writing process lead to change? In PPT, writing almost always happens in tandem with reflection—either by the client individually or facilitated by the clinician within the session. For example, in the *Gratitude Journal* practice, clients organize their personal and emotional experiences in a more intimate way, which allows them to reflect on experiences and emotions that are relevant to therapy. Thus, in this situation, writing works in tandem with *Positive Appraisal*. The process allows clients to organize their scrambled memories into sequential, somewhat structured, verbal language, within safe confines and in the presence (literally or metaphorically) of a clinician. A supportive therapeutic relationship helps clients to reframe or reappraise emotionally sensitive and often avoided experiences.

Reflection and writing also help clients to focus on the perspective of time. For example, the *Positive Introduction* practice highlights mastery *from the past* to boost self-efficacy *in the present*, while *A Better Version of Me* and *Positive Legacy* allow clients to use mastery, success, and resilience *from the past and present to visualize a meaningful future* that is based on the deliberate deployment of strengths.

The overarching umbrella of positive emotions throughout PPT increases the odds that clients will experience an increase in information processing, which, in turn, can help them to be more open and exploratory in their writing as they reappraise their experiences. There is already solid evidence that writing about traumatic experiences is beneficial for mental and physical health (Frattaroli, 2006; Kerner & Fitzpatrick, 2007; Phillips & Rolfe, 2016). Emerging evidence shows that writing about both negative and positive events helps clients to explore deeper dimensions of the experiences (Burton & King, 2004; Furnes & Dysvik, 2013). The changes we witnessed in our clients who completed PPT, individual and group, show that reflecting and writing about positives as well as negatives can be therapeutic.

Resource Activation (Using Strengths)

PPT is based on the resource-activation model (Flückiger & Grosse Holtforth, 2008) of psychotherapy, which applies clients' pre-existing resources—such as individual strengths, abilities, and readiness—to the very problems for which they seek therapy. PPT activities, such as exploring one's signature strengths—with collateral data from other practices, such as the *Gratitude Visit, Active Constructive Responding, Slow and Savor,* and the *Gift of Time*—activate resources, that is, translate strengths into concrete, personally applicable actions. Undertaking these practices helps clients experience abstract ideas in reality, which in turn changes client feelings. After all, clients seek therapy because they feel distressed, and putting their strengths and other PERMA elements into action deploys client cognitive resources (e.g., working memory, attention, selection, and filtration) on these activities which may not leave sufficient time to dwell on the negative aspects of life. More experiential engagement with positive experiences enhances self-efficacy and strengthens client self-confidence. Research has shown that strengths relate to life satisfaction due to an increased level of self-concept (Allan & Duffy, 2014; Douglass & Duffy, 2015).

Clinicians are able to foster resource activation as clients explicate their own competencies by exploring and owning their personal and interpersonal skills and resilience and by pursuing personally meaningful and relevant goals. For example:

> After Saima, a female client with depression, shared her Positive Introduction and completed her signature strengths practice, she said, "The years I spent in therapy looking only at what is missing in me, feels like I was wrapping myself in a false security blanket. . . . Just made me wallow more. . . . Now I see—and others also agree with me—that I am a spiritual, creative, and socially intelligent person. I feel as if that blanket, that veil, has been removed, and I am ready to move on." She was able to set specific goals through the practice of completing *A Better Version of Me.*

It appears that the more clients feel valued and in good hands, the more they might be willing and able to work on their presenting issues. Identification of strengths, we believe, helps clients to experience themselves as competent and self-trusting.

Experiential Skill Building (Meaning and Purpose)

PPT practices allow clients to develop their *signature strengths*. Symptomatic distress keeps these assets hidden, and clients coming for therapy are often unaware of their specific strengths. Unlike hedonic activities (i.e., pleasure-inducing activities, such as eating chocolates, having sex, going on vacations, or shopping), which are short-cuts, PPT practices are intentional activities that are time-order intensive (e.g., first writing about and then completing a *Gratitude Visit*, devising a plan to use signature strengths, writing three good things daily in a *Gratitude Journal*, arranging a savoring date, and giving a *Gift of Time*). Compared to hedonic pleasures that one gets used to (or adapted to) quickly, PPT activities last longer, involve quite a lot of thinking and interpretation, and do not habituate easily. For example, evidence shows that experiential activities predict higher well-being compared to shopping (Dittmar, Bond, Hurst, & Kasser, 2014; Kasser, 2002). Therefore, from the start of therapy, clients are told that happiness does not simply happen, but rather it is something that they must make happen. PPT practices change clients because any activity that taps the signature strengths of clients can be engaging (Allan & Duffy, 2014; Forest et al., 2012). For example, a client with the signature strength of creativity was asked to think of something that would use her creativity. She selected pottery—something she had always wanted to try.

Role of Moderator Variables in Therapeutic Change (Person-Intervention Fit)

A number of potential moderators can impact therapeutic change. Stephen Schuller (2010) has discussed at length the person-activity fit. In the context of PPT practices, this process essentially entails the clinician targeting specific practices to the needs of individual clients, taking into account their personality disposition and intrinsic motivation. For example: Is a client motivated toward change? If so, what is his level of commitment and sense of self-efficacy? Does a client perceive PPT in general and specific practices to be helpful? Does a client value PPT practices enough that despite challenges, her commitment level will not wane? If it wanes, does she have social support to help her re-engage? What are the overall contextual features in terms of the optimal level of intensity, timing, sequence, and integration of specific exercises? (Lyubomirsky & Layous, 2013; Schueller, Kashdan, & Parks, 2014). How much flexibility is allowed within each PPT practice to address unique personality, cultural features, and contextual features in creating individualized treatment packages, without comprising core treatment integrity? Part II of this manual discusses fit and flexibility for each PPT practice.

CAVEATS IN CONDUCTING PPT

Positive psychology has been criticized for not exploring people's troubles deeply enough and for quickly steering people to individually based positive notions (Coyne & Tennen, 2010; Ehrenreich, 2009; McNulty & Fincham, 2012). As reiterated throughout this chapter in various ways, the therapeutic aim of PPT does not deny negative emotions, nor does it encourage clients to quickly search for positives through rose-colored glasses. PPT is a scientific endeavor that gently encourages clients to explore their intact resources and learn to use them in overcoming their challenges. That said, in conducting PPT, it is important be mindful of the following caveats:

1. Despite emphasizing strengths, PPT is not prescriptive. Rather, it is a descriptive approach based on converging scientific evidence indicating that certain benefits accrue when individuals attend to the positive aspects of their experience. With time, specific lines of evidence will also accrue that positives and strengths play a causal role measured by biological and genetic markers. For example, doing well (not simply feeling good) is associated with the stronger expression of antibody and antiviral genes (Fredrickson et al., 2013). Similarly, tweets from people showing negative emotions such as anger, stress, and fatigue were associated with higher heart disease risk (Eichstaedt et al., 2015). The scientific base of PPT ideas and practices should be explained explicitly to the client to avoid it being perceived as a prescriptive approach.

2. It is clinically imprudent to apply PPT with clients experiencing acute symptoms of panic disorder, selective mutism, or paranoid personality disorder, as currently there is no evidence that PPT is effective for these disorders. Furthermore, some clients may have a strong feeling that their symptoms, not their strengths, ought to be the focus of treatment. Such clients may fear that expression or articulation of their weaknesses will be judged by the clinician. Others may have a deeply entrenched self-perception of being a victim and may not easily discover their agency. Yet for others, identification of character strengths may exaggerate narcissistic characteristics. Therefore, it is important that strengths be discussed within specific situational contexts and nuances be discussed thoroughly. For example, some clients may not benefit from being kind or forgiving in certain situations. Likewise, others may feel conflicted by being both authentic and socially intelligent. Some may face the dilemma of solving a complex challenge by being honest or empathic. Similarly, clients with a history of abuse and with a strengths profile of being humble, kind, and forgiving may not readily benefit from PPT until they develop the strength of perspective and critical thinking skills to understand situations more accurately and realistically. Clients with experiences of severe trauma and symptoms of posttraumatic stress may respond better initially to symptom-focused treatments

and may not be ready for PPT practices on posttraumatic growth. In summary, PPT is not a panacea. It may be more effective for some clinical issues than for others. It may also be more relevant to some clients than to others and may be relevant at specific times rather than all the time. The clinician must explore these dimensions to evaluate the client-treatment fit, and should also monitor this fit on an ongoing basis.

3. A clinician using PPT should not expect a linear progression of improvement because the motivation to change long-standing behavioral and emotional patterns fluctuates during the course of therapy. Clinicians should not assume that all residual negative emotions, hurts, pains, and sense of loss have been dealt with—because clients may not have mentioned everything. It is not uncommon for some PPT practices to generate negative and uncomfortable emotions. The nature of some of these practices encourages clients to explore pain (as well as potential growth) from difficult and traumatic experiences. When painful memories come up, the clinician should always be mindful to address these negative emotions in a timely manner, without trivializing or minimizing them for the sake of the positives, which could seriously undermine the therapeutic relationship. In particular, when historical traumas are reported and the clinician is aware of subsequent growth already achieved in therapy, the positive opportunities that trauma, loss, or adversity offer should not be pointed out too quickly or forcefully. However, drawing client attention toward potential growth should not be compromised by the clinician's worry of rupturing the therapeutic relationship.

4. Much like other treatments, clinician should be aware that PPT practices could cause unintended harm. For example, for a client with an inflated self-perception, use of strengths may further support her narcissism. And while it is important to underscore the balanced and situationally relevant use of strengths, the adaptive dimension of negative emotions should also be discussed. For example, the feelings of a client who expresses anger about blatant violations of human rights or who expresses sadness due to the loss of a communal resource (such as the closure of an independent book store or the loss of jobs to automation) should be acknowledged and validated. Genuine and authentic negative emotions should not be hastily replaced with positive ones.

5. Finally, positive emotions, character strengths, meaning, relationships, and accomplishments should be viewed from a cultural context. An emotive style of communication, interdependence on extended family members, or avoiding direct eye contact may convey zest, love, and respect (McGrath, 2015; Pedrotti, 2011), when viewed from the client's cultural perspective. For each session of PPT, we have outlined cultural considerations (Chapters 7–21).

PPT OUTCOME STUDIES

PPT has a growing body of empirical evidence. The practices in PPT were initially validated individually (Seligman, Steen, Park, & Peterson, 2005) before being coalesced into the PPT manual (Rashid & Seligman, 2019; Seligman, Rashid, & Parks, 2006), which has since been used in 20 studies (see Table 5.2: Summary of PPT Outcome Studies for a comprehensive list of studies). These studies have been conducted internationally and have addressed a variety of clinical populations (e.g., populations with depression, anxiety, borderline personality disorder, psychosis, and nicotine dependence). Most of these studies have been conducted in a group therapy format. Overall, PPT has been shown to significantly lower symptoms of distress and enhance well-being at posttreatment with medium to large effect sizes (see Table 5.2, for pre- to postmeasure score changes on outcome measures and effect sizes). Four of these studies, including two randomized controlled trials, compared PPT directly with dialectical behavior therapy and cognitive behavior therapy—two active and well-researched manualized treatments. PPT was found to perform equally well or exceed both treatments, notably on well-being measures (e.g., Carr, Finnegan, Griffin, Cotter, & Hyland, 2017; Ochoa, Casellas-Grau, Vives, Font, & Borràs, 2017; Schrank et al., 2016). More than half of the studies in Table 5.2 treated community samples (outpatients in hospital settings, community mental health clinics) from Canada, China, South Korea, Chile, France, Spain, Austria, Iran, and the United States and addressed clinical concerns, including depression, anxiety, borderline personality disorder, psychosis, and nicotine dependence.

Overall, PPT outcome studies report decreases in depression and increases in well-being compared to control or pretreatment scores. When compared to other established treatments such as cognitive behavior therapy or dialectical behavior therapy, PPT has performed with comparable effectiveness, notably on well-being measures. One important caution in reviewing these studies is that most have small sample sizes. This notwithstanding, these studies suggest that PPT's methods have merit and warrant further empirical examination to clarify previous findings and improve our understanding of the mechanisms of change. To this end, an outcome measure for PPT, the Positive Psychotherapy Inventory (PPTI; Guney, 2011) has been devised and validated. (The PPTI is reprinted in Appendix C at the end of this manual. It also appears in the client workbook and online at www.oup.com/ppt). PPTI is used to assess specific active ingredients of PPT, including positive emotions, engagement, meaning, and relationships (Bertisch, Rath, Long, Ashman, & Rashid, 2014; Rashid, Howes, & Louden, 2017). In addition, an Online Appendix of Positive Clinical Psychology Resources (which is available at www.oup.com/ppt) presents a comprehensive list of additional resources including an extensive bibliography of books related to positive clinical psychology, lists of clinical papers organized by topic, and relevant multimedia resources (YouTube videos, websites, and documentaries).

A systematic review examining the application of PPT in mental health care settings has recently been published (Walsh et al., 2016). Based on 12 studies, the review found that some PPT components are used widely (*Gratitude Journal*, character strengths, *Gratitude Letter* and *Visit*), while others are applied less frequently (e.g., *Toward Satisficing, Positive Appraisal, Tree of Positive Relationships*). As the clinical practice and research of PPT evolves, hopefully with the publication of this manual, longitudinal and multimethod research designs (e.g., experiential sampling or physiological and neurological indices) may uncover the effectiveness of PPT for specific disorders. We deem that it is essential that clinical application of PPT be informed continually by clinical research which will enrich and refine the repertoire of clinical practices.

We are theorizing, researching, and practicing clinicians. In Part I, we have attempted to lay a coherent theoretical framework of PPT. We have made our case for PPT—why it is necessary and from what specific strands of well-being it is informed. For almost a decade, evidence-based practice has been our abiding principal. Part I describes our attempts to explore the effectiveness of PPT with numerous clinical conditions and diverse samples. The theoretical strands described in Part I are turned into structured, sequenced, yet flexible and culturally responsive sessions in Part II.

Table 5.2

SUMMARY OF PPT OUTCOME STUDIES[a]

Randomized Controlled Trials

#	Authors and Publication Status	Description and Sample Characteristics	Outcome Measures	Key Findings
1	Seligman, Rashid, Parks, 2006, published	Individual PPT ($n = 11$), 12-14 sessions, with clients diagnosed with MDD, compared with TAU ($n = 9$) and TAUMED ($n = 12$); under- and postgraduate students seeking treatment at a university counseling center	Depression (ZDRS and Hamilton), overall psychiatric distress (OQ-45), life satisfaction (SWLS), and well-being (PPTI)	Post depression PPT < TAU (ZDRS and Hamilton $d = 1.12$ and 1.14) and PPT < TAUMED (ZDRS $d = 1.22$) and overall psychiatric distress (OQ-45 $d = 1.13$); post well-being PPT > TAU and TAUMED ($d = 1.26$ and 1.03).
2	Seligman, Rashid, & Parks, 2006, published	Group PPT ($n = 21$) with clients experiencing mild to moderate depressive symptoms compared with no-treatment control ($n = 21$) in six sessions; undergraduate students at a university	Depression and life satisfaction (SWLS)	Post depression PPT < Control (BDI-II $d = 0.48$), and at 3-, 6-, and 12-month follow-ups ($d = 0.67, 0.77,$ and 0.57, respectively) with a reduction of 0.96 points per week ($p <.003$), a rate of change that was significantly greater than that of the control group ($p < .05$).
3	Parks-Scheiner, 2009, dissertation	Individual ($n = 52$) completing six PPT exercises online, compared with no-treatment control group ($n = 69$), online sample	Depression (CES-D), life satisfaction (SWLS), and positive and negative affect (PANAS)	Post depression (CES-D $d = 0.21$, at the six-month follow-up); post PPT > positive and negative affect ($d = 0.16, 0.33,$ and 0.55 at three- and six-month follow up, respectively).
4	Asgharipoor et al., 2012, published	Group PPT ($n = 9$) for 12 weeks, with clients diagnosed with MDD, compared with CBT, also for 12 weeks, in a hospital setting in Iran	Depression (SCID and BDI-II), happiness (OTH), life satisfaction (SWLS), and psychological well-being (SWS)	Post happiness, PPT > CBT (OTH $d = 1.86$). On most measures both treatments did not differ.
5	Lü and Liu, 2013, published	Group PPT ($n = 16$), (two hours for 16 weekly sessions), compared with a no-treatment control group ($n = 18$), exploring the impact of positive affect on vagal tone in handling environmental challenges	Positive and negative affect (PANAS) and respiratory sinus arrhythmia	Depression, PPT < control, at the six-month follow-up ($d = 0.21$); positive and negative affect, PPT > control, at the postintervention and three- and six-month follow-ups ($d = 0.16, 0.33,$ and 0.55, respectively).

Table 5.2
CONTINUED

Randomized Controlled Trials

#	Authors and Publication Status	Description and Sample Characteristics	Outcome Measures	Key Findings
6	Rashid et al., 2013, published	Group PPT ($n = 9$), eight sessions, with Grade 6 and 7 students compared with no-treatment control ($n = 9$) at a public middle school	Social skills (SSRS), student satisfaction (SLSS), well-being (PPTI-C), and depression (CDI)	Post, PPT > Social Skills (SSRS-Composite-parent version ($d = 1.88$) and also on PPTI-C ($d = 0.90$)
7	Reinsch, 2014, presentation	Group PPT clients ($n = 9$), six sessions with clients seeking psychotherapy through employee assistance program, compared with no-treatment control group ($n = 8$)	Depression (CES-D) and well-being (PPTI)	Post depression (CES-D $d = 0.84$). Therapeutic gains maintained one month postintervention while no-treatment control with depression decreasing a statistically significant rate of 45%.
8	Schrank et al., 2016; published	Group WELLFOCUS PPT was completed ($n = 43$), for 11 weeks vs. TAU ($n = 41$), with community adults diagnosed with psychosis	Well-being (WEMWBS); psychiatric stress (Brief Psychiatric Rating Scale), Depression Scale, Happiness Scale, PPTI	Post WEMWBS ($d = 0.42$), depression ($d = 0.38$), and well-being according to the Positive Psychotherapy Inventory ($d = 0.30$). Secondary analysis adapting for therapy group further improved the results for symptom reduction ($d = 0.43$) and depression ($d = 0.41$) SDHS Depression
9	Uliaszek, Rashid, Williams, and Gulamani, 2016, published	Group PPT ($n = 27$) compared group dialectical behavior therapy ($n = 27$) with clients exhibiting symptoms of depression and borderline personality disorder at a university health center	Depression (SCID), psychiatric symptoms (SCL-90), emotion regulation (DER), distress tolerance (DTS), mindfulness (KIMS), well-being (PPTI) and life satisfaction (SWLS) and ways of coping (WOCCL), Working Alliance Inventory; PPTI PPT	Both PPT and dialectical behavior therapy differed significantly from pre- to posttreatment on all measures except the PPTI, SWLS, Working Alliance Inventory, and WOCCL maladaptive subscale with an average effect size of $d = 0.60$ and $d = 0.78$, respectively.
10	Dowlatabadi et al., 2016, published	36 infertile women who showed signs of mild to moderate depression were randomly placed into two groups: control ($n = 18$) and intervention ($n = 18$).	Depression (BDI-II) and life satisfaction (SWLS)	The results showed, compared to control group, the intervention group showed a significant increase in life satisfaction from 22.66 in pretest to 26.13 in posttest ($p < 0.001$).

(continued)

Table 5.2
CONTINUED

Randomized Controlled Trials

#	Authors and Publication Status	Description and Sample Characteristics	Outcome Measures	Key Findings
11	Dowlatabadi et al., 2016, published	This randomized controlled trail with breast cancer patients in the Oncology Center at Kermanshah, Iran, assigned 21 patients to the PPT and 21 to the control group. Five in PPT and 4 patients in the control condition did not complete the study.	The data were gathered before intervention and 10 weeks afterwards on depression (BDI-II) and Oxford's Happiness Inventory.	Post depression, PPT > control (BDI-II $d = 1.13$) and post happiness, PPT > control (Oxford's Happiness Inventory $d = 1.83$).
12	Carr et al., 2017, published	82 participants, from three diagnosed with MDD, from three public mental facilities, were assigned to Say Yes To Life (SYTL) a PPT integrated with CBT ($n = 40$), or TAU ($n = 42$). TAU included CBT supportive therapy, client-centered therapy, psychodynamic, psychotherapy, and integrative psychotherapy. Both treatments lasted for 20 two-hour weekly sessions	Depression: SCID; Depression Beck Depression Inventory-II (BDI-II), Hamilton Rating Scale for Depression (HRS-D), Montgomery–Asberg Depression Rating Scale (MADRS), cost-consequences evaluation	In both treatment completer and ITT analyses of Time 1, 2, and 3, the mean scores on the BDI-II, HAM-D, and MADRS using 2×3, Group $\times$ Time MANOVAs, there were significant Time effects. All effect sizes favored the SYTL group and ranged from small ($d = 0.12$) to medium ($d = 0.66$). A cost-consequence analysis showed that the average total cost of service usage in Euro per case in the SYTL group was significantly lower than that of the TAU group
13	Furchtlehner and Laireiter, 2016; presentation	Group PPT ($n = 44$) was compared with group CBT ($n = 44$) with patients diagnosed with depression, in small groups in two-hour sessions for 14 weeks.	SCID, depression (BDI-II, MADS), well-being (PPTI), life satisfaction (SWLS), and symptoms (BSI)	PPT fared better than CBT on all outcome measures with moderate to large effect sizes, depression ($d = 0.82$), MADS ($d = 0.33$), PPTI ($d = 0.58$), SWLS ($d = 0.85$), and BSI ($d = 0.95$).

Table 5.2
CONTINUED

Randomized Controlled Trials

#	Authors and Publication Status	Description and Sample Characteristics	Outcome Measures	Key Findings
14	Hwang, Kwon, and Hong, 2017; published	University students in Busan Metropolitan area, Korea were randomly assigned to receive three conditions, Individual modified (PPTm; $n = 8$), group neurofeedback aided meditation therapy (NFB; $n = 8$), and no treatment ($n = 8$)	Flourishing Scale (FS) to assess psychological and social well-being and the Scale of Positive and Negative experience (SPANE) to assess subjective affect.	Both PPTm and NFB aided meditation therapy showed significant positive effects on psychological wellbeing (FS) and Positive & Negative experiences (SPANE) compared to no-treatment group. At follow-up, the NFB meditation therapy showed a greater increase in subjective well-being compared to the mPPT, with an average effect size of $d = 1.08$, while the mPPT showed a greater increase in psychosocial well-being compared to the NFB meditation therapy, with average effect size $d = 1.36$.
15	Ochoa et al., 2017, published	126 female adult patients, consecutive survivors of breast cancer with high level of emotional distress were assigned to Positive Psychotherapy for Cancer (PPC; $n = 73$) in group format or waitlist control ($n = 53$). PPC conducted in 12 sessions, 90–120 minutes with each group comprising of 8–12 members	Hospital Anxiety and Depression Scale (HADS), Post-stress Disorder Checklist- Civilian Version (PCL-C), PTG, and Extreme Life Event Inventory	The PPC group obtained significantly better results after treatment than the control group, showing reduced distress, decreased posttraumatic symptoms, and increased PTG. The benefits were maintained at 3 and 12 months' follow-up.

Nonrandomized

#	Authors and Publication Status	Description and Sample Characteristics	Outcome Measures	Key Findings
16	Goodwin, 2010, dissertation	Group PPT ($n = 11$), in 10 sessions focused on increasing relationship satisfaction among anxious and stressed individuals; community sample at a training clinic	Anxiety (BAI), stress (PSS), relationship adjustment (DAS)	Post PPT < Anxiety (BAI $d = 1.48$), Stress < (PSS $d = 1.22$), no changes on relationship satisfaction (DAS)
17	Cuadra-Peralta et al., 2010, published	Group PPT ($n = 8$) in nine sessions with clients diagnosed with depression, compared with behavioral therapy ($n = 10$) at a community center in Chile	Depression (BDI-II and CES-D), happiness (AHI)	Post happiness (AHI, PPT > Behavior Therapy ($d = 0.72$); PPT group < on Depression, from pre-to-posttreatment (BDI-II $d = 0.90$ and CES-D $d = 0.93$)

(continued)

Table 5.2

CONTINUED

Randomized Controlled Trials

#	Authors and Publication Status	Description and Sample Characteristics	Outcome Measures	Key Findings
18	Bay, 2012, published	Group PPT ($n = 10$) compared with group CBT ($n = 8$) and medication ($n = 8$) with client experiencing symptoms of depression in a hospital setting in France	Depression (BDI-Shortened), depression and anxiety (HADS), happiness (SHS), Emotional Inventory (EQ-I), life satisfaction (SWLS), and positive and negative affect (PANAS)	Post depression, PPT < CBT ($d = 0.66$), happiness (SHS $d = 0.81$), life satisfaction (SWLS $d = 0.66$), optimism (LOT-R $d = 1.62$), and emotional intelligence (EQ-I $d = 1.04$). On most measures both PPT and CBT fared better than medication group.
19	Meyer et al., 2012, published	Group PPT in 10 sessions, with six exercises adapted for clients ($n = 16$) experiencing symptoms of schizophrenia at a hospital-affiliated clinic, with baseline, postintervention, three-month follow-up assessment	Psychological well-being (SWS), savoring (SBI), hope (DHS), recovery (RAS), symptoms (BSI), and social functioning (SFS)	Post PPT < CBT, depression (BDI $d = 0.66$), happiness (SHS $d = 0.81$), life satisfaction (SWLS $d = 0.66$), optimism (LOT-R $d = 1.62$), and EQ-I ($d = 1.04$). In most cases both PPT and CBT fared better than medication group.
20	Kahler et al., 2015, published	Group PPT ($n = 19$) in eight sessions was integrated with smoking cessation counseling and nicotine patch with at a community medical center	Depression (SCID, CES-D), nicotine dependence (FTND), positive and negative affect (PANAS)	Rate of session attendance and satisfaction with treatment were high, with most participants reporting using and benefitting from PPT exercises. Almost one-third (31.6%) of the sample sustained smoking abstinence for six months after their quit date

Note: PPT = positive psychotherapy; MDD = major depressive disorder; SWLS = satisfaction with life scale; TAU = treatment as usual; TAUMED = treatment as usual plus medication; CBT = cognitive behavioral therapy; MANOVA = multivariate analysis of variance; PTG = posttraumatic growth; ZDRS = Zung depression rating scale.

[a] *Chronologically ordered by year of publications and/or presentations.*

Outcome Measures

1. Beck Depression Inventory-II (BDI-II; Beck, Steer, & Brown, 1996)
2. Beck Depression Inventory-II-Short Form (BDI-SF; Chibnall & Tait, 1994)
3. Beck Anxiety Inventory (BAI; Beck, Epstein, & Steer, 1988)
4. Brief Symptom Inventory (BSI; Derogatis, 1993)

5. Brief Psychiatric Rating Scale (BPRS; Overall & Gorham, 1962)
6. Center for Epidemiological Studies Depression Scale (CES-D; Radloff, 1977)
7. Children Depression Inventory (CDI; Kovacs, 1992)
8. Client Satisfaction Questionnaire (CSQ-8; Larsen, Atkinson, Hargreaves, & Nguyen, 1979)
9. Difficulties in Emotion Regulation Scale (DERS; Gratz & Roemer, 2004)
10. Distress Tolerance Scale (DTS; Simons & Gaher, 2005)
11. Dyadic Adjustment Scale (DAS; Spanier, 1976)
12. Emotional Quotient Inventory (EQ-I; Dawda & Hart, 2000)
13. Fagerström Test for Nicotine Dependence (FTND; Heatherton, Kozlowski, Frecker, & Fagerström, 1991)
14. Hamilton Rating Scale for Depression (HRSD; Hamilton, 1960)
15. Health of the Nation Outcome Scale (HoNOS; Pirkins et al., 2005)
16. Hospital Anxiety and Depression Scale (HADS; Bjelland, Dahl, Haug, & Neckelmann, 2002)
17. Integrated Hope Scale (IHS; Schrank et al., 2012)
18. Kentucky Inventory of Mindfulness Skills (KIMS; Baer, Smith, & Allen, 2004).
19. Montgomery Asberg Depression Scale (MADS; Montgomery & Asberg, 1979)
20. Orientations to happiness (Peterson, Park, & Seligman, 2005)
21. Life Orientation Test–Revised (LOT-R; Scheier, Carver, & Bridges, 1994)
22. Outcome Questionnaire-45 (OQ-45; Lambert et al., 2003)
23. Positive Psychotherapy Inventory (PPTI; Rashid & Ostermann, 2009)
24. Positive Psychotherapy Inventory–Children Version (PPTI-C; Rashid & Anjum, 2008)
25. Post-Stress Disorder Checklist—Civilian Version (Costa-Requena, & Gil, 2010).
26. Post-traumatic Growth Inventory (PTGI; Tedesshi & Calhoune, 1996)
27. Recovery Assessment Scale (RAS; Corrigan, Salzer, Ralph, Sangster & Keck, 2004)
28. Respiratory sinus arrhythmia (RSA; Berntson et al., 1997); measures heart rate variability
29. Savoring Beliefs Inventory (SBI; Bryant, 2003)
30. Scales of Well-being (SWB; Ryff, 1989)
31. Short Depression-Happiness Scale (SDHS; Joseph & Linley, 2006)
32. Social Skills Rating System (SSRS; Gresham & Elliot, 1990)
33. Structured Clinical Interview for DSM-IV Axis I (SCID; First, Spitzer, Gibbon & Williams, 2007)
34. Students' Life Satisfaction Scale (SLSS; Huebner, 1991)
35. Social Functioning Scale (SFS; Birchwood, Smith, Cochrane & Wetton, 1990)
36. Values in Action–Youth (VIA-Youth; Park & Peterson, 2006)
37. Warwick-Edinburgh Mental Well-Being Scale, (WEMWBS; Tennant et al., 2007)
38. Zung Self-Rating Depression Scale (ZSRS; Zung, 1965).

SESSION-BY-SESSION PRACTICE

SESSIONS, PRACTICES, AND
THE THERAPEUTIC PROCESS

6

THE GOAL OF PART II OF THIS manual is to help clinicians from diverse professional backgrounds acquire, adapt, and hone therapeutic skills to deliver positive psychotherapy (PPT) in a variety of settings. Table 6.1: Positive Psychotherapy: Generic Session Structure outlines a typical PPT session, for individual and group settings. The authors have made every effort—from evidence and experience—to operationalize therapeutic conditions that foster positive emotions, engagement, fulfilling relationships, meaning, and goals toward recovery and resilience. The sessions in Part II offer clinicians skills and strategies that are gentle and clear, sequential and adaptable, and empathic and effective.

ORIENTATION TO POSITIVE PSYCHOTHERAPY

SUGGESTED SCRIPT FOR THE CLINICIAN

The following is a script you can use to introduce PPT to your clients:

Positive psychotherapy (PPT) is a therapeutic approach that attempts to counteract your symptoms with strengths, weaknesses with virtues, and deficits with skills, to help you understand complex situations and experiences in a balanced way.

The human brain pays more attention and responds more strongly to negatives than to positives. However, PPT helps by teaching us to build up our positives. To deal with the toughest challenges in life, we need our toughest internal resources, which in turn, will build our resilience. Much like health is better than sickness, mastery is better than stress, cooperation is better than conflict, hope is better than despair, and strengths are better than weaknesses.

The positives in PPT are primarily based on Dr. Martin Seligman's ideas of well-being. Dr. Seligman organized happiness and well-being into five scientifically measurable and teachable parts: (a) **P***ositive emotion; (b)* **E***ngagement; (c)* **R***elationships; (d)* **M***eaning; and (e)* **A***ccomplishment, with the first letters of each part forming the mnemonic* **PERMA** *[Seligman, 2012]. These elements are neither exhaustive nor exclusive, but it has been shown that fulfillment in these elements is associated with lower rates of distress and higher rates of life satisfaction.*

PPT practices will help you assess your strengths from multiple perspectives, followed by a series of practices that will help you develop what we call "practical wisdom." Examples include how to decide between taking a risky new initiative versus relying on the tried and tested; how to strike a balance between fairness and kindness; and how to show empathy to a friend but also be objective. The goal of practical wisdom is to help you better deal with challenging situations, that is, to choose the wise way when there are many options for how to deal with a challenge.

PPT teaches about strengths, but in context. In fact, under some circumstances, negatives such as sadness and anxiety may be more adaptive than positives, especially when survival is at stake. Similarly, anger—expressed as protest

Table 6.1

POSITIVE PSYCHOTHERAPY: GENERIC SESSION STRUCTURE

Core Concepts	Evidence-based core concepts are described in plain language that the clinician can read or paraphrase easily.
Relaxation Practice	Each session begins with a relaxation practice; typically clients are guided through a three- to five-minute relaxation practice.
Gratitude Journal	• Following the relaxation practice, clients share a good event or experience noted in their *Gratitude Journal* from the past week. • Clinician elicits anecdotes of strengths from clients. • Clients share positive emotions—big or small—and also a reflection about what caused them. • Clinician shares recent positive events reported in the media with clients.
Review	Clinician and clients review the previous session's core concept/s and practice. Clinician encourages clients to share their experiences, reactions, and reflections regarding the concept/s discussed and practiced during the previous session.
In-Session Practice	Each session has at least one in-session practice that continues between sessions with the hope that clients will continue to practice at home.
Reflection & Discussion	Questions directed to clients encourage them to reflect on and discuss the in-session practices.
Vignette	At least one vignette from the manual authors' clinical practice is presented, with all identifying information altered to protect client confidentiality.
Fit & Flexibility	PPT practice may not be effective for every clinical need, and flexibility is provided.
Cultural Considerations	Each session includes cultural considerations.
Maintenance	Specific strategies are presented which clients can use to maintain the benefits of each practice.
Resources	Resources, such as additional readings, websites, and videos, are listed.
Relaxation	We recommend that each session end with the same brief relaxation practice that started the session.

to work toward a greater good—is more adaptive than compliance. We will work together to understand your pain and hurts, and we will also look to find meaning from this pain.

Following this script, go over Table 5.1: Positive Psychotherapy: Session-by-Session Description, with your clients. Presenting this PPT overview will help you identify and address any concerns or confusion that clients have before confusion or concerns manifest during session. For example, if a client is confused or ambivalent (e.g., "I am not sure if positive psychotherapy can address my long-standing psychological problems," or "All these topics seem fine, but where and how will my specific symptoms be addressed?"), clarification will help the client benefit fully from the treatment approach, as chances are that he may not be in his best frame of mind or be familiar with this treatment approach.

You can use the following script to present an overview of PPT:

SUGGESTED SCRIPT FOR THE CLINICIAN
PPT can be divided into three phases:

- *Phase One focuses on helping you to come up with a balanced narrative by exploring your strengths from multiple perspectives. You will create meaningful goals using your signature strengths.*
- *Phase Two focuses on building positive emotions and, with support, dealing with negative memories, negative experiences, and negative feelings. These negatives may be keeping you stuck and not allowing you to move forward.*
- *Phase Three focuses on exploring your positive relationships and strengthening the processes that nurture these relationships. This final phase of PPT also allows you to explore the meaning and purpose of your life.*

THE THERAPEUTIC PROCESS

In this section, we discuss the finer aspects of psychotherapy in the context of PPT. These include facets such as establishing ground rules, fostering the therapeutic process, therapeutic alliance, engagement, motivation, process of change, intrinsic motivation, relapse prevention, feedback and outcome, therapist and client effects, and the process of change.

Establishing Ground Rules

It is important to agree on some ground rules to follow over the course of PPT. You and your clients should discuss these ground rules at the beginning of the treatment and update them continuously. However, if clients continue to balk, become passive, attempt to change the skills being taught, or avoid acquiring the skills altogether, acknowledge and empathize with clients and then inquire about the reasons for hesitation. It is ultimately your professional responsibility to manage the therapeutic process, and if clients, for any number of reasons, drift significantly from the intended purpose of the treatment, you should mindfully terminate the treatment or make appropriate referrals.

Confidentiality

Discuss the client's and your roles and responsibilities. Reassure clients about confidentiality of information according to your jurisdiction of practice. In group settings, where clients will be privy to each other's sensitive information, explain that specific details of stories and experiences must remain confidential within the group, but, outside the group, clients can share lessons learned in session.

Relaxation

Begin sessions with a brief (three – to five-minute) relaxation practice. Refer to Appendix A: Relaxation & Mindfulness Practices, which can be found at the end of this manual, as well as in the client workbook and online at www.oup.com/ppt. In group settings, you can play relaxing instrumental music just before each session of PPT. This may help set a soothing and safe therapeutic milieu for clients, encouraging them to delve deeper into issues that need to be solved.

Therapeutic Relationship

Like any other therapy, establishing and maintaining a genuinely warm, trusting, and collaborative relationship in PPT is crucial to keep clients motivated and clinicians engaged toward favorable therapeutic changes. Assess frequently to make sure that there are no ruptures in the relationship. Signs of rupture include client disagreement, lack of involvement with therapeutic tasks, lack of understanding therapeutic progress, halt in progress, and a breakdown in communication between clients and clinicians.

Intrinsic Motivation

Some clients lose motivation as they are unable to see immediate gains from their efforts. Others lack confidence in their abilities to successfully complete the practices. Still others lack the social support needed to successfully complete the practices (Ryan, Lynch, Vanstcckiste, & Deci, 2011). All of these conditions can diminish client motivation. Ryan and colleagues argue that most people are not intrinsically motivated for counseling. They don't look forward to counseling as a fun and recreational activity. Clients are more likely to value it if they perceive therapy as a path toward other valued outcomes, such as an improved career, more satisfying relationships, or a healthier lifestyle. Therefore, it is important to assess what specific outcomes each client most desires. Connecting these outcomes with deeper client values will help clients stay motivated to make necessary changes.

Active Engagement

PPT is an active treatment. It is not based on the assumption that a secure therapeutic relationship is sufficient, and detailed discussions of problems alone are unlikely to encourage clients to change undesired behavior. PPT is an active treatment that can yield optimal results when clients actively engage with clinicians by practicing and applying PPT skills to everyday life. Therefore, client participation in PPT practices, both in and out of session, is critical for an effective treatment outcome.

Instilling Hope

Instilling hope is an important facet in the process of human change. Across various theoretical orientations, hope serves as a unifying framework in therapy (Frank & Frank, 1991). In fact, Seligman (2002b) posits that instilling hope is a major and deep therapeutic strategy, which is often lumped under the derogatory misnomer of "nonspecifcs." Evidence shows that hope plays a pivotal role in fostering change in the early part of psychotherapy—within three to four sessions (Hanna, 2002; Schrank, Stanghellini, & Slade, 2008). When introduced early in therapy, hope may strengthen and empower clients to believe that a better future is possible (Frank & Frank, 1991). Beck and colleagues have described therapists as "purveyors of hope" (Newman, Leahy, Beck, Reilly-Harrington, & Gyulai, 2002, p. 86) and have advocated for therapeutic techniques and skills that specifically build a sense of hope in clients, who often enter therapy in a state of despair and hopelessness. Despite highlighting the importance of instilling hope, little empirical research has been done on how hope is promoted by psychotherapists (Larsen, Edey, & LeMay, 2007). In a case study focusing on translating hope into specific therapeutic practice, Larsen and Stege (2010) recommend an implicit use of hope, without actually using the word *hope* in psychotherapy. These authors recommend highlighting client resources, such as personal strengths, recent changes, and presence of social support. Clients can be asked to reflect on their own personal stories of strengths or change. From the start, PPT encourages clients to share their stories of strengths. The opening practice of *Positive Introduction* is about reflecting, writing, and sharing a story that brought out the best in the client. Similarly, assessment of strengths entails reflecting on life experiences that highlight client strengths in different situations. Furthermore, practices such as the *Gratitude Journal* and *Gratitude Letter, REACH, Forgiveness Letter, Expressive Writing,* and *Positive Legacy* elicit narratives of strengths and change. Hence, PPT can be conceptualized as a therapeutic approach that actively instills hope from the onset and maintains the wellspring of hope throughout the course of the treatment.

Simultaneous Treatments

Engage clients in discussing whether they are taking part in other related processes that include therapeutic elements and/or complementary or alternative medicine (e.g., herbal, homeopathic, Reiki) and which espouse specific guidelines or expectations about lifestyle. Discuss whether these are complementary to or competitive with PPT practices.

The Process of Change

Some clients may be motivated for external reasons—such as referral by significant others or mandated treatment—and such clients may be looking for a quick and easy therapeutic solution. Others may be genuinely interested due to acute stress, but, after learning that PPT is an active treatment requiring active client participation, such clients may find it hard to change long-term maladaptive behavioral patterns. Acknowledging the chronicity of patterns, it is important to build a solid therapeutic relationship that demonstrates empathy and clearly conveys to clients that they are capable of change and worthy of changing their long-term behavior. Help clients to conceptualize change in concrete, realistic, and optimistic ways that may take time.

Flexibility

PPT practices, as described in this manual, outline specific directions for effective implementation. However, if client motivation wanes, skilled clinicians can modify the practices to restore client interest and meet client needs. Make sure to carefully review the "Fit & Flexibility" section embedded within each session, which will allow you to be flexible in order to maintain client motivation.

Increasing Accessibility, Inclusion, and Effectiveness

Not all PPT practices can fully meet the needs of all clients. Unaddressed needs can undermine treatment. Therefore, having knowledge and experience of more than one treatment protocol can help you offer supplemental options. These options can introduce necessary modifications for specific clinical conditions, thereby making the treatment more accessible, inclusive, and effective.

Feedback

Psychotherapy—unlike parenting, mentoring, teaching, managing, or negotiating—is inherently an intimate interpersonal process that is only effective when the client actively participates. Therefore, it is important that clinicians engage clients in discussions and elicit frank feedback frequently to ensure that clients understand the rationale for PPT components. Actively elicit feedback about PPT from your clients during the course of the treatment. Discuss with clients what worked for them and what didn't. For things that worked, how did they work, and what changed? As PPT strives for a delicate balance between positives and negatives, be perceptive or explicitly ask how the client perceives session work and skill practices. Does she perceive skill acquisition as manageable and beneficial? Due to psychological stress, some clients may not fully appreciate the core concepts of specific topics or practices, so offer appropriate supports and flexibility as they acquire skills. Actively eliciting continuous feedback from clients can help you evaluate whether therapy is effective and if the client is improving or deteriorating, and this interaction provides opportunities to make necessary changes to the treatment (Lambert, Hansen, & Finch, 2001).

Monitoring Therapeutic Outcome

Throughout the course of conducting PPT, it is important that you remain vigilant—with the help of reliable outcome measures—to the possibility that clients may be deteriorating. As already discussed earlier in this manual, about 30% to 40% of clients realize no benefit from psychotherapy, and a small group of clients—between 5% and 10%—actually deteriorate during therapy (Lambert, 2007). Begin PPT with confidence, but understand that PPT may not work for everyone all the time. Supplementing your clinical judgment with regularly administered reliable and valid outcome measures will help you monitor progress (or the lack thereof) and improve timely clinical decision-making. If, through feedback, you learn that a client is not engaged, is not improving, or is deteriorating, assess his motivation and address disengagement with the client within session. Eliciting feedback from clients who drop out of treatment can be a tremendous help for you by clarifying nuances of treatment delivery that can be improved. We strongly encourage you to consult with your peers to gauge and adjust your engagement throughout the treatment.

Relapse Prevention

In any treatment, clients may relapse or revert to their symptomatic state. Clients may relapse due to multiple reasons, including diminished motivation. Relapse is a critical event. Discuss, in no uncertain terms, the cues and conditions that can lead to client vulnerability (e.g., anniversaries, specific places, or specific people). Often negative emotions and experiences make clients vulnerable, leading to relapse. Apply PPT practices in session (such as *Gratitude Journal, Slow and Savor*, or using signature strengths in a creative activity) to generate positive emotions. Research (Fredrickson, 2009) shows that positive emotions broaden mindsets. Clients are more likely to regain their motivation for treatment when they experience positive emotions. Joy, playful behavior, interest, and curiosity can produce more accurate information than initially negative attitudes like boredom and cynicism (Fredrickson & Losada, 2005). Positive emotions can also play a vital part in maintaining the motivation of clients, and PPT practices are meant to produce positive emotions. As clients engage in these practices, both in and out of session, engage in an authentic discussion about how experiencing positive emotions can make these practices intrinsically motivating for clients.

Progression

As also discussed in Chapter 5, do not expect a linear progression of improvement, because the motivation to change long-standing behavioral and emotional patterns fluctuates during the course of therapy. Also, client readiness to change fluctuates. Hence, it is important that you respond positively toward changes when they occur and remain open to adjust therapeutic goals. Making sure that goals are concrete and relevant to stressors and desired changes will improve client outcome.

Theoretical Foundations

Client motivation changes as circumstances change. You can explore plausible explanations for such changes with your clients, and you can consult, as needed, with your colleagues. It is important that you are familiar with the evidence-based theory of PPT. You will inevitably face uniquely idiosyncratic situations to which the structured practices described in this manual may not readily apply. A solid knowledge of PPT theory will help you to adapt PPT practices to unique situations. However, it is important that modification to PPT practices is done in collaboration with clients, offering them multiple pathways to achieve desired outcomes.

The rest of Part II of this manual presents 15 sessions with corresponding core concepts, practices, reflections, discussions, vignette/s, Fit & Flexibility Tips, cultural considerations, maintenance tips, and resources, which make up the heart of PPT.

SESSION ONE: *POSITIVE INTRODUCTION* AND *GRATITUDE JOURNAL*

7

SESSION ONE ORIENTS CLIENTS TO THE CLINICAL milieu and clarifies client and clinician roles and responsibilities. This session also teaches how to start the ongoing practice of cultivating gratitude through journaling positive experiences and appreciating the impact of gratitude on well-being. The two positive psychotherapy (PPT) practices covered in this session are *Positive Introduction* and *Gratitude Journal*.

SESSION ONE OUTLINE

Core Concepts (Part 1)
   In-Session Practice: *Positive Introduction*
   Reflection & Discussion
   Vignettes
   Fit & Flexibility
   Cultural Considerations
   Maintenance

Core Concepts (Part 2)
   In-Session Practice: *Gratitude Journal*
   Reflection & Discussion
   Vignette
   Fit & Flexibility
   Cultural Considerations
   Maintenance
Resources

CORE CONCEPTS (PART 1)

Psychotherapy is one of the few times in our lives when we have the opportunity to share our life stories in a way that no other social interaction offers (Adler & McAdams, 2007). If most of this psychotherapeutic interaction is spent recalling past hurts, offenses, and wounds, the opportunity to integrate parts of the self that might have slipped from our awareness due to rigid thinking, labile emotions, or insecure relationships is lost. By mindfully recalling a meaningful experience, weaving it into a story (the beginning, middle, and end), writing it down, and sharing it with someone, clients have the opportunity to reframe, reappraise, and refile important parts of the self from which they can draw personal strength. The practice of *Positive Introduction*, completed at the start of PPT, can be a catalyst to construct or restore a healthier and resilient self-concept. This practice allows both client and clinician to see the experience as part of a client's whole personality.

The *Positive Introduction* encourages clients to recall a significant event or experience that ended very well. Recall of positive memories plays an important role in mood regulation (Joormann, Siemer, & Gotlib, 2007). Reflecting, writing, sharing, and potentially reframing a personal high point, especially in the early phase of the therapeutic process, has the potential to generate positive emotions. Cultivation of positive emotions at the onset of the therapeutic process robustly predicts therapeutic change by enabling clients to consider new ideas and perspectives and to build long-term resources (Fitzpatrick & Stalikas, 2008).

Clients often enter psychotherapy with questions such as, "Why did I fail? Why have others treated me unfairly? Will I ever achieve my goals?" The act of writing (whether using a pen on paper, or a laptop or other electronic device) allows clients to be aware of their past efficacy (something done successfully in the past) and to compare their current state to any changes, subtle or significant, they may have experienced since the event they chose to write about occurred. Happy and mature people tend to highlight scenes of personal growth and redemption in their life stories (McAdam, 2008). The *Positive Introduction* can act as a guidepost (a high point in life) for clients from which to self-edit their narratives from the present to the future, to create more positive, successful experiences.

START-OF-SESSION RELAXATION

At the start of every session, begin with a brief relaxation exercise. Refer to Appendix A: Relaxation & Mindfulness Practices, which can be found at the end of this manual. A copy of this appendix also appears in the client workbook. To make additional copies, visit the companion website for this manual at www.oup.com/ppt.

IN-SESSION PRACTICE: *POSITIVE INTRODUCTION*

In this opening practice, clients introduce themselves through a real-life story. For encouragement, you can start with an example. A real-life story from one of the authors of this manual is presented as an illustration. A few video examples are listed in the Resources section at the end of this session. Any of these illustrations and examples will help clients to come up with their own stories. To begin, guide clients through the following script.

SUGGESTED SCRIPT FOR THE CLINICIAN

The following is a script you can use to introduce the *Positive Introduction* practice to your clients:

> *Please settle in your seats. Bring your back toward the back of the chair, with your feet flat on the floor and your hands resting on your thighs. Take three deep breaths. Recall a time or situation when you handled a tough situation in a positive way. You don't need to come up with a huge, life-changing event. Perhaps what comes to mind is a small event that called forth the best in you. Now open your eyes and, using Worksheet 1.1, write about this situation. Put it in the form of a story with a clear beginning, middle, and positive end.*

Allow three to four minutes for clients to recall the story. Then ask them to open their eyes and write down the event or anything about it, using Worksheet 1.1: *Positive Introduction*. Note that this and all worksheets (a) appear within the corresponding session of this manual, (b) are reprinted for the client in the accompanying client workbook, and (c) can be downloaded from the companion website at www.oup.com/ppt. Encourage your clients to write freely—without inhibition—and clarify for them that they don't have to share all the details of the story. Whatever they write is for their eyes only, and the act of writing something down can help us to make sense of our experiences, which sometimes define us. If you are conducting PPT in an individual session, ask your client to share the story or process of generating the story. In individual settings, clients almost always share their stories. If you are conducting PPT in a group setting, ask clients to share the story or process of generating the story with someone in the group with whom they feel comfortable. Ask receivers to listen carefully, as they might be reporting back to the larger group, but only if this sharing is permitted by the story writer. Although sharing is optional, the first person in a group who shares tends to instigate more sharing from the group.

Think about a time when you handled a tough situation in a positive way. You don't need to come up with a huge, life-changing event. Perhaps what comes to mind is a small event that called forth the best in you. Write about this situation. Make it in the form of a story with a clear beginning, middle, and a positive end. If you need more space, write on an additional piece of paper.

_____

_____

_____

_____

_____

_____

_____

_____

_____

_____

_____

_____

_____

_____

_____

_____

_____

_____

_____

REFLECTION & DISCUSSION

Ask clients to reflect on and answer the following questions in writing:

- Some stories become part of the way we perceive ourselves. How might this story have impacted your self-concept?
- What helped you to deal with the situation? Please describe specifics, such as:
  - Personal attributes, including persistence, optimism, or faith.
  - Environmental attributes, such as support from close friends, family members, or professional relationships.
- Are significant others in your life aware of this story in the same spirit or way that you recall it?

After the reflection and writing is complete, facilitate a discussion.

VIGNETTE: WHAT ARE YOU GOOD AT?

The following *Positive Introduction* was written by one of the manual authors. This is a true story that changed his orientation about human beings and convinced him to reframe his questions in therapy. The author doesn't typically share this story with his clients, but as a clinician, you may benefit from it by reframing your own questions.

Some years ago in Brooklyn, New York, amid the fading light and the falling autumn leaves, I was strolling blissfully toward my car after teaching a yoga class. Suddenly but quietly a cold metallic touch at my lower back halted my stroll. I turned around and found that it was a gun, held by a teenager. Another teen, presumably his partner in crime, quietly ushered me to my car and demanded the keys. At their order, I sat in the back seat, with one teen vigilantly keeping the gun nuzzled at my back, while his partner, now behind the wheel, drove rashly. Soon we had driven through two red lights. From a Zen-like calm, my body and mind catapulted into a full-blown panic state with sweaty palms and a pounding heart. I entertained only one catastrophic thought of my fate: from the dusty and dangerous streets of Lahore, Pakistan, my dream of getting a doctorate in clinical psychology will die on the streets of Brooklyn—in a police car chase.

My hosts demanded my wallet, which I promptly provided. Their eyes beamed when they saw a debit card. Their excitement about getting money perhaps accelerated the speed further, and another red light was ignored. I moved from panic to an ultra-panic state. Feeling utterly helpless, I resigned myself to a deep and long Ujjayi breath—a yogic technique to calm down emotions. The impact of this breath perhaps reached my mind sooner than my body and the clinician instinct in me encouraged me to say, in a stuttering voice, "You have my new car, my debit card, and I am ready to go and withdraw money from an ATM for you, so what's the rush? If you keep running red lights, cops will soon stop us." The police regularly patrolled this part of Brooklyn, especially after sunset. The instant reply from one of the teens was, "Shut your f***ing mouth, otherwise you will not see daylight again." I realized this was no time for me to exercise my clinician skills. After all, therapy can be harmful at times. Nonetheless, surprisingly, soon after, I noticed that they slowed down and even stopped at a red light. They were now searching actively for an ATM but couldn't find one where they could take me safely. I treated myself to another dose of Ujjayi breaths that perhaps calmed me and triggered the clinician instinct in me yet again. I did what most clinicians do—asked questions. Largely to distract my mind from the catastrophic thoughts, I initiated small talk with them.

I asked respectfully, "What do you do, I mean beside this (carjacking)?"

"Why you wanna know?" the driver replied.

"Just out of curiosity," I responded.

"This turf in Crooklyn" (he meant Brooklyn) "is ours . . . Anyone who tries to screw us, we take care of him . . . you know, so don't screw with us. You will not see daylight again."

I was only trying to build some rapport, although building rapport at gunpoint is not taught in most graduate-level clinical psychology programs. His response silenced me. But do most clinicians remain silent for long? I doubt it. I couldn't resist acting on my clinician instinct, and, out of nowhere, I asked them, "What are you good at?" Their first few responses are not worthy of writing here and are left to your imagination. However, the raw colloquial flavor of their responses did not offend the stubborn clinician inside me, and I persisted. I said, gently probing, "I am sure you are quite good at taking care of your turf, but are there other things you are good at?"

Now confused and slightly amused at the same time, the look on their faces seemed to say, "What have we got ourselves into?" After a long pause, with a sheepish smile, the fellow next to me pressed the gun a little harder into my gut. I took some more deep breaths and reframed the question: "You must be good at something." I anticipated some more pleasantries. Instead, the driver took a CD from the pocket of his jacket, inserted it into the CD player of the car, and cranked up the volume. Soon the confines of my car were reverberating with a cacophony of loud noise—I guess this is called music these days. One of my hosts shouted loudly, "We are good at music. When we are happy, we play music and we dance. . . . My buddy, back there, has really groovy songs."

With the music blasting and their upper bodies dancing, my hosts insisted that I join in with them, since I already looked like them and if we were moving to the music inside the car, no one would suspect anything. Dance, even in safe and secure settings, makes me nervous. At gunpoint, I imagined the headline the next day: dead man dancing. I told them I didn't know how to dance. My hosts graciously offered to teach me the "moves." They put an inverted baseball cap on my head and asked me to follow the moves. Soon, my upper body was moving in rhythms previously unknown to me. Having been raised on Bollywood tunes, I never thought that I would learn rap and reggae dance moves on the streets of Brooklyn with a gun pointed at me.

Somehow they forgot about making the trip to the ATM and made a detour to a deli for a snack. They offered to buy me something that I politely declined. We then visited a friend of theirs. After another 45 minutes, they left me on a dark Brooklyn street corner and drove away with my car. The next day, the police found my car with minor damage. My debit and credit cards had not been used and my laptop in the trunk was untouched. Ever since, I have never shied away from asking, "What are you good at?"

VIGNETTE: THREE POINTS IN THE FINAL BASKETBALL GAME

This is part of a *Positive Introduction* that Louis, a male client in his early 20s, shared in one-on-one psychotherapy. He presented with symptoms of social anxiety as well as a lack of motivation and confidence. For the first three sessions, clinician and client focused on managing his presenting distress. At the end of the third session, the clinician asked Louis to write a story about himself, using the directions given in the Clinician's Script. During the next session, Louis reluctantly read his story, making very little eye contact with the clinician.

The story discusses Louis's last year of high school when he was on the basketball team. He was athletic and always wanted to play, but, due to social anxiety, he always opted to sit on the bench. During the last game of the season, on the court of a rival school, three minutes before the end of the game with his team trailing by two points, a key player on the team got injured, and the coach had no choice but to ask Louis to come on the court. He stated that the very thought made him uncomfortable:

"Even though I was nervous before the game, I soon came to the realization that during the few minutes I was on court, I was totally immersed in the moment and experience. In the end it didn't matter to me how I looked or what others thought of my playing skills, I was just there to do my duty. In that moment, I was able to accomplish my duty and forgot the piercing eyes of judgment of others."

Louis ended the story, saying that he scored only three points the entire season, but these were enough to take his team to the play-offs.

FIT & FLEXIBILITY

Clients can use photographs, artifacts, souvenirs, or mementos such as awards, certificates, and letters of appreciation to anchor their stories. They can also tell their story through a montage of digital images, YouTube clips, and so on. Clients can submit stories in person or electronically.

Clients can be provided with an option to seal their *Positive Introduction* in an envelope, write their name and the date on the front, and give the envelope to you for safekeeping. You can tell clients that their introduction stories will be used in a future practice, as explained in Chapter 21, Session 15—but don't share the details. Do assure clients that the envelopes will be stored securely, that they will only be accessible to you, and that no one will read their stories.

Clients struggling to recall and write a *Positive Introduction* can ask close family members or friends to write a story about them.

Finally, if clients are unable to benefit from the options outlined here, they can write about any story or real-life event about overcoming challenges that they find inspiring. From this, they can gradually move toward their own real-life story or experience of resilience. Alternatively, clients can create an idealized introduction of themselves.

CULTURAL CONSIDERATIONS

Clients from non-Western cultures, where modesty is highly desired, may initially find the practice of *Positive Introduction* challenging. They may view it as an expression of self-congratulations, vanity, and immodesty; such clients may find this exercise to be incompatible with cultural expectations. One such client from an East Asian culture, an international student attending a world-renown business school, struggled to complete the exercise. However, one of her friends, with her permission, emailed a very moving story about the client.

If clients are reluctant to share a story verbally or in writing, ask them about culturally appropriate ways of self-expression. Invite them to share their story in a manner that suits them. For example, one of our clients, instead of writing a story, shared her sketchbook with the clinician. These sketches, drawn over a period of time, depicted a specific cultural motif with which the client identified closely. Encouraging the client to discuss this motif and her associations helped to generate her story. Helping clients to understand that the practice is about self-awareness, and not about showing off, helps to generate the story.

Lastly, to facilitate cultural appropriateness, clients can share a story of resilience that involves working with others.

MAINTENANCE

Discuss the following tips with your clients so that they can maintain their progress:

- A *Positive Introduction* can help you recall other stories of growth and triumph. We encourage you to share other similar stories. Sometimes the most important story comes after you and your clinician get to know one another better and you are more comfortable with the therapeutic process.

- Stories you tell about yourself are different parts of yourself. To extend the benefit of this practice, reflect on stories you tell, to yourself and others, about yourself. Is there a theme or themes? What are you trying to convey about yourself, through your stories? Are you vulnerable or resilient? Are you a victim or a survivor? Do your stories change, or change in nuance, according to the audience? What are your values? These questions will help you to clarify who you are (Mclean, Pasupathi, & Pals, 2007).

- Stories that we tell ourselves are shaped by the culture in which stories take place. One way to seek in-depth understanding of your culture is by exploring and sharing your stories, especially those of resilience, with your loved ones. Similarly, invite them to share their stories with you. This process will most likely cement your relationships with others, and you will also learn different ways of handling the same challenge.

Clinician Note

Most conversations in psychotherapy have the potential to form a sequence of stories and narratives. Pay close attention to each client's story. Inquire about and amplify it authentically. Take notes and remember details and the key theme in each story. These stories can be used in subsequent practices/sessions as running narratives. It might also be worthwhile to explore any disparity between the story narrated and current life circumstances.

Everyday stressors often deplete our energy and dampen our mood. Research shows that recalling positive autobiographical memories can help in shedding a negative mood (Joorman & Siemer, 2004). Encourage clients to keep a Gratitude Journal (as discussed later in this session) and revisit it periodically to notice changes in insights. Clients can also recall similar peak moments or experiences as a way to cope with stressors. Following the Positive Introduction practice, one client selected pictures of six similar experiences and kept them on her mobile phone as a reminder to help bounce back from stressors.

CORE CONCEPTS (PART 2)

Gratitude is an experience of thankfulness, which entails noticing and appreciating the positive things in life. In doing so, we acknowledge the value and meaning of positives. Gratitude broadens perspective and builds other positive emotions and positive reasoning (Emmons, 2007).

Clinically depressed individuals show significantly lower gratitude (nearly 50% less gratitude) than nondepressed controls (Watkins, Grimm, & Kolts, 2004). In fact, gratitude can protect clients against bouts of depression (Wood et al., 2008; Tsang, 2006).

Gratitude prompts clients to reframe negative experiences as positive whenever appropriate and realistic. This reframing in turn is associated with fewer psychological symptoms (Lambert, Fincham, & Stillman, 2012). Learning to be more grateful through sustained practices such as maintaining a *Gratitude Journal* can help clients to learn and use more positive coping strategies, which lower stress (Wood, Joseph, & Linley, 2007).

IN-SESSION PRACTICE: *GRATITUDE JOURNAL*
How We Benefit from Gratitude

Gratitude broadens our perspective and builds other positive emotions and attributes within us. According to Robert Emmons (Emmons & Mishra, 2012), a leading researcher in gratitude, research has shown that practicing gratitude can offer eight distinct benefits, including

- *Optimal Benefit:* Gratitude allows us to extract optimal benefit from a positive experience.
- *Self-Worth and Self-Esteem*: Gratitude bolsters our self-worth and self-esteem. It helps us to realize how much we and others have accomplished, which in turn makes us more confident and efficacious. Thus gratitude can help us unlearn negative habits like self-pity, which is the tendency to dwell or feel victimized.
- *Coping with Stress*: Gratitude can help us cope with stress and adversity. After an initial shock, gratitude can help us evaluate what is most important in our lives.
- *Helping Others*: Grateful people are more likely to help others. They become more aware of kind and caring acts and feel compelled to reciprocate. They are less likely to be materialistic and more likely to appreciate what they have.
- *Better Relationships*: Gratitude can strengthen our relationships. When we become truly aware of the value of our friends and family, we are likely to treat them better. When we treat them well, they treat us well.
- *Fewer Negative Comparisons*: Expressing gratitude decreases our likelihood of comparing ourselves to others. We become thankful and content with what we have (friends, family, home, health) and are less likely to feel bad for what we may not have.
- *Less Time for Negatives*: When we express gratitude, we are likely to spend less time dwelling on negative emotions. For example, when we feel grateful, it is less likely that we feel guilty, greedy, or angry.
- *Slower Adaptation*: How long does the joy of having a new possession last? Initially, we feel happy, but the joy doesn't last for very long. By appreciating the meaning and value of the object and experience, we can slow down this adaptation so that the experience of happiness continues for a longer time.

Distressed clients tend to compare themselves negatively with others. Such comparisons, as evidence shows, dent their self-worth and leave them feeling victimized and resentful (Nolen-Hoeksema & Davis, 1999). Gratitude, on the other hand, helps us become aware that we are recipients of goodness. One cannot be grateful without being thoughtful. Through this practice, we learn to think about the kindness of others, shifting our perspective from self-absorption to social expansion. In short, gratitude can build up our psychological capital, which can act as a buffer during tough times.

Gratitude has been uniquely related to total sleep quality, subjective sleep quality, sleep latency, sleep duration, and daytime dysfunction, after controlling for effects of the personality traits. It appears that presleep cognitions mediate the relationship between gratitude and sleep quality. When falling asleep, grateful people are less likely to think negative and worrisome thoughts and are more likely to think positive thoughts. It appears that negative presleep cognitions impair sleep, and gratitude reduces the likelihood of such thoughts, protecting sleep quality. Equally, it appears that positive presleep cognitions have a positive effect on sleep and that gratitude facilitates these thoughts, leading to better sleep quality (Wood, Joseph, Lloyd, & Atkins, 2009).

SUGGESTED SCRIPT FOR THE CLINICIAN

The following is a script you can use to introduce the *Gratitude Journal* practice to your clients:

> *Human evolution has seen to it that we remember failures more readily than successes. Our minds are naturally wired to focus more on negative events and experiences than those that are positive. This is called the "negativity bias." Most people spend far more time thinking about how they can fix something that has gone wrong (or is about to go wrong) than they do feeling good about what has gone right. We analyze bad events more thoroughly than good events, and we tend to dwell much more on the negatives than on the positives. This predisposition minimizes life satisfaction and maximizes psychological distress.*
>
> *We don't need much training to focus on negative experiences, but appreciating positive experiences requires special attention and effort from us. Complaining, being critical, and being cynical come easy to us, but practicing gratitude is hard. We are more likely to forget positive experiences and remember negatives ones. Therefore, it is important that we learn the skills and habits that allow us to appreciate what we have.*
>
> *Do not assume that all good things only happen because they are deserved. This leads to the feeling of entitlement and positive events being taken for granted. One way to avoid taking things for granted is to establish a daily practice of gratitude.*

Gratitude Journal

SUGGESTED SCRIPT FOR THE CLINICIAN

Please write three blessings (good things that happened today) each night before going to bed. Next to each blessing that you list, write at least one sentence about

- *Why this good thing happened today. What does this mean to you?*
- *What have you learned from taking the time to name this blessing or good thing?*
- *In what ways did you or others contribute to this blessing or good thing?*

Appendix B: *Gratitude Journal*, at the end of this manual, contains a template for a weekly *Gratitude Journal*. A copy of this journal also appears in the client workbook. To make additional copies, visit the companion website for this manual at www.oup.com/ppt.

The *Gratitude Journal* is an ongoing practice. Encourage your clients to complete this daily and to bring it to every session. Start the session by encouraging clients to share their journal entries. You will find that some clients will not keep up with their journal entries. To address this, bring a few extra copies of the *Gratitude Journal* to session. Encourage these clients to look back at the week and to reflect on positive things that may have happened, and ask them to record these positives during session. Clients can use a paper or digital version of a *Gratitude Journal*. There are also gratitude websites, some of which are listed in the Resources section at the end of this chapter. Every second week, use the Reflection & Discussion questions to engage clients in a discussion about the blessings they have written about. This discussion will help clients concretize the benefits of noticing and writing about good things in their lives.

REFLECTION & DISCUSSION

After completing this practice, ask clients to reflect and discuss:

- Did you have any difficulty recalling specific good events? If so, please specify.
- Did you notice any patterns in your good events or blessings? Family, friends, work, or nature?
- Was any aspect of your life clearly not represented in the good events or blessings, such as work or friends?
- Did you have an active role in the occurrence of good events or blessings, or did they mostly just happen to you?
- Do you find yourself reflecting more about good things after this practice?
- Do you find it a new way of looking at situations and people?
- Have you shared your good events or blessings with others?
- Did you find it hard to write them down? If so, why?

VIGNETTE: DEPRESSIVE SYMPTOMS AND *GRATITUDE JOURNAL*

Nabila, a 23-year-old female of South Asian descent, sought psychotherapy due to depressive symptoms, including feelings of melancholy, emptiness, excessive worry, and a lack of motivation. These symptoms, she stated, are chronic. She previously had sought treatment, both psychotherapy and antidepressant medication. The effectiveness of each round of treatment, she stated, sighing hopelessly, was limited, without a lasting recovery. When the clinician asked what motivated her to seek psychotherapy now, Nabila stated that, in her experience, the beginning phase of each treatment, psychotherapy or medication, is somewhat effective. Besides, positive psychotherapy intrigued her.

"Depression has been part of my life for a long time," Nabila recalled. She first experienced it at the onset of adolescence. Nabila stated that she comes from a conservative religious family that harbors a lot of negativity and what she called "drama." "My mother is most likely a chronically depressed individual. She has suffered both emotional and physical abuse at the hands of my overbearing and authoritarian father."

Nabila described her mother as a "passive person and I do not want to be like her." She continued, "In high school, I asserted myself, but it was my mother who turned against me. She was very hard on me and continues to be. I believe she took her suffering and frustration out on me because I am like her in many ways. When I started assuming more of my Canadian identity, she did not like it and wanted me to adhere to the strict cultural norms of India. She has not reconciled with the fact that I am not exactly like her. I am a Canadian of South Asian descent—not a South Asian living in Canada, as she is."

Nabila stated that, even though she loves her mother deeply, she expresses her anger in passive-aggressive ways. She explained, "My mother would not actively stop me from going out, wearing Western outfits, or befriending guys, but she would indirectly make me feel guilty as if I am doing something morally wrong."

Nabila continued, "At times my mother would report on me to my father, who now considers me to be rebellious, a disgrace to his family, and a bad influence on my two younger siblings."

Nabila said sadly that she is constantly surrounded by this negativity and that one comment triggers images and memories from the past. She then broods, which makes her feel more depressed and hopeless.

Nabila presents a typical pattern of depressive symptoms, which often takes clients down a spiral of negativity. Among other therapeutic practices, the clinician asked Nabila to start keeping a *Gratitude Journal*. She was given a handout that included recording space for writing down three good things every day for a week, with concrete illustrations. This helped her focus and not get distracted by incidental details of the practice, such as where to write the good experience and where to write the reflection. Nabila started the *Gratitude Journal* with some skepticism. Her first entry was about receiving a thank-you email from one of her close friends who is having a hard time with her husband and with whom Nabila met during the week for coffee. The clinician asked her:

CLINICIAN: What was in the email that you would consider as a blessing?
CLIENT: She and I recently spent some time together. She has been struggling with her husband.
CLINICIAN: What made her email you?
CLIENT: I know she is nice person, but this was not expected. . . . I also don't know exactly what I did that was helpful to her. Sometimes you just need to listen.

As Nabila progressed with her *Gratitude Journal*, her entries became more detailed regarding subtle aspects of her positive experiences. Discussing these entries in session also gave the clinician a rare opportunity to view aspects of her life and utilize them for therapeutic purposes. Nabila shared that she often goes for a walk with her sister, and the clinician and Nabila discussed how these instances demonstrate Nabila's positive attributes in action and how this is related to her wellness. These discussions helped Nabila to direct her attention to the good things already present in her life. Although she disclosed that she was initially skeptical about how merely writing about relatively small good things that happened could make a big difference in her chronic depression, she eventually came to find that this simple practice helped her to appreciate her own role in causing small but meaningful positive changes. Most surprising of all, Nabila started writing positive entries about her mother—a big step she never thought she would be able to take.

FIT & FLEXIBILITY

Some clients adapt to writing good things. We adapt to both positive and negatives (Lucas, 2007; Kahneman et al., 2006). Therefore, it is important to keep the gratitude strategy fresh by varying it and by avoiding overuse. The following are strategies to vary expressions of gratitude:

- Alternate this practice by writing in the journal for one week and, during the next week, by doing the practice orally, for example, by talking to a loved one.
- Express gratitude through art, such as photography, a weekly smartphone collage, or drawing or sketching instead of writing.
- Do the practice interactively with others, such as sharing positive events with family members before or after dinner or with colleagues at work, at the end of the workday, or via email.
- Purposely vary domains weekly or biweekly, focusing on family, work, leisure, nature, or positive events in the media.

Some clients may need more specific guidance: To address adaptation in completing the *Gratitude Journal* practice, provide such clients with prompts such as

- Today I noticed something beautiful. It was _____
- Today I experienced something that I did well. It was _____

- Today I was kind to someone or someone was kind to me. It was _____
- Today I heard good news. It was _____
- Today I saw something inspiring. It was _____

Some clients may forget to complete this assignment. Suggest the following strategies to help make this assignment more routine:

- Get a new notebook or journal for the practice so the client is more likely to notice it or feel it is special.
- Complete the practice at the same time each evening, and keep the *Gratitude Journal* in the same place.
- Set a daily reminder with a smartphone alarm.

Essential to this practice is deliberately paying attention to positive events, recording them systematically, and reflecting on them. We emphasize engaging in the *Gratitude Journal* practice during the evening, to be able to end each day on a positive note. However, some clients prefer to record their appreciations first thing in the morning, and that is fine. Their rationale may be that this practice sets a positive tone for the day. Another variation could be that, at the beginning of the day, clients write three good events likely to happen, and at the end of the day, they write three good events that actually happened.

Some clients may be going through very tough circumstances (e.g., death of a loved one, serious medical condition, break-up of a long-term relationship, or loss of a cherished job) that adversely impact their cognitive ability to concentrate on recalling positive events. These clients may not be able to do this practice authentically. In these cases, use a flexible approach, such as writing a negative and a positive statement, discussing any positive news in their lives, talking about positive events that took place in the public realm during the week, or, if appropriate, sharing positives in the aftermath of negative events, which might help clients to appreciate positives in a manner that is palatable to them.

CULTURAL CONSIDERATIONS

Clinicians should be mindful that expressions of gratitude vary from culture to culture. Some cultures prefer gestures of gratitude, instead of words, which might be difficult to capture in writing. Offer diverse ways to capture gratitude.

For clients from cultures that may have experienced extreme conditions (e.g., genocide, famine, epidemics, civil war, political oppression, or great natural disaster), the gratitude may be experienced by being away from these conditions, rather than by observing and acknowledging a positive experience. Likewise, positive appraisal of a negative event could also be considered an expression of gratitude.

Some clients may be going through life circumstances that make it very difficult for them to find something worth being grateful for in their everyday lives. For these clients, gently encourage them to think about past accomplishments for which they are grateful; encourage them to remember those who helped them succeed. If they simply cannot do this practice authentically outside of the sessions, then do not force it, and during sessions find opportunities to draw the attention of such clients toward experiences they might be thankful for.

Some clients from diverse cultural background may not be open to the Western ways of expressing gratitude, such as verbal or written expressions. In such situations, explore culturally specific and sensitive ways of expressing gratitude.

MAINTENANCE

Expressing gratitude every day maintains and enhances well-being. This expression can be as simple as a conscious and sincere "thank you" to someone who holds the door open for you or getting a positive email from your friend. Encourage clients to make it a habit to build gratitude into their daily schedules.

Discuss the following tips with your clients so that they can maintain their progress:

- Grateful people are less envious of others and are less likely to measure their success in terms of material gains. When we are genuinely thankful and appreciative for what we have (e.g., family, friends, health, home), we are less likely to pay close attention to what our neighbors have (Finlay & Lyons, 2000; Froh et al., 2011). Grateful people are also more likely to help others. When we become aware of the kind and caring acts of others, we naturally feel like reciprocating (Watkins, 2010). In this way, gratitude reinforces other favorable consequences, increasing and strengthening it. What other favorable changes happen when you start practicing gratitude?
- A pervasive sense of gratitude contributes to positive interpretations of life events. That is, grateful people tend to look at life events in a more positive way. After practicing gratitude (by consistently maintaining a *Gratitude Journal*), whenever you recall past hurts and painful memories, we encourage you to discuss with your clinician if your interpretation of these events have changed after practicing gratitude.
- Observe if a blessing or a good thing is related to your strengths, qualities, or talents; that is, has being grateful also helped you to appreciate your other attributes, such as kindness, social and personal intelligence, and appreciation of beauty?
- You can express your gratitude through art (e.g., painting, sketching, photography, collage, or scrapbooking).
- Instead of writing, for a few weeks you can share your blessings with your partner and encourage him or her to share with you.
- On days you may be gripped by a negative or sad mood and don't feel like writing in your *Gratitude Journal*, just review previous entries.

END-OF-SESSION RELAXATION

We recommend that each session end with the same brief relaxation practice that started the session.

RESOURCES FOR *POSITIVE INTRODUCTION*

Readings

- Bauer, J. J., McAdams, D. P., & Sakaeda, A. R. (2005). Interpreting the good life: Growth memories in the lives of mature, happy people. *Journal of Personality and Social Psychology, 88*, 203–217.
- Burns, G. (2001). *101 Healing Stories: Using Metaphors in Therapy.* New York: Wiley.
- McAdams, D. P. (2001). The psychology of life stories. *Review of General Psychology, 5*, 100–122.
- Pals, J. L. (2006). Narrative identity processing of difficult life experiences: Pathways of personality development and positive self-transformation in adulthood. *Journal of Personality, 74*, 1079–1110.

Videos

- First author's positive introduction: Tayyab Rashid on Using Strengths at a Time of Trauma: https://youtu.be/Pucs6MUpKng

Websites

- Readers' Digest section on true and inspiring stories:
  http://www.rd.com/true-stories/
- Inspiring stories including amazing, short, moral, funny, positive, touching, positive, and spiritual stories:
  http://www.inspirationalstories.eu

RESOURCES FOR *GRATITUDE JOURNAL*

Readings

- Emmons, R. A., & Stern, R. (2013). Gratitude as a psychotherapeutic intervention: Gratitude. *Journal of Clinical Psychology, 69*(8), 846–855.
- Kaczmarek, L. D., Kashdan, T. B., Kleiman, E., Baczkowski, B., Enko, B., Siebers, A., et al. (2013). Who self-initiates gratitude interventions in daily life? An examination of intentions, curiosity, depressive symptoms, and life satisfaction. *Personality and Individual Differences, 55*, 805–810.
- Krysinska, K., Lester, D., Lyke, J., & Corveleyn, J. (2015). Trait gratitude and suicidal ideation and behavior: An exploratory study. *Crisis: The Journal of Crisis Intervention and Suicide Prevention, 36*(4), 291–296. http://dx.doi.org/10.1027/0227-5910/a000320
- O'Connell, B. H., O'Shea, D., & Gallagher, S. (2017). Feeling thanks and saying thanks: A randomized controlled trial examining if and how socially oriented gratitude journals work. *Journal of Clinical Psychology, 73*(10), 1280–1300.
- Wood, A. M., Froh, J. J., & Geraghty, A. W. A. (2010). Gratitude and well-being: A review and theoretical integration. *Clinical Psychology Review, 30*, 890–905.

Videos

- Martin Seligman explains Three Blessing Exercise:
  https://youtu.be/RT2vKMyIQwc
- Robert Emmons on evidence-based practices of cultivating gratitude:
  https://youtu.be/8964envYh58
- Louie Schwartzberg's TED Talk on gratitude showing stunning time-lapse photography:
  https://youtu.be/gXDMoiEkyuQ

Websites

- Explore what good is happening in the world through these websites:
  www.selfgrowth.com/news
  www.happynews.com
  www.optimistworld.com

## 8

SESSION TWO: *CHARACTER STRENGTHS* AND *SIGNATURE STRENGTHS*

SESSION TWO IS THE FIRST OF THREE sessions focusing on *Character Strengths* and *Signature Strengths*, which are positive traits that can be developed through practice and can contribute to personal growth and wellness. Taken together, Sessions Two to Four cover assessing strengths; understanding their contextualized, situation-specific usage; and how specific strengths can be utilized to create a desired or better version of the self.

SESSION TWO OUTLINE
Core Concepts
    In-Session Practice: *Character Strengths Assessment*
    Reflection & Discussion
    Vignettes
    Fit & Flexibility
    Cultural Considerations
    Maintenance
Resources

CORE CONCEPTS
To help us gauge a client's psychological distress, traditional therapy has valid and reliable ways to assess stressors, symptoms, dysfunctions, deficits, and disorders. Positive psychotherapy (PPT) offers valid and reliable tools to assess the character strengths of clients, so that they can understand and discover many different ways in which they can be good, sane, and positive.

PPT focuses on character strengths. Whereas symptoms and their severity help us understand the stress, sadness, anger, and anxiety of clients, character strengths such as gratitude, hope, love, kindness, and curiosity help us understand the ways in which clients can be good, sane, and high functioning. Just as psychology has shown that individuals who experience negative emotions such as anger, hostility, vengeance, or narcissistic traits are more likely to develop a host of psychological problems, individuals who experience gratitude, forgiveness, humility, love, and kindness are more likely to report being happier and more satisfied with life (Trompetter et al., 2017). Hence, assessing strengths along with symptoms is critical for a balanced and holistic clinical practice, and for understanding that psychotherapy is as much about cultivation of thriving as it is about alleviation of distress.

Assessment of strengths from a clinical perspective was discussed in detail in Part I of this manual. The following core points will help clients to focus explicitly on strengths:

- Fixing weaknesses is remediation, whereas nurturing strengths produces growth and more well-being. While there is great value to listening to and helping clients interpret their problems, mere interpretation and insight don't necessarily make clients emotionally stronger. Discussion and elaboration of strengths, in relation to symptoms and stress, improve clients' self-efficacy because strengths offer them diverse ways to be good, kind, playful, industrious, curious, creative, and grateful.

- Strengths essentially come from being and doing good, not only from feeling good. One often feels good when one does good. But doing good is not limited to trite, feel-good statements, such as "You can do anything if you work hard enough" and "The sky's the limit." In contrast, doing good comes from specific, realistic actions.
- Evidence shows that strengths can act as buffers against mental illness. PPT assumes that psychopathology occurs due to a lack of certain strengths. For example, evidence shows that people low on hope, optimism, gratitude, zest, love, and curiosity are most likely to experience depression (Trompetter et al., 2017), whereas high scores on hope and gratitude are associated with positive mental health and greater life satisfaction (Macaskill & Denovan, 2014).
- In a recent study, clinicians reported that strengths helped them to broaden client perspectives, instilled hope and increased motivation, helped to create a positive meaning through reframing and metaphors, and also improved the therapeutic process (Scheel, Davis, & Henderson, 2012). Another study showed that when the clinician derived positive emotions from the client's input in the therapy, it improved the client's resourcefulness (Vandenberghe & Silvestre, 2013).
- Using strengths increases client self-efficacy and confidence over and above self-esteem (Linley et al., 2010). Strengths offer ways to facilitate being good, kind, humorous, industrious, curious, creative, and grateful. Using strengths shows significant stress reduction, more positive emotions, and vitality (Wood et al., 2011).

START-OF-SESSION RELAXATION

At the start of every session, begin with a brief relaxation exercise. Refer to Appendix A: Relaxation & Mindfulness Practices, which can be found at the end of this manual. A copy of this appendix also appears in the client workbook. To make additional copies, visit the companion website for this manual at www.oup.com/ppt. Continue the session with a review of the client's *Gratitude Journal* as well as a review of the core concepts taught in the previous session.

IN-SESSION PRACTICE: *CHARACTER STRENGTHS ASSESSMENT*

After discussing the notion of character strengths, clients complete a number of exercises to explore their *own* strengths. Rather than a simplistic approach of identifying and using more of their top five strengths, PPT adapts a comprehensive strengths assessment approach, in which clients collect information about their top five or six strengths from multiple perspectives. In Chapter 4 of this manual, the section called "Incorporating Strengths in PPT" describes numerous ways of assessing a client's character strengths. Recent data and clinical experience have demonstrated that this comprehensive form of strengths assessment is valuable, and clients have found it helpful (Uliaszek, Rashid, Williams, & Gulamani, 2016). Being able to see discrepancies between the results of the different modes of strength assessment presents an excellent opportunity for clients to think critically about their strengths and for clinicians to engage clients in discussion of how they feel about their strengths in a dynamic and concrete manner.

SUGGESTED SCRIPT FOR THE CLINICIAN

The following is a script you can use to help your clients figure out their signature strengths. This script involves Worksheets 2.1 to 2.6. Note that these and all worksheets (a) appear within the corresponding session of this manual, (b) are reprinted for the client in the accompanying client workbook, and (c) can be downloaded from the companion website at www.oup.com/ppt. Some of the following steps can be completed in-session, while others will be done between sessions.

Today we begin the process of identifying your own signature strengths, which are at the heart of PPT. We do this from multiple perspectives, so let's begin.

1. **Step One:** *You will watch a video clip, and, using Worksheet 2.1, you will identify and record five strengths that best represent you. Please follow the specific worksheet instructions to make sure that this step is done correctly. When you have completed Worksheet 2.1, transfer the identified strengths to column 2 of Worksheet 2.6.*

2. **Step Two:** *On Worksheet 2.2, please read the descriptions of 24 strengths and select exactly five (no less, no more) that best represent you. Take your time with this exercise. When you have completed Worksheet 2.2, transfer the identified strengths to column 3 of Worksheet 2.6.*

3. **Step Three:** *Please plot your strengths as identified in Steps One and Two using Worksheet 2.3. Worksheet 2.1 strengths roughly correspond to your emotions or your heart, since responses are based on a rapid audiovisual presentation of strengths. Worksheet 2.2 strengths are based on your thinking or your head, since you were given ample time to think and select five strengths. Although there is no evidence to suggest that a heart and head match is desirable, the whole process is meant to engage your self-awareness from two different perspectives— something we rarely do. There is no need to transfer these strengths to Worksheet 2.6. The purpose of Worksheet 2.3 is to allow you to see if there is any overlap between you heart and head strengths.*

4. **Step Four:** *Using Worksheets 2.4 and 2.5, ask two sources—one close friend and one family member—to identify five character strengths that they think best represent your personality. Please ask them to identify your strengths only by using checkmarks and to keep their answers confidential. You will be provided envelopes for the completed worksheets. Please bring those in to your next session or as soon as they are ready. When you have completed Worksheet 2.4, transfer the identified strengths to column 4 of Worksheet 2.6, and when you have completed Worksheet 2.5, transfer the identified strengths to column 5 of Worksheet 2.6.*

5. **Step Five:** *At home, you will be completing a free online Signature Strengths Questionnaire (SSQ-72; www.tayyabrashid.com), which identifies your five or six top strengths (based on your five or six highest scores). Transfer these strengths to column 6 of Worksheet 2.6.*

6. **Step Six:** *After Worksheets 2.1 to 2.5 are done and you have completed Step Five, you can continue working on Worksheet 2.6: Your Signature Strengths Profile. Complete column 7 by adding the scores across each row.*

7. **Step Seven:** *Go to column 8 on Worksheet 2.6 and identify strengths you Underuse (U) and Overuse (O). You can expand your selection to other strengths, even if these are not your signature strengths.*

8. **Step Eight:** *Keeping in mind why you came to therapy, fill out column 9 of Worksheet 2.6 (Desired) by identifying which strengths, either from your signature strengths or others, can help you solve your problems or to be the kind of person you always wanted to be.*

WORKSHEET 2.1   WHAT ARE YOUR "HEART" STRENGTHS?

You will watch a video showing pictures of the strengths listed here. Each picture will be labeled with the name of one of these strengths, and each picture will appear for a very brief period. Without focusing on whether the picture best represents the strength, please tune in to your emotions as sharply as you can. Keep your pen ready and with minimal thinking, if the strength represents your personality, please circle it or put an "x" in the right-hand column. Try to keep your selections limited to five strengths that best describe you. If you end up choosing more than five, you will have an opportunity to cross out any extra ones after the video is over.

	Character Strengths	**Represents You**
1	Creativity	
2	Curiosity	
3	Open-mindedness	
4	Love of Learning	
5	Perspective	
6	Bravery	
7	Persistence	
8	Integrity	
9	Vitality & Zest	
10	Love	
11	Kindness	
12	Social intelligence	
13	Citizenship & Teamwork	
14	Fairness	
15	Leadership	
16	Forgiveness & Mercy	
17	Humility & Modesty	
18	Prudence	
19	Self-regulation	
20	Appreciation of Beauty and Excellence	
21	Gratitude	
22	Hope & Optimism	
23	Humor & Playfulness	
24	Spirituality	

When you have completed Worksheet 2.1, transfer the identified strengths to column 2 of Worksheet 2.6.

WORKSHEET 2.2   WHAT ARE YOUR "HEAD" STRENGTHS?

*Read the following descriptions of 24 positive character strengths. Select the **five** that **most often** characterize you, by placing a checkmark in the Signature Strengths column.*

	Description	Signature Strengths
1	I am good at thinking of new and better ways of doing things.	
2	I love to explore things, ask questions, and am open to different experiences and activities.	
3	I am flexible and open-minded; I think through and examine all sides before deciding.	
4	I love to learn new ideas, concepts, and facts in school or on my own.	
5	Friends consult with me on important matters, as they consider me to be wise beyond my age.	
6	I do not give up in the face of hardship or challenge, even when I am afraid.	
7	I finish most things, even if get distracted; I am able to refocus and complete the task.	
8	I consider myself to be a genuine and honest person, known to be trustworthy. I act consistent with my values.	
9	I am energetic, cheerful, and full of life.	
10	Showing and receiving genuine love and affection come naturally to me.	
11	I love to do kind acts for others, often without being asked.	
12	I manage myself well in social situations and am known to have good interpersonal skills.	
13	I am an active community or team member, and I contribute to the success of my group.	
14	I stand up for others when they are treated unfairly, bullied, or ridiculed.	
15	Others often choose me as a leader as I am known to lead well.	
16	I do not hold grudges; I forgive easily those who offend me.	
17	I don't like to be the center of attention and prefer others to shine.	
18	I am careful and cautious; I can anticipate risks and problems of my actions and respond accordingly.	
19	I manage my feelings and behaviors even in challenging situations; I generally follow rules and routines.	
20	I am moved deeply by beauty in nature, in art (e.g., painting, music, theatre) and/or in excellence in many fields of life.	
21	I express thankfulness for good things through words and actions.	
22	I hope and believe that more good things will happen than bad ones.	
23	I am playful and funny, and I use humor to connect with others.	
24	I believe in a higher power and participate in religious or spiritual practices (e.g., prayer, meditation) willingly.	

When you have completed Worksheet 2.2, transfer the identified strengths to column 3 of Worksheet 2.6.

WORKSHEET 2.3   YOUR *CHARACTER STRENGTHS*: HEART VS. HEAD

	Character Strength	Heart	Head
1	Creativity		
2	Curiosity		
3	Open-mindedness		
4	Love of Learning		
5	Perspective		
6	Bravery		
7	Persistence		
8	Integrity		
9	Vitality & Zest		
10	Love		
11	Kindness		
12	Social Intelligence		
13	Citizenship & Teamwork		
14	Fairness		
15	Leadership		
16	Forgiveness & Mercy		
17	Humility & Modesty		
18	Prudence		
19	Self-regulation		
20	Appreciation of Beauty and Excellence		
21	Gratitude		
22	Hope & Optimism		
23	Humor & Playfulness		
24	Spirituality		

In the heart column, mark the strengths identified on Worksheet 2.1, and in the head column, mark the strengths identified on Worksheet 2.2. There is no need to transfer these strengths to Worksheet 2.6. The purpose of Worksheet 2.3 is to allow you to see if there is any overlap between you heart and head strengths.

To be completed by a family member

Please read the following descriptions of 24 positive character traits. Then select with a checkmark exactly *five* (no less, no more) you find **most often** characterize _____.

Description		Signature Strengths
1	Is good at thinking of new and better ways of doing things	
2	Loves to explore things, asks questions, is open to different experiences and activities	
3	Is flexible and open-minded; thinks through and examines all sides before deciding	
4	Loves to learn new ideas, concepts, and facts in school or on her/his own	
5	Friends consult him/her regarding important matters; is considered to be wise beyond age	
6	Does not give up in face of hardship or challenge, even when afraid	
7	Finishes most things; is able to refocus when distracted and complete the task	
8	Is a genuine and honest person, is known to be trustworthy; acts consistent with her/his values	
9	Is energetic, cheerful, and full of life	
10	Both loving and being loved comes natural to him/her; values close relationships with others	
11	Loves to do kind acts for others, often without being asked	
12	Manages her/himself well in social situations and is known to have good interpersonal skills	
13	Is an active community or team member, and contributes to the success of the group	
14	Stands up for others when they are treated unfairly, bullied, or ridiculed	
15	Is often chosen by others as a leader; is known to lead well	
16	Forgives easily those who offend him/her; does not hold grudges	
17	Doesn't like to be the center of attention and prefers others to shine	
18	Is careful and cautious, can anticipate risks and problems of his/her actions and responds accordingly	
19	Manages feelings and behaviors well in challenging situations; generally follows rules and routines	
20	Is moved deeply by beauty in nature, in art (e.g., painting, music, theatre) and/or in excellence in many fields of life	
21	Expresses thankfulness for good things through words and actions	
22	Hopes and believe that more good things will happen than bad ones	
23	Is playful and funny, and uses humor to connect with others	
24	Believes in a higher power and participates in religious or spiritual practices (e.g., prayer, meditation) willingly	

When you have completed Worksheet 2.4, transfer the identified strengths to column 4 of Worksheet 2.6.

To be completed by a friend

*Please read the following descriptions of 24 positive character traits. Then select with a checkmark exactly **five** (no less, no more) you find **most often** characterize _____.*

Description		Signature Strengths
1	Is good at thinking of new and better ways of doing things	
2	Loves to explore things, asks questions, is open to different experiences and activities	
3	Is flexible and open-minded; thinks through and examines all sides before deciding	
4	Loves to learn new ideas, concepts, and facts in school or on her/his own	
5	Friends consult him/her regarding important matters; is considered to be wise beyond age	
6	Does not give up in face of hardship or challenge, even when afraid	
7	Finishes most things; is able to refocus when distracted and complete the task	
8	Is a genuine and honest person, is known to be trustworthy; acts consistent with her/his values	
9	Is energetic, cheerful, and full of life	
10	Both loving and being loved comes natural to him/her; values close relationships with others	
11	Loves to do kind acts for others, often without being asked	
12	Manages her/himself well in social situations and is known to have good interpersonal skills	
13	Is an active community or team member, and contributes to the success of the group	
14	Stands up for others when they are treated unfairly, bullied, or ridiculed	
15	Is often chosen by others as a leader; is known to lead well	
16	Forgives easily those who offend him/her; does not hold grudges	
17	Doesn't like to be the center of attention and prefers others to shine	
18	Is careful and cautious, can anticipate risks and problems of his/her actions and responds accordingly	
19	Manages feelings and behaviors well in challenging situations; generally follows rules and routines	
20	Is moved deeply by beauty in nature, in art (e.g., painting, music, theatre) and/or in excellence in many fields of life	
21	Expresses thankfulness for good things through words and actions	
22	Hopes and believe that more good things will happen than bad ones	
23	Is playful and funny, and uses humor to connect with others	
24	Believes in a higher power and participates in religious or spiritual practices (e.g., prayer, meditation) willingly	

When you have completed Worksheet 2.5, transfer the identified strengths to column 5 of Worksheet 2.6.

WORKSHEET 2.6   COMPILE YOUR SIGNATURE STRENGTHS

This worksheet has columns for you to fill out. Each column is independent of the others.

Column 2 and 3: *Record the five strengths you self-identified from Worksheets 2.1 and 2.2.*

Column 4 and 5: *Record the five strengths identified by your family member from Worksheet 2.4 and the five strengths identified by your friend from Worksheet 2.5.*

Column 6: *Record your top five or six strengths identified from the Signature Strengths Questionnaire:* www.tayyabrashid.com.

Column 7: *Add the scores across each row.*

Column 8: *Identify five strengths that you may be lacking (Underuse) or have in excess (Overuse).*

Column 9: *Identify five strengths that you would like to possess.*

Signature Strengths Profile

Column 1		Column 2	Column 3	Column 4	Column 5	Column 6	Column 7	Column 8	Column 9
Strengths		WS2.1 Heart	WS2.2 Head	WS2.4 Family	WS2.5 Friend	SSQ- 72	Totals	U/O	Desired
1	Creativity & Originality								
2	Curiosity, Interest in the World								
3	Open-Mindedness, Critical Thinking								
4	Love of Learning								
5	Perspective & Wisdom								
6	Bravery & Valor								
7	Persistence, Diligence & Industry								
8	Integrity, Authenticity & Honesty								
9	Vitality, Zest, Enthusiasm & Energy								
10	Love: Capacity to Love and Be Loved								
11	Kindness & Generosity								
12	Social Intelligence								
13	Citizenship, Teamwork & Loyalty								
14	Fairness, Equity & Justice								
15	Leadership								
16	Forgiveness & Mercy								
17	Humility & Modesty								
18	Prudence, Caution & Discretion								
19	Self-Regulation & Self-Control								
20	Appreciation of Beauty								
21	Gratitude								
22	Hope & Optimism								
23	Humor & Playfulness								
24	Spirituality & Religiousness								

REFLECTION & DISCUSSION

After completing this practice, ask clients to reflect and discuss:

- After considering various perspectives, how well do your signature strengths reflect your personality? Would your signature strengths adequately describe your personality to someone who knows nothing about you?
- Are there significant differences among your perspective and those of your family, friend, and the questionnaire (SSQ-72)? Did multiple people identify the same specific strengths? Explain.
- After compiling your profile, did you find out that you display specific strengths with specific people or in specific situations? Explain.
- When you think about your life thus far, which of your strengths have always existed? Which strengths are new? What can you learn from this?
- How do your strengths work together in synergy?

After reflecting on and discussing these questions, clients should complete Worksheet 2.7: Markers of Your *Signature Strength*s. Explain to clients that the purpose of this worksheet is to help them explore the authenticity of their signature strengths. Are the strengths identified by a client's signature profile (Worksheet 2.6) *really* his own, true strengths? We can resolve complex situations in everyday life when we understand our true strengths. Knowing that the five or six identified strengths are truly our own signature strengths is very important so that we can take ownership of them.

In the space provided, first list your signature strengths taken from your signature strengths profile. Next, using the provided questions, briefly write about specific experiences, including anecdotes about one or more of your signature strengths. Note that the questions will help to highlight key markers (authenticity) of your signature strengths.

My Signature Strengths, according to my profile are:

1.

2.

3.

4.

5.

6.

QUESTIONS to Determine Key Markers of Signature Strengths

1. **Authenticity:** Is this strength a core part of me?

2. **Excitement:** When I use my signature strength(s), do I feel excited?

3. **Learning:** Is it natural and effortless for me to use this strength?

4. **Finding new ways to use**: Do I yearn to find new ways to use my strength(s)?

5. **Persistence:** Do I find it difficult to stop an activity that fully uses this strength?

6. **Invigoration:** Does using this strength make me feel invigorated instead of exhausted?

7. **Projects to Use the Strength:** Do I create personal projects designed to make use of this strength?

8. **Enthusiastic:** Do I feel joyous, zestful, and enthusiastic while using this strength?

REFLECTION & DISCUSSION (CONTINUED)
After completing Worksheet 2.7, ask clients to reflect and discuss:

- Which signature strength stood out for you in terms of specific markers (e.g., authenticity, learning, or invigoration)? Please explain why.
- After completing this worksheet, how confident do you feel about your signature strengths?
- Please review all 24 strengths. Are there strengths not identified by your profile that you feel should be there, in terms of the markers listed in Worksheet 2.7? Why did these strengths not make the list of your top five or six signature strengths?

Now that clients know about their signature strengths, the next step is to develop self-awareness about the under- and overuse of their strengths, as well as which strengths they lack. Ask clients to complete Worksheet 2.8: Under- and Overuse of Strengths.

Read the following description of the strengths. Put a minus sign next to three strengths you might be underusing (or lacking altogether). Put a plus sign next to three strengths you overuse. (Note that these strengths do not have to be one of your signature strengths.)

Then for each of your signature strengths, specify a corresponding lack/underuse and excess/overuse, if applicable.

Character Strength		Description	Underuse or Lacking	Overuse or Excess
1	Creativity & Originality	Thinking of new and better ways of doing things; not being content with doing things in conventional ways		
2	Curiosity & Openness to Experience	Being driven to explore things; asking questions, not tolerating ambiguity easily; being open to different experiences and activities		
3	Open-Mindedness & Critical Thinking	Thinking through and examining all sides before deciding; consulting with trusted others; being flexible to change one's mind when necessary		
4	Love of Learning	Loving to learn many things, concepts, ideas, and facts in school or on one's own		
5	Perspective (wisdom)	Putting things together to understand underlying meaning; settling disputes among friends; learning from mistakes		
6	Bravery & Valor	Overcoming fears to do what needs to be done; not giving up in the face of a hardship or challenge		
7	Perseverance, Persistence, & Industry	Finishing most things; being able to refocus when distracted and completing the task without complaining; overcoming challenges to complete the task		
8	Integrity, Authenticity, & Honesty	Not pretending to be someone one is not; coming across as a genuine and honest person		
9	Vitality, Zest, Enthusiasm, & Energy	Being energetic, cheerful, and full of life; being chosen by others to hang out with		
10	Love: Capacity to Love and Be Loved	Having warm and caring relationships with family and friends; showing genuine love and affection through actions regularly		
11	Kindness & Generosity	Doing kind deeds for others, often without asking; helping others regularly; being known as a kind person		
12	Social Intelligence	Easily understanding others' feelings; managing oneself well in social situations; displaying excellent interpersonal skills		
13	Citizenship, Teamwork, & Loyalty	Relating well with teammates or group members; contributing to the success of the group		
14	Fairness, Equity, & Justice	Standing up for others when they are treated unfairly, bullied, or ridiculed; day-to-day actions show a sense of fairness		
15	Leadership	Organizing activities that include others; being someone others like to follow; being often chosen to lead by peers		

Character Strength		Description	Underuse or Lacking	Overuse or Excess
16	Forgiveness & Mercy	Forgiving easily those who offend; not holding grudges		
17	Humility & Modesty	Not liking to be the center of attention; not acting special; admitting shortcomings readily; knowing what one can and cannot do. Letting others shine.		
18	Prudence, Caution, & Discretion	Being careful and cautious; avoid taking undue risks; not easily yielding to external pressures		
19	Self-Regulation & Self-Control	Managing feelings and behavior well; gladly following rules and routines		
20	Appreciation of Beauty & Excellence	Being moved deeply by beauty in nature, in art (painting, music, theatre, etc.), or in excellence in any field of life		
21	Gratitude	Expressing thankfulness for good things through words and actions; not taking things for granted		
22	Hope, Optimism, & Future-mindedness	Hoping and believing that more good things will happen than bad ones; recovering quickly from setbacks and taking concrete steps to overcome them		
23	Humor & Playfulness	Being playful, funny, and using humor to connect with others		
24	Religiousness & Spirituality	Believing in God or a higher power; liking to participate in religious or spiritual practices, e.g., prayer, meditation		

REFLECTION & DISCUSSION (CONTINUED)

After completing Worksheet 2.8, ask clients to reflect and discuss:

1. Sometimes, what we think of as a negative behavior in others can be under- or overuse of strengths. Reflect on these common scenarios and discuss which might be a reflection of the under or over usage of a strength:[1]
    a. Someone feeling sad and slow
    b. Someone worrying too much about small things or worrying about minute details that may not be critical
    c. Someone always being in a playful and humorous mood
    d. Someone who fails to confront his friend for inappropriate behavior
    e. Someone who may be taking too many projects or assignments

2. Often it is not clear cut or straightforward to distinguish a balanced use of a strength from its over- or underuse. Take curiosity as an example. Curiosity entails actively seeking knowledge to open oneself to new experiences. Its underuse (disinterest, apathy, or boredom) may be easily recognizable, but its overuse may be difficult to spot. One could actively seek knowledge for many purposes, including Facebook stalking others. The latter behavior would most likely be nosiness. Similarly, zest can encompass displaying vitality and enthusiasm to manic, hysterical, or frantic behavior. Consider your signature strengths and reflect on what specific behaviors and actions may let you know if you are under- or overusing a strength.

3. Are there any specific situations or circumstances that reinforce under- or overuse of one of your signature strengths?

4. Are there some cultural factors that endorse under- or overuse of specific strengths? For example, some cultures put greater emphasis on humility, while others emphasize teamwork or social intelligence.

5. If you over use one of your signature strengths—say creativity—can you think of other strengths (such as self-regulation, modesty, or prudence) that may not be your signature strengths but can still help you to use creativity in a balanced way?

VIGNETTE: MELISSA

Melissa, a 34-year-old female, completed a PPT group. She had been referred to the group for moderate to severe symptoms of depression and anxiety. After completing her signature strength profile, Melissa shared the following reflections with the group:

"I shared the signature strengths worksheet with my fiancé, my colleague at work, and a friend whom I have known since high school. My fiancé and I matched in four out of five strengths, which is surprising since we have quite different perspectives on many issues. It was also surprising because I realized that he actually knows me well and values my strengths.

"My colleague at work highlighted leadership, which was kind of a surprise because I have never deliberately taken any leadership role. However, after she identified it as a strength, I started thinking perhaps one day I may enjoy leading an initiative—maybe not at my current job though. My long-time friend identified integrity and persistence. I wasn't surprised about these. I usually don't take additional

---

[1] (a) Underutilizing zest and positive emotions, given there are no other extenuating circumstances to explain sadness; (b) lack of perspective or overuse of prudence; (c) overuse of humor and playfulness; (d) lack of courage or fairness; (e) lack of self-regulation.

work, until I finish what I am working on. I am told I am an honest person and never compromise on this, even though I have to sacrifice some important things. . . . In fact, sometimes I am called, mostly by my mother, "too honest."

"I loved the aspect of incorporating others' perspectives . . . otherwise, we become too sure of ourselves and dismiss dissenting information."

VIGNETTE: MOREEZ

Moreez, a 21-year-old male undergraduate student, sought individual psychotherapy for severe symptoms of depression and feeling isolated. He reported a history of depressive symptoms starting in the early years of high school. Initially Moreez was not motivated enough to fully engage in psychotherapy, and his academic functioning was low. Introverted and quiet by nature, his affective range was restricted. He rarely smiled during the sessions.

As the therapeutic rapport developed, he reluctantly agreed to explore his signature strengths. It took him about three sessions to gather all the collateral information about his strengths. He opted to ask two friends—instead of a family member—to identify his strengths, as he felt too shy to ask a family member for input. However, each step increased his interest. When tallied across different sources, humility, prudence, kindness, social intelligence, and teamwork turned out to be his signature strengths. His clinician was intrigued and asked Moreez to share his insights about social intelligence, teamwork, and perspective. He stated that he is known, among his friends, to be a good listener. Moreez said, "When everybody needs someone to hear their problems, I am always there." He added that not only does he listen well, but whenever two friends argue, or a friend finds him- or herself in conflict with someone else, "I am the first one, from whom they seek advice. I am known to be the voice of reason." Explaining his signature strength of teamwork, he stated that he is a good team player, and, for group assignments, he is often asked to join a group.

Moreez wasn't very surprised to learn about his signature strengths, as he already intuitively knew what they were. He said that although he is available for others when they need him, no one is there for him. He said that he is not very expressive of his needs, and most of his friends don't ask or ask deeply enough about how he is doing.

After listening empathically, the clinician fully acknowledged Moreez's struggles and feelings of isolation, as well as highlighted the courage it took to share these feelings in therapy. The clinician gently and tentatively commented that Moreez's ability to listen to others and his ability to consider all aspects of the situation well enough to offer reasoned counsel make him socially intelligent, and that these strengths, with some adaptations, may serve him well in the long run. After being asked by the clinician, Moreez shared numerous illustrations of using these strengths. Emphasizing his strength of perspective, the clinician drew the client's attention to how his kindness and social skills help others in many ways. Moreez found this interpretation of his signature strengths very helpful and stated that he always considered these aspects of his personality more of a weakness. However, seeing them as strengths made him feel better. As he was able to reframe his perceived liabilities as his assets, his mood improved. His loneliness did not totally diminish, but he started feeling more efficacious and believed that his strengths helped him to relate with others.

Later in this manual, we explain how this client was able to learn a more nuanced and adaptive use of his strengths; however, the process of identifying his strengths in itself lifted his mood out of depression.

FIT & FLEXIBILITY

As a clinician conducting PPT, you are likely to come across numerous challenges when working from a strengths-based perspective. Some clients will be skeptical about strengths in therapy, as they will have entrenched ideas that therapy is a place to discuss troubles, and hence a focus on strengths is irrelevant and a waste of time. Others may find comfort in their role as victim. In working from a strengths-based approach with hundreds of clients for many years—always focusing on the therapeutic relationship and therapeutic process—we have learned to be patient and to find ways to use these strategies:

- When clients report being overwhelmed or are in crisis, they need your strengths of empathy and relatedness and your ability to tolerate their distress. Focus on these first.
- Ask clients how they typically cope with a crisis, note any strengths, and discuss these strengths whenever you feel clients are ready to engage in such a discussion.
- Acknowledge and appreciate clients' willingness to share their struggles. When appropriate, call it courage and the ability to trust the clinician.
- Keep the hope and quest for change ignited, and then introduce strengths as essential ingredients to facilitate the change.
- Whenever appropriate, reframe the problem through the lens of strengths. For example, in solving problems, people learn to consult with others (social interaction), try different things (initiative, creativity, persistence), weigh options (prudence), explore what is solvable and realistic (perspective), and follow a course and try to stick with it (self-regulation).
- Be concrete in spotting client strengths. Formal assessment comes alive when the clinician elicits concrete actions, habits, experiences, skills, stories, and accomplishments implicating client strengths.
- Some clients dismiss strengths because they may have what is known as lingering *Freudophobia* (Wilson, 2009). That is, clients believe that the real causes of their problems are unacceptable sexual and aggressive drives. Pervasive in popular culture, this belief is a wishy-washy idea that keeps clients stuck in fear and skepticism about their signature strengths. Discuss with them that these ideas are not only impossible to test empirically but also that these are mired in recollection bias (Wilson & Gilbert, 2003).
- A number of clients may focus, and a few may hyperfocus, on strengths for which they scored low. Avoid steering their attention toward their top strengths, and ask them what explains their lower score on specific strengths. The narratives that follow will offer you invaluable insight into the client's self-concept—present and desired. Client information on their bottom strengths often unpacks unprocessed traumas, hurts, injuries, and insults. This is a golden opportunity for you to enrich clients' narratives, which they shared in the *Positive Introduction*. Furthermore, explanation of bottom strengths can help both clients and clinicians clarify the therapeutic goals and how a client's top strengths can be synthesized to accomplish these goals.

Clinician Note

- *Be aware that, for some clients, labeling and assessment of strengths can reinforce their tendencies to locate causes of their problem primarily in others and in the environment. This enables them to evade the personal responsibility that is needed in order to recover. For example, for clients raised in interdependent cultural milieus, the responsibility for both successes*

> *and failures is perceived collectively and is hence attributed to more interpersonally based strengths such as love, social intelligence, or teamwork. In addition to culture, personality traits may play a role. For example, a client with an inflated self-view and narcissistic tendencies may use strengths to further bolster her self-view. It is important to spend ample time with such clients explaining the contextual and adaptive use of strengths.*
>
> - *Most clients seeking therapy have been raised on a steady diet of criticism from their parents, siblings, colleagues, and bosses. Criticism is a culturally influenced construct and often works as a double-edge sword. For example, depending on cultural norms and familial cultural norms, criticism coupled with compliments, genuine affection, and care can be adaptive, as seen in close-knit families. However, when a diet of criticism is coupled with the negativity bias, this may reinforce ruminative thinking in clients, and, preoccupied with rumination, such clients may accept strengths at face value but continue to brood on their weaknesses. Even after two significant others affirm client strengths, such clients may continue to perceive themselves as incompetent, deeply flawed, and underachievers. Explore cultural roots of criticism and be open to using other therapeutic approaches—such as cognitive behavior therapy, emotion-focused therapy, or acceptance commitment therapy—to treat negative thinking. At the same time, engaging clients in moderately complex exercises which get them thinking about their positive experiences could automatically cut the time they spend thinking about their failures and setbacks. Almost all PPT practices include comprehensive thinking about positives.*

CULTURAL CONSIDERATIONS

Partly due to cultural norms, some clients may not view their signature strengths credibly or may give them less importance. For example, clients from a collectivist cultural ethos may undervalue strengths such as creativity because conformity is desired in their culture; they may undervalue zest when their culture values humility; or they may undervalue leadership when their culture values teamwork more.

Explore culture-specific expression of these strengths. One client—a Muslim female from a conservative family—entered therapy while going through a divorce after a very short marriage. She cited overbearing in-laws and gender-based discrimination as prime reasons for the separation. Born and raised in North America, the client was convinced that it was the right decision, despite the fact that the marriage was completely her choice. Nonetheless, she was extremely worried about the probing questions her extended family might ask her about the decision to get a divorce. Perspective, bravery, and fairness turned out to be her signature strengths. Fairness was especially endorsed by both a family member and a close friend. A discussion about the culturally appropriate expressions of fairness revealed that fairness includes standing up when someone is being treated unfairly, including oneself. This helped her feel confident that her decision was an expression of one of her cardinal strengths, which is valued in the culture that she and her family identify with. When standing up for herself against cultural pressures, she called on her strength of bravery to persist in her pursuit of what she deemed to be fair.

Be sensitive and responsive to client stories that show resilience and the use of specific strengths when this use of strengths comes at a heavy social, financial, and/or emotional cost due to cultural factors. For example, a client shared that after years of emotional and physical abuse at the hands of his father, he finally mustered the courage—defying cultural norms—to stand up to his father, and eventually this client left home. Another client was loving and very kind with her live-in partner. The eight years she spent with him were filled with playfulness, zest, and gratitude. One day, she discovered that during all of those years, her partner had been cheating on her with her best friend. Clinicians should be sensitive to and prudent about the therapeutic pace in discussing strengths, as a premature discussion of strengths may further erode clients' faith in strengths. Proceed slowly to first establish a solid therapeutic relationship, and then introduce elements of PPT or a strengths-based approach, focusing on equipping clients with practical wisdom, as discussed in the next session.

MAINTENANCE

Discuss the following tips with your clients so that they can maintain their progress:

As human beings, our ability to spot negativity within ourselves—and around ourselves—is far sharper, deeper and stubborn than our ability to note positives. This tendency grows whenever we experience negative events.

If you don't do anything about this negativity bias, you will likely remain stuck in negativity and in turn, it will stick with you, often manifesting through chronic anxiety, sadness, anger, ambivalence, and isolation. You probably assume, like most of us, that psychotherapy is the place to discuss these negatives, and indeed it is. However, psychotherapy is also a place where you can also explore what makes you resilient, without ignoring your vulnerabilities; where you can discover your hopes and dreams, without dismissing your despair and illusions; and where you can acquire skills to build your strengths, without ignoring your weaknesses. Engaging in such an effort in a sustained way can reset your negativity lens. The systematic ways you learn to spot and use your strengths can prepare you to apply this learning in other areas of your life such as at work and at home and can expand your general outlook toward life. The following is an example:

> Karen, a young female client, found it very difficult to think of herself in strengths terms. She perceived herself as an "undesirable package" with a history of hospitalization for chronic suicidal ideation, psychotic breaks, and a preoccupation with negative memories of the past, including emotional abuse and loss of close family members. After much skepticism, Karen began to explore her strengths. Love of learning, curiosity, creativity, bravery, and leadership turned out to be her signature strengths. When asked to share concrete experiences related to each strength, this young woman stated that she entered college as one of the top scholars in her province, with a full scholarship. Despite all these challenges, Karen was able to maintain her academic standing and always made the "Dean's List." She has given talks to many high school girls about overcoming the stigma of seeking timely help. Just sharing these concrete events shifted her mood, and she said, "I just realized, my life is not that bad, I can still do some things."

Can you identify with Karen in some ways? Ask yourself, what sorts of stories do you tell yourself? What is the underlying theme of your stories? Much like the *Positive Introduction* practice in which you recalled an event that brought out the best in you, and your daily *Gratitude Journal* practice of looking at good things that happen, this practice of acknowledging your strengths can help you orient your mindset toward more positive aspects within you and around you. We are good at attributing negatives (e.g., "his dishonesty caused the embezzlement"), and knowledge of strengths will help you make positive attributions in daily life (e.g., "her kindness helped her friend with a place to stay after she had to leave an abusive relationship").

PPT practices will help you to know and understand your strengths in depth. From mere labels, you will learn to internalize your strengths. Following are some illustrations of client self-descriptions at the start of therapy and then after exploring strengths; these statements demonstrate how these clients internalized the strengths perspective into their personality.

Client 1
At the start of therapy:

I am hopeless, I don't think I will ever find a person who would understand me. Soon after a first date, I start seeing their real and negative side. . . . Perhaps I am only good at attracting the wrong person.

After exploring strengths:

I feel better that others have spotted some strengths in me. I never thought that despite not being able to find the right person, I am perceived as a kind, socially intelligent, prudent, and humble person. This was quite helpful. As soon as I start dating, I know that I need not worry too much and overuse my prudence in judging the person too quickly. Instead, I will use my kindness and social intelligence to understand the other person.

Client 2
At the start of therapy:

Many a times, I have asked myself, is that it?

After exploring strengths:
I never realized that I get moved deeply by the wonders of nature. The last time I was close to nature, I was in absolute awe; my mind, body, and spirit were all at ease. Perhaps there is more to life than I think.

Client 3
At the start of therapy:

I am known to be a lively person who never escapes from challenges; I embrace them. But lately, I cannot seem to get it right. . . . Often I do the right thing but at the wrong time or the right thing with the wrong person. . . .

After exploring strengths:

I can put things in perspective. . . . Knowing that zest is one of my signature strengths, and that others see it too makes sense; I am easily inspired, passionate, and throw everything into the activities that I undertake. Perhaps a little prudence can serve me better.

Client 4
At the start of therapy:

I deliberately hold off expressing my love and affection to my partner. Perhaps I am afraid I may come across to the person I am dating as weak, dependent, and insecure.

After exploring strengths:

I didn't realize that I am overly cautious; I need to open up in order to give and receive love. . . . . I didn't realize that it is a strength. . . . I used to think that too much expression of love could make me vulnerable.

Client 5
At the start of therapy:

I cannot grow until I get rid of all my faults.

After exploring strengths:

I have spent hundreds, if not thousands, of hours with therapists, life coaches, amazing motivational speakers, and spiritual gurus to correct my weaknesses, but always felt I couldn't get rid of them. . . . I always felt due to my weaknesses, I would never measure up to the expectations of my high achieving father. . . . Identifying my strengths has made a serious dent in my thinking: perhaps I would be better off building my strengths than trying to get rid of my faults.

END-OF-SESSION RELAXATION

We recommend that each session end with the same brief relaxation practice that started the session.

RESOURCES

Readings

- Joseph, S., & Wood, A. (2010). Assessment of positive functioning in clinical psychology: Theoretical and practical issues. *Clinical Psychology Review, 30*(7), 830–838.
- Quinlan, D. M., Swain, N., Cameron, C., & Vella-Brodrick, D. A. (2015). How "other people matter" in a classroom-based strengths intervention: Exploring interpersonal strategies and classroom outcomes. *The Journal of Positive Psychology, 10*(1), 77–89. doi:10.1080/17439760.2014.920407
- Rashid, T. & Ostermann, R. F. (2009). Strength-based assessment in clinical practice. *Journal of Clinical Psychology, 65*, 488–498.
- Rashid, T. (2015) Strength-based assessment. In S. Joseph (Ed.), *Positive psychology in practice* (2nd ed., pp. 519–544). New York: Wiley. doi: 10.1002/9781118996874.ch31
- Scheel, M. J., Davis, C. K., & Henderson, J. D. (2012). Therapist use of client strengths: A qualitative study of positive processes. *The Counseling Psychologist, 41*(3), 392–427. doi:10.1177/0011000012439427
- Tedeshi, R. G. & Kilmer, R. P. (2005). Assessing strengths, resilience, and growth to guide clinical interventions. *Professional Psychology: Research and Practice, 36*, 230–237.

Videos

- What Are Your Character Strengths? A brief video to assess character strengths (Worksheet 1; Heart, page x):
  https://youtu.be/K-3IjNr1gCg
- TED Talk on importance of character strengths in psychotherapy by Tayyab Rashid:
  https://youtu.be/Q6W5IrZH7tc
- The Science of Character: an eight-minute documentary presenting a compelling case for character strengths toward a fulfilling life:
  https://youtu.be/p0fK4837Bgg

Websites

- The VIA Institute on Character offers invaluable resources on both the science and practice of character, with free measure of character strengths:
  http://www.viacharacter.org

## 9

SESSION THREE: PRACTICAL WISDOM

SESSION THREE PRESENTS THE SKILLS OF PRACTICAL WISDOM. These skills teach us how to adaptively apply our signature strengths in a balanced way to solve problems. The central positive psychotherapy (PPT) practice covered in this session is *Know-How of Strengths*.

SESSION THREE OUTLINE

Core Concepts
    In-Session Practice: *Know-How of Strengths*
    Reflection & Discussion
    Additional Exercises to Build Practical Wisdom Skills
    Vignette
    Fit & Flexibility
    Cultural Considerations
    Maintenance
Resources

CORE CONCEPTS

The core feature of this segment of PPT is to teach clients the Aristotelian notion of practical wisdom, that is, the adaptive use of strengths to be used to live a good, meaningful, and virtuous life. The core concepts of the adaptive use of strengths are presented later in this session, in the section "Learn about Practical Wisdom—The *Know-How* of Strengths," with the help of illustrative vignettes. Through these skills, clients can learn to apply their strengths to overcome their stressors and negative emotions and experiences. These skills help clients pursue a deeply personal goal toward their growth.

START-OF-SESSION RELAXATION

At the start of every session, begin with a brief relaxation exercise. Refer to Appendix A: Relaxation & Mindfulness Practices, which can be found at the end of this manual. A copy of this appendix also appears in the client workbook. Continue the session with a review of the client's *Gratitude Journal* as well as a review of the core concepts taught in the previous session.

IN-SESSION PRACTICE: *KNOW-HOW OF STRENGTHS*

Nurturing Practical Wisdom
SEEK SPECIFICITY
First and foremost, the abstract idea of a signature strength must be translated into concrete actions so that clients better understand what that strength means for them in their daily lives. Complex real-life situations and challenges do not present themselves with clear instructions for which action best represents a specific strength. One way to calibrate specificity is the outcome. For example, if the outcome of using your signature strength of love of learning is to increase your knowledge, you can translate the outcome in specific terms

(e.g., reading a specific number of books or articles to increase knowledge). If the outcome of using your signature strength of spirituality is to be connected with something larger than the self, then both the quality and quantity of specific activities deemed to represent spirituality can be identified.

Specificity of one's actions representing signature strengths also depends on context. Creativity, for example, can represent itself in creative problem-solving in the context of challenges, or it can be undertaking a novel way of doing things. Note that strengths are not mutually exclusive, and, if fact, strengths are more likely to overlap than to stand alone.

To help you grasp the nuances of signature strengths and translate them into concrete actions, see Appendix D: Building Your Strengths, for actions, popular movies, and songs. (This appendix also appears in the client workbook and online at www.oup.com/ppt.)

FIND RELEVANCE

The second and more difficult skill is to know if your signature strength is relevant to the situation at hand. For example, later in this session we discuss a female client, Michelle, who has a signature strength of forgiveness. The relevance of applying this signature strength is contingent upon contextual and interpersonal factors. Strengths such as forgiveness may be best used in a specific situation or with specific individuals but not with everyone in every situation. Michelle would benefit from honing her skills of relevance by considering the impact of forgiveness on herself and others. Past experience can help her decide whether forgiveness is relevant in a specific context.

Sandro, another client, is a middle-aged male who harbored strong resentment against his ex-wife, who had been his partner for more than 20 years. She had engaged in an extramarital affair with another woman throughout the course of her marriage to Sandro. He stated that she waited until the youngest of their children turned 18 and left home for college before leaving him. Sandro believed that he was unable to forgive her. When the clinician asked why, Sandro stated, "I want her to realize that what she did was wrong. If I forgave her, it would not make her realize what she had done." The clinician responded with, "Yet, I see you wallowing in your own pain. . . The forgiveness is not for her; it is for you. You don't even need to communicate it to her." This client, however, was not ready to forgive, so his clinician did not force the issue. Use of forgiveness in this case, at that time in therapy, was not appropriate.

Real-life challenges do not come with a ticker tape running across the screen of a television news channel, suggesting that a specific strength is relevant in a specific situation. Therefore, in deciding relevance, help the client to consider which strength, or set of strengths, will produce an adaptive and healthy outcome.

Let's consider the issue of fairness, which is needed to be an effective leader. One client, Rachael, was a senior HR manager who considered herself to be an effective leader and was therefore surprised when leadership was not one of her top strengths. A detailed discussion about the qualities of leadership helped her realize that she lacks the ability to work effectively with other people who do not share her point of view. Rachael doesn't have the trust of the people she works with, and she is unable to bring out the best in everyone on her staff, despite her efforts. Discussions with her clinician about using other strengths, such as social intelligence, fairness, and teamwork, helped Rachael to use these strengths in order to reinforce her leadership qualities.

Also, in deciding relevance, we need to *Put Things into Perspective*, which allows us to decide where, where, with whom, and how our signature strengths might be most useful, for us, and for others. For example, May, a married female client, reported feeling overwhelmingly that her partner's happiness is her primary responsibility. She often stated that pleasing him is far more important than listening to her own needs. Helping May see that her signature strengths are not most effective for her own well-being was initially a challenging part of therapy, but eventually this was an eye-opening realization for the client.

RESOLVE CONFLICT

The third skill in nurturing practical wisdom is developing an understanding, and possibly resolving the situation, when two strengths (or signature strengths) conflict with one another. For example, one of our clients, Jia, often experienced conflict between her creativity and prudence. She wanted to become an artist, but her parents, both physicians, often subtly and sometimes strongly encouraged her to pursue a "sound and safe career" in medicine. Jia's sense of caution persuaded her to forgo painting (her passion), and she is currently enrolled in medical school. Our therapeutic work was not very effective as she became more keenly aware of the conflict between her two signature strengths.

Conflict can be resolved, however, by deciding which signature strength is more closely aligned with one's core values or which signature strength will yield the optimal outcome. For example, if Jia's core value is self-expression, and she comes alive and feels authentic to herself when she realizes her creative or optimal potential, she might be happier if she is able to find a creative niche or outlet in any endeavor. On the other hand, if her core value is to ensure employment, as well as preserve a stable relationship with her parents—which, in her case, is a cultural expectation—Jia might be better off pursuing a career that offers employment security. Start backward with the desired outcome and evaluate which strength will lead to that outcome. This may not only help to resolve the conflict but also to develop a deeper understanding of which strength might help clients to attain their goals.

REFLECT

Practical wisdom requires us to reflect on what impact our signature strengths will have on others. What are the moral implications of exercising our signature strengths on a larger scale? Consider the following cases we have encountered in clinical practice: Maria, a young female student with the signature strengths of prudence, fairness, and social intelligence, misinterpreted messages posted about her on her Facebook page by friends. Maria assumed that someone might be conspiring against her and possibly against all females from her cultural background. Out of care and caution, she posted a message on Facebook and on several other social media sites warning other women that their safety may be in jeopardy. The campus authorities became alarmed, and a cascade of safety protocols was set into motion, inconveniencing a large number of students. Once the dust settled, in individual session, Maria and her clinician processed the incident. Maria realized that, without much reflection, she overused her signature strengths.

Another client, a graduate student, continued to invest lab resources into a project that his supervisor had told him to change. This persistence cost him and his lab partners needless time and effort, demonstrating an overuse of persistence. These two illustrations show how strengths can result in negative outcomes when they are overused.

Moreover, an essential part of practical wisdom is developing awareness of our motives. We should be aware of our own failures and be willing to admit to them. Admitting our own failures, however, is not easy, and requires courage and humility (two strengths). One way to hone this skill is to stand back and impartially judge our own role and responsibilities, and how we can learn from mistakes and missteps, especially those that have an impact on others.

CALIBRATE

To nurture practical wisdom skills, we also need to regularly stay attuned to the situation, sense change, and calibrate and recalibrate the use of our strengths to suit the demands of the situation. Many individuals are unable to solve their problems, as they keep on trying ineffective solutions or do not change their approach. For example, think about a health care professional. Doctors need to balance the time commitment they devote to their patients with their own professional needs, like seeing enough patients to meet office expenses, being on time for the next patient, and so on. How should a cancer specialist adjust and calibrate the desire to tell the truth to parents of child with terminal cancer

(Schwartz & Sharpe, 2010)? The multiplicity and complexity of life often create numerous grey areas. Not all rules, guidelines, policies, and regulations can capture the shades of grey. Rigid and narrow application of rules—no matter how well intentioned—depletes the motivation of individuals who find themselves trapped in these rules.

Keep in mind that the signature strengths profile of clients and subsequent PPT practices help clients to sharpen their skills to use strengths appropriately given the challenges at hand. Take your time and help clients to complete the signature strengths profile as much as they can, as it is the foundation for clients to know themselves and others better.

SUGGESTED SCRIPT FOR THE CLINICIAN
The following is a script you can use to help your clients begin to understand the importance of utilizing practical wisdom skills to effectively apply signature strengths in their daily lives (Kaitlin et al., 2017; Ronningstam, 2016).

Much as psychological symptoms (such as sadness, anger, or anxiety) indicate stress, strengths (such as gratitude, hope, love, kindness, and curiosity) display well-being, satisfaction, interest, engagement, purpose, and meaning in life.

Research and clinical experience tell us that individuals who experience negative emotions such as anger, hostility, and vengeance, or those who show narcissistic traits, are more likely to develop a number of psychological problems, whereas individuals who experience gratitude, forgiveness, kindness, and love are more likely to report being satisfied with life. You know your signature strengths. Now we focus on how you can use your signature strengths to be happier as well as to develop skills to use your strengths to manage your negatives. First let's focus on how to develop the skills of using your strengths to manage your stressors. Let's begin by exploring how you feel about your signature strengths.

Under- and Overuse of Strengths
Using Worksheet 3.1: Illustrating Your Under- and Overuse of Strengths, ask clients to continue exploring specific ways they over- or underuse their strengths. Note that this and all worksheets (a) appear within the corresponding session of this manual, (b) are reprinted for the client in the accompanying client workbook, and (c) can be downloaded from the companion website at www.oup.com/ppt.

Use the following illustration to diagram your strengths by turning your strengths into behaviors (the actions, activities, and habits you do when displaying your strengths). Select larger circles to indicate the strengths you overuse and smaller circles for strengths you underuse. Use intersecting circles to indicate strengths that overlap with one another.

Learn about Practical Wisdom—The *Know-How of Strengths*

Now that you have identified your signature strengths, identify your over- and underuse of strengths. In this step, we will deepen our understanding by looking at common problems with under- and overuse of strengths and learn about practical wisdom, or the "Know-How of Strengths." Let's look at three scenarios from real-life PPT sessions.

Discuss each scenario with your clients and elicit their responses in terms of over- and/or underuse of strengths.

- *Saleem, a middle-aged male client, is a retail manager with the signature strength of fairness, who weighed every situation from that standpoint. He perceived even benign gestures from his staff and colleagues as "unfair" and became isolated.*
- *Michelle, a young female client with the signature strengths of forgiveness, kindness, and humility, overused her strengths and let others take advantage of her; eventually she stated that she had become a "doormat" for others.*
- *Akeela, a female client with the signature strengths of curiosity and love of learning, found it increasingly difficult to complete her tasks at school and at work, as she spent an inordinate amount of time "researching" everything.*

These scenarios show good intentions. However, having good intentions and knowledge of signature strengths is not enough. We need skills and the willingness to use these skills to solve our problems. In PPT, this skill set is called the "Know-How of Strengths"; the more formal term for this is "practical wisdom." Next we will discuss in detail what practical wisdom is and how it can be nurtured.

To use strengths, whether these are your signature or non-signature strengths, PPT teaches practical wisdom, which is about using strengths to make things better. From the perspective of practical wisdom, strengths should not be treated in isolation. Also, more is not necessarily better—nurturing a single strength to the exclusion of others can produce undesirable results.

Looking at the scenarios about the three clients just presented, fairness could be adaptive; a lack of it would result in unfair treatment of others, but it could help Michelle if she were to stand up for herself. Curiosity may not be good for Akeela in completing school assignments or work-related tasks; she may benefit more from self-regulation and persistence. Saleem would benefit by building perspective, knowing how to read social context, and moving beyond black-and-white rules to see that sometimes the best way to deal with others lies in the grey. In addition, Michelle could benefit from strengths that would help her to tune in to her own emotions. She could feel, intuit, and gradually become assertive so that she could feel and state, "This doesn't feel right to me," instead of feeling like a "doormat." Finally, it would help Akeela to understand timing. Using her signature strength of curiosity may serve her better when she has ample time on her hands to explore, but perhaps not when she faces a deadline to submit an assignment or project.

Next we turn to Worksheet 3.2: Developing Practical Wisdom Skills. We describe these skills and explore how scenarios can be resolved or handled through applying these skills.

WORKSHEET 3.2   DEVELOPING PRACTICAL WISDOM SKILLS

Following are five strategies for building practical wisdom, or Know-How of Strengths:

1. **Seek Specificity:** Complex real-life situations and challenges do not present themselves with clear instructions for which actions best represent a specific strength. One way to seek specificity is to consider the outcome. For example, if for you the outcome of using your love of learning is to increase knowledge, you can translate the outcome in specific terms, such as reading a specific number of books or articles to increase knowledge.

    To help you grasp the nuances of signature strengths and translate them into concrete actions, consult Appendix D: Building Your Strengths, which appears at the end of this workbook. This appendix offers multiple behavioral ways of using strengths.

2. **Find Relevance:** Explore if your signature strength is relevant to the situation at hand. For example, kindness and forgiveness may not be relevant in situations that need to be dealt with using fairness or courage. In some situations, your signature strengths of humility or playfulness may be very relevant, but in situations that need you to assert your rights, humility may not work; in situations that require us to empathize with others who may have just experienced a trauma, playfulness may not be appropriate.

3. **Resolve Conflict:** The third skill is understanding how to resolve a situation in which the use of two signature strengths may conflict with one another. For example, you are doing a project and want to do the best possible job. You want to utilize your signature strength of creativity or persistence. At the same time, your closest friend needs your time and company (signature strength: love). Or your signature strengths of zest and self-regulation may pull you in different directions. Resolve these conflicts by deciding which signature strength is more closely aligned with your core values or which signature strength will yield the optimal outcome.

4. **Reflect:** Practical wisdom requires you to reflect on what impact your signature strengths will have on others. What are the moral implications on a larger scale of exercising your signature strengths? For example, exercising spirituality from a specific tradition, in the public realm, may alienate those who don't subscribe to that specific tradition. Or exercising love of learning may negatively impact the self-confidence of those who struggle with learning due to an inherent learning disability.

5. **Calibrate:** To nurture practical wisdom skills, you also need to regularly stay attuned to the situation, sense change, and calibrate and recalibrate (i.e., fine-tune) your use of strengths to suit the demands of the situation. Many people are unable to solve their problems, as they keep trying ineffective solutions or do not change their approach as the situation changes.

Now read the following three scenarios and under each one write the specific advice you would give to each person:

Accommodating and Considerate: Early in Jane's relationship with Jimmy, Jane understood that Jimmy becomes insecure and jealous as soon as he sees her talking to another guy, especially someone who Jimmy feels is "better" than he. But Jane is finding it hard to break up with Jimmy as she is known to be one of the most "accommodating" and "considerate" people around.

> *Your Advice:*
>
> _____
>
> _____
>
> _____

All I want is to be happy: Lee, a young man in his mid-20s, often repeated the same thing in therapy. Followed by a long list of positives, such as "I work very hard; I was hired even before I finished my undergraduate degree; I am told that I am good-looking, funny, sporty, and helpful. I never hurt anyone, I have never argued with anyone (in my adult life) . . .," Lee would conclude with, "but I don't feel happy."

    Your Advice:

_____

_____

_____

Just Talking Helps: Heena, a 21-year-old female, is making no progress in therapy—by all indicators (objective and clinical). Heena continues to report suicidal ideation although she has never made any attempt, and she resists any change and wants to continue therapy. She states that "just talking to someone helps."

    Your Advice:

_____

_____

_____

To continue learning about practical wisdom skills, ask your client to now turn to Worksheet 3.3: The Challenge.

Write about a current challenge you are facing and may have been trying to resolve. Describe it in concrete terms: What it is? When did it start, and how long has it been going on? In what ways has it been challenging?

The Challenge	Your Reflections
Describe a current challenge that needs to be solved.	
When did it start? How long has it lasted?	
What are its effects?	
Is it due to overuse of your strengths? Which ones? How?	
What aspects of this challenge would you like to change?	
Which specific practical wisdom strategy can you use to make adaptive changes?	

REFLECTION & DISCUSSION

The following questions are a follow-up to the challenge identified in Worksheet 3.3:

- Let's assume that you are able to use one of the practical wisdom strategies effectively in resolving the problem identified in Worksheet 3.3. What would it look like if this problem is resolved? What specific behaviors you would be doing? And what behaviors would stop? Try to answer as concretely as possible.
- Keeping the desirable behaviors in mind, what small, manageable, specific, and concrete steps can help you remain engaged and motivated in these behaviors?
- The practical wisdom strategy or strategies you have identified will most likely require support from others. Who will support you? If you are unable get this support, what alternative supports can you think of?

ADDITIONAL EXERCISES TO BUILD PRACTICAL WISDOM SKILLS

Encourage clients to pick one of the following exercises to build their practical wisdom:

- Discuss with a close, trusted, and wise friend how to reallocate mental, emotional, and physical resources (i.e., how much effort should be used) to solve the challenge identified in Worksheet 3.3. Also consider whether your strengths can be used more adaptively elsewhere, instead of working on aspects of the challenge that cannot be changed.
- Identify new real-life opportunities that can help you regulate your signature strengths adaptively.
- Develop tolerance and an attitude of acceptance that incorporates apparent contradictions, such as accepting loved ones who display strengths and also act selfishly, insensitively, or uncaringly.
- Balance competing desires and needs when two signature strengths can be used together to solve a problem or to respond adaptively to a challenge. For example, can forgiveness and fairness be integrated creatively to encourage some forgiveness and, at the same time, ensure that fairness is not compromised?

VIGNETTE

Marc is a 36-year-old successful professional, working fulltime and pursuing his MBA part-time. He sought therapy for work-related stress. The following dialog with his clinician shows Marc's understanding of his signature strengths and how he can develop his practical wisdom skills to optimally use his signature strengths:

CLINICIAN: Marc, what did you learn about yourself after completing your Signature Strengths Profile?
MARC: Well, a lot. . . I see myself a little differently than my loved ones do. . . The things that I choose . . . I mean on that heart, head, and online questionnaire, I selected love of learning, fairness, and authenticity—these three were in all three options, while appreciation of beauty was in two.
CLINICIAN: Do you see these as core parts of your personality?
MARC: Yes, indeed. I don't compromise on fairness, I am what you see—there is no hidden side.
CLINICIAN: What strengths did others spot, any different ones?
MARCH: They selected perspective, and to my surprise, they also picked two strengths I didn't know I possess.

CLINICIAN: Which ones were these?

MARC: My partner of over 10 years picked social intelligence and bravery, while my oldest friend from high school picked courage and humor.

CLINICIAN: What was surprising about these strengths?

MARC: I am a very practical, clear-thinking, and decisive person. I don't think I am particularly socially intelligent or humorous. . . I am not a social butterfly. I rather keep myself to myself.

CLINICIAN: Well, sometimes others see within us, that which we don't. What other strengths did your high school friend spot in you?

MARC: Fairness and authenticity.

CLINICIAN: Well, it looks like your selection of fairness and authenticity got endorsement from at least one other person who knows you well. It must be central to you. Is it?

MARC: It is, as I explained. . . However, I also worry that my work team doesn't see my fairness as actually being fairness. Instead, they see it as stubbornness and a bit of coldness. That's why they remain a bit distant from me.

CLINICIAN: Can you give a recent example?

MARC: Hmmm . . . two weeks ago, during a staff meeting, someone made a homophobic comment—not explicit—and I called the person out, right in the moment.

CLINICIAN: What happened?

MARC: Well, I thought I went a bit overboard . . . I later heard that this person felt very embarrassed and later stated that it wasn't his intent . . .

CLINICIAN: Do you think he really didn't mean it?

MARC: In retrospect, I do. He has never said or done anything like that before. In fact, he is quite a gentleman . . . I could have handled it differently.

CLINICIAN: What strategy can you draw from practical wisdom?

MARC: I am not sure. . . Was this not a situation in which to use fairness?

[CLINICIAN DRAWS MARC'S ATTENTION TO WORKSHEET 2.6: Compile Your Signature Strengths.]

MARC: [After a pause] Both relevance and specificity could be applicable here.

CLINICIAN: How so?

MARC: Well, I should have considered the interpersonal and contextual features. It was the first time that person made a homophobic comment, at least to my knowledge. . . I could have been a bit more subtle or I could have asked him to explain the comment one on one, after the meeting.

CLINICIAN: Well, right now, you are using another practical wisdom strategy—reflection. You are looking at the impact of your signature strength on others.

MARC: Yeah. I wasn't aware . . .

CLINICIAN: What other strength or strengths could you have used in this situation?

MARC: I am not sure which one . . .

CLINICIAN: What did your partner spot in you?

MARC: [Pauses] Social intelligence . . . I see, . . . it is all about the tact, the nuances. The mantra in the corporate world is emotional intelligence.

CLINICIAN: Yeah, but beyond the clichéd mantra . . . let's go one step deeper. Social intelligence also includes knowing the emotional subtleties of others and also of your own, such as, what made you to react in a certain way? As far as I know, you are quite a level-headed person.

MARC: You are right. When it comes to the issue of sexual orientation, I become slightly more sensitive. My fairness antenna activates very quickly, and I cannot stand it when someone is treated unfairly . . . I went through a lot of bullying in high school over my sexuality.

CLINICIAN: I know well what you had to endure, and I commend your commitment to equality. The art of practical wisdom is when our strengths don't bring an optimal outcome, we always can try another one. Where fairness may not work, try social intelligence, or combine them. I'm confident that you have the perspective to integrate the two to find an optimal solution.

MARC: Good to know. I will certainly try.

FIT & FLEXIBILITY

While equipping clients with knowledge about their strengths, make sure you do not inadvertently give them this message that their signature strengths profile is final and complete. For some clients, this may be a closure on these strengths. They may stop striving actively to enhance these strengths and may focus on their lesser strengths or on their weaknesses. Due to the inherent negativity bias, lesser or lower strengths may be perceived as an area of weakness. Therefore, it is critical to help clients understand that strengths are dynamic. There is always room for growth. The use of one strength in adolescence or young adulthood may look different than it looks in middle or later life. Periodically check with clients about how they feel about their top strengths. In imparting practical wisdom strategies, especially those of specificity, relevance, and calibration, make sure clients perceive this as development of a strength, not merely as use of a well-developed strength (Biswas-Diener et al., 2011).

Practical wisdom is about using strengths in concert, rather than in isolation. Having more of a strength is not necessarily better. In fact, nurturing a single strength can produce undesirable results. A challenging situation, such as dealing with a bully or standing up to emotional abuse, can be tackled with multiple strengths such as courage, persistence, fairness, prudence, and hope. Likewise, more than one practical wisdom strategy, such as specificity or relevance, can translate strengths into concrete and responsible actions (perspective). Also, when working in small groups, such as sports teams, health teams, or project specific teams, try to work with the signature strengths of individual members (i.e., collate results of all and determine which strengths are most common in the group). This will likely increase trust in the group process.

Some clinicians may encourage clients to use their practical wisdom strategies rather prematurely assuming that clients fully understand their strengths. Indeed, from the *Positive Introduction* to compiling one's signature strengths, clients have multiple opportunities to understand their strengths at a deeper level. However, make sure that clients *understand* their strengths and are able to demonstrate under which conditions their signature strengths are most helpful and under which conditions they are least helpful. To highlight this, you can quickly generate ideas about the use of another affiliated strength (e.g., curiosity instead of creativity, wisdom instead of love of learning, courage instead of authenticity). Similarly, it is important that client and clinician discuss specific actions which will demonstrate that the intended strength is being maximally expressed through these actions.

CULTURAL CONSIDERATIONS

Cultures differ in expressing strengths, much like with other emotions. Practical wisdom requires that we explore at a deeper level, avoiding surface-level expression. For example, sometimes what we think of as negative behaviors in individuals from different cultures or person with different abilities might actually be very much within their cultural norms or the sphere of possibilities. For example, we may perceive someone as being arrogant when, instead, this may be his cultural expression of being confident. Or someone who worries too much about small things may not always be a perfectionist. She might have been taught by her familial or the larger culture to do things meticulously. She may perceive that her worth depends on being meticulous. Likewise, some cultures deal with serious situations in a fatalistic or humorous way. While this may be perceived as being less serious or nonchalant by some, it may be a culturally appropriate way of dealing with things that cannot be fixed easily.

For another example, one of the authors worked for many years as a school psychologist, and one of his students was a six-year-old boy named Pavel, who was suspected of having an underlying autistic spectrum disorder. Along with being given traditional assessments, Pavel's strengths were also assessed, including reports from his teachers and his after-school caregivers. Indeed, assessment confirmed autism. However, Pavel's teachers also reported that he is creative and when he finds something to be interesting, he can complete the task without becoming distracted. During the feedback session, when the child's mother heard that her son's teachers think the boy's creativity is a strength, she cried and said, "I had accepted that Pavel is who he is, but I guess I was wrong. There are some things I can certainly help him to further develop." She ended with a profound observation, "It was my eyes that did not look beyond the symptoms in my son."

Some clients may be unsure about which signature strength to use or how to use a specific signature strength in their own cultural context. Rather than exploring rationale ways of using signatures strengths, encourage such clients, if they are open to this discussion, to rely on their emotions to first hear and feel what the situation demands. Once they can explore their culturally informed gut responses, encourage them to align their emotions with common sense. For example, standing up to ongoing abuse at home may make a client angry, but she may not be able to express her anger due to familial honor in the local community. Helping this client to feel her anger and find a rationale way to express this anger may be one way of using practical wisdom in a culturally informed manner. For example, discussing the problem with a trustworthy community elder or seeking support from a religious or spiritual leader could be beneficial.

Not all situations or challenges with cultural contexts can be resolved by the practical wisdom strategies discussed here. Encourage clients not to be afraid of experimenting with alternative and culturally appropriate ways of finding solutions. Enhancing clients' understanding about specificity, relevance, reflection, and calibration offers them sufficient information to find an appropriate cultural fit.

MAINTENANCE

Blaine Fowers (2005) offers specific strategies which can help us to reinforce practical wisdom. Discuss these tips with your clients so that they can maintain their progress:

- Sometimes your signature strengths may conflict with one another. For example, your courage may want you to take risks and explore a new and unknown route, and your prudence may caution against it. You may want to be kind to your friend, and your fairness demands that you ought to confront him over an ethical violation that impacts others. You want be empathic with your subordinate and also feel compelled to let her know that her job may be cut. Or you want to be authentic with yourself, and social and cultural norms force you against it. Use the strategies listed in Worksheet 3.2 to resolve these conflicts through the use of practical wisdom strategies. Also, use your signature (and other) strengths to build perspective, one you may not see from simply following rules and regulations.
- When unsure which signature strength to use in a given context, rely on emotions to first hear and feel what the situation demands. Before acting, make emotion a partner with reason; educate emotions through other strengths.
- Make sure that you are using your signature strengths to do the right thing. Consult with wise minds about what is the right thing to do within the circumstances.
- Understand that not every situation can be resolved by using signature strengths. Don't be afraid to experiment with your alternative strengths, skills, abilities, and talents.

END-OF-SESSION RELAXATION

We recommend that each session end with the same brief relaxation practice that started the session.

RESOURCES

Readings

- Allan, B. A. (2015). Balance among character strengths and meaning in life. *Journal of Happiness Studies, 16*(5), 1247–1261. doi:10.1007/s10902-014-9557-9
- Cassar, J., Ross, J., Dahne, J., Ewer, P., Teesson, M., Hopko, D., et al. (2016). Therapist tips for the brief behavioural activation therapy for depression—Revised (BATD-R) treatment manual practical wisdom and clinical nuance. *Clinical Psychologist, 20*(1), 46–53.
- Vervaeke, J., & Ferrarro, L. (2013). *Relevance, Meaning and the Cognitive Science of Wisdom: The Scientific Study of Personal Wisdom: From Contemplative Traditions to Neuroscience.* Edited by M. Ferrarri & N. Weststrate. New York: Springer.
- Walsh, R. (2015). What is wisdom? Cross-cultural and cross-disciplinary syntheses. *Review of General Psychology, 19*(3), 278–293.
- Yang, S. (2013). Wisdom and good lives: A process perspective. *New Ideas in Psychology, 31*(3), 194.

Videos

- TED Talk: Barry Schwartz: Using our Practical Wisdom:
  https://youtu.be/IDS-ieLCmS4
- TED Talk: Joshua Prager: Wisdom from Great Writers on Every Year of Our Life:
  https://www.ted.com/talks/joshua_prager_wisdom_from_great_writers_on_every_year_of_life

Websites

- Centre for Practical Wisdom: University of Chicago:
  http://wisdomresearch.org/
- Podcast: A Word to the Wise: Canadian Broadcasting Cooperation's Program Ideas:
  http://www.cbc.ca/radio/ideas/a-word-to-the-wise-part-1-1.2913730

SESSION FOUR: *A BETTER VERSION OF ME*

10

SESSION FOUR, THE LAST OF THE SESSIONS focusing on character strengths, looks at articulating and implementing a written plan of positive, pragmatic, and persistent self-development. The central positive psychotherapy (PPT) practice covered in this session is *A Better Version of Me.*

SESSION FOUR OUTLINE
Core Concepts
  In-Session Practice: *A Better Version of Me*
  Reflection & Discussion
  Vignettes
  Fit & Flexibility
  Cultural Considerations
  Maintenance
Resources

CORE CONCEPTS
Many of us are motivated to improve ourselves, to overcome our challenges, and to boost our well-being. However, the time needed for the self-reflection necessary for self-improvement and moving from intention to action is increasingly difficult to find because of our busy lives, filled with evermore gadgets and external stressors. Judging, however, by the billions in sales for self-help products (such as books, videos, workshops, retreats, and apps), our appetite for self-improvement is not diminished. The notion of creating a better or best possible future self—whether in the domain of health, work, relationships, or creative endeavors—can help us redirect our strengths, skills, and abilities to achieve our goals.

A "best self" is created by imagining and then striving toward personal goals. People are more likely to strive toward their goals when these goals are consistent with their needs, and when circumstances are somewhat favorable for goal striving. Do not wait for your clients to articulate goals; instead, Michalak and Holtforth (2006) suggest that clinicians actively make the effort to assess the content and structure of client goals and review the relationships among goals, symptoms, and treatment motivation as soon as possible. Also, periodically review goal progress with clients and help them to refine the process if necessary.

Articulating and then writing goals (on paper or digitally) is important. Therapeutic benefits of writing are well documented. The seminal work of James Pennebaker (1997) has shown that writing about traumatic, negative, or difficult experiences can not only help individuals find a safe disclosure process but also help them to develop better coping mechanisms. Laura King, another researcher in narrative psychology, has found that writing about positive experiences also improves health by allowing us to make better sense of our emotions and thereby offering us a greater sense of control (King & Milner, 2000).

Our best selves are created by pursuing what we really want. Research shows that people who write down their goals, share this information with a friend, and send weekly updates to that friend about their goal progress are 33% more likely to be successful in accomplishing their goals (Hortop, Wrosch, & Gagné, 2013; Sheldon, Ryan, Deci, & Kasser, 2004).

START-OF-SESSION RELAXATION

At the start of every session, begin with a brief relaxation exercise. Refer to Appendix A: Relaxation & Mindfulness Practices, which can be found at the end of this manual. A copy of this appendix also appears in the client workbook. Continue the session with a review of the client's *Gratitude Journal* as well as a review of the core concepts taught in the previous session.

IN-SESSION PRACTICE: *A BETTER VERSION OF ME*

SUGGESTED SCRIPT FOR THE CLINICIAN

The following is a script you can use to engage clients in discussing the purpose of psychotherapy.

> *You may not articulate this. But wouldn't you agree that you want more joy, hope and optimism, courage and love in your life, not simply less sadness, fear, anger, or boredom?*
>
> *Do you want to explore, express, and enhance your strengths, and not just remediate your weaknesses and guard against your vulnerabilities? Do you want your life imbued with purpose and meaning? There is enormous interest in ways to foster growth and flourishing. Too common are recipes for self-development, proposing everything from positive thinking to aromatherapy (Weiten, 2006). But rare are psychotherapy approaches that focus equally on your symptoms **and** your strengths. Positive psychotherapy is one such approach, and looking at both strengths and symptoms is central to this treatment.*
>
> *In previous sessions you have learned about your signature strengths, and in this session you will learn to articulate and implement a written plan of positive, pragmatic, and persistent self-development. Before I describe the upcoming practice, I would like you to keep in mind a few important considerations: Why and how would you like to pursue such a plan? What are some considerations for striving toward a better version of yourself? Let's do an exercise that is based on a core PPT assumption: that we each have an inherent capacity toward growth, well-being, and flourishing.*
>
> *As human beings, we constantly pursue goals: becoming richer, thinner, more famous, or influential. PPT is not necessarily opposed to these goals, but the focus is to help you frame goals that best use your signature strengths and your interests, talents, needs, and, more importantly, your core values.*
>
> *Researchers of personal growth agree that personal goals predicting happiness are called "self-concordant goals." These are the goals you choose on your own, rather than being asked to do something, no matter how well intentioned it might be. You will be the best judge of what you want.*
>
> *Sometimes, however, symptoms of depression or anxiety can inhibit your ability to articulate what you want. I hope that after the previous practices through which you explored your deepest assets (your signature strengths), and where you worked on a current challenge (Worksheet 3.3), you will have a fair idea of what you want and what kind of person you want to be.*
>
> *If you are still unclear about what kind of person you want to be, the following visualization, derived from research on intrinsic motivation (things you really want), will help you visualize with clarity what kind of person you want to be. Based on what would be a better version of you, I will ask you to write your self-growth plan—a plan that is based on who you are, and who you want to be,*

in terms of concrete and attainable goals. Evidence shows that you are more likely to accomplish your goals if you write them and share them with a friend for periodic updates.

Ask clients to:

- Turn to Worksheet 4.1: *A Better Version of Me*, and have a pen or pencil handy. Note that this and all worksheets (a) appear within the corresponding session of this manual, (b) are reprinted for the client in the accompanying client workbook, and (c) can be downloaded from the companion website at www.oup.com/ppt.
- Clear the space around clients. If they are seated around a large table, extra items are to be put in a bag or put aside, and mobile devices are to be turned off.
- Have them bring their backs to the back of the chair/seat, with head, neck, and trunk in a relaxed alignment, feet flat on the floor, and hands on or close to their thighs.
- Have them settle in and take three deep breaths. As they breathe, they can slowly and gently close their eyes (preferred, although not required).

Then read the following script verbatim:

Visualize a better version of yourself. What would be a better version of you? Select one specific theme: more relaxed, more grounded, more enthusiastic, more energized, more engaged, more creative, more connected, more reflective, happier, healthier.

Remember, this version will be good for you only if you:

- *Believe it will make you happier or more satisfied*
- *Believe this version of you is good for you*
- *Believe that you want to be this sort of person*
- *Believe you have to be this sort of person*

Now visualize details in more concrete terms. How can you move toward this better version? Think of it as a journey. What path do you need to travel through to be this better version? To pursue this path, what exactly do you need to do?

Think about your signature strengths. In visualizing your signature strengths, focus on your interests, talents, skills, and abilities that are related to these signature strengths.

Visualize specific actions, behaviors, routines, and habits that express your signature strengths. Is it specific acts of kindness, expressing love in certain ways, feeling grateful for specific things in your life, or specific creative endeavors?

Connect, if you can, some actions to achieving the better version you just visualized. How can your signature strengths, and the actions that express them, help you to be the better version of you?

If you have a clear or somewhat clear list of actions, activities, routines, or habits that will help you to be the better version, can you commit to doing some?

Select the ones you are willing to commit to for the next three months.

Visualize potential barriers that could halt your progress--barriers internal to you or barriers from outside.

Think of what you can do to overcome these barriers. Who can support you in overcoming these barriers?

Now, visualize what might happen if you are able to progress to a better version of you. What would change in your life, in your daily routine? Be specific.

Allow clients sufficient time on each of these questions. Then continue:

When you are ready, bring your attention back to the room.

Now please complete Worksheet 4.1: A Better Version of Me. Without thinking much, please record your responses as your visualized them.

The Plan

Set Realistic Goals

What would be a better version of me on [Day,   Month,   Year   ]?

Set goals that are:	Specify some changes you want to see:
• Concrete and observable through behaviors, actions, and habits • Well integrated with your current life situation • Not in conflict with your values • Supported by your social networks	• More relaxed? More grounded? • More enthusiastic? More energized? • More engaged? More creative? • More connected? More reflective? • More social? More relaxed? • Happier? Healthier?

Complete these Sentences

This *Better Version of Me* will make me happier or more satisfied because

_____

It is something good for me because

_____

It is someone I always wanted to be because

_____

It is someone I have to be because

_____

Create a Timeline

Date of Plan: _____

Date of Anticipated Completion: _____

Mid-point (insert approximate date): _____

Partner with Someone

Name of friend who is willing to support me: _____

How frequently will the person check with me about my progress? _____

How will we communicate?   By Phone?   By Email?   In Person?

Examples of Goals for A Better Version of Me

Emotional Resilience	Social Resilience
More relaxed/grounded	More deeply connected with friends
• I will start a relaxation routine (e.g., breathe deeply a couple times a day, attend a weekly yoga/meditation class) • I will incorporate deliberate idle time (at least 15 minutes daily) when I will do nothing • Next time I become upset, I will take a break before reacting, breathe deeply, consult with someone who can give me an impartial perspective, or try to ask more questions to understand the context • I will eliminate at least one thing that distracts me from being focused and productive • I will take time to do/play something that I really enjoy	• I will spot the specific strengths, abilities, skills of others and compliment them • I will ask a friend who I care about, yet have not emotionally understood, specific ways in which I can better connect with him or her • I will engage in a meaningful yet fun activity with my friend which is mutually appealing to us (e.g., snow shoeing, rock climbing, playing a board game, going to a sporting event/performance together) • I will have a one-on-one lunch or dinner date with my close friend, during which electronic devices will be off • I will do one kind act (big or small) for my friend without being asked
Physical Resilience	Work Place Resilience
More Energized/Healthier	More Engaged
• I will create an exercise routine that I can maintain on a regular basis (three times a week) • I will add at least one healthy snack to my daily eating plan • I will vow not to sit for X amount of time, and will incorporate physical activity every X (hour) into my routine • I will improve my sleep by doing at least one thing consistently (e.g., stop eating at least two hours before bedtime, stop looking at a screen at least one hour before going to bed, say no to events/activities that consistently impact my sleep adversely) • I will adopt at least one habit that will improve my physical health (e.g., wash hands, have regular checkups)	• I will familiarize myself with my work/job requirements by reviewing tasks required, deadlines, etc. • I will give each project the time and effort it deserves and will make it optimally engaging • If procrastination is a problem, I will change my inner dialogue for at least two of these: I have to TO *I choose to* I must finish TO *Where and when can I start?* The project is too large TO *I can divide the assignment into small steps* My project must be perfect TO *Not all of my projects can be perfect, I will strive for what is humanly possible, not perfect*

SESSION-BY-SESSION PRACTICE

REFLECTION & DISCUSSION

After completing this practice, ask clients to reflect and discuss:

- This was a long visualization. How would you describe the overall experience of visualizing a better version of yourself? Were you able to follow along or did you experienced some challenges? Please share.
- How was the experience of writing about what your visualized? Were you able to capture what you visualized or did you struggle?
- Did this exercise help you to generate concrete ideas for a better version of yourself?
- How concrete are the ideas you generated? This practice works better when you are able to formulate concreate ideas which are realistic, and which you can manage reasonably well.
- In case you struggled to generate concrete ideas, having a clear picture of a better version of yourself can still work. In our experience, having a clear image or perception of what a person wants to be—even if he or she has difficulty coming up with concrete ideas of how to get there—allows that person to focus on the process and ultimate goal. For you, what worked—a clear image of a better version, or concrete paths that lead to this better version, or both?

VIGNETTE: JOHN

John, 38, was seen in individual therapy for symptoms of generalized anxiety. The following is his description of *A Better Version of Me*.

"*A Better Version of Me*: In my high school years, I was a cross-country runner and won many races. In college, I participated at the varsity level. But then things took a turn for the worse. The economic meltdown five years ago hurt me on so many levels. I lost my job and, a year later, my marriage broke up. I started experiencing anxiety attacks. When I visualize a *Better Version of Me*, I have no problem in seeing just one thing—a calmer and more relaxed version of me. To be so, I selected to use my strengths of self-regulation and persistence, as I am not sure how zest, social intelligence, and curiosity might help me feel calmer; they may actually have an opposite effect. My goal is to start running again. I will start with a goal of running a 10K within three months and eventually a half-marathon by next summer.

"**My plan:** I plan to run three times a week starting with 30 minutes in the first month, and then progress to 40 minutes. I am lucky to have a job again, but it requires me to sit for long periods of time doing deskwork, staring at a computer screen almost nonstop. It will be nice to run in the morning to be energetic for the rest of the day.

"**Who will support me?** I have a friend who lives nearby. We used to play baseball together, and he has expressed his interest in running, as he feels he has put on some weight. He also used to run, and the last time we met at the supermarket, he asked me if I would like to go biking or running. I will call him to see if he would like to join me. Our schedules are not likely to match every time, but whenever possible, I will text him the night before to see if he is available the next morning.

"**What would be different if I achieve that goal?** I don't think it will change my life dramatically, but this is something I have wanted to do because when I used to run, it was a calming experience like nothing else. Even after long runs, I did not feel tired; it also helped me stop worrying about my problems. I am hoping that if I am able to get back to running, it will get me back to my calmer and less anxious side—even a tiny bit will help."

Outcome: Soon after devising the plan, John was able to connect with his friend and both ran together—more often than John anticipated. He stated, "My running partner has now become one of my close friends, as he has been going through a difficult breakup," and both were able to share their struggles, often after running. Therapy ended as John's insurance coverage for therapy was exhausted. Just before the last session, John and his friend successfully completed a 10K, and they were training to run a half-marathon within a year.

VIGNETTE: SALLY

Sally, 46, a human resource manager, was seen in individual therapy for recurrent depression. The following is her description of *A Better Version of Me*.

"I must say I was quite skeptical about this whole strength thing, and *A Better Version of Me*—it sounded so cheesy and New Age-y. I thought therapy has become a room full of self-help recipes—only very expensive. After all, I am used to therapy that for so many years has focused on my self-esteem and lack of confidence issues.

"The goal of my action plan was to use my strengths to focus on me becoming a more loving (even though it came out as my top signature strength), more connected and grounded person. These strengths were not surprising for me, as I knew myself. However, I was surprised that spirituality did not come as one of my signature strengths, even though I consider myself spiritually inclined. I decided to find something that somehow could connect me with spirituality, but also something that made me feel alive. Following my initial plan, I tried meditation, volunteering at a women's shelter, and a book club, but I did not feel alive and connected deeply. I had given up on this plan. One night, I went to pick up one of my friends from her choir practice. I spent less than 10 minutes listening to the practice and loved it. My friend urged me to join (in return she got a free ride and plenty of time to update me on neighborhood gossip). I was deemed good enough to join the group. On practice nights, my husband agreed to cook dinner and take care of house chores. In return, I took over backyard cleaning and gardening, which he used to do but never enjoyed. Surprisingly, I found the experiencing of pulling out weeds and planting and nurturing flowers and plants very rewarding and almost spiritual.

"My husband and children noticed a difference, especially the nights I came home from choir practice. I was told I appeared more cheerful and my mood began to improve gradually. By Christmas, I felt more engaged, alive, and loved the experiencing of singing in unison with others . . . . On numerous occasions, during choir performances, time stopped for me and I felt part of something larger than myself—a feeling never experienced before. For me, this was spirituality; although it was not my signature strength, still it gave me the deepest fulfillment. Perhaps spirituality encompasses many dimensions. At work, my staff also noticed the difference and commented that I have become less intense and no longer look like an 'overstretched, overworked boss.'

"I never thought that I could be off of medication, but I am weaning off. Six months on, I don't know if I have developed a better version of myself. I cannot judge it, but I do feel lighter and more alive—like I used to feel when I was very young and played in the country, singing in the valley to birds and trees."

FIT & FLEXIBILITY

The *A Better Version of Me* practice can be a huge undertaking and may not be completed within the timeframe of treatment. Personal change often requires unlearning the old and ineffective habits and acquiring and practicing a new skill set. One needs to line up supports and resources for reinforcement, refinement, and realignment with other existing skills. For example, one of our clients successfully created a new version of himself following a serious suicide attempt. This journey started about four years ago, when the client began by seeking residential drug treatment and attending individual and group PPT for two years. Today, at the time of writing this manuscript, he has just published his first scientific paper in a prestigious journal and is likely to graduate with honors. However, this successful creation of a much better version has taken four years, with many stops and starts and, more importantly, with significant social and physical changes (e.g., in his living arrangement and employment), and with this specific client, existential changes (in his mindset). All of this has taken time. While we have a few very successful cases, and many moderately effective cases, also piled in our clinical charts are numerous attempts that did not progress much. Therefore clinicians should be patient and able to tolerate starts and stops, progression and regression.

CULTURAL CONSIDERATIONS

In facilitating this practice, a clinician needs to be aware of cultural biases. For example, the core of *A Better Version of Me* is based on the concept of self-development, which varies from culture to culture. The Western concept of self-development encompasses personal growth, taking new and largely individual initiatives, and finding new appreciation for life. The vignettes described earlier highlight these themes. Self-development in Eastern (and most non-European) cultures emphasizes investing in relationships; improving social interaction; and contributing to preserving family, group, and tribal traditions. Despite increasing cultural diversity, research shows that these differences hold. An important implication of these differences is that clients from an Eastern cultural background may select a goal and use their signature strengths for *A Better Version of Me* that entails better relationships with others. Restoring or improving relationships in an interdependent culture requires more effort and more complex interactions over a longer period of time, whereas *A Better Version of Me* focused on improving individual strengths or taking a new initiative may require a relatively shorter amount of time. Therefore, consider each case independently, even when this intervention is administered in group settings.

At the same time, pursuing an individualized, relatively more autonomous sense of self might be the desired goal for a client from a conservative culture, which was the case for one of our clients participating in group PPT. This client, from a conservative, religious, South Asian background, desired to develop a better version of herself by learning to recalibrate her social intelligence, modesty, and prudence (overused strengths).

Ultimately, it is important that you provide your clients a therapeutic milieu where they are able to select personally meaningful, engaging, and culturally and socially relevant goals.

MAINTENANCE

Discuss the following tips with your clients so that they can maintain their progress:

- We each have many selves, including some that we like and desire to develop further and others that we dislike and want to change (Markus & Nuruis, 2008). The practice of *A Better Version of Me* offers you a structured way to develop a self you want to develop. You can repeat or revise this practice as many times as you want as long as you are clear about *which* specific desirable self you are moving toward.

- In developing a better version of yourself, select activities that you find realistic and relevant and that you can sustain over a period of time. (For examples, see the suggestions toward the end of Worksheet 4.1.) Sustenance doesn't mean that you don't allow yourself to deviate. Some situations may require to you alter your routine. These may include skipping exercise to help a friend who needs timely help, being less creative if a project needs to be completed within a specific time and budget, and curtailing courageous actions if these bring more chaos than calm.

- Although *A Better Version of Me* requires specific details (concrete actions to be done, when, how, where, and with frequency), it is also okay that you initiate this process (of becoming a better person) without having all relevant details. Sometimes, the mere commitment to become a better person is sufficient, and you can add relevant details as you go along. In other words, it is fine that you enjoy the process, as long as you remain committed to the outcome.

- Sometimes your negativity bias, which may be well entrenched in your self-concept, can impede your progress—and may be something you cannot change. You can postpone this practice and move on to other PPT practices that may help you undo the negativity bias, hopefully motivating you to take on the challenge of creating a better version of yourself.

- You should also keep in mind that the *A Better Version of Me* practice encourages you to create a *better*—not necessarily the *best*—version of yourself. It may take a while to create the best version. In the meantime, you can create multiple better versions. The cumulative effects of these versions may help you eventually to create and sustain the most desirable version of yourself.

- While pursuing this practice, a setback or an acute challenge may derail your progress. Remind yourself that the ultimate judge of your better version is *you*. As long as you are putting forth your best effort—a better version of yourself will take shape.

END-OF-SESSION RELAXATION

We recommend that each session end with the same brief relaxation practice that started the session.

RESOURCES

Readings

- Meevissen, Y. M. C., Peters, M. L., & Alberts, H. J. E. M. (2011). Become more optimistic by imagining a best possible self: Effects of a two-week intervention. *Journal of Behavior Therapy* and *Experimental Psychiatry, 42*, 371–378.
- Owens, R. L., & Patterson, M. M. (2013) Positive psychological interventions for children: A comparison of gratitude and best possible selves approaches. *The Journal of Genetic Psychology, 174*(4), 403–428, doi:10.1080/00221325.2012.697496
- Renner, F., Schwarz, P., Peters, M. L., & Huibers, M. J. H. (2016). Effects of a best-possible-self mental imagery exercise on mood and dysfunctional attitudes. *Psychiatry Research, 215*(1), 105–110.
- Sheldon, K. M., & Lyubomirsky, S. (2006). How to increase and sustain positive emotion: The effects of expressing gratitude and visualizing best possible selves. *The Journal of Positive Psychology, 2*, 73.

Videos

- Barry Schwartz makes a passionate call for "practical wisdom" as an antidote to a society gone mad with bureaucracy. He argues powerfully that rules often fail us, incentives often backfire, and practical, everyday wisdom will help rebuild our world:
  https://www.ted.com/talks/barry_schwartz_on_our_loss_of_wisdom
- Elizabeth Lindsey, a fellow of the National Geographic Society, discusses indigenous wisdom and traditions:
  http://www.ted.com/speakers/elizabeth_lindsey

Websites

- The Max Planck Society's website. Eighty-three institutes of this Germany-based society, including a wisdom institute, conduct basic research in the service of the general public in the natural sciences, life sciences, social sciences, and the humanities:
  http://www.mpg.de/institutes
- The Science of Older and Wiser:
  http://www.nytimes.com/2014/03/13/business/retirementspecial/the-science-of-older-and-wiser.html?_r=0
- Practical wisdom as the master virtue:
  http://www.artofmanliness.com/2011/12/19/practical-wisdom/
- Ryan M. Niemiec: The Best Possible Self Exercise (Boosts Hope):
  http://blogs.psychcentral.com/character-strengths/2012/09/the-best-possible-self-exercise-boosts-hope/

## 11

SESSION FIVE: OPEN AND CLOSED MEMORIES

IN SESSION FIVE, WHICH IS THE START of Phase Two of positive psychotherapy (PPT), clients recall, write, and process their open and closed memories. They learn to develop skills for dealing with open or negative memories through the PPT practice of *Positive Appraisal.*

SESSION FIVE OUTLINE
Core Concepts
    In-Session Practice: *Open Memories*
    Reflection & Discussion
    In-Session Practice: *A Closed Memory*
    Reflection & Discussion
    Positive Appraisal
    Practice: *Positive Appraisal*
    Reflection & Discussion
    Vignette
    Fit & Flexibility
    Cultural Considerations
    Maintenance
Resources

CORE CONCEPTS
In PPT, we refer to memories that are not fully understood and those that trigger negative emotional responses as "open memories." Memories that ended somewhat conclusively with a positive outcome, even those entailing past challenges or difficulties, are referred to as "closed memories."

Clients entering psychotherapy often say, "I am carrying a lot of baggage from the past, which I cannot get rid of." Or, "My past won't let me move forward." Most forms of traditional therapy, especially those influenced by the psychodynamic view, place a therapeutic premium on venting anger and frustration about past hurts. Thus the bulk of therapeutic strategies are geared toward releasing pent-up anger, using a rather untested assumption that, once anger is released, the client will automatically gain therapeutic insight. This assumption has significantly influenced psychotherapy and is also widespread in popular culture, expressed in phrases such as, "blow off steam," "let it out," and "get if off your chest."

Venting of open or negative memories is unlikely to bring about therapeutic change in a depressed client. In some cases, it can be harmful (Bushman, Baumeister, & Phillips, 2001). Evidence also shows that when participants vented their anger by hitting a punching bag, they actually felt angrier and were likely to engage in aggressive action. Furthermore, venting anger produces more heart disease and resentment (Anderson & Bushman, 2002; Chida & Steptoe, 2009). Repeated focus on negative memories of the past maintains and even escalates depression (Nolen-Hoeksema, Wisco, & Lybomirsky, 2008).

Recalling open and negative memories promotes pessimistic and fatalistic thinking and increases stress. If we do not express these feelings at the right time in an appropriate manner, the feelings begin to settle in and develop into bitterness toward others. Then, due to the negativity bias, we may label others as completely bad, and we may not be able to focus on the specifics that engendered the negative feelings in the first place. It is harmful for ourselves when we begin to develop bitter feelings for others. Clients may see these others in black-and-white terms, and they may needlessly and endlessly ponder why the others have offended them. Such clients often ask, "Why would someone do this to me?" They may talk about this obsessively with friends, which is a form of rumination. Clients assume that rumination offers insight, whereas it actually ends up damaging them more than those who offended. Such rumination on open and negative memories can also deplete our social support because those around us may not want to constantly hear us rehashing the past (Calmes & Roberts, 2008).

Evidence shows that bearing negative memories, such as grudges, is linked to hypertension in adults and adolescents. People who hold grudges tend to have higher rates of heart disease, high blood pressure, heart attacks, and chronic pain (Andreassen, 2001; Messias, Saini, Sinato, & Welch, 2010). Negative memories and holding a grudge often consist of negative, resentful, and cyclical (repeated) thinking. This type of thinking depletes cognitive resources over time, which limits our problem-solving abilities.

Clinician Note

Please review the contents of this session before presenting it to your clients. It is important to ensure that clients are sufficiently emotionally and psychologically stable to handle the topic. You can always return to this topic at a later stage in treatment.

Also, Positive Appraisal may not be relevant for every client, given their presenting concerns.

START-OF-SESSION RELAXATION

At the start of every session, begin with a brief relaxation exercise. Refer to Appendix A: Relaxation & Mindfulness Practices, which can be found at the end of this manual. A copy of this appendix also appears in the client workbook. Continue the session with a review of the client's *Gratitude Journal* as well as a review of the core concepts taught in the previous session.

IN-SESSION PRACTICE: *OPEN MEMORIES*

SUGGESTED SCRIPT FOR THE CLINICIAN

The following is a script you can use to introduce the concept of open (negative) memories and their psychological, social, and physiological impact.

When the average person hears the word "psychotherapy," what do they associate it with? Answers may include: A place to vent anger and frustration from the past. Or a place where people go who have a lot of problems, which they want to get rid of, but cannot. In fact, new clients often say, "My past won't let me move forward." Many forms of traditional psychotherapy are based on the process of releasing our pent-up anger with a rather untested assumption that, once the anger dies down, the client will automatically gain therapeutic insight. This assumption has significantly influenced psychotherapy and is also widespread in popular culture, expressed in phrases such as, "blow off steam," "let it out," and "get if off your chest."

Evidence shows, however, that venting negative memories is unlikely to bring about a therapeutic change in someone with depression (Anderson et al., 2006), and, in some cases, it can even be harmful. Evidence shows that when participants vented their anger by hitting a punching bag, they actually felt angrier and were likely to engage in aggressive action. Furthermore, venting anger can lead to more heart disease and resentment. That said, there is no denying that a repeated focus on negative memories of the past maintains depression and can make it worse.

Recalling negative memories promotes pessimistic and fatalistic thinking and increases stress. If we do not express these feelings at the right time in an appropriate manner, they begin to settle in us. It becomes harmful if we begin to develop bitter feelings for someone. As a result, we might label that person as "bad," rather than focusing on the specifics that made us feel that way.

Not only may we judge the whole person, we often needlessly and endlessly try to understand why that person offended us. We may ask, "Why would that person do this to me?" If we talk about this obsessively with our friends, it is called rumination. We assume that this process offers us insight, but in fact it ends up damaging us.

Ruminating on negative memories can hurt our friendships and social support, because other people may not want to associate with us if we appear to be crippled by our negative memories or if we are preoccupied by our negative past.

Research has shown that holding on to negative memories, such as grudges, is linked to hypertension in adults and adolescents. People who hold grudges tend to have higher rates of heart disease, high blood pressure, and chronic pain.

Negative memories and holding a grudge often consist of negative, resentful, and cyclical (repeated) thinking. Over time, this type of thinking uses up our cognitive resources, and this limits our problem-solving abilities.

We will now engage in a short practice regarding these concepts.

Practice: Step-by-Step Details

To convey care for clients and to offer them sufficient scaffolding so that they are able to courageously encounter upsetting memories, we encourage clinicians to proceed with this practice using the following steps.

- **Step 1:** After completing a relaxation exercise, clients recall an open memory—an adverse experience that, whenever it is recalled, triggers negative experiences and feelings. Clients feel that something is still "open," like "unfinished business," when they recall this disturbing memory.
- **Step 2:** Clients recall a closed memory—of a difficult experience, which at the time was tough to go through, but now looking back, the client feels that it offered opportunities for growth. The recall of this experience brings a sense of closure and satisfaction.
- **Step 3:** Through reflection and discussion, clients compare these two experiences.
- **Step 4:** Clients learn about *Positive Cognitive Appraisal* skills and try to use one or more to deal with the open memory.

SUGGESTED SCRIPT FOR THE CLINICIAN
The following is a script you can use to prompt the client to select an open memory.

Sit in a comfortable position with your arms resting on your thighs and your head, neck, and chest in a relaxed straight line. Your feet are resting flat on the floor.

Pay attention to your breathing; notice when you inhale and exhale, when your chest expands and contracts. Gently bring your breath into your belly. Repeat this cycle. Inhale and exhale 10 times, on your own count, quietly.

Continue repeating this breathing cycle. Try to make each breath in and out last for ten seconds. Start over after each count.

If your attention wavers, don't worry. Start your count over.

Allow at least one to two minutes to center clients. Then read the following script verbatim:

Recall in your mind a memory that you feel you have not fully understood. Whenever you think of this memory, the experience is not pleasant and you feel you have some unfinished business associated with it. This is called an open memory. Try to pick a memory not associated with shame and guilt or those associated with profound sadness, loss, rejection, anger, anxiety, or frustration.

Ask clients to open their eyes. Once they open, facilitate a discussion using the following questions.

REFLECTION & DISCUSSION

After completing this practice, ask clients to reflect and discuss:

- If an open or negative memory entails harm and hurt done by someone else, do you find yourself thinking about this person or about the causes and consequences of his or her actions? Would you describe this process as reflective, brooding, wallowing, conclusive, and so on? What are the benefits and disadvantages of this process?
- Have you discussed this negative memory with someone else? If you have, what was the outcome? Did you get another's perspective or vent your feelings?
- What are the long-term effects on your emotional well-being of harboring this negative memory? What can you do to lessen these effects?

IN-SESSION PRACTICE: *A CLOSED MEMORY*

Complete the next practice soon after discussing these questions. We recommend that the open and closed memory practices be completed in one session. Read the following script verbatim.

Think of a difficult situation that you had to endure. Sometimes, even when bad things happen, ultimately they have positive consequences—things we can now be grateful for. Try to focus on the positive aspects of this difficult experience. What kinds of things do you now feel thankful or grateful for? This is called a closed memory.

Ask clients to open their eyes. Once they open, facilitate a discussion using the following questions.

REFLECTION & DISCUSSION

After completing this practice, ask clients to reflect and discuss:

- How has this experience benefited you as a person?
- Were there personal strengths that grew out of this experience?
- How has the event put your life into perspective?
- How has this event helped you appreciate the truly important people and things in your life? In sum, how can you be thankful for the beneficial consequences that have resulted from this event?

POSITIVE APPRAISAL

The open and closed memories practices help clients understand that the person who is impacted by open memories is the client, not the person who offended, harmed, or hurt him. The client's open memories—which initially produced strong negative emotions—remain unprocessed and eventually evolve into symptomatic complexities (Harvey et al., 2004). By holding on to these memories, clients adversely impact their own emotional health because often these memories paralyze them, especially at times when clients want to do something important. PPT uses *Positive Appraisal*, a meaning-based coping approach that reinterprets events or situations in a positive manner (Cooney et al., 2007; Folkman & Moskowtiz, 2000; Van Dillen et al., 2007).

The following are examples of negative memories that clients have found to be persistent and distressing:

- *Whenever I try to do something good, my spouse does something which reminds me of a painful incident from the past.*
- *Whenever I accomplish something I feel good, yet failures of the past remind me that there is so much more that I have to achieve, in order to measure up.*
- *I want to do good, but resentment of the past holds me back; my good actions have been taken for granted.*
- *I have forgiven my spouse for hurting me but still find it hard to trust him again.*
- *I feel angry that my dearest friend did not stand up for me when it really mattered.*

Recalling negative memories brings an array of negative emotions such as anger, bitterness, confusion, or sadness. These feelings may be more intense if someone close to us does the hurt or harm. We may harbor a grudge and wish the offender to be punished, degraded, humiliated, or disempowered so that some sense of justice is restored. Fully acknowledging and mindfully validating these feelings, PPT posits that when open memories are not addressed actively, they often evolve into resentment, vengeance, and hostility. Unfortunately, the first and foremost victim is not the person toward whom the client holds the grudge but the client herself. PPT helps clients to deal with open, bitter, and negative memories in an affirmative manner, through following four skills.

PRACTICE: *POSITIVE APPRAISAL*

Worksheet 5.1: *Positive Appraisal*, lists four strategies encompassing the practice of *Positive Appraisal* in PPT. Note that this and all worksheets (a) appear within the corresponding session of this manual, (b) are reprinted for the client in the accompanying client workbook, and (c) can be downloaded from the companion website at www.oup.com/ppt. First discuss these strategies with your clients, and then encourage them to complete the worksheet in order to deal with open and negative memories head-on.

1. *Create Psychological Space:* *You can create psychological space between your lingering negative memory and yourself. One way to do this is to describe the bitter memory from a third person's perspective—that is, without using "I." This will allow you to create some distance between yourself and the open memory, offering you an opportunity to revise your feelings and the meaning of the memory rather than rehashing it.*

Practice: Imagine you are journalist, photographer, or documentary filmmaker, and in the following space, describe your open memory or grudge from a third-person vantage point. Try to keep the third-person expression less personalized and more neutral.

_____

_____

_____

2. *Reconsolidation:* *When you are immersed in the negative memory, you are unlikely to pay attention to all aspects of the situation because your thinking becomes narrow. Do the following practice when you are in a calm state and not overwhelmed by a current stressor.*

Practice: Take deep breaths. Recall all the finer and subtle aspects of your open and bitter memory. Try to reinterpret it in the following space, deliberately recalling any positive aspects that you might have missed. Keep negative aspects at bay—as much as you can—because the focus of the practice is to acknowledge and write about the positive aspects of the open memory that you might have missed initially. In doing so, think of your most important values in life, and infuse them in your revised memory (Folkman & Moskowitze, 2000; Van Dillen et al., 2007; Vázquez, 2015).

_____

_____

_____

3. *Mindful Self-focus:* *This practice encourages you to develop a nonjudgmental and sustained mental state whenever an open memory pops up. With a receptive mind, shift your attention to internal and external events and experiences evoked by the negative memory. As the open and negative memory unfolds, try to observe it than react to it.*

Practice: Step back, and let your open and negative memory unfold in front of your eyes, as if you are watching a film. Be an observer, rather than being swept away by the emotions of memory. Your job is to let unpleasant memories pass by. Repeat this practice a couple of times, and note in the following spaces if your observations help you get used to the open memory and feel less upset.

_____

_____

_____

4. *Diversion:* *We encourage you to sharpen your antenna to promptly recognize cues that activate the recall of your open and bitter memories, and, as soon as that recall begins, immediately try to draw your attention away and engage in a physical or cognitive task that interests you. The sooner you move your attention to a different task, the easier it may be to stop the recall of your open memory. The more often you are able to divert your attention, the better you will learn to recognize the external cues that activate bitter memories. You will then be able to catch them quickly and steer your attention to healthier and more adaptive behaviors.*

Practice: As soon as an open memory is triggered, try to draw your attention away and engage in a physical or cognitive task that interests you. In the following spaces, write down three experiential, engaging, hands-on, and complex activities that can divert your attention from negative memories.

_____

_____

_____

REFLECTION & DISCUSSION

After completing this practice, ask clients to reflect and discuss:

- Of the four positive appraisal strategies, which one(s) do you find to be the most relevant to your open memories?
- After reviewing these four strategies, do you feel that your open memories can be changed, modified, or repacked in a different way that could work for you?
- Reflect upon your open memories. Which ones do you feel are not amenable to *Positive Appraisal*? Remember, you don't have to force yourself to deal with an open memory through *Positive Appraisal*.
- In applying one or more of the *Positive Appraisal* strategies, what sort of social supports will you need? Can you think of an alternative, in case such a support is not available?
- In what ways can these strategies help you in the future, as you encounter complex, ambivalent, or conflictual situations?

VIGNETTE: ANNA AND HER UNFINISHED BUSINESS

Anna, a 53-year-old, single mother of two adult children, experienced chronic symptoms of depression and was also embittered by memories of her past. Most of these memories were about the emotional abuse Anna suffered at the hands of her ex-husband, Doug, during their 12-year marriage, which was marked by arguments, fights, and a lot of unhappiness. Divorced for almost a decade, Anna was still struggling with these memories when she entered therapy. Anna reported that these memories are triggered unexpectedly and leave her angry, sad, and isolated. Anna had been in therapy previously, but she felt that she still has some "unfinished business" with these memories; this became the primary focus of her therapy.

Most of us reflect on our setbacks and struggles. This reflection may make us sad—but for most of us we don't become paralyzed. We are able to put the past in perspective, refocus on our present, and move on with our daily lives. This, however, was not the case for Anna. She not only thought almost constantly about the negative experiences of the past, but she also tried to draw new insights from them. Anna, however, was only circling around the causes and consequences of her emotional abuse—a process commonly known as ruminating. In the first few sessions, while listening empathically to Anna's bitter memories, her clinician gently nudged her to become an observer of her own thinking while she dwelt in past memories. To become an observer of her own thinking was not an easy task for Anna. To make the process easier and more concrete, at the clinician's suggestion, Anna kept a written log of time spent on these negative memories and also how she felt during and afterward. She reported that whenever she dwelled on the negative memories of her past, her mood darkened, she felt stressed, and she was unable to focus well, consequently hurting the quality of her work and home life.

Rather than discussing the content of Anna's negative memories in detail, the clinician asked her to actively observe and reflect upon wallowing—one of the major causes of her depression. Anna agreed, and it helped her to notice that dwelling in the past, although somewhat tempting and soothing, didn't help her. She gained no new insights into her past miseries, and often thinking about these bitter memories made her angry and sad. Furthermore, she realized that she continued to harbor a grudge against her ex-husband, which, at times, prompted a strong desire to take revenge—something she would never do otherwise. However, this desire to take revenge led to more mistrust of others, including of her children. She did not trust her colleagues and couldn't delegate work that others could easily do. In addition,

Anna noted that she had been told that she had become hypersensitive, interpreting the rather benign comments of others in a negative way and taking them personally.

After developing awareness about the consequences of holding on to negative memories, Anna focused on developing the skill of letting go. Anna felt—and rightly so—that she was a victim, a punching bag, and a doormat. She had lived most of her life under the influence of two personalities, a strong and assertive mother and a domineering husband. Anna felt that her prolonged emotional abuse had left deep scars on her personality that could not be healed. The clinician drew Anna's attention to the present, where the abuse has stopped because Anna has been divorced for nearly 10 years and is in the process of moving from victim to survivor.

The clinician and Anna discussed that the past, as painful as it is, cannot be changed, but the past should not dictate the present and future. If Anna allows the past to continue to dictate or direct her present and future, she will most likely continue to experience sadness, feel empty, and remain isolated and unhappy. This victim role kept her from growing and exploring new ways of being. After much discussion, Anna has begun to see herself as a survivor who has the potential to grow.

FIT & FLEXIBILITY

Some negative memories are so powerful (e.g., sexual or physical abuse, the tragic loss of a loved one, an accident, natural disasters, or crimes against humanity) that they continue to elicit strong emotions whenever the memory is revisited. Although *Positive Appraisal* can help people deal with such powerful memories, it is best that clients start with relatively less intense memories and move gradually toward more severe and emotionally charged ones.

A negative memory caused by an authority figure or institution (e.g., teacher, school, house of worship) may not be easy to deal with, especially if the memory entails violation of personal rights. Therefore, we advise clients not to use them in *Positive Appraisal*, because such memories may evoke other related memories, which could then trigger a crisis or a cascade of emotions that may be difficult to contain.

Positive Appraisal is also not advisable for those who have experienced a recent trauma or are likely to re-experience intensity of trauma-related symptoms. Not every trauma needs an appraisal. In some cases, attempting to hurriedly deal with a trauma may, in fact, backfire. Before starting this practice, let your clients know that this could be a challenging session and you will therefore proceed slowly.

Explore and apply appropriate weight to specific personality factors that may interact with this practice. For example, one of our clients tended to be very sensitive and focused on relatively small social slights (e.g., not getting a turn, nonverbal disapproval, not being invited to a party). She lacked the resources to put such minor transgressions into perspective: prior discussion of and ways of using the character strength of wisdom allowed her to put things into perspective and engage with *Positive Appraisal*.

A negative memory may have multiple versions or copies. For example, if the negative memory entails not being able to stand up for oneself—often the case with depressed clients—help the client to select the most characteristic version and use the strategies described previously to deal adaptively with the memory. After the client is able to work through the memory, help him to apply the strategy to similar past episodes.

Use relaxation techniques such as deep breathing, progressive muscle relaxation, and positive imagery with clients who may become anxious during recall or appraisal. Once relaxed, it is much easier to untangle the negatives from authentic positives.

Some clients may perceive distraction as avoidance or suppression—the name may imply such. Rather than engaging in deeper work to deal with the negative memory adaptively, they may hurriedly suppress or avoid the negative emotions associated with the memory and may then assert that they have completely dealt with the memory. To guard against a hurried approach, periodically ask the client about the reduction in adverse impact of the negative memory. For example, a client with a short temper may use the diversion strategy to cope with her penchant for anger by playing a game that involves physical movement or playing a game on her smartphone, or she may divert her attention to a physical chore to be completed at home.

Some clients may not readily want to deal adaptively with the negative memory; such clients may prefer to vent, because they have held onto to this memory for so long and thinking about it makes them feel alive. Or they may see letting go of a negative memory, grudge, resentment, or revenge as a sign of weakness. Others like to have easy access to these memories in order to continue in a self-pitying or victim role. With such clients, a more detailed discussion, conveyed with warmth, genuineness, and empathy, can help them evaluate the adverse impact of holding onto negative memories and can underscore the importance of change. And, when appropriate, letting such clients vent their anger in a safe manner may prepare them to better engage in therapeutic endeavors.

Furthermore, make sure that clients don't feel forced or coerced to undertake *Positive Appraisal*. Doing so may compromise clients' feelings of autonomy and control. On the other hand, therapeutic warmth, genuineness, and empathy can encourage clients to confront difficult and chronic issues which they may have been avoiding.

The processing of negative memories may only be temporary if a similar occurrence or an adverse encounter with the same person brings back negative memories, especially if the offense is serious (e.g., abuse, aggression, deliberate moral infractions). Because letting go of such a grudge may run the risk minimizing the offense, forgetting it in the short term, or even partially denying or avoiding painful emotions, encourage clients to choose an open memory that doesn't involve a serious offense, especially when learning to develop and maintain the skills.

For more serious offenses, merely letting go of the open and negative memories may not be sufficient. An active, committed, and difficult process of forgiveness may be required, and this process is discussed in Chapter 12 (Session Six: Forgiveness). Some clients may need to know more about grudges, however, and may be interested in forgiveness. Discussing the content and process of forgiveness requires considerable time; it may open memories and issues that might be dealt with better in a more forgiveness-focused practice. Sometimes the therapeutic effects of *Positive Appraisal* will not be maintained as symptoms may return or get worse.

CULTURAL CONSIDERATIONS

Culture has an impact on how negative experiences, traumas, and challenges manifest. Be mindful in exploring how the idiom of stress is conceptualized within the culture of the client. Be aware that there are variations within cultures, largely due to familial and financial factors. Some clients may not be able to articulate an open memory, as it may unravel cultural stress, which they may not be able to handle. Furthermore, culturally expected roles and duty may prevent some clients from opening up, or the trauma itself may be influenced by a factor unique to the culture. For example, one of our clients, Latifah, a female from an interdependent culture, was sexually abused by a close family member. Years later, when she told her mother about the abuse, her mother (although she empathized with the daughter fully) eventually advised Latifah to remain quiet and not to share the information with anyone, even though Latifah had to occasionally encounter her abuser at social gatherings. Latifah found her mother's response to be much more traumatic than the abuse itself or encountering the abuser in social situations. Be aware that cultural norms can sometime shape the content of a traumatic experience.

Some clients may face cultural barriers to the recall and articulation of a negative memory, especially if the memory involves someone close to them. In Western culture, sharing difficult emotions is perceived as a sign of competence and courage. However, this may not be the case in non-Western cultures, so cultural context should be considered with clients who may have similar views about expression of negative memory.

MAINTENANCE

Discuss the following tips with your clients so that they can maintain their progress:

- When an open memory keeps revisiting you, especially if it pops up unexpectedly in situations where you least desire it, use the skills learned in this session. If your experience with the practice of *Positive Appraisal* has helped you, consider handling a different open memory—preferably something that still disturbs you but that is not too traumatic. Find a comfortable and quiet place. Start with a mindfulness practice of your choosing—something you have already been doing in PPT. Recall the open memory. Take a couple of deep breaths. Monitor your emotional state. If you are not feeling overwhelmed or emotionally numb, proceed. Remember, the goal is to focus on negative feelings without being overwhelmed by them. If you don't feel overwhelmed, through reflection, elaborate on the memory by adding context from the past (any historical reasons related to this negative experience), from the present (has the situation changed since the incidence?), and related to the future (what are odds that the incident will recur?). Write about any meaning you can extract from the experience that is personally relevant to your well-being. Ask yourself if you can relate to the negative experience in a different way.
- If the open memories keep on disturbing you, using the process described here, try to recall any positive aspects that you might have overlooked at the time of the incident, due to stressful circumstances. Due to negativity biases, positive or adaptive aspects of the situation often escape our attention. Recall the details to explore if you overlooked any positives. You can also recall similar situations that may help you to spot overlooked positives.
- Going forward, in stressful or negative situations, try distraction as discussed in the practice of *Positive Appraisal*. Although distraction is not always easy to do, try to shift your focus to a moderately complex cognitive task that engages you (like reading or baking your favorite chocolate cake).

END-OF-SESSION RELAXATION

We recommend that each session end with the same brief relaxation practice that started the session.

RESOURCES

Readings

- Ayduk, Ö., & Kross, E. (2010). From a distance: Implications of spontaneous self-distancing for adaptive self-reflection. *Journal of Personality and Social Psychology, 98*(5), 809–829. doi:10.1037/a0019205
- Denkova, E., Dolcos, S., & Dolcos, F. (2015). Neural correlates of 'distracting' from emotion during autobiographical recollection. *Social Cognitive and Affective Neuroscience, 10*(2), 219–230. doi:10.1093/scan/nsu039
- Huffziger, S., & Kuehner, C. (2009). Rumination, distraction, and mindful self-focus in depressed patients. *Behaviour Research and Therapy, 47*(3), 224–230. doi:10.1016/j.brat.2008.12.005
- Joormann, J., Hertel, P. T., Brozovich, F., & Gotlib, I. H. (2005). Remembering the good, forgetting the bad: intentional forgetting of emotional material in depression. *Journal of Abnormal Psychology, 114*(4), 640–648. doi:10.1037/0021-843X.114.4.640
- Messias, E., Saini, A., Sinato, P., & Welch, S. (2010). Bearing grudges and physical health: Relationship to smoking, cardiovascular health and ulcers. *Social Psychiatry and Psychiatric Epidemiology, 45*(2), 183–187.
- Redondo, R. L., Kim, J., Arons, A. L., Ramirez, S., Liu, X., & Tonegawa, S. (2014). Bidirectional switch of the valence associated with a hippocampal contextual memory engram. *Nature, 513*, 426–430. doi:10.1038/nature13725

Videos

- A role-play demonstration about dealing with negative memories and grudges:
  http://www.webmd.com/mental-health/features/forgive-forget
- Cognitive restructuring in cognitive behavioral therapy, a video from the Beck Institute for Cognitive Therapy:
  https://youtu.be/orPPdMvaNGA
- Quiet Positive Distractions—Explained by Crabtree Innovations:
  https://youtu.be/GhMaliATDNI
- Author and therapist Paul Gilbert explores how awareness of how our own minds work can help break negative thought patterns and help us to become more compassionate:
  https://youtu.be/pz9Fr_v9Okw

Websites

- MIT Technology Review: Repairing Bad Memories, June 17, 2013:
  http://www.technologyreview.com/featuredstory/515981/repairing-bad-memories/
- The Science of Happiness—An Experiment in Gratitude:
  https://youtu.be/oHv6vTKD6lg?list=PL373A068F767AD185

## 12

SESSION SIX: FORGIVENESS

SESSION SIX TEACHES THAT FORGIVENESS IS A process for change rather than an event. This session explains what forgiveness is and what it is not. The central positive psychotherapy (PPT) practices covered in this session are *REACH*, which is an approach to forgiveness, and writing a *Forgiveness Letter.*

SESSION SIX OUTLINE

Core Concepts
    In-Session Practice: *REACH*
    Reflection & Discussion
    A Second Practice: The *Forgiveness Letter*
    Reflection & Discussion
    Vignettes
    Fit & Flexibility
    Cultural Considerations
    Maintenance
Resources

CORE CONCEPTS

Forgiveness is a process of change rather than an event. It is a process of decreasing negative resentment-based emotions, motivations, and cognitions (Worthington, 2005). Clients willingly decide not to seek revenge and instead offer the offending person their kindness and compassion.

Rather than becoming locked into a cycle of hatred; harboring grudges; and dwelling on open, negative memories, forgiveness offers clients an alternative to revenge. Grudge-collecting is an ongoing and often complicated emotional process, marked by hostility, residual anger, fearfulness, and depression (Worthington & Wade, 1999). Forgiveness asks clients to make an informed choice by changing their relationship to the past from a destructive to a constructive one (McCullough et al., 2014).

Forgiveness aids psychological healing through positive change in affect, improves physical and mental health, restores a victim's sense of personal power, helps bring about reconciliation between offended and offender, and promotes hope for the resolution of real-world intergroup conflicts (Cornish & Wade, 2015; Fehr, Gelfand, & Nag, 2010; Toussaint & Webb, 2005; Van Tongeren et al., 2014).

Forgiveness may give the impression of many things, but it is important for clients to understand that forgiveness does *not* mean (Enright & Fitzgibbons, 2015; Worthington, Witvliet, Pietrini, & Miller, 2007):

- Pardoning the offender;
- Relaxing the demands for justice through socially acceptable means;
- Forgetting the wrong;
- Condoning and excusing (putting up with an offense or letting go of the offense);
- Justifying—that is, starting to believe that what the offender did was right;
- Assuming that time will heal;

- Ignoring the natural consequences of the offense by replacing negative thoughts or emotions with neutral or positive ones;
- Balancing the scales—that is, getting back at the offender by doing something else.

Comparable to the notions described here, in the context of PPT, forgiveness is a psychological skill that clients can use, in addition to *Positive Appraisal*, in order to deal with negative memories, emotional wounds, and hurts.

START-OF-SESSION RELAXATION

At the start of every session, begin with a brief relaxation exercise. Refer to Appendix A: Relaxation & Mindfulness Practices, which can be found at the end of this manual. A copy of this appendix also appears in the client workbook. Continue the session with a review of the client's *Gratitude Journal* as well as a review of the core concepts taught in the previous session.

IN-SESSION PRACTICE: *REACH*
How to Forgive?
Worthington (2006) suggests a five-step process (albeit not an easy or quick one) that he calls ***REACH***.

Clinician Note

While going through the REACH steps with your clients, ask them to respond to each step using Worksheet 6.1: REACH. Note that this and all worksheets (a) appear within the corresponding session of this manual, (b) are reprinted for the client in the accompanying client workbook, and (c) can be downloaded from the companion website at www.oup.com/ppt.

SUGGESTED SCRIPT FOR THE CLINICIAN
The following is a script you can use to introduce the *REACH* steps to your clients:

We are going to begin a practice about forgiveness. This practice is called REACH, and I would like you to go through each step, in sequence. This will require a substantial amount of time and effort, but given the enormous benefits it may bring as you complete these steps, I would suggest giving this practice a serious try. Please do not hesitate to discuss this if needed—even when we have moved on to other topics.

*Step One: **R = Recall** an event: You can close your eyes if you feel comfortable. Think of a person who hurt you, and you continue to feel the ill effect of the hurt. Do not wallow in self-pity. Take deep, slow, and calming breaths as you visualize the event. (Allow clients two to three minutes.)*

Please open your eyes. In the spaces provided on Worksheet 6.1, describe the event, incident, or offense. You don't have to use actual names. You can use the person's initials or a pseudonym that you can remember.

*Step Two: **E = Empathize** from the perpetrator's point of view: When survival is being threatened, a perpetrator may hurt innocent people. Keep in mind that empathy is a key ingredient of forgiveness. Empathy involves identifying* *emotionally and experientially with the other—without evaluating. To help you do this, remember the following:*

- *When others feel their survival is threatened, they may hurt innocent people.*
- *People who attack others are themselves usually in a state of fear, worry, and hurt.*
- *The situation people find themselves in—not necessarily their underlying personalities—can lead to hurting.*
- *People often don't think when they hurt others; they just lash out.*

Step Two is not easy to accomplish, but try to make up a plausible story that the perpetrator might tell if challenged to justify his or her actions. In the spaces provided on Worksheet 6.1, please write down what you think your offender was thinking.

Step Three: A = Altruistic *gift of forgiveness: This is another difficult step. First, recall a time when you transgressed, felt guilty, and were forgiven. This was a gift you were given by another person because you needed it, and you were grateful for this gift. In the spaces provided on Worksheet 6.1, please write a description of the event.*

Step Four: C = Commit *yourself to forgive publicly: Ways to forgive yourself publicly include writing a "certificate of forgiveness," writing a letter of forgiveness, writing it in your diary, writing a poem or song, or telling a trusted friend what you have done. These are all contracts of forgiveness that lead to the final step in the REACH process. Of these, which contract are you willing to undertake publicly to express your commitment to forgiveness? In the spaces provided, write how you would like to publicly show your commitment to forgiveness.*

Step Five: H = Hold *onto forgiveness: This is another difficult step because memories of the event will certainly recur. Forgiveness is not erasure; rather it is a change in the tag lines that a memory carries. It is important to realize that the memories do not mean that you have not forgiven that person. Don't dwell vengefully on the memories, and don't allow yourself to wallow in them. Remind yourself that you have forgiven, and read the document you composed in Step Four.*

On the lines provided on Worksheet 6.1, please list things that may help you to hold on to your forgiveness as well as things that may interfere with or weaken your resolve to hold on to forgiveness.

Step One: *R = Recall* *an event:* You can close your eyes if you feel comfortable. Think of a person who hurt you and you continue to feel the ill effect of the hurt. Do not wallow in self-pity. Take deep, slow, and calming breaths as you visualize the event. When you are ready, open your eyes, and in the following spaces, describe the event, incident, or offense. You don't have to use actual names. You can use the person's initials or a pseudonym that you can remember.

_____

_____

_____

_____

_____

Step Two: *E = Empathize* *from the perpetrator's point of view:* When survival is being threatened, a perpetrator may hurt innocent people. Keep in mind that *empathy* is a key ingredient of forgiveness. Empathy involves identifying emotionally and experientially with the other—without evaluating. To help you do this, remember the following:

• When others feel their survival is threatened, they may hurt innocent people.
• People who attack others are themselves usually in a state of fear, worry, and hurt.
• The situation people find themselves in—not necessarily their underlying personalities—can lead to hurting.
• People often don't think when they hurt others; they just lash out.

Step Two is not easy to accomplish, but try to make up a plausible story that the perpetrator might tell if challenged to justify his or her actions. In the following spaces, please write down what you think your offender was thinking.

_____

_____

_____

_____

_____

Step Three: *A = Altruistic* *gift of forgiveness:* This is another difficult step. First, recall a time when you transgressed, felt guilty, and were forgiven. This was a gift you were given by another person because you needed it, and you were grateful for this gift. In the following spaces, please write a description of the event.

_____

_____

_____

_____

_____

Step Four: *C = Commit* *yourself to forgive publicly:* Ways to forgive yourself publicly include writing a "certificate of forgiveness," writing a letter of forgiveness, writing it in your diary, writing a poem or song, or telling a trusted friend what you have done. These are all contracts of forgiveness that lead to the final step in the *REACH* process. Of these, which contract are you willing to undertake publicly to express your commitment to forgiveness? In the following spaces, write how you would like to publicly show your commitment to forgiveness.

_____

_____

_____

_____

_____

Step Five: *H = Hold* *onto forgiveness:* This is another difficult step because memories of the event will certainly recur. Forgiveness is not erasure; rather it is a change in the tag lines that a memory carries. It is important to realize that the memories do not mean that you have not forgiven that person. Don't dwell vengefully on the memories, and don't allow yourself to wallow in them. Remind yourself that you have forgiven, and read the document you composed in Step Four.

Then in the following spaces, list things that may help you to hold on to your forgiveness as well as things that may interfere with or weaken your resolve to hold on to forgiveness.

List things that may help you to hold on to your forgiveness:

1. _____

2. _____

3. _____

List things that may interfere with or weaken your resolve to hold on to forgiveness:

1. _____

2. _____

3. _____

Encourage your clients to clarify any questions they may have about implementing *REACH*.

REFLECTION & DISCUSSION

If clients are able to attempt or complete the *REACH* practice, encourage them to learn the process of forgiveness through the following questions:

- How honestly and thoroughly were you able to follow the *REACH* practice?
- During the steps outlined, did anger, disappointment, and/or hostility arise? If you felt any of these emotions, what specific step of the practice, or anything else, helped you to keep moving forward?
- Which step of the practice did you find most difficult?
- If you can you anticipate any experience that could derail your resolve to forgive, what might it be?
- Some people forgive but don't act in a forgiving way. How would you describe your forgiveness?
- How would you compare superficial forgiveness with genuine forgiveness?
- If you feel that you could not forgive fully at this point, what might help you achieve a greater level of forgiveness?

A SECOND PRACTICE: THE *FORGIVENESS LETTER*

REACH may take some time to achieve, and PPT also offers a second practice of forgiveness, as described in Worksheet 6.2.

WORKSHEET 6.2   WRITING A *FORGIVENESS LETTER*

For this practice, think of people who have wronged you in the past and who you have never explicitly forgiven. Which of these experiences persist in your memory and generate negative emotions from which you would like to free yourself? Choose one person you would like to forgive, and write a letter of forgiveness to that person. Do not mail the letter—this practice is for you, not for him or her. You may even write to a person no longer living.

In the letter describe in concrete terms how you were wronged by this person. How were you affected by the original transgression? How have you continued to be hurt by the memory of the event? Be sure to end with an explicit declaration of forgiveness.

To consolidate this practice, consider two further options:

1. *You can design a ceremony in which you symbolically forgive the perpetrator/ transgressor and get rid of your rage or bitterness. For example, you may read the letter out loud (to yourself) and then bury it in the backyard or place it in a special envelope and seal it.*
2. *If you would like to continue your work on forgiveness, keep a Forgiveness Journal. In this journal, record those instances when painful memories of past wrongdoing intrude into the present. Reflect on how your life might be different if you were free of the anger and resentment that accompanies these memories. Use your journal to write forgiveness letters or briefer forgiveness declarations as needed.*

REFLECTION & DISCUSSION

After completing this practice, ask clients to reflect and discuss:

- Writing about difficult memories and difficult situations, although challenging, is eventually therapeutic. In what ways was this process therapeutic for you?
- What was the most difficult part of writing this letter?
- In what ways is the writing process different from just holding onto the memories of the offense in your head?

VIGNETTE: LIA AND HER *FORGIVENESS LETTER*

As noted, in addition to the practice of *REACH*, clients can write a *Letter of Forgiveness*. Clients can be asked to complete a draft forgiveness letter in session and then to rewrite the letter later in the week. Below is a final version of such a letter written by one of our clients, Lia, a female in her mid-20s. (Note that Lia wrote her Letter of Forgiveness but did not deliver it. In this specific case, Lia, wrote a forgiveness letter to her deceased father.)

My Dearest Daddy,

May God rest your soul and may he grant you his endless kindness on the other side. I've written you a letter, Daddy, in the hope that it brings both of us peace and to enable me to clear some space in my heart so I can fill it with more love for you.

Daddy, you may not know this, as I've never vocalized these thoughts to you, but I want you to know that I forgive you for not making Mama, my two sisters, and me a constant priority on your responsibility list. I know you held nothing but love and pride for us in your heart, but sometimes actions don't necessarily translate into intentions, and because of my knowledge of that, I am able today, to say with a smile, that I forgive you.

You see, for as long as I could remember, I wondered why your preference in spending your money and at times your time was always outwardly focused towards others while we, your family, were always left starved and devoid of attention. As a little girl, I remember my embarrassment every school year, when at some point or other, we were escorted out of the building because our fees weren't paid. As a teenager that embarrassment turned into anger every time I saw my mother collect our belongings in black garbage bags because we were evicted from our house yet again. I was angry a lot of the time back then and turned very quiet. I internalized all of my emotions and frustrations and, in a way, started breeding an animal of negativity that made its home in my chest for many years.

I remember a point in my late teens when I decided that the life we were living was not a healthy one. I knew you had been in jail a few times before, but no one ever clearly told me this. I knew very well that we couldn't afford basic meals, or running water and electricity because you were unable to plan our lives efficiently. I also knew that your sisters and their families in Sudan were living a much better life than we were, because you supported them fully. I knew.

That animal I started breeding in my chest years before had turned into a well-fed 10-foot monster that was ready to devour anything in its way. For so long, I only knew how to expect the worst from you. I was certain that bills would never get paid, respect to my mother would never be shown, and the saddest part was that I was sure that your tyranny and anger would turn towards my sisters and me.

In spite of all of that, I forgive you—as I have been forgiven by those who I have wronged or misjudged in my life. I am able to reflect and relive certain scenarios where I was the perpetrator and the other person was able to see through my wrongdoing and grant me their forgiveness. Those are the relationships that today make me a better person and a more grounded contributor. Being forgiven by someone else represents a dear gift that is handed to me, and today I'd like to hand you that gift of forgiveness.

What I forgot to mention to you earlier is that alongside the dark monster there was a creature of light and love residing in my heart that grew larger every time I heard your voice or saw your face. I'm grateful for the light that allowed me to see that you are like anyone else who may have never received wisdom on how to cherish your wife and children but knew how to care for your siblings who you grew up with. That particular characteristic of yours is the reason why you will always be the most generous person I have ever known. Where that generosity is delivered is not the central point, but rather your ability to give unconditionally.

It has been a challenging ride for my rational, analytical brain to come to peace with who you are. Until now, and I assume for years to come, I will wonder what drove you to prioritize others. I may wonder, but I will never judge you again.

It has been *five* years since we buried you, and there isn't a day that passes without me being grateful for you being my father and for all the wonderful things you instilled in me: your love for education, your rebellion against the status quo, your sensitive heart that you hid behind mountains of rocks, and most of all, your pride. As an adult, I choose to live the best parts of you and to consciously remember attributes that I will fight against acquiring. You will always be my father and I will always love you.

Rest well my dear Daddy.
Your daughter and confidant,
Lia

Clinician Note

PPT recommends that the Forgiveness Letter is written but not necessarily delivered. Clients need to evaluate whether delivering the letter is appropriate at the time and for the person it is intended. Clients should be made aware of the possibility of an angry or otherwise emotional reaction from the target of the Forgiveness Letter.

VIGNETTE: KYU MEIN

Kyu Mein, a 27-year-old male, sought therapy for persistent depressive and social anxiety symptoms. During the course of therapy, he reported having resentment toward his uncle who physically abused him by applying pressure to his chest when Kyu Mein was very young. The client has been holding on to this resentment ever since. Kyu Mein tried to use *REACH* to forgive his uncle, but it didn't work for him. The clinician suggested that Kyu Mein listen to a podcast on dealing with anger and resentment in different ways. After listening to the podcast, Kyu Mein stated that he doesn't have to forgive his uncle. He said, "I can be compassionate towards him. I can give him the gift of my compassion. And my being compassionate doesn't mean I need to forgive him."

FIT & FLEXIBILITY

Clients may be angry for any number of reasons, including poor living conditions, impoverished neighborhoods, and racial discrimination. The *REACH* practice and the Forgiveness Letter, however, are not aimed at addressing social conditions. Clients may want to work on injuries perpetrated by a specific person, but these might be rooted in a wider social context (e.g., discrimination based on race, sexual orientation, ability, or ethnicity). PPT doesn't speak to people as representatives of groups that may hold historical grievances (e.g., a radicalized minority that has been historically mistreated, such as Blacks or Indigenous Americans). Nonetheless, without involving others, PPT can help clients experience forgiveness as a unilateral process; that is, clients can gain from forgiveness without expecting an apology or acknowledgment from the offender.

Sometimes the process of forgiveness is not effective, as clients are trying to forgive something that should not be forgiven, such as abuse, gross and repeated violation of one's rights, or offenses that hurt the client but the actual victim may be someone else.

Maintaining forgiveness depends on the client's personality and the acuteness of symptoms. For example, maintaining forgiveness for a client with acute or resurfaced symptoms of a trauma or with severe symptoms of depression may be difficult. The following are two examples from our practice: (a) Lien forgave a family member for the emotional abuse he had inflicted on her for years. This abuse had left Lien with chronic symptoms of depression and anxiety. At a family gathering, a small skirmish reignited Lien's bitter memories of abuse, and all her forgiveness vanished. She now hates the family member even more than before. (b) Instead of moving through the forgiveness process, Francesca started blaming the offender online. A strong retaliation from the offender has now made the situation worse.

Clients with unresolved trauma may resort to forgiveness as a way to move on. Help such clients understand that forgiveness is a unique process and is distinct from processes that may sound like forgiveness but which are not. As long as clients are ready to engage in the process with an open mind, the process may result in forgiveness, or it may not.

> **Clinician Note**
> *It is not advisable for clients to use forgiveness for every offense. Offenses may need to be discussed with you, and the person forgiving frequently should be cautioned about what Michael McCullough (2008, p. 87) calls becoming "everybody's doormat." Revisit the skills of practical wisdom (see Chapter 9, Session 3 in this manual) with such clients.*

CULTURAL CONSIDERATIONS

Cultural, religious, and familial expectations and explanations can facilitate or inhibit forgiveness in numerous ways. For example, cultural expectations may encourage forgiveness for social desirability to appease family or clan. Make sure that the client is able to find ways to reconcile any possible conflicts. In some cultural communities, forgiveness is conceptualized as a process that is not, in fact, forgiveness. It may be pardoning, relaxing the demands for justice, forgetting, ignoring, or forcibly normalizing the offense.

The cultural context may offer a different meaning to forgiveness, which may or may not work for clients. Help them understand what forgiveness is and what it is not. For example, one of our clients assumed that God had taken revenge on her behalf when the person who offended her got into a terrible situation. Another client accepted an unrelated explanation from the person who offended him and subsequently forgave her, only to re-experience a similar offense from the same person less than a year later.

MAINTENANCE

Discuss the following tips with your clients so that they can maintain their progress:

- Maintenance of forgiveness may depend on whether the perpetrator refrains from future offenses, especially if you and the offender are likely to see each other in the future. Solicited, weak, and insincere apologies may give the impression of forgiveness, but they may be insufficient to maintain forgiveness.

- If you are unable to forgive and continue to hold on to open and negative memories or grudges, note that those who hold grudges are likely to develop hypertension and have higher rates of heart disease, high blood pressure, heart attacks, and chronic pain. Choosing forgiveness is beneficial for your overall well-being.

- To maintain forgiveness, periodically review the five *REACH* steps (shown on Worksheet 6.1) and reaffirm your commitment, preferably with a trusted confidant.

- To maintain forgiveness or to extend its benefits, make a list of individuals against whom you hold a grudge, and then either meet them personally to discuss it or visualize how you can apply *REACH* with them. Don't forget to put the original offense into its proper context and perspective.

- You may initially forgive an offense or offender but may not be able to maintain the forgiveness and may, in fact, resort to passive means of maintaining the grudge, offense, or hurt. Therefore it is important to go through the forgiveness process for lasting change.

END-OF-SESSION RELAXATION

We recommend that each session end with the same brief relaxation practice that started the session.

RESOURCES

Readings

- Baskin, T. W., & Enright, R. D. (2004). Intervention studies on forgiveness: A meta-analysis. *Journal of Counseling and Development, 82*, 79–80.
- Harris, A. H. S., Luskin, F., Norman, S. B., Standard, S., Bruning, J., Evans, S., & Thoresen, C. E. (2006). Effects of a group forgiveness intervention on forgiveness, perceived stress, and trait-anger. *Journal of Clinical Psychology, 62*(6), 715–733. doi:10.1002/jclp.20264
- Pronk, T. M., Karremans, J. C., Overbeek, G., Vermulst, A. A., & Wigboldus, D. H. J. (2010). What it takes to forgive: When and why executive functioning facilitates forgiveness. *Journal of Personality and Social Psychology, 98*(1), 119–131. doi:10.1037/a0017875
- Worthington, E. L. Jr., & Wade, N. G. (1999). The psychology of unforgiveness and forgiveness and implications for clinical practice. *Journal of Social and Clinical Psychology, 18*, 385–418.

Videos

- TED Talk: The mothers who found forgiveness, friendship, one who lost a son on 9/11 and one whose son was convicted:
  https://www.ted.com/talks/9_11_healing_the_mothers_who_found_forgiveness_friendship
- Nelson Mandela: Message of Forgiveness—The Making Of Mandela:
  https://youtu.be/S2RyxVURHoY
- *Shawshank Redemption*: The moment when Red finally stands up to the system and asserts his own terms of redemption:
  https://youtu.be/KtwXlIwozog

Websites

- Psychologist Everett Worthington, a leader in the forgiveness research:
  http://www.evworthington-forgiveness.com/
- Ten Extraordinary Examples of Forgiveness:
  http://listverse.com/2013/10/31/10-extraordinary-examples-of-forgiveness/
- Valuable resources about forgiveness:
  www.forgiving.org/

Podcast

- A Better Way to Be Angry: advice from philosopher Martha Nussbaum:
  http://www.cbc.ca/radio/tapestry/anger-and-forgiveness-1.3997934/a-better-way-to-be-angry-advice-from-philosopher-martha-nussbaum-1.3997950

SESSION SEVEN: MAXIMIZING VERSUS SATISFICING

## 13

SESSION SEVEN PRESENTS THE CONCEPTS OF MAXIMIZING (aiming to make the best possible choice) and satisficing (making a "good enough" choice). The central positive psychotherapy (PPT) practice covered in this session is *Toward Satisficing*.

SESSION SEVEN OUTLINE

Core Concepts
    In-Session Practice: *Are You a Maximizer or a Satisficer?*
    Reflection & Discussion
    In-Session Practice: *Toward Satisficing*
    Reflection & Discussion
    Vignettes
    Fit & Flexibility
    Cultural Considerations
    Maintenance
Resources

CORE CONCEPTS

An essential part of our well-being includes exercising control over our environment and being able to produce desired outcomes. Availability of choices plays a critical role in exerting control and in shaping desired outcomes (Leotti et al., 2010). Despite having specific environmental barriers, we enjoy varying degrees of choices. Individuals use this choice in different ways. According to psychologist Barry Schwartz (2004), *maximizers* always aim to make the best possible choice, comparing products both before and after making purchasing decisions, and taking their time in deciding what to buy. They exert enormous effort reading labels, checking out consumer magazines, and trying new products. They also spend more time comparing their purchasing decisions with those of others. In contrast, *satisficers* aim for "good enough," whether or not better selections might be out there, and when an item meets their standards, they stop looking.

Schwartz (2004) argues that choices are a mixed blessing. It is difficult to gather adequate information about options needed to make a choice, and as our range of options expands, the standards of what is an acceptable outcome rise. (For example, walk down the aisle of many super markets today, and you will see a wide variety of breakfast cereals. How do you make a decision when there are so many choices?) As our options expand, we may come to believe that any unacceptable result is our fault, because with so many choices, we should be able to find the best one. Schwartz's research indicates that although maximizers are more likely to make better objective choices than satisficers, maximizers get less satisfaction from their choices. When they are asked to end the search and compromise, maximizers feel apprehensive. Schwartz found that the greatest maximizers are the least happy with their efforts. When compared to others, they get little pleasure from finding out that they did better and feel substantially more dissatisfaction when finding out that they did worse. They are also more prone to experiencing regret after a purchase, and if their purchase disappoints them, they take much longer to recover. Furthermore, maximizers tend to brood or ruminate more than do satisficers.

Maximizers are more prone to depression and perfectionism due to overly high expectations and self-fulfilling fears of regret. Perfectionists, like maximizers, seek to achieve the best, as both have very high standards. Perfectionists have high standards that they don't expect to meet, whereas maximizers have very high standards that they do expect to meet, and, when they are unable to meet them, they become depressed (Chowdhury, Ratneshwar, & Mohanty, 2009; Schwartz et al., 2002).

Our lives present us with a wide range of choices, from everyday decisions such as what to eat, what to wear, and what image to set as a desktop background to more important decisions such as who to date, which university to attend, what career to pursue, and where to move or buy a house. No matter how big or small, each choice reinforces our beliefs about control. However, Schwartz's research shows that too much choice, though it may sometimes produce a better decision, exacts a heavy price for the maximizer and underestimates the emotional impact of maximizing.

START-OF-SESSION RELAXATION

At the start of every session, begin with a brief relaxation exercise. Refer to Appendix A: Relaxation & Mindfulness Practices, which can be found at the end of this manual. A copy of this appendix also appears in the client workbook. Continue the session with a review of the client's *Gratitude Journal* as well as a review of the core concepts taught in the previous session.

IN-SESSION PRACTICE: *ARE YOU A MAXIMIZER OR A SATISFICER?*

Ask clients to complete Worksheet 7.1. This practice will help to assess if your client is a maximizer or a satisficer. Note that this and all worksheets (a) appear within the corresponding session of this manual, (b) are reprinted for the client in the accompanying client workbook, and (c) can be downloaded from the companion website at www.oup.com/ppt.

WORKSHEET 7.1   ARE YOU A MAXIMIZER OR A SATISFICER?

Using the following scale, please rate yourself and explore where you fall on the Satisficer–Maximizer continuum.[1]

1 – Completely disagree   2 – Disagree   3 – Somewhat Disagree
4 – Neutral   5 – Somewhat agree   6 – Agree   7 – Strongly Agree

	Statement	Response
1	Whenever I'm faced with a choice, I try to imagine what all the other possibilities are, even ones that aren't present at the moment.	
2	No matter how satisfied I am with my job, it's only right for me to be on the lookout for better opportunities.	
3	When I am in the car listening to the radio, I often check other stations to see if something better is playing, even if I am relatively satisfied with what I'm listening to.	
4	When I watch TV, I channel surf, often scanning through the available options even while attempting to watch one program.	
5	I treat relationships like clothing; I expect to try a lot on before I get the perfect fit.	
6	I often find it difficult to shop for a gift for a friend.	
7	Renting videos is really difficult. I am always struggling to pick the best one.	
8	When shopping, I have a hard time finding clothing that I really love.	
9	I'm a big fan of lists that attempt to rank things (the best movies, the best singers, the best athletes, the best novels, etc.).	
10	I find that writing is very difficult, even if it's just writing a letter to a friend, because it's so hard to word things just right. I often do several drafts of even simple things.	
11	No matter what I do, I have the highest standard for myself.	
12	I never settle for second best.	
13	I often fantasize about living in ways that are quite different from my actual life.	

After completing the worksheet, compute the total score (the sum of all 13 items). The average score on this scale is 50. The high score is 75 or above and the low is 25 or below. There are no gender differences. If you scored 65 or higher, then you have maximizing behaviors or habits that have adverse impact on your well-being. If you scored 40 or lower, you are on the satisficing end of the scale.

[1] Reprinted with permission. Schwartz et al., 2002.

REFLECTION & DISCUSSION

After completing this practice, ask clients to reflect and discuss:

- What does your score indicate about you?
- If you scored high (50 or higher), in what way will this awareness help you make some meaningful changes toward satisficing?
- If you scored high, how aware are you of the costs (economic, emotional, and physical) of maximizing?
- No one maximizes in all areas of life. In which do you maximize and in which do you satisfice? Please recall and compare your emotional reactions in both situations.
- Have you found yourself engaged in more product comparison than satisficers?
- Some people want to *have* choices, while others want to *make* choices. Which describes you better?

IN-SESSION PRACTICE: *TOWARD SATISFICING*

The alternative to maximizing is satisficing. A satisficer has criteria and standards, but a satisficer is not worried about the possibility that there might be something better. Whether your clients generally maximize or satisfice, ask them to complete Worksheet 7.2: Ten Ways to Increase Satisficing, which lists strategies derived from Barry Schwartz's work. Present these strategies with clients in session and help them write a personalized goal at the end of each strategy on the worksheet. Discuss how this goal can be reached both by maximizing and by satisficing and what might be the cost or benefit of each approach.

No.	Strategy
1	***Be a Chooser, Not a Picker:*** Choosers are people who are able to reflect on what makes a decision important, on whether, perhaps, none of the options should be chosen, on whether a new option should be created, and on what a particular choice says about the chooser as an individual. *You can be a Chooser, not a Picker in following areas:* • Shorten or eliminate deliberations about decisions that are unimportant to you. • Use some of the time you have freed up to ask yourself what you really want in the areas of your life where decisions matters. If none of the options work, you will try: _____ _____
2	***Satisfice More and Maximize Less:*** To embrace satisficing, you will try to: • Think about occasions in life when you settled comfortably for "good enough." • Scrutinize how you chose in those areas. • Apply that strategy more broadly. If these options don't work, you will try: _____ _____
3	***Think about the Opportunity Costs:*** You can avoid the disappointment that comes from thinking about opportunity costs by trying the following: • Unless you are truly dissatisfied, you will stick with what you usually buy. • You will resist being tempted by "new and improved." • You will adopt the attitude "don't scratch unless there is an itch." • You will not worry that you'll miss out on all the new things that the world has to offer. If these strategies don't work, you will try: _____ _____
4	***Make Your Decision Nonreversible:*** When a decision is final, we engage in a variety of psychological processes that enhance our feelings about the choice we made relative to alternatives. If a decision is reversible, we don't engage these processes to the same degree. List examples of your reversible decisions: a. _____ b. _____ c. _____ Now list nonreversible decisions you will make in the following areas of your life: a. _____ b. _____ c. _____

No.	Strategy
5	*Practice an "Attitude of Gratitude"*: You can vastly improve your subjective experience by consciously striving to be grateful more often for what is good about a choice and to be disappointed less by what is bad about it. You will practice an attitude of gratitude about your following choices: a. _____ b. _____ c. _____
6	*Regret Less:* The sting of regret (either actual or potential) colors many decisions and sometimes influences us to avoid making decisions at all. Although regret is often appropriate and instructive, when it becomes so pronounced that it poisons or even prevents decisions, you can make an effort to minimize it. You will lessen regret by trying to: • Adopt the standards of a satisficer rather than a maximizer. • Reduce the number of options you consider before making a decision. • Focus on what is good in a decision rather than focusing on your disappointments with what is bad. If these strategies don't work, you will try: _____ _____
7.	*Anticipate Adaptation:* We regularly adapt to almost everything we experience. In tough times, adaptation enables us to avoid the full brunt of the hardship; in good times, adaptation puts us on a "hedonic treadmill," robbing us of the full measure of satisfaction we expect from each positive experience. We can't prevent adaptation. You will develop realistic expectations about how experiences change with time: • If you buy a new gadget, you will be aware that the thrill won't last beyond two months. • You will spend less time looking for the perfect thing (maximizing), so that you won't have huge search costs to be "amortized" against the satisfaction you derive from what you choose. • You will remind yourself of how good things actually are instead of focusing on how they're less good than they were at first. If these strategies don't work, you will try: _____ _____
8	*Control Expectations:* Our evaluation of experience is substantially influenced by how it compares with our expectations. So what may be the easiest route to increasing satisfaction with the results of decisions is to lower excessively high expectations about them. To make the task of lowering expectations easier, you will: • Reduce the number of options you will consider. • Be a satisficer rather than a maximizer. • Allow for serendipity. If these strategies don't work, you will try: _____ _____

No.	Strategy
9	***Curtail Social Comparison:*** We evaluate the quality of our experiences by social comparisons. Although useful, this often reduces our satisfaction. You will try the following: • You will remember that "He who dies with the most toys wins" is a bumper sticker, not wisdom. • You will focus on what makes you happy and what gives meaning to your life. If these strategies don't work, you will try: _____ _____
10	***Learn to Love Constraints:*** As choices increase, freedom of choice eventually becomes a tyranny of choice. Routine decisions take so much time and attention that it becomes difficult to get through the day. In many circumstances, learn to view limits on possibilities as liberating, not constraining. Society provides rules, standards, and norms for making choices, and individual experience creates habits. By deciding to follow a rule (e.g., always wear a seat belt, never drink more than two glasses of wine in one evening), we avoid having to make a deliberate decision again and again. This kind of rule-following frees up time and attention that can be devoted to thinking about choices and decisions to which rules don't apply. You will follow these rules: a._____ b._____ c._____

[2] Schwartz (2004).

REFLECTION & DISCUSSION

After completing this practice, ask clients to reflect and discuss:

- Of the satisficing strategies discussed here, which ones are you able to implement relatively independently?
- Of the satisficing strategies discussed here, for which ones do you need cooperation or support from others to succeed?
- Some choices or decisions such as where to move, which job to take, or who to marry would benefit from maximizing. What areas in your life would benefit from maximizing?
- Maximizing behavior and decision-making often rely on outside validation, such as something being highly ranked, recommended by experts, socially desirable, or favored or followed by many. Does your decision making depend on these types of measures?

VIGNETTE: JESSIE AND HIS SAUCONYS

The following excerpt is from one of our clients, Jessie, who describes his understanding of maximizing and satisficing after these concepts were discussed in detail during one-on-one therapy.

"Last week a thin slice of sock began revealing itself through a hole in my shoe. I had put it off long enough; it was time to buy another pair. So I googled 'buy running shoes,' and suddenly had 27,000 shoe stores to choose from. Surely I'd find the perfect pair. But maybe it's not so great to have thousands of footwear options. Considering many choices, and having to forego many attractive features of things not chosen, causes regret. I love my new shoes, but there are Nike aeration and cushioning features that my new Sauconys aren't equipped with. The more choices available, the more desirable features I can regret passing up."

VIGNETTE: ANASTASIA AND HER TRIPS TO THE MALL

Anastasia, a senior in college with symptoms of anxiety, describes the experience of using one of the satisficing strategies:

"Before completing the exercise, I would go to the mall to buy clothes. I would spend a lot time going from store to store, looking at similar items in the same price range. I would take pictures on my cell, compare the items with online options . . . and eventually I would make the purchase. . . . But then at home, soon my mind would dwell on the imperfections of my purchase, and I would return the items. . . . It was a constant cycle of search, purchase, and return; search, purchase, and return. Last weekend, I deliberately went out of my way, to the furthest outlet mall, and I purchased sale items that are not returnable. When I came home, I felt a strange sense of closure."

FIT & FLEXIBILITY

Some clients who score high on the maximizing dimension may merely be high achievers who have more success and superior credentials, and they have learned to expect more from themselves. Therefore, it is important to go beyond the scores and explore whether the client is a maximizer or a high achiever or both.

It is also important to understand the interaction between the client's personality and maximizing/satisficing. For example, clients with good analytical abilities coupled with an abiding sense of curiosity may be more likely to maximize than clients who have strengths such as agreeableness, humility, and gratitude. These strengths seem to be more linked with satisficing than with maximizing.

CULTURAL CONSIDERATIONS

Maximizing can also be a behavioral strategy learned from a client's family of origin. For example, in a family that has emigrated from impoverished economic conditions to a Western society that abounds in material goods and opportunities, maximizing can be a process of acculturation for the family. That is, before making any decision, the family wants to explore all options, as this process enables them to acculturate.

Before immigrating to an affluent Western country, if a family from a diverse cultural background experienced severe economic hardship, such as famine, war, or other trauma, maximizing tendencies can be a way to alleviate anxiety about the possibility of a potential future disaster.

Some families or individuals go to great lengths to find the best and least expensive deal not because they are maximizing but rather because they need to survive on a tight budget.

Some immigrant families, especially those with parents who work hard to ensure a brighter academic or professional future for their children, tend to live vicariously through their children. They fear that in order to realize the "American Dream," their children have to excel in all domains. Therefore, they strongly "encourage" their children to maximize every opportunity. For a few other well-accomplished, high-achieving families, the maximizing tendencies instilled in children are, in part, due to the fear that the children have to maximize opportunities in order to maintain the socioeconomic social standing, especially in their cultural communities.

A recent graduate or a newly laid off worker applying for dozens of jobs is less likely to satisfice and more likely to maximize while looking for a survival job.

MAINTENANCE

In addition to the strategies highlighted in Worksheet 7.2, discuss the following tips with your clients so that they can maintain their progress:

- Maximizers are more likely to engage in social comparisons, especially to assess standards, and evaluate the relative status of their own experiences or possessions. To promote satisficing, rather than relying on external standards, develop your own anchors, that is, your own internal standards.
- To promote satisficing, savor experiences. Rather than trying to cultivate many experiences of very high quality (high in pleasure value), try to keep such experiences relatively rare and exclusive. This will thwart adaptation, and you will be less prone to up the ante after every pleasurable experience.
- By exploring a large number of options, maximizers tend to believe that they can control many areas of their lives—from their education to their employment and from selecting partners to creating social identities. However, research shows that the net gain (in terms of additional information) has little or no impact on the outcome (Schwartz et al., 2002). In other words, the pursuit to control or manage a perfect outcome gives maximizers the impression that they are in control, but the result is almost inconsequential. Also, all of the effort used to manage the control process deprives maximizers of enjoying the process.

END-OF-SESSION RELAXATION

We recommend that each session end with the same brief relaxation practice that started the session.

RESOURCES

Reading

- Jain, K., Bearden, J. N., & Filipowicz, A. (2013). Do maximizers predict better than satisficers? *Journal of Behavioral Decision Making, 26*(1), 41–50. doi:10.1002/bdm.763
- Kahneman, D., & Tversky, A. (1984). Choices, values, and frames. *American Psychologist, 39,* 341–350.
- Schwartz, B. (2004). *The Paradox of Choice: Why More Is Less.* New York: Ecco/HarperCollins.
- Schwartz, B., Ward, A., Monterosso, J., Lyubomirsky, S., White, K., & Lehman, D. R. (2002). Maximizing versus satisficing: Happiness is a matter of choice. *Journal of Personality and Social Psychology, 83*(5), 1178–1197. doi:10.1037/0022-3514.83.5.1178

Videos

- TED Talk: Barry Schwartz, author of *The Paradox of Choice,* discusses how more choices paralyze us and deplete our happiness:
  https://www.ted.com/talks/barry_schwartz_on_the_paradox_of_choice
- TED Talk: Shyeena Iynger discusses how people choose and what makes us think that we are good at it:
  https://www.ted.com/speakers/sheena_iyengar
- TED Talk: Dan Gilbert discusses how our beliefs of what makes us happy are often wrong:
  http://www.ted.com/talks/dan_gilbert_researches_happiness
- To assess if you are maximize or satisficer, take a free online test:
  http://www.nicholasreese.com/decide/

Websites

- Elizabeth Bernstein: How You Make Decisions Says a Lot About How Happy You Are "Maximizers" Check All Options, "Satisficers" Make the Best Decision Quickly: Guess Who's Happier? (*The Wall Street Journal*):
  http://www.wsj.com/articles/how-you-make-decisions-says-a-lot-about-how-happy-you-are-1412614997

SESSION EIGHT: GRATITUDE

14

SESSION EIGHT, WHICH IS THE FINAL SESSION in Phase Two of positive psychotherapy (PPT), expands the concept of gratitude—which was first introduced in Session One in the form of the *Gratitude Journal*. Session Eight facilitates recalling and writing to someone who is alive now and who in the past did something positive but who the client has never fully thanked. The PPT practices covered in this session are the *Gratitude Letter* and *Gratitude Visit*.

SESSION EIGHT OUTLINE

Core Concepts
    In-Session Practices: *Gratitude Letter* and *Gratitude Visit*
    Reflection & Discussion
    Vignettes
    Fit & Flexibility
    Cultural Considerations
    Maintenance
Resources

CORE CONCEPTS

The following core concepts are identical to those presented in Chapter 7, Session One, where we introduced the *Gratitude Journal*.

Gratitude is an experience of thankfulness, which entails noticing and appreciating the positive things in life. In doing so, we acknowledge the value and meaning of positives. Gratitude broadens perspective and builds other positive emotions and positive reasoning (Emmons, 2007).

Clinically depressed individuals show significantly lower gratitude (nearly 50% less gratitude) than nondepressed controls (Watkins, Grimm, & Kolts, 2004). In fact, gratitude can protect clients against bouts of depression (Tsang, 2006; Wood et al., 2008).

Gratitude prompts clients to reframe negative experiences as positive whenever appropriate and realistic. This reframing in turn is associated with fewer psychological symptoms (Lambert, Fincham, & Stllman, 2012). Learning to be more grateful through sustained practices such as maintaining a *Gratitude Journal* can help clients to learn and use more positive coping strategies, which lower stress (Wood, Joseph, & Linley, 2007).

START-OF-SESSION RELAXATION

At the start of every session, begin with a brief relaxation exercise. Refer to Appendix A: Relaxation & Mindfulness Practices, which can be found at the end of this manual. A copy of this appendix also appears in the client workbook. Continue the session with a review of the client's *Gratitude Journal* as well as a review of the core concepts taught in the previous session.

IN-SESSION PRACTICES: *GRATITUDE LETTER AND GRATITUDE VISIT*

SUGGESTED SCRIPT FOR THE CLINICIAN

The following is a script you can use to introduce the *Gratitude Letter* to your clients:

Sit in a comfortable position with your arms resting on your thighs and your head, neck, and chest in a relaxed straight line. Your feet are resting flat on the floor.

Pay attention to your breathing; notice when you inhale and exhale, when your chest expands and contracts. Gently bring your breath into your belly. Repeat this cycle. Inhale and exhale 10 times, on your own count, quietly.

Continue repeating this breathing cycle. Try to make each breath in and out last for 10 seconds. Start over after each count.

Close your eyes. Call up the face of someone still alive who years ago did something that changed your life for the better, someone who you never properly thanked; someone you could meet face-to-face next week or so. Got a face? (From Flourish, Seligman, 2012, p. 30)

Open your eyes and, without delay, turn to Worksheet 8.1 and please write a roughly 300-word letter to the person whose face you recalled. Express your thanks by saying in concrete terms whatever the person did that helped you. Don't worry about style or grammar; this is only the first draft. Honor your emotions and capture them as you recall them.

Note that this and all worksheets (a) appear within the corresponding session of this manual, (b) are reprinted for the client in the accompanying client workbook, and (c) can be downloaded from our companion website at www.oup.com/ppt.

Write your initial draft:

Dear _____

_____

_____

_____

_____

_____

_____

_____

_____

_____

_____

_____

_____

_____

_____

_____

After you have completed the draft letter, please continue this exercise at home, as instructed:

Gratitude Letter and *Gratitude Visit*

- *Please polish the Gratitude Letter you drafted in session. Write and rewrite it, describing in specific terms why you are grateful. The letter should specify what the person did for you and clearly explain exactly how this action affected your life. In the letter, tell the person what you are doing now and how you often remember his or her efforts.*
- *Once you have finished the final version of the letter, sign and laminate it, to signify its importance.*
- *Next, make a date to visit that person. Invite her or him to your home, or travel to that person's home.*
- *It is important that you complete the next step of this exercise face to face, not just in writing or by phone. Do not explain the purpose of the visit in advance; a simple "I just want to see you" is enough.*
- *Wine and cheese do not matter, but bring the laminated version of your testimonial with you as a gift. When you and the person are all settled down, read your testimonial aloud slowly, with expression, and with eye contact. Then let other person react unhurriedly. Reminisce together about the concrete events that make this person so important to you.*

> **Clinician Note**
>
> *The Gratitude Letter and Visit practice requires considerable effort and time to manage the logistics of arranging a visit. Therefore, provide clients adequate time to complete this practice over the course of therapy. Discuss the anticipated timeline for completing this exercise with clients, and periodically remind them to get this done.*
>
> *Encourage clients to read their Gratitude Letters in session as a dry run or rehearsal so that they can experience writing it and reading it out loud. This will help clients make any necessary changes to the Gratitude Letter, and, in group PPT, this will motivate other clients to follow suit. Make sure that clients also have the opportunity to share their experiences of the Gratitude Visit. If this practice is done in a group context, ask clients to complete this before the group ends.*

REFLECTION & DISCUSSION

After completing both the letter and visit, ask clients to reflect and discuss:

*   How did you feel as you wrote your letter?
*   What was the easiest part to write and what was the toughest part?
*   How did the other person react to your expression of gratitude? And how were you affected by their reaction?
*   How long did these feelings last after you presented your letter?
*   Did you recall the experience in the days that followed the reading of the letter? If so, how did this recollection affect your mood?

VIGNETTES

Following are three vignettes. The first two are from clients who completed PPT in group settings, while the third is a process note about the practice from a client seen in individual therapy. The first letter is the initial draft, written during the session. It is not known if the letter was delivered. The second vignette is a final letter, and it was delivered in person and read to the recipient in person.

VIGNETTE: INITIAL DRAFT OF A *GRATITUDE LETTER*

"Dear Sally,

This letter is to thank you, with genuine gratitude, for the loving acts you bestowed upon me during my high school years. At a time when I felt misunderstood, angry, and lonely, you offered me your compassionate ear and voice. The time you devoted to helping me, though it may seem small in your eyes, has had a big effect on the person I am constantly becoming. When others were trying to preach with words and advice, you taught me through action and care. Do you remember the time when you picked me up in your van and talked to me for over an hour while we sat on the side of the road? It may seem like a little gesture, but the words I am using to describe your actions here are hopelessly inadequate to explain the effect it had on me. You made me feel wanted and worth caring about, and this is the greatest gift you ever gave me. This letter is as much for me as it is for you: I truly am thankful for all you have done and I hope you can now appreciate how much it meant to me."

VIGNETTE: *GRATITUDE LETTER* AND *GRATITUDE VISIT*

The following illustrates a *Gratitude Letter* and *Gratitude Visit*. A 23-year-old female wrote this letter. During the course of individual therapy, this client brought the recipient of the letter to the therapy office and read the letter in the presence of the clinician and other members of the PPT group, with, of course, their consent.

"Dear Friend,

In life we are faced with events and stumble upon many people for reasons that might be so beyond our understanding. German poet Rainer Maria Rilke said, "Be patient toward all that is unsolved in your heart and try to love the questions themselves, do not now seek the answers which cannot be given to you because you would not be able to live them . . . and the point is to live everything. Live the questions now." I decided that even though I might not know entirely why my life circumstances have been the way they are, out of these circumstances I decided to take many chances over the course of the past few years and open myself up to changes. In particular, one of the most important changes and chances I have taken was with you, and I am writing you this letter as an attempt to show you the gratitude that is growing inside me every day.

"Boiling thankfulness down to specifics isn't an easy task when your realization of how much gratitude you have is enough to immerse you entirely, but I'll try. I want to thank you for quietly stepping into my life while I was feeling lost. You didn't expect to be noticed, but you were. I can't really fathom how much comfort I feel when you are around, my tension slowly wilts and I know that I am surrounded by care. Sometimes you build homes in people, and I made one in you, a nest of love and mutual joy.

"Thank you for bringing a refreshing change in a time where I felt that most of my life was turned upside down and things felt like they were caving in due to my unstable sense of self and long history of a resurfacing depression, invalidating environments, and affiliations with toxic people. You made me feel safe and wanted. The chaos that I silently endured, I could now share with you and I do. There is a particular ease one feels when they can reveal their stories, their truths (be it big or small), but even more so, their hurt. Awareness that suffering doesn't need to be immediately displaced nor suppressed is something very important that I have learned. Thank you for noticing and accepting that I am not a neatly wrapped package (as many would quickly assume). I am a person with desires and strengths (and weaknesses too), but you never let my weaknesses alter how you felt about me and who I am to you. Thank you for being there, daily, as I share my life with you.

"In particular, I want to thank you for helping me with the stepping stones on my journey to mental health. I want to thank you for holding my hand as I cross bridges into new territories of self-awareness but also for letting go when you knew it was needed. Thank you for not being idle and unresponsive when I go through my hardest times. After the few scariest and draining weeks of last year, leaving me at a terrifying edge, you were not afraid to point out to me the consequences of letting myself continuously go through breakdowns and episodes of sorts. You gave me honesty in how much you were able to help me get through my illnesses, and you pointed me to a different path of aid, that of therapy. You motivated me to stop putting up with years of silence, mistreatment towards myself, and abuse. You were a very big help in bringing me here to counseling, to group, to find safe spaces where it is okay to speak my mind. You accept my entirety (including my weaknesses and my illness) and even try to go beyond mere acceptance, by trying to understand (through continuous research of information on mental health and coping strategies.) You aren't afraid to show me the mirror of reality and endlessly tell me that there is something better for me, and that I deserve to treat myself the best that I can.

"I am growing continuously, and that doesn't mean my problems have dispersed entirely, actually it's quite the opposite. But I do know for a fact that I have gotten much better at accepting that some answers aren't always going to be so explicit and easy to figure out. Poet e. e. Cummings states, 'The eyes of my eyes are opened,' and that perfectly embodies how I feel in relation to gratitude, thank you."

VIGNETTE: IMPACT OF DELIVERING A GRATITUDE LETTER

"Dear Dr. Rashid,

I hope this note finds you doing well, as I'm writing to you regarding my *Gratitude Letter* and *Gratitude Visit*, which I was not able to do earlier but promised I would. Well, today was the day. . . . I was skeptical of this exercise, but a week ago I was really upset . . . same old stuff you know. I happened to receive a note from a person I least expected, and I changed, in fact that unexpected note made my day, and the effect lasted for several days. I thought that if a simple note could make me so happy, writing a *Gratitude Letter* to my half-sister would not hurt, and so I wrote it.

"Today I visited her—after many years—and shared my letter. Reading it aloud sounded very strange in the beginning and I wanted to get into it as soon as possible, but then, I went into some sort of a zone—a place of me I never knew I had. Soon, I forgot everything, and the letter and the person were all I could see and hear. . . . Reading the letter aloud was a little awkward in the beginning, overwhelming. Soon tears streamed down her eyes and tears were also in my eyes.

"Somehow without falling to pieces, I finished the letter. While writing it, I had felt as though I was not capturing its spirit. But reading it felt like . . .

"Afterward, I came to know, as much as she helped me, that the experience itself helped her tremendously as she was herself dealing with some serious personal issues. I am glad I did this."

FIT & FLEXIBILITY

- *The Gratitude Letter* and *Visit* is a powerful practice that can pose challenges for some clients. They may find writing and personally delivering the letter overwhelmingly awkward, and this practice could even make them feel vulnerable. Acknowledge these challenges, and allow such clients some flexibility: We strongly emphasize that clients personally deliver the letter. However, this may not be possible for a number of reasons (e.g., geographical distance, cost, or difficulty getting together one on one due to familial/social constraints). In such cases, the letter can be mailed with a request for the recipient to open it while the person expressing gratitude calls on the phone or is on a video chat. Alternatively, the letter can be mailed and can be followed up with a phone call or in-person chat.

- Some clients may have mixed emotions about the person they are writing to. Along with the deepfelt sense of gratitude, such clients may also feel resentment, anger, or even envy toward this person. This dynamic occurs frequently when the recipient of a *Gratitude Visit* is a close family member or a person with whom there is ongoing and frequent interaction. In such cases, remind the client that this is a *Gratitude Letter* and *Visit*, not an opportunity to settle a grudge. The intent of this practice is to focus exclusively on the positives, not on any negatives. We can experience both negative and positive emotions for the same person. Nevertheless, if clients are unable to keep negatives at bay in an adaptive manner, they ought to pick someone else.

- This practice may not work effectively if the recipient of the *Gratitude Letter* and *Visit* feels that gratitude is his or her right and privilege. By the same token, some clients may think that no one in their lives deserves this and that they themselves ought to be the recipient of gratitude. Other clients may state that an emotional expression is not necessary, as the person (to be thanked) already knows that they are grateful. Help such clients understand that fostering a positive and genuine expression of thankfulness further strengthens relationships.

- Instead of visiting, clients can also host a "gratitude night," inviting a guest who has been important in their lives and who they have not properly thanked or who has not been told how his or her help changed the life of the person expressing gratitude. Or clients can read their letter publicly. Clients can also choose a special occasion, such as a promotion, the receipt of an award or trophy, or recognition of a milestone, to publicly or privately thank the person who helped them achieve this honor.

- If the gratitude recipient is unavailable for any reason, including death, the good deed can be acknowledged by reading the *Gratitude Letter* in front of close friends and family members.

- Some clients may be going through difficult life circumstances that make it very hard for them to find something worth being grateful for. For these clients, gently encourage them to think of past accomplishments for which they are grateful; encourage them to remember those who helped them succeed. If they simply cannot do this practice authentically, then do not force them.

CULTURAL CONSIDERATIONS

The expression of gratitude can be different across cultures. Some people do not express gratitude through words or may not have the vocabulary to do so; as such, it may be difficult for these clients to capture their sentiments through writing. Allow them to express their gratitude however they are best able. Some clients may feel guilty while doing this practice, because they may feel bad for those around them who do not enjoy the luxuries they have.

Clients from diverse cultural backgrounds may also find this practice to be challenging; for such clients, modesty and prudence are more important and culturally relevant than gratitude. Furthermore, they may feel that the sanctity of the good deed would be diluted by the recalling and retelling. Explore with these clients how gratitude is expressed in their culture and how this practice can be tweaked to a culturally friendly perspective.

MAINTENANCE

Discuss the following tips with your clients so that they can maintain their progress:

- Socialize more with people who are grateful and less with those who are not. An emotion expressed within a group has a ripple effect and becomes shared by the group. Happy and grateful people have a contagious effect.

- The words we use create reality. Grateful people have a particular linguistic style. They use a language of gifts, giving, fortune, abundance, satisfaction, blessing, and blessedness. Ungrateful people use expressions of deprivation, regrets, lack, need, scarcity, and loss. The expressions of depressed people who are low in gratitude are somewhat similar and focus on the self, such as, "I am a loser," and "no one loves me." If you want to cultivate gratitude, self-monitor your words. We are not suggesting that you inflate yourself with superficial compliments but that you pay attention to the good things people have done for you.

- If your experience with the *Gratitude Letter* and *Visit* has been powerful, have you thought of others with whom you wish to share your gratitude? Think of the people—parents, friends, teachers, coaches, teammates, employers—who have been especially kind to you but have never heard you express your gratitude. Your gratitude may be long overdue.
- Express gratitude directly to another. Gratitude is an interpersonal attribute that is most effective when done directly—face to face, by phone, or by letter. Avoid the mere lip service of "thank you." Express your appreciation in concrete terms to, for example, the teacher who recognized your ability and connected with you in ways that brought out the best in you, or your favorite uncle who guided you through the tough terrain of adolescence when no else could understand you, or an old friend who stood by you when you were bullied. Write to them and express your gratitude in concrete terms. If it is appropriate and affordable, give that person a gift of something you two can do together, such as having dinner together, or going to see a musical, a concert, an art exhibition, or a sporting event.

END-OF-SESSION RELAXATION

We recommend that each session end with the same brief relaxation practice that started the session.

RESOURCES

Readings

- Emmons, R. A., & Stern, R. (2013). Gratitude as a psychotherapeutic intervention. *Journal of Clinical Psychology*, *69*(8), 846–855.
- Kaczmarek, L. D., Kashdan, T. B., Drążkowski, D., & Enko, J. (2015). Why do people prefer gratitude journaling over gratitude letters? The influence of individual differences in motivation and personality on web-based interventions. *Personality and Individual Differences*, *75*, 1–6.
- Post, S., & Neimark, J. (2007). *Why Good Things Happen to Good People: The Exciting New Research that Proves the Link between Doing Good and Living a Longer, Healthier, Happier Life*. New York: Random House.
- Toepfer, S. M., & Walker, K. (2009). Letters of gratitude: Improving well-being through expressive writing. *Journal of Writing Research*, *1*(3), 181–198.

Videos

- Science of Happiness: An Experiment in Gratitude, the power of writing and sharing gratitude letter:
  https://youtu.be/oHv6vTKD6lg
- Virtual *Gratitude Visit*: Dr. Daniel Tomasulo discusses how to conduct a virtual gratitude visit:
  https://youtu.be/iptEvstz6_M

Websites

- Website of Robert Emmons, one of the most eminent researchers of gratitude:
  http://emmons.faculty.ucdavis.edu
- Stories of Gratitude: stories about the extraordinary power of gratitude:
  http://365grateful.com

## 15

SESSION NINE: HOPE AND OPTIMISM

IN SESSION NINE, WHICH IS THE START of Phase Three of positive psychotherapy (PPT), clients learn to see the best possible, realistic outcomes. They learn that challenges are temporary and how to develop a sense of hope. The central PPT practice covered in this session is *One Door Closes, Another Door Opens*.

SESSION NINE OUTLINE

Core Concepts
    In-Session Practice: *One Door Closes, Another Door Opens*
    Reflection & Discussion
    Vignettes
    Fit & Flexibility
    Cultural Considerations
    Maintenance
Resources

CORE CONCEPTS

Thinking about a different and desirable future and finding paths to achieve that future are one of the most remarkable human capacities. Hope and optimism are inherent in this capacity. We often hear statements from our clients, such as: "I feel stuck; my work doesn't allow me to grow;" "I want to feel good about myself but all I find are weaknesses;" "I have tried everything but nothing seems to work." In dealing with a deep sense of despair, hope is considered a central and worthy goal across different psychotherapy traditions (Frank & Frank, 1991) because hope and optimism play a vital role in combating psychological distress. They are strongly associated with better physical, emotional, and psychological health (Snyder, Cheavens, & Michael, 2005; Segerstrom, 2007; Seligman, 1991; Visser et al., 2013).

Hope is the perception that one can reach desired goals (Snyder, 1994). Hopeful thinking entails the belief that one can find pathways to desired goals, and finding pathways motivates one to use those pathways (Snyder, Rand, & Sigmon, 2002). Optimism can be defined as an attribution, that is, the way we explain causes of events to ourselves (Seligman, 1991). When explaining the causes of a failure, optimists (a) generally attribute causes more to external factors rather than blaming themselves entirely, (b) relate causes to specific events instead of to all events in their lives, and (c) perceive the failure as temporary instead of permanent. Optimism, according to another theoretical stream, is a goal-directed disposition, which enables individuals to perceive themselves as being able to move toward desirable goals (Scheier & Carver, 1994). Despite differences in these core concepts, hope and optimism research offers a common theme; that is, hope and optimism—rather than blaming oneself for all the wrongs—are routes or paths toward desired goals, and systematically changing one's attributions results in creating attainable paths and goals. We believe that psychotherapy essentially is about changing self-sabotaging attributions and cultivating desirable routes and routines. Here we present some salient findings from hope and optimism research:

- Evidence suggests that, when times are tough, optimists report less distress because they cope in ways that yield better outcomes and they take necessary steps to ensure that their future continues to remain bright. There is remarkably little evidence suggesting that optimists are ever worse off than pessimists.
- Hope and optimism are quite well understood, and they serve us best when we encounter a setback or adversity. Optimism and hope have been the subjects of thousands of scientific studies that have uncovered critical elements and processes that can build attributes to treat and prevent depression (Cheavens, Michael, & Snyder, 2005; Seligman, 1991). Building hope and optimism is one of the most potent antidotes for depression; optimists and pessimists differ in ways that have a big impact on their lives. They differ in how they encounter problems and cope with adversity.
- Optimism is linked to good morals; effective problem-solving; academic, athletic, military, occupational, and political success; popularity; good health; and even long life and freedom from trauma (Alarcon, Bowling, & Khazon, 2013; Nes & Segerstrom, 2006).

START-OF-SESSION RELAXATION

At the start of every session, begin with a brief relaxation exercise. Refer to Appendix A: Relaxation & Mindfulness Practices, which can be found at the end of this manual. A copy of this appendix also appears in the client workbook. Continue the session with a review of the client's *Gratitude Journal* as well as a review of the core concepts taught in the previous session.

IN-SESSION PRACTICE: *ONE DOOR CLOSES, ANOTHER DOOR OPENS*

SUGGESTED SCRIPT FOR THE CLINICIAN

The following is a script you can use to introduce this practice to your clients:

Consider this quote by Winston Churchill: "A pessimist sees the difficulty in every opportunity; an optimist sees the opportunity in every difficulty." What does this quote mean to you? Do you tend to act like a pessimist or an optimist?

Optimism entails positive emotions about the future as well as about the present. The optimist sees the good in the bad. Being optimistic does not make a person foolish or naïve. Indeed, optimism can be hard work, as Worksheet 9.1: Doors Opening, suggests. Think of times when you failed to get a job you wanted or when you were rejected by someone you loved. When one door closes, another one almost always opens (Pine & Houston, 1993).

Note that this and all worksheets (a) appear within the corresponding session of this manual, (b) are reprinted for the client in the accompanying client workbook, and (c) can be downloaded from our companion website at www.oup.com/ppt.

Step One:

In the following blanks, write about your experiences with doors opening and closing. Did you see the open door immediately, or did it take a while? Did your disappointment, sadness, bitterness, or other negative feelings resulting from the closed door make it harder to find an open door? Are there things you can do in the future to find the open door more readily?

Consider three doors that closed on you. What other doors opened? Try to fill in the blanks:

(1) The most important door that ever closed on me was _____

and the door that opened was _____

(2) A door that closed on me through bad luck or missed opportunity was _____

and the door that opened was _____

(3) A door that closed on me through loss, rejection, or death was _____

and the door that opened was _____

Step Two:

In this step, you will explore how you explain to yourself the reasoning behind why the door closed. Pick one of the three illustrations from Step One and respond to the statements by selecting a numeric response that best represents your reasoning for both closed and open doors. (On the scales, 1= Very untrue of you, while 7= Very true of you.)

The Door that Closed was Door Number____

1.	This door closed mostly due to me	1..... 3..... 5..... 7.....
OR		
2.	This door closed mostly due to other people or circumstances	1..... 3..... 5..... 7.....
3.	This or similar doors will always remain closed	1..... 3..... 5..... 7.....
OR		
4.	This door is closed temporarily	1..... 3..... 5..... 7.....
5.	This closed door will ruin everything in my life	1..... 3..... 5..... 7.....
OR		
6.	This door influences just this one aspect of my life	1..... 3..... 5..... 7.....

If you score high (12 or higher) on items 1, 3, and 5, this indicates that your explanations for closed doors (setbacks, failures, and adversities) are personalized (largely due to you), are permanent (will not change), and are pervasive (one closed door will close many other things in life).

If you score high on items 2, 4, and 6, this indicates that your explanations for closed doors are not personalized, are temporary, and are localized (not impacting all areas of your life). According to Seligman's theory of attributions (Forgeard & Seligman, 2012; Seligman, 1991), such explanations are associated with more adaptive functioning in the wake of negative experiences.

REFLECTION & DISCUSSION

After completing this practice, ask clients to reflect and discuss:

- When people hold themselves solely responsible for a setback and perceive it as doom and gloom in almost all aspects of their lives that will last forever, they become vulnerable to depression and a host of other psychological problems. How do you explain causes of failure to yourself, especially when a door closes (i.e., a setback, missed opportunity, or adversity)?
- What was the impact of doors that closed? What were the negatives and positives regarding your happiness and well-being? Was the impact all-encompassing or long-lasting?
- Did this impact bring something positive to you? What was it?
- In what way has the *One Door Closes, Another Door Opens* practice enhanced your flexibility and adaptability?
- Do you think that deliberate focus on the brighter side (*Door Opens*) might encourage you to minimize or overlook tough realizations that you need to face?
- What led to a door closing, and what helped you to open another door?
- How easy or hard was it for you to see if a door opened, even just a crack?
- What does the closed door represent for you now?
- Did you grow from doors that opened? Is there room for more growth? What might this growth look like?
- Reflect on one or two people who helped you to open the doors or who held the opened doors for you to enter.
- Would you still like the door that closed to be opened, or do you not care about it now?

VIGNETTE: ANTOINE

While under the influence of alcohol and drugs, Antoine, a 37-year-old male, had unprotected sex with another male. Six months later, Antoine was diagnosed as HIV positive. A successful sales person at an art gallery, Antoine initially was shocked, felt guilty, and was overwhelmed by what he perceived to be a door closing on his future, and he found himself on the verge of suicide. He made an attempt but was saved by a good Samaritan. Feeling hopeless and angry at himself, Antoine just wanted to wait for his death.

During trauma-focused work in therapy, Antoine also assessed his strengths. Creativity and appreciation of beauty were salient. He had always wanted to become a photographer. Antoine sold his house, moved to a smaller apartment, and started taking photography classes. This long-term client, with symptoms well-managed, now travels the world to capture day-to-day triumphs and turbulences of males infected with the AIDS virus.

VIGNETTE: LAUREN

Lauren, a 23-year-old female diagnosed with borderline personality disorder, shared that the most important door that closed on her was when she was kicked out of her family home. Initially scared and feeling abandoned, she found menial jobs, supported herself, and also paid for her studies. Lauren learned to cook, clean, and live on a meager budget. When the door of home was closed on her, the door of self-sustenance opened for her. Lauren graduated this year, not with high grades but with high hopes.

FIT & FLEXIBILITY

The biggest challenge that clients face when approaching a task or challenge with optimism is to know in which situations optimism is the appropriate approach to use. There are many situations in life that warrant thoughtful use of prudence and critical thinking. PPT encourages clients to develop flexible or complex optimism. Clients can choose to use optimism when they judge that less depression, more achievement, or better health is the issue. But they can also choose not to use optimism when they judge that clear sight or taking responsibility is called for. Learning optimism does not erode our sense of values or our judgment. Rather, it frees us to achieve the goals we set. However, optimism's benefits are not unbounded.

Pessimism also has a role to play, both in society at large and in our own lives; we must have the courage to endure pessimism when its perspective is valuable (Seligman, 1991, p. 292). For example, pessimism promotes our readiness to identify, anticipate, and prepare for potential dangers, skills that are especially important in relation to dangerous situations. For example, depending on the weather, a pessimistic person might be motivated to de-ice an airplane a second time before taking off because she is thinking of the worst possible outcome, while an optimist might consider this unnecessary. Similarly for firefighters and surgeons, focused thinking and a selective set of behaviors directly related to the tasks at hand are important. Pessimism is adaptive if it is directed toward things that are specific and select; diffuse or universal pessimism is not functional.

It is important that, as the clinician, you are able to assess and build a genuine sense of hope and optimism in clients. Some clients, due to a preponderance of negative attitudes toward mental health, may minimize their symptoms of depression, overestimate their chances of recovery, or dismiss or minimize subtle yet important nuances of emotional health (Hunt, Auriemma, & Cashaw, 2003; Tong, 2014). Others may come with an unrealistic optimism, also known as optimistic bias (Sedikides & Gregg, 2008). This is a tendency when individuals, depressed or otherwise, judge themselves to be at less risk of experiencing unfavorable events when compared to the "average" other.

Hope and optimism work better when clients have realistic appraisals of things that can be changed. Some clients may have an unbridled sense of optimism that anything and everything is possible as long as one perseveres with positive thinking. PPT is about changing things that can be changed (e.g., thinking, action, ways of responding and interacting). Hope and optimism are not fantasies of changing things that cannot be changed. Such indulgence distracts clients from engaging in realistically achievable pursuits (Oettingen & Gollwitzer, 2009).

CULTURAL CONSIDERATIONS

Some clients who worry, especially those from an East Asian background, may appear quite pessimistic due to cultural factors that cultivate prudence and self-regulation more than hope and zest. Such clients may have operated and survived well working with their pessimism. They set low expectations and presume that things might turn out poorly; they review all the negative or bad outcomes that may occur. They then mentally rehearse ways to deal with various challenges, and they do that until they get a clear picture of how things will turn out and what precautions they need to minimize the chances of failure. This strategy, generally known as defensive pessimism, sometimes works well, especially for those who are anxious as well as depressed (Norem & Chang, 2000).

Keeping cultural factors in mind, instead of utilizing defensive pessimism, clients may respond better to the strengths of prudence and caution. Hence, it is important for you to deeply understand the signature strength profile of your clients so that you are able to help them let go of negatives and deficit-based labels about themselves and use more strength-based language to understand themselves.

It is also important to evaluate optimism and hope within the cultural context. The Chinese sense of optimism, for example, entails being able to accept conditions in one's life, rather than expecting that more good things will happen in the future (Lai & Yue, 2000) and interdependent orientation (suggesting a collective orientation) could lead to higher modesty and self-effacement.

MAINTENANCE

Discuss the following tips with your clients so that they can maintain their progress:

- The next time you help a friend with a problem, look for the positive aspects of the situation. Instead of using clichés like "look on the bright side," try to help your friend find specific, concrete opportunities that he might otherwise overlook.
- To maintain hope and optimism, especially in tough times after therapy, remember how you were able to benefit from psychotherapy—which is essentially a hope-enhancing process. People may seek therapy because they lack skills to change undesirable aspects of their behavior or because they have skills but lack confidence regarding how to creatively apply these skills. The therapeutic process, if effective, allows you to understand your skills and to harness or enhance them, if additional skills are needed. If you have skills, the therapeutic process will help you to gain or regain the confidence and motivation to apply those skills by devising a plan to accomplish specific goals. The next time you find yourself lacking hope and optimism, recall how psychotherapy effectively worked for you—if it did. Such a reflection will enable you to transfer skills learned in therapy to solve new challenges you may encounter in life.
- Maintaining hope and optimism also requires social support and a supportive social environment. Ensure that you surround yourself with people who are future-minded and optimistic. If you encounter a serious setback, failure, or adversity, an optimistic and hopeful friend can be an asset to help boost your mood. Likewise, if your friends encounter problems, you can lift their spirits.

END-OF-SESSION RELAXATION

We recommend that each session end with the same brief relaxation practice that started the session.

RESOURCES

Readings

- Caprara, G. V, Steca, P., Alessandri, G., Abela, J. R, & McWhinnie, C. M. (2010). Positive orientation: explorations on what is common to life satisfaction, self-esteem, and optimism. *Epidemiologia E Psichiatria Sociale, 19,* 63–71.
- Carver, C. S., Scheier, M. F., & Segerstrom, S. C. (2010). Optimism. *Clinical Psychology Review, 30*(7), 879–889. doi:10.1016/j.cpr.2010.01.006.
- Gilman, R., Schumm, J. A., & Chard, K. M. (2012). Hope as a change mechanism in the treatment of posttraumatic stress disorder. *Psychological Trauma: Theory, Research, Practice, and Policy, 4,* 270–277. doi:10.1037/a0024252
- Giltay, E. J., Geleijnse, J. M., Zitman, F. G., Hoekstra, T., & Schouten, E. G. (2004). Dispositional optimism and all-cause and cardiovascular mortality in a prospective cohort of elderly Dutch men and women. *Archives of General Psychiatry, 61,* 1126–1135.
- Jarcheski, A., & Mahon, N. E. (2016). Meta-analyses of predictors of hope in adolescents. *Western Journal of Nursing Research, 38*(3), 345–368. doi:10.1177/0193945914559545
- Weis, R., & Speridakos, E. C. (2011). A meta-analysis of hope enhancement strategies in clinical and community settings. *Psychology of Well-Being: Theory, Research and Practice, 1*(1), 5. http://doi.org/10.1186/2211-1522-1-5.
- Yarcheski, A., & Mahon, N. E. (2016). Meta-analyses of predictors of hope in adolescents. *Western Journal of Nursing Research, 38*(3), 345–368. doi:10.1177/0193945914559545

Videos

- Explanatory style: Learn how your thinking habits can affect your ability to bounce back from stressful circumstances:
  https://youtu.be/q8UiXudooh8
- TED Talk: Neil Pasricha speaks on spreading little optimism everyday about things which make life worth living:
  http://www.ted.com/speakers/neil_pasricha; retrieved November 24, 2015
- Seligman on Optimism: at BBC's Hardtalk:
  https://youtu.be/nFzlaCGvoLY?list=PLB9036743C2E1866F
- Positive Emotions, by Barbara Fredrickson; positivity focuses on what "positivity" is and why it needs to be heartfelt to be effective:
  https://youtu.be/Ds_9Df6dK7c

Websites

- A website about awesome things:
  http://1000awesomethings.com
- Positive Psychology Daily News: To stay updated about positive psychology events:
  http://positivepsychologynews.com
- Positivity Ratio: Learn about your positive to negative emotion ratio, also called the positivity ratio, at Barbara Fredrickson's website:
  www.positivityratio.com

## 16

SESSION TEN: POSTTRAUMATIC GROWTH

SESSION TEN INVITES CLIENTS TO EXPLORE THEIR deep feelings and thoughts about a traumatic experience that continues to bother them. The central positive psychotherapy (PPT) practice covered in this session is *Expressive Writing*.

SESSION TEN OUTLINE

Core Concepts
    In-Session Practice: *Expressive Writing*
    Reflection & Discussion
    Vignettes
    Fit & Flexibility
    Cultural Considerations
    Maintenance
Resources

CORE CONCEPTS

Following trauma, some individuals develop posttraumatic stress disorder (PTSD), a serious condition requiring serious treatment. However, following trauma, most people also develop what is called posttraumatic growth (PTG). PTG entails a change of insight into the meaning of life and the importance of relationships. This growth often helps mitigate the feelings of loss or helplessness engendered by the trauma (Calhoun & Tedeschi, 2006). Research shows that PTG can lead to improved relationships, greater appreciation of life, and enhanced personal strength and spirituality (Grace, Kinsella, Muldoon, & Fortune, 2015; Roepke, 2015; Jayawickreme & Blackie, 2014). Research also shows that people experiencing PTG

- Develop a renewed belief in their abilities to endure and prevail.
- Achieve improved relationships—in particular, discovering who their true friends are and who they can really count on. Some relationships pass the test, while others fail.
- Feel more comfortable with intimacy and have a greater sense of compassion for others who suffer.
- Develop a deeper, more sophisticated, and more satisfying philosophy of life.

Other things to consider (Fazio, Rashid, & Hayward, 2008):

- Spirituality, gratitude, kindness, hope, and bravery facilitate PTG.
- PTG is not all rosy. It enables survivors to see "who their real friends are" or "who their fair-weather friends are."
- Problem-focused coping, positive reinterpretation, and positive religious coping facilitate PTG.
- Time itself doesn't influence PTG, but intervening events and processes facilitate growth, and PTG tends to be stable over time.

START-OF-SESSION RELAXATION

At the start of every session, begin with a brief relaxation exercise. Refer to Appendix A: Relaxation & Mindfulness Practices, which can be found at the end of this manual. A copy of this appendix also appears in the client workbook. Continue the session with a review of the client's *Gratitude Journal* as well as a review of the core concepts taught in the previous session.

IN-SESSION PRACTICE: *EXPRESSIVE WRITING*

For more than two decades, James Pennebaker has been exploring how writing about a traumatic or upsetting experience can affect people's health and well-being. Pennebaker's strategy, known as *Writing Therapy* (Pennebaker & Evans, 2014), has been explore in more than 200 studies and includes writing with the assurance of confidentiality (Smyth & Pennebaker, 2008). He asks his students to write about one of their most distressing or traumatic life experiences. The students are instructed to describe the experience in detail and to fully explore their personal reactions and deepest emotions. Each writing session lasts 15 to 30 minutes, and the students are asked to continue writing for a total of three to five consecutive days.

Pennebaker and others have found that expressive writing about past traumatic events has many beneficial consequences (Park & Blumberg, 2002; Pennebaker, 1997). Individuals who spend three days exploring, in a journal, their deepest thoughts and feelings about ordeals or traumas make fewer visits to a doctor in the months following the writing, show enhanced immune function, report less depression and distress, get higher grades, and are more likely to find new jobs after unemployment. Writing about personal and meaningful experiences can have positive effects on mental health (Cooper & Frattaroli, 2006). Disclosing information may help people to make sense of upsetting events, better regulate their emotions, and improve their connection with the social world, which leads to positive effects on health and well-being (Neimeyer, Burke, Mackay, & van Dyke Stringer, 2010). These effects have been found cross-culturally.

The critical mechanism appears to be the nature of the writing process itself, which helps individuals to comprehend, come to terms with, and make sense of trauma. Finding meaning in the trauma through writing also appears to reduce how often and how intensely individuals experience intrusive thoughts about it.

SUGGESTED SCRIPT FOR THE CLINICIAN

The following is a script you can use to introduce clients to the *Expressive Writing* practice.

The very act of writing about your deepest traumatic experience may inhibit your expression because you may feel that someone will read this. To alleviate your apprehension, keep your writings in a secure place that no one else has access to. If you live with your partner, you may want to explain about the nature and purpose of this exercise and request privacy.

Following the instructions on Worksheet 10.1, spend at least 15 to 20 minutes a day for four consecutive days writing a detailed account of a trauma you experienced.

This may not be an easy practice to do, but, we have already handled some difficult topics in session, such as reflecting and writing about a challenging situation as well as revisiting open and negative memories. Hopefully, those practices have enhanced your confidence to handle difficult issues within the safe therapeutic confines. The goal is to help you gain new insight from these practices—insight that is geared toward your personal growth.

While you are writing, if you become overwhelmed by your feelings and thoughts, take a short break (two to five minutes at most). Refresh yourself and promptly return. Try your best not to leave the practice incomplete or partially finished, such as writing for only one or two days.

Note that this and all worksheets (a) appear within the corresponding session of this manual, (b) are reprinted for the client in the accompanying client workbook, and (c) can be downloaded from our companion website at www.oup.com/ppt.

WORKSHEET 10.1 *EXPRESSIVE WRITING*

Using a note pad or journal, please write a detailed account of a trauma you experienced. Continue this exercise for at least 15 to 20 minutes a day for four consecutive days. Make sure you keep your writings in a safe, secure place that only you have access to.

In your writing, try to let go and explore your deepest thoughts and feelings about the traumatic experience in your life. You can tie this experience to other parts of your life, or keep it focused on one specific area. You can write about the same experience on all four days or you can write about different experiences.

At the end of four days, after describing the experience, please write if the experience has helped you:

- *understand what it means to you*
- *understand your ability to handle similar situations*
- *understand your relationships in a different light*

REFLECTION & DISCUSSION

After completing this practice, ask clients to reflect and discuss:

- What was the most difficult part of writing? Do you agree that even though it may have been difficult, it was still worth writing?
- Some reactions to the trauma, adversity, or losses can be so strong that we deliberately avoid associated feelings. Did the writing process help you see this avoidance, if any?
- Did writing help you to visualize growth in terms of your perspective on life?
- Did you experience healing or growth, despite having the lingering pain of the trauma or loss?
- Write about some concrete actions or behaviors you have undertaken, or you plan to do, which signify PTG.
- Did the structure of the writing process help you to see the causal chain of the traumatic experience differently? If so, what different causal links did you discover?
- Do you see your character strengths reflected in your PTG?

VIGNETTE: KANE

Kane, a 20-year-old male client, was first seen in individual and then group PPT. Kane made an effective, successful recovery. Six months after the last session, he described his recovery and growth:

"The process of recovering and growth of a clear and adaptive sense of self is like following the sun on a cloudy day. The sun is true self. The natural response for people to feel when they cannot get a clear vision of themselves is distress, but there are signs that we can pick up on, that lead us closer to finding the sun. It is these signs that we must pay attention to, but never trust wholeheartedly. There is nothing more shattering than engaging in a directed pursuit only to find, in a moment of clarity, that the sun reveals itself to be in a location completely different from the direction of your pursuit. I think this is the source of much of the initial instability from which recovery must take place. Therefore, it is of vital importance that such a mistake is not made again. This is not to say that we should not pursue our intuitions, it is just to say that we should not assume our intuitions are correct. When the object of the pursuit is of such importance as a coherent sense of self, the emotion that accompanies such intuitions can be deceiving. It is the emotion attached to the importance of the goal that makes the incentive of the intuition so great. It is not necessarily the intuition itself. This is a mistake that can prove to be detrimental for recovery.

"Finally, the largest and most intrusive cloud in most people's lives is likely an inability to forgive and accept themselves. It is one thing to finally see one's self clearly, but it is another thing altogether to look favorably upon what is seen. To address this, all I can say is that you are worth accepting. There is nothing intrinsically wrong with you, no matter how deeply you might believe this to be so. To forgive yourself is to free yourself. There are no shackles more constraining than the judgments we impose on ourselves. We restrict ourselves to continually behaving and thinking in an unhelpful way until we learn to accept ourselves for who we are. Free yourself, you deserve that much."

VIGNETTE: THE MEANDERING PATH TO PERSPECTIVE

Annie, 23, a South Asian female, recently graduated with a major in art and creative writing. She participated in group PPT in her first year, but she couldn't bring herself to do the *Expressive Writing* practice. Almost three years later, Annie came in for a few individual sessions just prior to her graduation and stated that she was finally able to write about her trauma and in the process, produced insight. (Perspective was one of Annie's signature strengths, and, without any prompting, she integrated her perspective into this narrative.)

"Each of us possesses a world, ever revolving around a centrally constructed 'I' that bears witness and affixes narrative meaning. Thrusted against the currents of life—I attempt to hold on. This is a promise, an ongoing act of withstanding, that I have made to myself since I was a young girl. As a child, I felt that I swallowed a heaviness that remained in my belly. I remember after long days of enduring bullying at school and arriving home to violent screaming matches, I would slink into my room. I would stare out the window at the dusty yellow street lights as the night hummed on. Each night my small body trembled with quiet tears and shame as I prayed for an *elsewhere* to escape to and a metamorphosis from my familiar ugliness. More than a decade later, my body has grown, skin has stretched and shed, prayers have wavered.

"I realized my persistence on movement was integral to carving out a path for myself. It is the path that begins and returns to the young girl, who I no longer mourn but instead whose hand I gently take. Moving inwards has thus been a process of returning. Perspective is inextricably attached to vision—belonging both to the *eye* and *I*. Possessing sensitive heart and natural inquisitiveness made me attuned to the inner workings of myself. I have used writing as a means of mapping the dimensions and shifts in my reflections and self-perception. By the end of each summer I would fill about two notebooks worth of archived confessions and bundled experiences.

"Through writing, I can envision myself, propped up on a stage with only one witness: myself. A blank page is what lies between dislodging knives out of wounds. Moving inwards initially allowed me to centralize my yearning, despair, and hopes. Yet, after many years, I am teaching myself to **move through** and **be present** in midst of feeling itself. I conceive of perspective as the ability to simultaneously move inside and outside of oneself. It is often in such ordinary moments that we might catch a flickering glimpse of our own growth. It is our duty to let our spirit persist. As Rainer Maria Rilke beautifully asserts:

"Let everything happen to you
Beauty and terror
Just keep going
No feeling is final"

VIGNETTE: HENRY

The following is a story written by one of our young clients, Henry, who, under very challenging circumstances, completed his degree and eventually was able to get full-time employment. Henry first engaged in group and then individual PPT.

> from a pristine childhood
> in a distant land, one-day war of creed and class unleashed
> and swept his dreams
> he saw human debris
> leaving indelible scars on his soul
> his home shattered to pieces

his family was scattered in three continents, in numerous refugee camps
for almost a decade, he waited, in cold corners
with a tiny warmth of hope
which finally landed him on the cold but secure Canadian soil
he landed within one foot in snow and the other in a supermarket
stood there, week after week, every week for sixty hours
also on weekends, when his peers played and partied
But he, worked and gave each penny to pay the rent of a crowded apartment
and paid for groceries—for everyone
he said, I fed them, but still
with a tired body, whenever he stepped into the apartment,
tirades and troubles of family welcomed him
often he thought, is that it . . . ?
one of his colleagues thought the same, and exited life
leaving him at edge of existence, which found no meaning nor means to live
"is that it" . . . this thought brought him to a windowless, cold psychiatric rooms
a number of times
for weeks . . . he lived in the hospital
his spirit quieted, by a cocktail of drugs
and soul tattered with a cocktail of diagnoses
depression, PTSD, social anxiety
he started PPT group with great skepticism
his opening story, ended with a line, "I never quit"
he thought he has only stressors and no strengths
but was surprised when others spotted his grit and resilience
still skeptical he started thinking about these strengths
he re-told his story, this time sparkled with strengths, along with stressors
while he told the story, many strains and struggles crossed his path
but every time he told himself, "I never quit."

FIT & FLEXIBILITY

Anne Marie Roepke (2015), who recently reviewed the literature relevant to PTG, suggests that clinicians should pay close attention to growth themes because subtle or inadvertent comments or gestures can quash growth or promote it by encouraging clients to discuss it.

Growth promotion exercises—especially those dealing with trauma—run the risk of building the expectation in clients that they *have to grow* after completing such exercises. Reduce this pressure to grow by focusing on the process rather than on the outcome.

Although certain themes regarding the manifestation of trauma can be delineated from prior findings, the nature and timeline of trauma manifestation may vary from person to person, especially in contemporary urban and diverse societies. Clinicians conducting PPT should be mindful that completing this practice as part of the protocol and sequence is far less important than adapting the protocol as necessary to promote optimal clinical care for each client. If you sense that this practice may potentially cause harm or interfere in the natural healing or recovery process, proceed with caution. However, it is also important to be aware that many clients will avoid processing trauma, and the *Expressive Writing* practice may allow them to finally deal with it through a structured process. Discuss with clients that the practice has the potential to offer them a clearer perspective, which may help clients bring closure to a painful experience and enable them to acknowledge the positive gains they may have acquired.

Sometimes we deliberately don't want to dig into our past if it involves traumatic memories because confronting the trauma and associated emotions is not only uncomfortable but also makes us feel vulnerable. If that is the case with your clients, ask them to choose a setting that offers them feelings of safety or trusted social support, or a time of day or season of the year during which they feel rejuvenated (e.g., spring or summer) or when they are not overwhelmed by external stressors (i.e., a stressful work week, holidays, family members in transition, or medical challenges) to do this practice (Jelinek et al., 2010). If clients feel more comfortable, they can do the first writing session in the therapy room, with the option of the clinician departing temporarily.

Be mindful that the worst moments of a trauma often contain disorganized or unfinished thoughts that the client may not articulate clearly or accurately through this PTG practice. This does not imply that the exercise should not be undertaken, and during the course of the exercise (before, during, or after), encourage such clients to appraise the accuracy of their recall.

Also be mindful that current external factors (such as world events, scandals in the news, and so on) may impact the expressive writing process. For example, a client recently shared that the increasing number of accounts of sexual assaults by prominent celebrities and public figures has triggered memories. Without being able to recall precisely, she feels that she may have experienced a trauma when she was quite young. Clinicians should proceed carefully to ensure that client experiences of trauma—based on autobiographical memories—neither underestimate nor overestimate the impact. Significant external stressors can overwhelm most of us, rendering the practice less than optimal.

Clinician Note

It is not reasonable to expect that changes that come as a result of PTG-focused practices will last forever or will result in a total personal transformation.

1. *It may be difficult to establish discrete start and end points that mark when growth from trauma has started or ended.*
2. *Keep in mind that some clients might not continue to experience growth on a long-term basis due to any number of reasons that may be beyond their control. A periodic assessment using a valid and reliable measure may provide you with a yardstick to gauge changes in growth.*
3. *Continue discussing therapeutic changes with clients without explicitly asking about growth. This can help you understand the context in which clients are deeply embedded.*
4. *Moreover, an ongoing discussion focused on themes of change may help you identify when additional resources or supports are needed to maintain and amplify PTG.*

In the past decade, we have worked with hundreds of clients in individual and group settings. The following is a snapshot of a client who showed PTG:

Erica, a female in her late 20s, experienced years of emotional and at times physical abuse from her husband. The relationship took a turn for the worse after their child was diagnosed with a developmental disability. While her husband couldn't accept this painful reality, Erica accepted it and left no stone unturned in seeking the best possible support services for her child. In the process, while her relationship with her husband worsened, she became an advocate for parents of children with similar developmental challenges.

CULTURAL CONSIDERATIONS

It is imperative that you listen carefully to the language and psychological responses of clients within the cultural context. Rather than just being listened to empathically, clients from some cultures may ask you for explicit advice, suggestions, coping strategies, or culturally appropriate resources. Respond in a way that meets their needs or refer to someone who understands the contextual features of trauma including the client's immediate cultural, religious, social, and economic circumstances.

While engaging in this practice, be aware of culturally sensitive emotional expressions, especially those associated with trauma. Cultures differ in their ways to clearly differentiate specific emotions. For example, interpersonal emotions are more frequently articulated in interdependent cultures, whereas intrapersonal emotions are more clearly differentiated in individualistic cultures (Cordaro et al., 2018). While engaged in the PTG practice, pay close attention to how clients from diverse cultural backgrounds express emotions, amplify the physiological states associated with emotions, and how they interpret the emotions related to both trauma and growth.

Also, listen carefully, without judging client experiences from any one specific cultural lens. This is a good opportunity for clinicians to exercise their strengths of open-mindedness, curiosity, and social intelligence.

MAINTENANCE

Discuss the following tips with your clients so that they can maintain their progress:

- Writing about a traumatic event can be extremely challenging. However, keeping the trauma inside—without expressing it in an adaptive manner—can be very harmful for you. Therefore, it is important that before and after the *Expressive Writing* practice, you remind yourself that your intent is to break the mental block, stop the cycle of thinking about the trauma, and, more importantly, explore if the trauma also brought about any positive changes in you.
- This practice is both individual and interpersonal. The therapeutic groundwork done so far, with the help of your clinician, is critical in preparing you to undertake this PTG endeavor. You will most likely use your strengths of courage, social intelligence, and self-regulation to undertake this work. However, to gain and maintain perspective, especially in interpreting its meaning and potential growth, you will greatly benefit from the continuation of therapeutic support. Confiding your feelings with your clinician, putting such feelings into words, and drawing insights about potential growth is best done in a safe, interpersonal context. We recommend that to maintain the benefits of this practice, you keep engaging in therapy for a while.
- It is also important that you do not force yourself to find growth or expect that surviving a trauma will yield major positive changes in your life. Growth from a trauma, although a more frequent phenomenon than acknowledged and recognized, may take its due time and course to manifest. Rather than searching for a discrete expression of growth, focus more on changes that might have organically occurred within you. For example, after surviving a traumatic event, most individuals report experiencing three things (Roepke, 2015):
  - Renewed belief in one's ability to endure and prevail.
  - Improved relationships—in particular, discovering who one's true friends are and on whom one can really count and how critical one's relationships are compared to material goods.
  - Feeling more comfortable with intimacy and feeling a greater sense of compassion for others who suffer.

Periodically reflect if these or similar changes have taken place in you.

END-OF-SESSION RELAXATION

We recommend that each session end with the same brief relaxation practice that started the session.

RESOURCES

Readings

- Bonanno, G. A., & Mancini, A. D. (2012). Beyond resilience and PTSD: Mapping the heterogeneity of responses to potential trauma. *Psychological Trauma, 4,* 74–83.
- Fazio, R., Rashid, T., & Hayward, H. (2008). Growth from trauma, loss, and adversity. In S. J. Lopez (Ed.), *Positive Psychology: Exploring the Best in People.* Westport, CT: Greenwood.
- Jin, Y., Xu, J., & Liu, D. (2014). The relationship between post traumatic stress disorder and post traumatic growth: Gender differences in PTG and PTSD subgroups. *Social Psychiatry and Psychiatric Epidemiology, 49*(12), 1903–1910.
- Pennebaker, J. W. (2004). *Writing to Heal: A Guided Journal for Recovering from Trauma and Emotional Upheaval.* Oakland, CA: New Harbinger.
- Roepke, A. M. (2015). Psychosocial interventions and posttraumatic growth: A meta-analysis. *Journal of Consulting and Clinical Psychology, 83*(1), 129–142. http://dx.doi.org/10.1037/a0036872
- Tedeschi, R. G. & McNally, R. J. (2011). Can we facilitate posttraumatic growth in combat veterans? *American Psychologist, 66,* 19–24.

Videos

- Dr. Randy Pausch's inspirational speech: The Last Lecture:
  https://youtu.be/p1CEhH5gnvg
- Team Hoy: I Can Only Imagine, the story of Dick and Rick Hoyt, one of the most inspirational father and son team to race in an Ironman competition:
  https://youtu.be/cxqe77-Am3w
- TED Talk: Andrew Solomon: How the worst moments help us know who we are:
  http://www.ted.com/talks/andrew_solomon_how_the_worst_moments_in_our_lives_make_us_who_we_are; Retrieved November 24, 2015

Websites

- Home Page of James Pennebaker, pioneer in processing trauma through writing:
  https://liberalarts.utexas.edu/psychology/faculty/pennebak
- Manitoba Trauma Information & Education Centre:
  http://trauma-recovery.ca/resiliency/post-traumatic-growth/
- What doesn't kill us:
  http://www.huffingtonpost.com/stephen-joseph/what-doesnt-kill-us-post_b_2862726.html
- Mobile apps related to trauma:
  www.veterans.gc.ca/eng/stay-connected/mobile-app/ptsd-coach-canada

SESSION ELEVEN: SLOWNESS AND SAVORING

17

IN SESSION ELEVEN, CLIENTS LEARN HOW TO deliberately slow down and develop an awareness of how to savor. In so doing, they learn to attend mindfully to the positives. The central positive psychotherapy (PPT) practices covered in this session are *Slow and Savor*.

SESSION ELEVEN OUTLINE
Core Concepts: Slow
    In-Session Practice: *Slow*
    Reflection & Discussion
Core Concepts: Savor
    In-Session Practice: *Savor*
    Reflection & Discussion
    In-Session Practice: *Planned Savoring Activity*
    Reflection & Discussion
    Homework Practice: *A Savoring Date*
    Reflection & Discussion
    Vignettes
    Fit & Flexibility
    Cultural Considerations
    Maintenance
Resources

CORE CONCEPTS: SLOW
In this time of multitasking, speed has become the ultimate desire, and Canadian journalist Carl Honore (2005) contends that we live in a multitasking era where we have become addicted to speed. We cram more and more into every minute of our lives, such as:

- speed dieting and speed dating,
- instant messaging, tweeting,
- drive-throughs,
- microwave dinners,
- crash courses to master skills, and
- speed yoga and speed meditation.

We live turbo-charged lives in which every moment feels like a race against the clock. This attitude of impatience has infected every corner of our culture, and we are all desperate for a cure. This kind of life takes a toll on everything from our health, diet, and work to our communities, relationships, and the environment. Evidence shows that people who are cognitively busy are also more likely to act selfishly, use sexist language, and make erroneous judgment in social situations (Kahneman, 2011).

    Many clients report that despite doing many things each day, most of which are done quickly, they still feel stressed, underaccomplished, and tired. They never seem to reach the end of their "to-do" list. They feel like they are racing through life rather than actually

195

living it. For at least five decades, Western culture (and now, much of the rest of the world) has been misguided by believing that speed is good. Going faster may be desirable in some cases, but in recent years we have entered a phase of "diminishing returns." Despite speeding up almost everything, including human maturation, we are not any happier or healthier. That is why the "Slow Movement" is attracting attention.

Everywhere people are waking up to the folly of living in fast-forward and discovering that by slowing down judiciously, they do everything better and enjoy everything more. The latest neuroscience shows that when people are in a relaxed, mellow state, the brain slips into a deeper, richer, more nuanced mode of thought (Kahneman, 2011). Psychologists actually call this "Slow Thinking." Artists have always known that you cannot hurry the act of creation, and, increasingly, businesses are realizing the same thing. Workers need moments to relax, unplug, and be silent in order to be creative and productive. Without digressing much, let us clarify here that slowness is not anti-speed. High-speed Internet is good, we would not enjoy ice-hockey if it were slow (maybe a touch more polite though), and there are deadlines for projects that propel us to increase our pace.

Multitasking is ubiquitous in our society as well. However, for most high-order activities, the human brain is not designed to multitask; rather what the brain actually does is sequentially toggle between activities, and it becomes good at going back and forth (Carrier et al., 2015). Research indicates that this kind of toggling between activities is not very productive, and, in fact, tasks can take more than twice as long to complete when performed this way (Minear et al., 2013). This is why projects and tasks we work on can take longer to complete when we are constantly inundated with instant messages, Facebook alerts, and breaking news.

START-OF-SESSION RELAXATION

At the start of every session, begin with a brief relaxation exercise. Refer to Appendix A: Relaxation & Mindfulness Practices, which can be found at the end of this manual. A copy of this appendix also appears in the client workbook. Continue the session with a review of the client's *Gratitude Journal* as well as a review of the core concepts taught in the previous session.

IN-SESSION PRACTICE: *SLOW*

Worksheet 11.1 offers six strategies to help us slow down. Discuss each one with clients. This psychoeducational approach will help clients to grasp the concept of slowing down with concrete suggestions. While discussing, ask clients how they relate to each strategy. Note that this and all worksheets (a) appear within the corresponding session of this manual, (b) are reprinted for the client in the accompanying client workbook, and (c) can be downloaded from our companion website at www.oup.com/ppt.

How can you shift gears and slow down a little? Here are some suggestions. Please select one that you feel you can easily implement. In the space at the end of this worksheet, indicate which option you selected. Then write about why you selected this option.

Start Small and Gradually Decelerate: An incremental and gradual slowing down of pace is better than screeching to a halt. Start with a small decrease and gradually decelerate.

Start with a Few Areas: Pick one or two areas you usually hurry through and slow those areas down. Some examples could be eating at least three meals slowly in a week, walking slowly at least once a week, or having a media/technology-free evening once a week.

Get Involved: Deliberately focus on peaceful experiences, such as following floating clouds with your eyes, watching the sunset, feeling the breeze, or hearing and enjoying wind chimes. You may find that the rhythms of nature are slow but deeply satisfying.

Educate: Talk to your family and friends about the adverse consequences of speed(e.g., accidents, injuries, stress, and anxiety).

Gadget-Free Zones: Create gadget-free times or zones (e.g., no cell phones after 6 PM or no TV in the bedroom).

Learn to Say No: Learn to say no and avoid overscheduling.

Selected Option:
Why did you select this option?

Actions:
What specific actions you will take?

How often?

What sort of social support do you think you need to implement this strategy?

If this strategy works, what would be different in three months?

REFLECTION & DISCUSSION

After completing this practice, ask clients to reflect and discuss:

- If you find yourself constantly busy, how does this business manifest in your daily life? Do you find yourself constantly short on time, and do you multitask?
- Do you feel that information overload, time crunch, overstimulation, underperforming, and multitasking are some of the signs of being busy and living life in the fast track? Which ones of these do you experience?
- What drives your busy behavior? Do you believe that these are internal, external, or a combination of both? Examples of internal behavior are anxious personality disposition and experiencing symptoms of anxiety.
- How does the slowness strategy you selected on Worksheet 11.1 relate to your specific signs?
- All of the strategies to slow down mentioned here require active engagement. What specific actions will you take, or who will support or inhibit your active engagement?
- Which strengths (either from your profile or otherwise) can you use to ensure that your selected strategy is successful?

CORE CONCEPTS: SAVOR

Fred Bryant (2003), a pioneer in savoring, defines savoring as a mindful process of attending to and appreciating the positive experiences in one's life. Bryant describes various aspects of savoring:

- There are four types of savoring: basking, thanksgiving, marveling, and luxuriating. Savoring fosters positive emotions and increases well-being.
- By savoring objects or experiences with friends and family, we can deepen our connection to the meaningful people in our lives.
- Savoring requires effort—we have to work against the pressures to multitask and "move, move, move."
- Savoring becomes a more natural feeling the more we practice it.

IN-SESSION PRACTICE: *SAVOR*

There are numerous kinds of savoring experiences that clients can attend, appreciate, and have to enhance positive experiences. Some of these are outlined in Worksheet 11.2. Also included are techniques to experience specific kinds of savoring. Discuss the different kinds of savoring experiences and techniques with your clients, and see if they relate more to certain experiences and techniques than to others.

Savoring is mindfully combining the positive sensations, emotions, perceptions, thoughts, and beliefs to appreciate the experience. This worksheet lists different kinds of savoring experiences, followed by techniques you can use to savor. In the space at the end of this worksheet, select a savoring technique you would like to try. Then write about when, where, and how often you can use this technique in your daily life.

Kinds of Savoring Experiences
Basking: Taking great pleasure or satisfaction in one's accomplishments, good fortune, and blessings.
Thanksgiving: Giving thanks; expressing gratitude.
Luxuriating: Taking great pleasure (and showing no restraint) in enjoying physical comforts and sensations.
Marveling: Becoming filled with wonder or astonishment. Beauty often induces marveling. Exercising virtue may also inspire marveling. For example, one might marvel at a person's strength in facing and overcoming adversity.
Mindfulness: The state of being aware, attentive, and observant of oneself, one's surroundings and other people.
Savoring Techniques
Sharing With Others: You can seek out others to share an experience and tell others how much you value the moment. This is the single strongest predictor of pleasure.
Memory Building: Take mental photographs or even a physical souvenir of an event and reminisce about it later with others.
Self-praise: Don't be afraid of pride. Share your achievements with others. This is about being authentic and honest in celebrating your persistence in maintaining focus and verve in achieving something meaningful to you.
Sharpening Perceptions: This involves focusing on certain elements and blocking out others. For example, most people spend far more time thinking about how they can correct something that has gone wrong (or is about to go wrong) than they do basking in what has gone right.
Select one of these savoring techniques. When, where, and how frequently can you use it to increase positive emotions in your daily life?

REFLECTION & DISCUSSION

After completing this practice, ask clients to reflect and discuss:

- Of the four kinds of savoring (basking, thanksgiving, luxuriating, and marveling), which one would you use most frequently and in what situations?
- Is there any additional kind of savoring you utilized that is not listed here?
- Are there any factors that inhibit you from using any of the kinds of savoring listed in Worksheet 11.2?
- Savoring requires practice. What specific actions can you undertake to solidify your savoring practice?

IN-SESSION PRACTICE: *PLANNED SAVORING ACTIVITY*

Prior to the start of this session, collect an array of items (e.g., souvenirs, stones, something that produces melodic sounds, feather, flowers, food, pictures or postcards of natural beauty and wonder). If you are conducting PPT in group format, check ahead of time for allergies. Place the items on a table for group PPT or next to the client for individual PPT.

- Discuss the different kinds of savoring experiences and techniques, with the help of Worksheet 11.2.
- Ask clients to select at least one of the objects and to savor the object using one or more of the savoring techniques.
- Ask clients to mentally record what they notice as they savor.
- Ask them to use as many of their senses as possible (different kinds, as well as techniques).
- Allow clients three to five minutes to savor the selected item/s.

The next step is to share with someone. In group PPT, clients can share with the person next to them. In individual PPT, the client can share with the clinician. Ask clients to discuss the kind of sharing experience and the technique they used for this exercise. Then ask clients to reflect and discuss using the following questions.

REFLECTION & DISCUSSION

- How many of your senses did you involve as you were savoring the items of your choice?
- Did you try to focus on certain sensory properties of the items while blocking others?
- While you were savoring, did you feel the urge to leave one item and rush to another?
- Were you able to make yourself comfortable and relaxed to do this activity? What did you do to relax? Do you do this often?
- While savoring, did you think that the specific item could have been better? What prompted that thought?
- Did you have a good experience? What led to it?

HOMEWORK PRACTICE: *A SAVORING DATE*

To amplify the savoring practice, ask your clients to do the following activity at home and then to reflect on the questions.

Plan and execute a "savoring date." You can do this activity with your partner, a friend, or a family member. For example, you can invite a friend over for ice cream (sampling a few different kinds together); you can watch a favorite movie together or listen to favorite music (with the goal of paying as close attention as possible and using as many senses as feasible to fully appreciate the film or song); you can sit outside and savor the nature around you or, if possible, start a fire in the fireplace; or simply set aside time to talk with the other person (while being curious, attentive, and appreciative during the time shared). Be creative with this exercise and plan an activity that requires at least an hour with the other person. Then, when it is over, write an account of the experience, using the Reflection & Discussion questions.

REFLECTION & DISCUSSION

- How much did you enjoy your savoring date? If you didn't, what prevented you from enjoying it?
- Did deliberate planning affect the joy or pleasure? Do you think that doing this spontaneously would produce a different outcome?
- How rare is this type of date in your life?
- Did you try to take in every sensory property of the savoring date (sights, sounds, smells, etc.)?
- During the savoring date, did you think about other things that were hanging over you, such as problems, worries, or chores that you still must face?

VIGNETTE: SOPHIA SAVORS BY COOKING A DINNER

Sophia, a 23-year-old client with symptoms of borderline personality disorder, participated in a PPT group intervention. She reported frequent irritability and restlessness. After completing most PPT practices, and finding them moderately helpful, Sophia found savoring to be most beneficial. She was having frequent arguments with her boyfriend over trivial issues, from exactly where to put the silverware while emptying the dishwasher to which television program to watch. Although their relationship on the whole was stable, these daily hassles were hurting the quality of their time together. Sophia loved to cook. She surprised her boyfriend, Sami, by cooking his favorite Indian cuisine. She described the experience as follows:

"After learning the various forms of savoring, I decided to select something that I would like and Sami would also like. Last weekend, he was working all day. It allowed me to first go to the Indian supermarket and select the ingredients. I especially loved smells of spices, from sharp cumin seeds to subtle turmeric power—all sharpened my senses. I purchased as many original ingredients as I could. When I got back to our apartment, I decided to cook only one dish at a time to enjoy the aroma and process. With my favorite instrumental Indian music playing in the background, I ground whole Garum Masala. The entire kitchen filled with distinct aromas. I took my time, cleaned vegetables, chopped them, prepared them, and followed each step slowly. Sami was pleasantly surprised. We had a slow meal, enjoying every bite of it. It was such a good experience that Sami and I decided to take turns and cook one such meal every month.

"*Reflection:* I know one meal is not going to change my life, or that of Sami, but I realize that one meal at a time can help me to manage my mood better. I have always loved cooking and trying new recipes. I had stopped after minor irritations spoilt my mood the last time I was cooking and I decided not to try. But this weekend's experience helped me to understand two subtle things. First, I can have a good time on my own. I don't need others and not a lot of fancy things to feel good. I feel good when I am doing something hands on, and it requires some effort. Second, I realize that our weekend dinner was so good that the next day, I was able to handle minor hassles better. Perhaps I need to deliberately plan these good moments to have good days."

VIGNETTE: AYSEEHA DEALS WITH HER DEPRESSIVE SYMPTOMS BY LEARNING TO SAVOR

Twenty-four-year-old Ayseeha, a client with perfectionistic tendencies, sought individual therapy for severe and recurrent symptoms of depression. After some reluctance, she agreed to start a *Gratitude Journal*. The following are some of her journal entries, listing Ayseeha's savoring experiences.

Sunday	• Savored that my mother bought the prettiest scarf from my favorite shop • My brother introduced me to a yummy, possibly addictive, form of jalapeño and cheddar cheese dip
Monday	• Rain: Love it, as if entire city of dust has taken a bath • All buses, trains, and streetcars on time, wow!
Tuesday	• Continued to enjoy rain • Purchased a new and expensive brand of Greek yogurt and enjoyed it with granola, so tasty
Wednesday	• Appreciated acknowledgment from my mother that I am a grown-up woman now and no longer a child • Savored the thought that I can choose the course of my life without feeling guilty
Thursday	• Got to class on time • Had a good discussion on one of my favorite topics in the class; was surprised to hear the level of maturity of some students—I had thought they were quite oblivious to these issues
Friday	• Thank God it is Friday and I didn't have to go to school, and slept late
Saturday	• Enjoyed doing nothing
Sunday	• Slept late and then enjoyed going to the mall with my sister and mom

FIT & FLEXIBILITY

Although savoring may be appealing to some, depressed clients may find the task daunting if they do not perceive themselves as having control over their negative attribution style (e.g., such clients may be discouraged by the task if they find themselves distracted during the short period of time that they are ask to be mindful). Assess what might be holding clients back from engaging in savoring practices, and discuss this with them if they aren't sure what might be holding them back.

Enjoying an experience is a more important aspect of savoring than perceiving that one has control. Help clients attend to and appreciate their positive feelings that emerge from the homework activities.

Clients having difficulty savoring because they are used to speed and pace can be taught to intentionally slow down by specifically defining how slow to go (e.g., two bites a minute). In addition to breaking down by time, an experience can be broken into smaller units. An inventory of all sensory experiences can be created ahead of the experience, with the client going through each aspect.

Some experiences, by nature, are fleeting (e.g., spotting a shooting star, glimpsing a rare bird that quickly flies away). Therefore, keep the natural pace of the experience in mind. That said, it is also important to keep in mind that clients may place differential importance on certain aspects of an experience, such as savoring wine versus cheese.

Likewise, individual personality disposition may moderate the savoring experiences. For some, climbing to the summit of a mountain and enjoying the vista is the ultimate savoring experience; for others, it is surfing the crest of a wave. For some, it is the chopping, cleaning, grating, simmering, and seasoning of ingredients for a favorite soup. A savoring experience can be complex or simple. Some clients may focus sharply on one or two aspects of an experience, while others may experience all of the elements synergistically (e.g., a majestic panoramic view of nature, a performance by a virtuoso, a Broadway musical).

Some depressed clients may struggle to savor a pleasant experience due to attentional difficulties. Attention is a finite resource. Pay close attention to how clients are deploying their available attentional resources on savoring. Teaching clients to either eliminate or ignore distractions may help them to closely and completely focus on some aspects of the experience. This may lower their anxiety and minimize their misguided expectations that they must attend to all aspects. Remind clients that savoring, by definition, is a slow experience.

CULTURAL CONSIDERATIONS

Clients surrounded by cultures driven by fast-paced technology may find it difficult to understand the value of slowing down when their success at work seems to be defined and determined by their ability to move at a rapid pace. It is important for such clients to understand that one can be fast-paced at times when productivity is necessary and that they also need to find time to slow down to take care of themselves and enjoy their activities and experiences.

Not all cultures are as time-bound and fast-paced as North American. Clients from diverse cultural backgrounds may already be familiar with and accustomed to a slower pace at home. Assess and modify instructions according to cultural expectations.

Psychologically distressed clients from diverse cultural backgrounds display different savoring preferences. For example, compared to East Asians, North Americans strongly endorse cognitive and behavioral savoring responses that aim to amplify or extend positive experiences (e.g., self-congratulations, behavioral activation; Nisbett, 2008). For example, the preparation for and anticipation of holiday festivities, such as Valentine's Day, Halloween, Thanksgiving, and Christmas, start weeks before the holiday, extending the period of celebration. Clients from East and South Asian, Latin, Middle Eastern, and East European cultural backgrounds may have their own cultural celebrations such as Deewalli, Eid, Kwanza, and Hanukkah and may feel the same anticipation about their celebrations.

MAINTENANCE

Discuss the following tips with your clients so that they can maintain their progress:

- Savoring requires practice. Reflect and write your personal list of actions which can sustain and enhance savoring.
- Some of us may struggle with savoring practices because we overthink experiences, which interferes with our ability to notice and attend to our senses, such as touch, smell, or hearing.
- Attend mindfully to all aspects of a savoring experience, including its cognitive, affective, and behavioral aspects. However, tuning in too much to feelings or thoughts may backfire and could interfere, eventually dampening the savoring experience.
- The focus of the *Slow and Savor* practices is positive. If you are feeling distressed, see if you are able to put aside your negative thoughts and feelings for a while, so that you will benefit more from these practices. You can use the diversion strategy (from Session Five: Open and Closed Memories) to optimally benefit from your savoring experience.

- One way to maintain savoring is to diversify it. Spend quality time with one of your favorite family members or friends. Pick an activity that both of you enjoy. It could be as simple as having a conversation in a distraction-free environment, watching a movie together, or going for a walk. Try to be in the "here and now" with that person without worrying about the past or the future.
- Spend some time by yourself. This could be for half an hour or an entire day. You could choose to listen to favorite songs, explore a park, go to a new restaurant, or simply read a book of your choice. Pay close attention to your senses while you are engaged in the activity. What do you see, smell, and hear around you?
- Speed is not always bad, nor always good. Sometimes it is good to work quickly, but, for the most part, when we work in a relaxed state, our brain becomes more creative and more productive in performing complex tasks.
- To maintain and enhance savoring, you can also replicate the in-session practice with friends and family members, especially on special occasions and celebrations.

Following is a suggested list of items to savor. The items on this list are designed to target each of the senses and to broaden the notion of savoring to include items beside food: dark chocolate; smooth rocks and sea shells; bags of various ground coffees or loose teas; kaleidoscope; CDs with different genres of music such as opera, jazz, hip hop; various nuts; wind chimes; flowers; pine cones; honey suckle; cotton; sandpaper, gauze; a poem.

END-OF-SESSION RELAXATION

End this session with a short mindfulness-based exercise, followed by showing the following TED Talk: Nature. Beauty. Gratitude: Louis Schwartzberg's stunning time-lapse photography.

RESOURCES

Readings

- Bryant, F. B., & Veroff, J. (2007). *Savoring: A New Model of Positive Experience*. Mahwah, NJ: Lawrence Erlbaum Associates.
- Honoré, C. (2005). *In Praise of Slowness: How a Worldwide Movement Is Challenging the Cult of Speed*. San Francisco: Harper.
- Howell, A. J., Passmore, H. A., & Buro, K. (2013). Meaning in nature: Meaning in life as a mediator of the relationship between nature connectedness and well-being. *Journal of Happiness Studies*, *14*(6), 1681–1696. doi:10.1007/s10902-012-9403-x
- Hurley, D. B., & Kwon, P. (2012). Results of a study to increase savoring the moment: Differential impact on positive and negative outcomes. *Journal of Happiness Studies*, *13*(4), 579–588. doi:10.1007/s10902-011-9280-8

Videos

- TED Talk: Nature. Beauty. Gratitude: Louis Schwartzberg's stunning time-lapse photography:
  http://www.ted.com/talks/louie_schwartzberg_nature_beauty_gratitude
- TED Talk: David Griffin: How photography connects us:
  http://www.ted.com/playlists/30/natural_wonder
- TED Talk: Julian Treasure lays out an eight-step plan to restore our relationship with sound:
  http://www.ted.com/talks/julian_treasure_shh_sound_health_in_8_steps

Websites

- National Geographic's official website:
  http://www.nationalgeographic.com

18

SESSION TWELVE: POSITIVE RELATIONSHIPS

IN SESSION TWELVE, CLIENTS LEARN THE SIGNIFICANCE of recognizing the strengths of their loved ones. The central positive psychotherapy (PPT) practice covered in this session is creating a *Tree of Positive Relationships*.

SESSION TWELVE OUTLINE
Navigating PPT
Core Concepts
    In-Session Practice: *Tree of Positive Relationships*
    Reflection & Discussion
    Vignette
    Fit & Flexibility
    Cultural Considerations
    Maintenance
Resources

Clinician Note

On the following pages, the notion of family is used broadly. We are not limiting it to biologically related family but rather use the term for any constellation of positive, mutually respectful, and loving relationships.

NAVIGATING PPT
So far, our PPT voyage has focused on unfolding the inner resourcefulness of clients. We hope that our practices have helped your clients use their own positive resources to further build their resilience. Together, you and your clients have traveled the peaks and valleys of emotions and experiences—from spotting the good in the moment (*Gratitude Journal*) to revisiting experiences that brought out the goodness within; from calming meandering minds to composing a rich, textured, and holistic self-concept (Signature Strengths Profile); from encountering with courage the pain of open and negative memories to expressing an enduring sense of thankfulness (*Gratitude Letter* and *Visit*). All of these positive emotions and experiences have broadened clients' mindset. From this point onwards, PPT practices focus primarily on interpersonal, social, and communal resourcefulness. We start with positive relationships.

CORE CONCEPTS
We are essentially gregarious beings. Most of us spend the bulk of our time in the active or passive company of others (Bureau of Labor Statistics, 2016). The *quality* of time spent with others also matters, and evidence clearly shows that positive interaction with others acts as a buffer against a number of psychological problems, especially against depression (Fisher & Robinson, 2009). Hence, there is consensus that when our gregarious drive is

thwarted, depression—among other ills—ensues. And when our positive interactions with others find its expression, we flourish. Emerging evidence shows that secure relationships are strongly associated with health indicators. A meta-analysis of 148 studies showed that irrespective of age, sex, initial health status, and cause of death, adults with stronger social ties had at least a 50% increased likelihood of survival (Holt-Lunstad, Smith, & Layton, 2010).

Positive relationships come in many forms. Let's start with family. Biological or otherwise, all family members possess strengths and resources. Due to negative attributions and negativity bias, these strengths may be less prominent. PPT helps clients to explore not only their own strengths but also the strengths of their loved ones. Therefore, in this phase, PPT moves to overcome these challenges. Susan Sheridan and her colleagues (2004) define "positive family" as a unit that is able to access and mobilize strengths and resources to acquire and build skills and competencies, through specific behaviors, to meet members' needs and challenges.

According to Barbara Fredrickson (2014), the eminent researcher of positive emotions, the key strength in meeting challenges is love. Fredrickson contents that love enables us to see another person, holistically, with care, concern, and compassion. Within each moment of loving connection, one becomes sincerely invested in the well-being of the other person, simply for the sake of that person. Such feelings, in genuine love, are mutual. Evidence shows that such mutual care is the hallmark of intimate relationships.

There are many ways of systematically cultivating genuine care. From the vantage point of PPT, learning about one another's strengths is an important way because this promotes empathy and fosters greater appreciation for each person's actions and intentions. For example, when a mother discovers that some of her son's top strengths are honesty, fairness, and bravery, she is better able to understand why he drives all the way across town to return the extra dollar he was accidentally given when checking out at a grocery store, even though he will spend more than a dollar in gas in the process of driving to and from the store. Rather than seeing illogical behavior, the mom can see that her son is simply acting according to his defining character strengths. Likewise, understanding that signature strengths of one's family member are authenticity and honesty may offer a perspective on her comments, remarks, or responses which could be perceived by others as blunt or rude. Cohesion is the hallmark of a positive family including a sense of connectedness or emotional bonding among family members. Research by Houltberg and colleagues (2011) has shown that connectedness in family protects against depressed mood (Tabassum, Mohan, & Smith, 2016; Vazsonyi & Belliston, 2006).

START-OF-SESSION RELAXATION

At the start of every session, begin with a brief relaxation exercise. Refer to Appendix A: Relaxation & Mindfulness Practices, which can be found at the end of this manual. A copy of this appendix also appears in the client workbook. Continue the session with a review of the client's *Gratitude Journal* as well as a review of the core concepts taught in the previous session.

IN-SESSION PRACTICE: *TREE OF POSITIVE RELATIONSHIPS*

Discuss the following questions with your clients in session:

- Who in your immediate or extended relationships always appears to be the most hopeful and optimistic person?
- Who in your relationship circles has the most humorous and playful disposition?

- Who in your relations is the most creative person?
- Who in your relations is always cheerful, bubbly, and smiley?
- Who in your relations is the most curious person?
- Who always treats others fairly and squarely?
- Who is the most loving person in your family or friends?
- Who among your loved ones loves to create new things?
- Who among your loved ones was or is a good leader?
- Who in your relations is the most forgiving person?
- Who among your loved ones shows balanced self-regulation?

Homework

After discussing these questions in session, ask clients to read and complete Worksheet 12.1: *Tree of Positive Relationships*, as homework. Note that this and all worksheets (a) appear within the corresponding session of this manual, (b) are reprinted for the client in the accompanying client workbook, and (c) can be downloaded from our companion website at www.oup.com/ppt.

One way to foster positive relationships is by realizing the importance of understanding and acknowledging the highest strengths of your loved ones and how you fit into your larger family and friend network. When you recognize the strengths of your friends and family members, you are more likely to appreciate them and to build stronger connections. In addition, learning about one another's strengths may potentially help you to gain new insights into the behavior of your loved ones that you previously misunderstood. For example, when Beverley discovers that several of her husband Jackson's top strengths are honesty, fairness, and bravery, she is better able to understand why he would drive all the way across town to return an extra dollar he was accidentally given when checking out at a grocery store— even though he will spend over a dollar in gas in the process of driving to and from the store. Rather than seeing Jackson's behavior as illogical, Beverley can see that he is simply acting according to his strengths of character. Likewise, parents who come to understand that a signature strength of their child is curiosity and interest in the world are better able to tolerate, and even come to enjoy, the abundance of questions posed by the child about how and why things work the way they do.

The Tree of Positive Relationships is designed to help you and people you are close with to gain greater insight into each other's strengths. In order to complete this homework, please ask your family members to complete the Signature Strengths Questionnaire (SSQ-72) available at: www.tayyabrashid.com, or the Values in Action survey available at: http://www.viacharacter.org/

After your loved ones have determined their strengths and have shared these results with you, please complete the blank tree here. We have provided an example of a completed tree for your reference.

Sample *Tree of Positive Relationships*

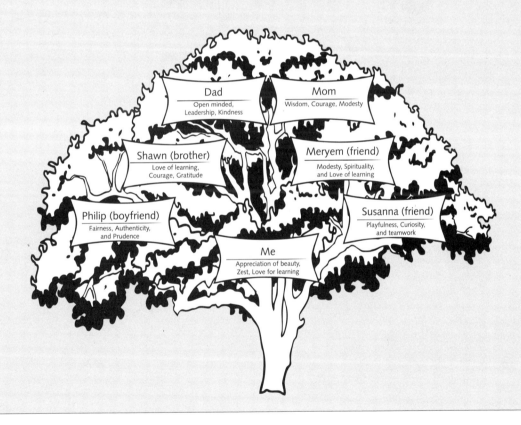

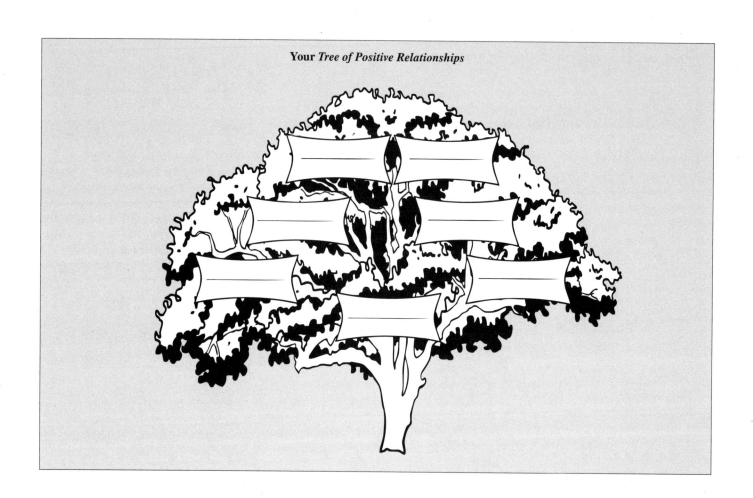

REFLECTION & DISCUSSION

After the assignment has been completed, the questions in Worksheet 12.2: Reflecting on Your *Tree of Positive Relationships*, can help clients facilitate discussion within their families. Ask them to complete the worksheet and share with you during the next session.

After you have completed your Tree of Positive Relationships, fill out this worksheet and bring it to your next session:

1. What specific events exemplify strengths of your loved ones?
    *   Example 1: *My father is kind because he always tries to do nice things for me without me even asking for them.*
    *   Example 2: *My best friend is brave because she stands up for others when people say mean things.*

    Example:

    _____

    _____

    Example:

    _____

    _____

    _____

    Example:

    _____

    _____

2. Can you identify people in your tree who have helped you develop your strengths?

    _____

    _____

3. Do you have any strengths that are also in your loved ones' top five?

    _____

    _____

4. Are there any specific patterns in terms of strengths among your close relationships?

    _____

    _____

5. Do you have any strengths that no one else in your tree of strengths has?

    _____

    _____

6. How can you use your strengths together to make relationships stronger?

    _____

    _____

VIGNETTE: SARAH AND HER *TREE OF POSITIVE RELATIONSHIPS*

Sarah, a 47-year-old mother of two, completed the *Tree of Positive Relationships* practice as part of individual PPT. She sought psychotherapy because of the lack of support she received from her son and husband, while she worked full-time and was completing her studies. After doing this practice, Sarah discussed her insights with her clinician:

CLINICIAN: How did you find the *Tree of Positive Relationships* practice?

SARAH: You know I am a private person. For me the idea of constructing a tree of my positive relationships seemed almost funny.

CLINICIAN: What felt funny about it?

SARAH: It sounded grand and a bit silly. You know my struggles with my husband and son. And I also did not have the best childhood. My father was stubborn, an introvert, and my mother, ah . . . I think she has undiagnosed depression and anxiety . . . so I was not sure if there is a tree of positive relationships in my life . . . I doubted. I thought I might be able to find some shoots . . .

CLINICIAN: What did you find?

SARAH: Well, my first attempt to have my husband and son complete the online strengths test failed. They both ridiculed me. They know I am in therapy. My husband remarked that it must be my shrink who wants to see "how crazy we are." . . . So they refused.

CLINICIAN: Were you able to complete the exercise at all?

SARAH: Yes, two weeks ago, I had a big assignment due and my work is super busy these days. I asked my husband to take care of dinner for just three days and asked my son to do the dishes.

CLINICIAN: So?.

SARAH: Well, the first day I came home after meeting my group for the assignment, I found both of them watching their favorite sports channel. Dinner was nowhere in insight. Instead, they had finished all the snacks at home.

CLINICIAN: How did you respond?

SARAH: I sulked, remained quiet, and quickly fixed the dinner. However, after dinner, I couldn't keep my composure and expressed my disappointment. Both were somewhat embarrassed. My husband agreed that it's not fair that I have to work, study, and then come home and cook dinner. They would like to make it up to me by taking care of dinner for rest of the week. After thinking this over, I said, rather than cooking dinner, if they want to make amends, they could help me complete the *Tree of Positive Relationships* practice. I already was seeing positive changes in my life from previously done practices, and I wanted them to complete the online strengths test, in an honest way.

CLINICIAN: I like you how you used your strength of fairness to share family responsibilities [fairness was identified as one of Sarah's signature strengths].

SARAH: Yes, but I think they completed it more out of guilt. Anyway, last weekend, I cooked their favorite meal. Right after the meal, everyone went online and completed the signature strengths survey. We regrouped at dessert and shared feedback about our strengths. Next, I placed a flip chart sheet in the center of the table and drew a large tree. I went first and plotted my signature strengths on the tree. My husband and son followed and within 10 minutes, everyone's signature strengths filled the tree.

CLINICIAN: I am curious what happened next.

SARAH: It surprised us that all three of us share at least one strength—persistence. My husband is high on teamwork, prudence, and perspective, while my son has humor and playfulness, zest, creativity, and love of learning. Both agreed that these strengths describe them well.

CLINICIAN: Did you discuss how strengths can support you as a well-functioning family?

SARAH: Yes, I am glad that we had discussed practical wisdom previously. First we all shared how we use persistence. All three of us use it in different ways and in different contexts. For example, my son is very persistent in sports, and my husband is very persistent at work—sometimes too persistent. I said it would be great if both of them can show more persistence with chores around the house. I continued by saying that if I can persist and continue working and also going to school, they can persist at home by finishing their chores. Both were able to appreciate what I was saying. My husband quickly pointed out, "Honey, you are persistent and fair, actually, you are persistently fair." We laughed. My husband was able to put things in perspective and for the first time in his life—instead of arguing about my insistence on an equitable distribution of work and everyone pitching in around the house—he was able to appreciate my expression of fairness.

CLINICIAN: How about your son?

SARAH: Knowing Matt's strengths was perhaps the biggest surprise. He is 21. He has always been an active kid. He is full of energy, he is adventurous, loves outdoor sports. When he was young, he was not very coordinated; he still isn't. My husband and I always suspected that Matt has ADHD. In elementary school, his teachers also suspected that, and he was tested, and the assessment found that he has some features but not full-blown ADHD. If something grabs Matt's attention, he can focus well and he persists. But for all of these years, I feared that he does have ADHD, and the assessment just wasn't detailed enough to catch it . . . [Sarah clearly looked dejected.]

CLINICIAN: Indeed it saddens you because you want the best for you son . . . . Let me ask you something, has this fear that Matt has "undiagnosed" ADHD impacted your relationship with him?

SARAH: For sure, it has. I have perceived him as inadequate . . . and many times, I have blamed myself and my husband for not spending enough time with Matt when he was younger, doing things which would build his focus, and concentration. [Tears welled in her eyes, and there was a pause.]

CLINICIAN: I can only imagine . . . and you have been experiencing these emotions all along. [Pause]

SARAH: After completing the *Tree of Positive Relationships* practice, it was the first time I actually understood that I look at my son—and also maybe at my husband—from a place of inadequacies. I did the same to myself—for years—until I assessed my own strengths in this treatment and started believing in them. I think I need to start doing that for my loved ones too.

CLINICIAN: Indeed. It gives so much satisfaction to see how you are integrating various parts of your life. And how do you see Matt now? Has this changed your relationship with him?

SARAH: I no longer believe that he has undiagnosed ADHD. Instead of seeing symptoms of hyperactivity, I see Matt as having lots of zest, vitality, energy. And if I look back, for the most part, he has used his zest in productive ways. He never studied a lot, but he always got good grades. I now see that his energy attracts many friends. He has always been the life of the party.

CLINICIAN: How does this new insight about Matt impact family interaction?

SARAH: After knowing Matt's strengths, my husband remarked that his own father was like Matt. But in those days, the term ADHD was not in fashion. So people looked at him as a "jolly good" guy who always wanted to do great things. And he did too. He was an accomplished sailor.

CLINICIAN: I hope this is just the start of this practice and that your loved ones will spot each other's strengths without feeling silly.

[Sarah smiled.]

FIT & FLEXIBILITY

In addition to discovering a loved one's strengths, another way to understand these strengths is to hear their stories of resilience. Exploring how our loved ones have overcome challenges in the past enables us to understand their strengths in a deeper way.

Some clients may struggle with completing this practice because their relationships or families may not be functioning well. Perhaps they have financial struggles or mismanagement, relationship discord, drug or alcohol problems, or work-family imbalance. In such cases, encourage your clients to look for dyads that may be functioning better than the large group—dyads such as mother–adolescent, father–adolescent, child–grandparent, or sibling subgroups. Strengths can be spotted through smaller groups.

Be sure to remind clients that they can include in their *Tree of Positive Relationships* anyone they consider family. Clients who come from broken, dispersed, deceased, or dysfunctional families may find this activity emotionally difficult. Encourage them to use any loved ones in their lives.

Some clients are not able to make positive changes due to biological, cultural, or economic barriers. Instead of focusing on correcting weaknesses, these clients would benefit from developing growth-producing behaviors that emphasize strengths, assets, and skills. This focus can in turn foster stronger connections, competence, and confidence.

CULTURAL CONSIDERATIONS

In the past, families were often molded on the "traditional" model (i.e., nuclear family, heterosexual couple, with two dependent children). Contemporary families are far more diverse, with single-parent families, blended families, same-sex partnership families, multiracial families, multiethnic families, families divided by immigration statutes (e.g., parents not allowed to stay in the country with their children), and so on. Characteristics of healthy family functioning may differ based on these diverse compositions.

Families from some cultural backgrounds are more likely to share narratives that demonstrate collective strengths, such as caring for parents, helping younger siblings, and expressing a preference for interdependent goals and pursuits. Therefore, it is important that if you are working with clients from diverse cultural backgrounds you are aware of how interpersonal strengths—such as teamwork, social intelligence, or kindness—manifest within specific cultural contexts, as these attributes can easily be perceived as weaknesses. For example, pursuing family goals, instead of personal ones, may prompt some clinicians to suggest that the client ought to focus on expressing individual agency. Or others may ask clients to consider self-compassion. Likewise, kindness of older siblings—as displayed by caring for younger siblings or helping them with homework—may be perceived as exploitation by parents, and clients may be told, even implicitly or explicitly, that they are being treated unfairly.

While working with first-generation clients, it is helpful to be aware of guilt—a psychological phenomenon that some first-generation young adults in Western countries may entertain that they escaped the hardships and impoverishment their parents endured in their native countries. As a result, an explicit display of positive emotions such as zest, vitality, and playfulness may not come naturally or may be subdued (Carrier et al., 2015).

Cultures also differ on goals. For example, in Chinese culture, the goal of maintaining harmonious family relationships is preferred to individual goals. Likewise, the well-being of family and the overall functioning of family as a unit take precedence over individual well-being. Therefore, it is important that when doing this practice you discuss with clients how individual strengths contribute to collective goals.

Finally, positive relationships are created, developed, and sustained within specific cultural norms, traditions, and routines. Expression of strengths ought to be viewed within these normative and cultural contexts.

MAINTENANCE

Discuss the following tips with your clients so that they can maintain their progress:

- One way to build positive relationships is by spotting, naming, and celebrating the strengths of our loved ones. When you recognize the strengths of your loved ones, on the spot, it creates a positive resonance, which could, in turn, strengthen relationships.
- Focus on activities that develop bonds among family members; that establish routines, traditions, and communication patterns; and that happen on a regular basis. These are core family leisure activities.

- From spotting, acknowledging, and celebrating strengths, it is important to create both spontaneous and structured activities. Spontaneous activities are ones that require minimal planning, are informal, and are inclusive of everyone or most family members. Examples of spontaneous activities include family dinner in the park; shopping for ingredients together and then trying them in a new recipe; playing board or digital games; or casually doing sports together, such as shooting hoops in the driveway, playing badminton in the backyard, or enjoying ping pong in the basement. Examples of structured family activities include family vacations; outdoor adventures such as picnics, camping, attending sporting or cultural events; and visiting extended family or close friends in another city, state, province, or country (Morganson, Litano, & O'Neill, 2014). For some families, structured activities may also include visiting specific places or sites of religious, spiritual, artistic, political, or cultural significance. Both spontaneous and structured activities that involve loved ones cement positive relationships like nothing else. Consider this quote from Kelly (1997):

  > Life is not composed of theme parks and cruises. It is composed of dinner table talk, vacations together, getting the home and yard in shape, kidding around, caring for each other, goofing off, dreaming, and all the minutiae of the day and the hour. That is the real life in real conditions that is important to us all. (p. 3)

- Try to have an uninterrupted chat with every member of your family at least once a week. Periodically ask yourself, "Am I listening to my loved one the way I would like to be listened to?"
- Learning about one another's strengths may also help clients to gain new insights into the behaviors of family members that they previously misunderstood. This knowledge will enable family members to know, acknowledge, and celebrate each other's strengths and promote interactions and family-centered activities around those strengths. For instance, if you learn that your partner has the strengths of appreciation of beauty and excellence, then a creative or performing arts center would be a great place to visit when you are on vacation. If some of your family members love sports, a family excursion around a sporting event may allow the display of multiple strengths, including playfulness and humor (having fun together), teamwork (coordination of the event), and love of learning (knowledge about sports).
- Investing in positive relationships within one's family, chosen family, and/or circle of significant others takes time, skill, and effort. This effort can lead to greater happiness.
- In cultivating positive relationships among significant others, it is important to recognize the strengths of these others and to engage in activities that allow all parties to use their strengths.
- Taking the time to remember the strengths and other positive qualities of loved ones is important for preserving positive relationships. Over time, we can get so used to these positive qualities that we do not notice them as much as we once did.

END-OF-SESSION RELAXATION

We recommend that each session end with the same brief relaxation practice that started the session.

RESOURCES

Readings

- Davis, M., & Suveg, C. (2014). Focusing on the positive: A review of the role of child positive affect in developmental psychopathology. *Clinical Child and Family Psychology Review, 17*(2), 97–124.
- Ho, H. C. Y., Mui, M., Wan, A., Ng, Y., Stewart, S. M., Yew, C., et al. (2016). Happy family kitchen II: A cluster randomized controlled trial of a community-based positive psychology family intervention for subjective happiness and health-related quality of life in Hong Kong. *Trials, 17*(1), 367.
- Sheridan, S. M., Warnes, E. D., Cowan, R. J., Schemm, A. V., & Clarke, B. L. (2004). Family-centered positive psychology: Focusing on strengths to build student success. *Psychology in the Schools, 41*(1), 7–17. doi:10.1002/pits.10134

Videos

- YouTube: Let's Eat Rice Daddy: 2012 Chinese New Year commercial by BERNAS: https://youtu.be/LzP8E8KSgPc
- Positive Parenting: Lea Waters on Strength Based Parenting: https://youtu.be/RMhVopiQYzM
- TED Talk: Andrew Solomon: What Does Family Mean? https://www.ted.com/talks/andrew_solomon_love_no_matter_what?referrer=playlist-what_does_family_mean
- YouTube: Father, Son and a Sparrow: https://youtu.be/fOYpFhxEptE

Websites

- Institute of Family Studies: https://ifstudies.org/
- Better Together: http://robertdputnam.com/better-together/
- Centre for Family Studies, University of Oxford: https://www.cfr.cam.ac.uk/

## 19

SESSION THIRTEEN: POSITIVE COMMUNICATION

IN SESSION THIRTEEN, CLIENTS LEARN ABOUT FOUR styles of responding to good news. Of these styles, only *Active Constructive Responding (ACR)*—the central practice covered in this session—predicts relationship satisfaction.

SESSION THIRTEEN OUTLINE

Core Concepts
    In-Session Practice: *Active Constructive Responding*
    Reflection & Discussion
    Homework Practice: *Identify Your Partner's Strengths*
    Reflection & Discussion
    Vignettes
    Fit & Flexibility
    Cultural Considerations
    Maintenance
Resources

CORE CONCEPTS

Consider this Swedish proverb:

Shared joy is a double joy; shared sorrow is a half sorrow.

Both good and bad things happen to people. Some of us try to reframe a negative event to put it into perspective. Others have a hard time letting go of a negative event and continue to ruminate. Research indicates that people experience positive emotions 2.5 times more often than we experience negative emotions, and we also frequently experience positive and negative emotions simultaneously (Trampe, Quoidbach, & Taquet, 2015). However, the potency of negatives, especially the ruminative or "stickiness" of them, keeps us stuck. Some people even hesitate to disclose positive events.

When we experience adversities, challenges, hassles, and traumas, for the most part (if not always), people seek out their spouses, partners, friends, family, and community for support. Research shows that social support is beneficial, emotionally and physically, for coping. As a clinician, this is likely not new to you. However, have you considered the other side of the coin? Good things also happen, and, for most of us, good things happen more than bad things. Ironically, psychotherapists are less likely to ask their clients, "What do you do when things go right?," especially with their partner. Self-disclosure of positive events is critical for secure bonding and for the development of intimacy. In this session of positive psychotherapy (PPT), a specific type of self-disclosure is presented. This self-disclosure is done in a constructive and positive manner.

Shelly Gable and her colleagues (Gable et al., 2004; Maisel & Gable, 2009) have explored the intrapersonal and interpersonal consequences of self-disclosure and seeking out others when good things happen to us. Langston (1994) found that when people experience a positive event and share its news with others, they experience greater positive affect, beyond increases associated with the valence of the positive event itself. Langston termed this "capitalization," a term that Gable adopted to denote the process of sharing positive news with another person and thereby deriving additional benefit from it. Capitalization is a process of being seen, felt, valued, and expanded. The sum of these components is greater since both the sharer and the responder feel validated. Capitalization offers a skill to regulate our responses.

Gable and her colleagues (2004) have delineated responding into four distinct styles. Of these styles, which are shown in Box 19.1, ACR was associated with increased daily positive affect and well-being, above and beyond the impact of the positive event itself and other daily events.

Gable and her colleagues found that when others were perceived to respond actively and constructively (and not passively or destructively) to capitalization attempts, the benefits were further enhanced. Moreover, close relationships in which one's partner typically responds to capitalization attempts enthusiastically was associated with higher relationship well-being (e.g., intimacy, daily marital satisfaction). Emerging lines of research have shown that ACR to a positive event enhances intimacy of the couple, increases

---

BOX 19.1   FOUR WAYS OF RESPONDING TO A GOOD EVENT SHARED BY A LOVED ONE

	Constructive	Destructive
Active	Enthusiastic support, elaborates the experience; person feels validated and understood; the event is relived, expanded; specific and relevant questions about the unfolding of the event and reasons why the event took place are asked; what additional positive events may happen associated with it is also asked *Illustration:* "That is wonderful! I'm so happy for you. You would be excellent in that new position." *Display:* maintaining eye contact, smiling, displaying positive emotions	Quashing the event, brings conversation to a halt; person feels ashamed, embarrassed, guilty or angry *Illustration:* "If you get the promotion, you are going to have to be at work all week and on Saturday mornings too." *Display:* Pointing out the downside; displaying negative emotions through grimace, tense forehead, etc. and through nonverbal cues
Passive	Quiet, understated support; conversation fizzles out; person feels unimportant, misunderstood, embarrassed, and guilty *Illustration:* "That's nice that you are being considered for the promotion." *Display:* happy, but subdued expressions lacking enthusiasm; downplaying; little to no active emotional expressions	Ignoring the event; conversation never starts; person feels confused, guilty, or disappointed *Illustration:* "A promotion, huh? Well, hurry up and get changed so that we can get some dinner. I am starving." *Display:* little or no eye contact, lacking interest, turning away, leaving the room

daily happiness, and reduces conflicts. Both self-disclosure and partner responsiveness contribute to the experience of intimacy in interactions. Specifically, capitalization states that (Lemay, Clark, & Feeney, 2007)

- Partners and other people who share good news feel validated. Capitalization gives them the message that they are important.
- When people tell others about positive events, they experience more positive emotions and feel greater life satisfaction than when they cannot or choose not to tell others about these positive events.
- The benefits of sharing are above and beyond the positive emotions and life satisfaction that are experienced with the event itself.
- Sharing positive events entails questions about the event, discussions about the important aspects of the event, and the implications of the event—all of which cement relationships.

In PPT, we recommend that one way to build positive relationships is by understanding and acknowledging the highest strengths of our family members and how they fit into our larger family network. When we recognize the strengths of our family members, we are more likely to appreciate one another and to build stronger connections. Learning about one another's strengths may also help us gain new insights into the behaviors of our family members that we previously misunderstood. This will enable family members to know, acknowledge, and celebrate one another's strengths and promote interactions and family-centered activities around those strengths. For instance, if a client learns that his brother has a great love of history, then a trip to a history museum would be a great place to visit when the family goes on vacation. Learning about one another's strengths enables us to have insights about each other that will most likely remove misunderstandings and will promote empathy and greater appreciation for each other's actions and intentions.

Engaging in self-disclosure is critical for secure bonding and for the development of intimacy. In PPT, a specific sort of self-disclosure is encouraged. This self-disclosure is done in a constructive and positive manner. Positive events have a nurturing, broadening, or building potential (Fredrickson, 2001) and are rarely irreversible. In contrast, negative events leave long-lasting damage, require quicker responses, and can be potentially fatal as they require regulation to change aversive situations (Pratto & John, 1991).

START-OF-SESSION RELAXATION

At the start of every session, begin with a brief relaxation exercise. Refer to Appendix A: Relaxation & Mindfulness Practices, which can be found at the end of this manual. A copy of this appendix also appears in the client workbook. Continue the session with a review of the client's *Gratitude Journal* as well as a review of the core concepts taught in the previous session.

IN-SESSION PRACTICE: *ACTIVE CONSTRUCTIVE RESPONDING*

Worksheet 13.1 starts with examples of the four responding styles, followed by an in-session exercise. Note that this and all worksheets (a) appear within the corresponding session of this manual, (b) are reprinted for the client in the accompanying client work-book, and (c) can be downloaded from our companion website at www.oup.com/ppt. The examples in Worksheet 13.1 come from both clinical and nonclinical settings. Present this worksheet to your clients. Ask them to read about the various responding styles and to select ones that represent their own situations, most of the time, by marking an X in the column labeled Response.

Please read about the following different styles of responding and put an X in the Response column for the ones that apply to you most of the time.

Active/Constructive	Response
My partner usually reacts to my good fortune enthusiastically.	
I sometimes get the sense that my partner is even more happy and excited than I am.	
My partner often asks a lot of questions and shows genuine interest about the good event.	
Passive/Constructive	
My partner tries not to make a big deal out of it but is happy for me.	
My partner is usually silently supportive of the good things that occur to me.	
My partner says little, but I know he/she is happy for me.	
Active/Destructive	
My partner often finds a problem with it.	
My partner reminds me that most good things have their bad aspects as well.	
He/she points out the potential downsides of the good event.	
Passive/Destructive	
Sometimes I get the impression that he/she doesn't care much.	
My partner doesn't pay much attention to me.	
My partner often seems uninterested.	

- *Now it's your turn to try ACR today in-session. Take turns with a partner (or with your clinician if you are in individual therapy).*
- *As the **Sharer,** think of something meaningful and positive that happened to you, or that you noticed in the last week. Share this with your partner.*
- *As the **Responder**, think about your strengths and explore how you can use your strengths in the Active Constructive Responses you offer (e.g., curiosity to guide your question, optimism, social intelligence).*
- *Then switch roles between sharer and responder. When this practice is complete, your clinician will ask you some reflection questions.*

REFLECTION & DISCUSSION

After completing this practice, ask clients to reflect and discuss:

- What was comfortable in doing this practice?
- What was uncomfortable in doing this practice?
- Are there any subjective or objective barriers (such as your personality style, preferences, family of origin, culture, beliefs, or interpersonal dynamics) that hinder you in engaging in *ACR*?
- If you already do some sort of *ACR*, what can you do to take it to a higher level?
- If you find that *ACR* doesn't come naturally to you, what small steps can you take to adopt some aspects of this practice that are consistent with your disposition?
- Identify individuals or situations that display all four responding styles. What effects do you notice of each style both on sharer and responder?
- What can you learn about yourself from identifying your response style?

HOMEWORK PRACTICE: *IDENTIFY YOUR PARTNER'S STRENGTHS*

To amplify the *ARC* practice, ask your clients to complete Worksheet 13.2 at home, and then to reflect on the following questions.

Earlier in therapy, you completed practices that enabled you to determine your own signature strengths, and now you are quite familiar with these strengths. To complete this homework assignment, you will need two copies of this worksheet. Set aside at least 30 minutes for this practice with your partner. In a relaxed environment, ask your partner to fill out the worksheet by identifying five strengths that best represent you, without ranking them. While your partner is completing the worksheet, you complete one for your partner. When finished, exchange worksheets and continue with the Reflect & Discuss questions.

	Description	Signature Strengths
1	Is good at thinking of new and better ways of doing things	
2	Loves to explore things, asks questions, is open to different experiences and activities	
3	Is flexible and open-minded; thinks through and examines all sides before deciding	
4	Loves to learn new ideas, concepts, and facts in school or on her/his own	
5	Friends consult him/her regarding important matters; is considered to be wise beyond age	
6	Does not give up in face of hardship or challenge, even when afraid	
7	Finishes most things; is able to refocus when distracted and complete the task	
8	Is a genuine and honest person, is known to be trustworthy; acts consistent with her/his values	
9	Is energetic, cheerful, and full of life	
10	Both loving and being loved comes natural to him/her; values close relationships with others	
11	Loves to do kind acts for others, often without being asked	
12	Manages her/himself well in social situations and is known to have good interpersonal skills	
13	Is an active community or team member, and contributes to the success of the group	
14	Stands up for others when they are treated unfairly, bullied, or ridiculed	
15	Is often chosen by others as a leader; is known to lead well	
16	Forgives easily those who offend him/her; does not hold grudges	
17	Doesn't like to be the center of attention and prefers others to shine	
18	Is careful and cautious, can anticipate risks and problems of his/her actions and responds accordingly	
19	Manages feelings and behaviors well in challenging situations; generally follows rules and routines	
20	Is moved deeply by beauty in nature, in art (e.g., painting, music, theatre) and/or in excellence in many fields of life	
21	Expresses thankfulness for good things through words and actions	
22	Hopes and believe that more good things will happen than bad ones	
23	Is playful and funny, and uses humor to connect with others	
24	Believes in a higher power and participates in religious or spiritual practices (e.g., prayer, meditation) willingly	

REFLECTION & DISCUSSION

After completing this practice with your partner, reflect and discuss:

- How was the process of labeling and affirming each other's strengths? Have you done similar things with your partner before?
- What behaviors, actions, or habits does your partner exhibit to denote the strengths you identified?
- Do you share strengths with each other? Discuss any your share as well as ones you don't.
- In what ways do your strengths complement each other?
- Did you also look at your partner's and your bottom strengths? What can you learn from those?

VIGNETTE: SABRINA TRIES *ACTIVE CONSTRUCTIVE RESPONDING*

Sabrina, a 33-year-old, married, Hispanic female, sought psychotherapy for being constantly criticized and feeling unappreciated by her husband, Jose. Sabrina and Jose met when both were doing their full-time internship; they dated for more than two years before getting married. Sabrina recalled that, before marriage, Jose appreciated her intelligence, attention to detail, commitment to work, and professional integrity. Sabrina stated that she works as hard as Jose does and earns more than he does, yet lately she has been feeling unvalued and inadequate, and she is getting tired of being hurt by him. Sharing a specific experience, Sabrina stated that the previous week, she had secured a major corporate account for which she had worked very hard. Everyone in her office congratulated her, and her boss rewarded her with a bonus and two days off. Feeling accomplished and elated, Sabrina enthusiastically shared the news with Jose as soon as she got home. Jose, whose eyes were glued to a baseball game on the television, congratulated her in a lukewarm tone without making eye contact and added that this would be a difficult client for her. He then quickly shifted the topic to dinner.

With her joy dampened, Sabrina distracted herself in preparing dinner while Jose remained fixed on the television. Struggling to find words to express herself, Sabrina simmered inside for the next few days, thinking that her accomplishments and feelings didn't matter to Jose and wondering if he still loved her.

Considering that Sabrina finds it difficult to express herself, she asked Jose if he would like to join her in psychotherapy for a few sessions. After initial hesitation, Jose agreed to attend a few sessions but kept on insisting that the couple was doing just fine. Instead of blaming and shaming Jose, initially the therapy focused on creating a caring space where both were able to share with each other times when they felt valued and not valued, appreciated and unappreciated. As expected, Sabrina had far more to share than Jose.

Listening to Sabrina's reflections, Jose was surprised. He had thought that everything was working well. Just listening to Sabrina's issues in the presence of an impartial professional, Jose became aware of two things: first, that he constantly communicated with Sabrina—whether with or without words, whether he smiled or made a poker face, whether he made eye contact or avoided it, and whether he reached out and touched Sabrina or physically withdrew from her. Jose communicated with Sabrina, who in turn was attaching meaning to everything he communicated. Second, Jose also realized that his communication style was causing Sabrina a great deal of stress. Rather than correcting this communication style, the clinician asked Jose to engage in *ACR*. To put the skill into practice, Sabrina was asked to share something important and positive that happened to her during the past two weeks.

Jose, in turn, was asked to respond enthusiastically in a way that felt authentic to him and would also make Sabrina feel understood and validated. Jose's first few responses were either enthusiastic or authentic but not both. It took some coaching before he was able to offer his wife a response that made her feel both validated and supported.

Jose was somewhat dismayed. He stated that he cannot change, and said, "This is the way I am." Nonetheless, he was reassured that even though it may feel a bit awkward initially since he is used to responding in a typical way, with time and with sincere effort, ACR would eventually become easier and seem more natural to him. Furthermore, he doesn't have to practice ACR with everyone and in every situation. The aim of the practice is to connect genuinely with loved ones, not with everyone.

As human beings, we are hardwired to detect negative facial expressions, tones, gestures, and postures with more efficiency than with positives ones, and we are often unaware of this tendency. Indeed, this negativity bias can sharpen our critical thinking, but, if overused in our intimate relationships, it can cause harm. Fortunately, we are also blessed with the psychological sophistication to override this hardwiring and make an effort to offer positive and constructive responses to make our relationships more fulfilling—something Sabrina and Jose have begun to do.

VIGNETTE: SHERRY AND COUNTERING SHAME WITH HUMOR

Sherry, a 38-year-old female client, recently attended a PPT workshop during which participants were asked to close their eyes and engage in a meditative practice whereby they would envision a time in their lives when they had some kind of challenge and managed to overcome it in a positive way. Here is Sherry's reflection on the practice:

"As I closed my eyes, it was a bit challenging to choose one event because there have been many in my life. I'm sure that's no different than anyone else. Within moments, my mind came to rest on a pleasant memory regarding my mother. My relationship with her had always been somewhat strained. And at this point in my life, I had made a commitment to work through my 'mother issues' as I learned to create a healthier and happier relationship with her.

"I recalled a time when I was about 35 years old. I'd been in counseling on and off for about seven years, focusing on resolving various difficulties in my life, including my relationship with mom. I was learning about assertiveness, personal boundaries, and expressing my thoughts and feelings in healthier ways, instead of being reactive and lashing out in anger or fear or shame as I had become accustomed to doing when I felt threatened.

"Back in the present, as I sat in this quiet room with 20 other workshop participants, my eyes closed, my breathing regulated to a nice, slow, easy pace, my mind drifted back to a memory. The phone was ringing. "Hello?' I said. My mom was calling to ask me to do something for her. At that time in my life I was a newly single parent raising two young children and going to college full-time to become a social worker. So needless to say, I was very, very busy. I really didn't have time to help my mom, nor did I want to do whatever it was that she was asking for. It wasn't anything really important, and either she could do it for herself, or one of my less busy siblings could take care of it. I was taking care of the kids and studying, along with a plethora of other household duties that a single parent must contend with. So I said, 'No, I won't be able to help.' I then braced myself for the litany that would typically ensue as a result of my refusing to comply with her wishes. 'You are selfish!'

'You think of no one but yourself!' and 'You are just like your father!' (Never a good thing in her book.)

"My parents had been divorced for many years, and mom still harbored a great deal of anger and resentment toward Dad. I found myself reacting in anger, fear, and/or shame whenever Mom told me how selfish and self-centered I was, and how I was like my father. This time was different though. For the first time I didn't have that emotional attachment to what she was saying. I didn't buy into her beliefs about me or her accusations, and I was really surprised by that! What happened instead was that I felt nothing but peace. That was very interesting! As I looked at it, I realized with a flash of insight that this has been a pattern my mother had been using all of my life. This communication dynamic was a way for her to manipulate us kids into doing what she wanted us to do. The clarity of that awareness was like the clouds parting and heaven opening up with celestial music and the angels singing Hallelujah!!! Ha ha—not really, but that's what I imagined. I was just overcome with this awareness and how it had influenced me all my life! I started laughing! I wasn't laughing at her. I was just laughing at the wonder of it all and how I couldn't believe I hadn't seen this sooner.

"Mom went really quiet. Then she said with a really harsh voice, 'What are you laughing at???' I was still kind of laughing and giggling and said, 'Oh my God, Mom! I'm just seeing this for the very first time! You have been using this as a manipulation for me and my sibs for all our lives. You know you are manipulating me by getting me angry and telling me how selfish and self-centered I am. You try to make me feel guilty to get me to do what you want me to do!' Mom went really quiet again, and I thought, 'Oh boy here it comes. She is going to get really mad at me.' Then she started laughing!!! I couldn't believe what I was hearing!!!! I just waited . . . and she said, 'Well it took you long enough!!!'

"I think that conversation was the birthplace of an adult relationship between my mother and me. No longer did she treat me like I was a little girl, and she seemed to have a renewed respect for me as a grown woman. She started relating to me as such and, you know, I started being kinder and patient, and gentler with her as well. I was able to see my mom as an adult and as a single parent who had her own challenges to contend with under some very trying circumstances.

"I shared this story during the workshop, and I was told that I was able to use the strengths of playfulness and humor to address this challenging problem with my mother."

FIT & FLEXIBILITY

Some clients may state, as one of our clients did, "But I am not a very enthusiastic, celebrating person to begin with" or "I am not very extraverted whereas ACR sounds very extraverted." ACR is not about the *volume* of client responses; rather, ACR is about *depth* and interest. It is not about the precision of verbal expression, but it is about sincerity of the emotions. A client can be an introvert, yet in the comfort of her disposition and demeanor, she can ask questions to go deeper, to let the other person know that she is genuinely interested and happy about the good news.

Since all forms of responding to good or bad news are highly subjective, how can we determine what is a real ACR? Furthermore, it is possible that some people might be satisfied with a gentle smile, while others may not be satisfied even with unbridled enthusiasm. Shelley Gable and her colleagues (2004) found that objective ratings of ACR correlate with how the responder feels after the discussion; specifically, when outside observers rate the response as being active and constructive, sharers also felt more satisfied with their partners and closer to their partners. Thus it seems that the actual response matters, and it is not just that some people see any response as active (or passive) and constructive (or destructive). There usually is a gut sense of delivered or received authenticity.

A few clients may report that it feels fake, ostentatious, or flamboyant to celebrate even minor successes. Indeed, one cannot offer *ACR* for every good event. Frequent or overuse of *ACR* dilutes its authenticity. Therefore, one must respond actively and constructively to events that are meaningful and important. Moreover, some situational factors may not lend one to offer *ACR* immediately when the good event is shared. It can be delayed, if situational factors do not allow the responder to offer an authentic *ACR*, such as attending to someone's medical needs, responding to a phone call that needs an immediate response, adding final touches to a project with an approaching deadline, or when in the company of others who may not understand your response. Finally, *ACR* is about specificity. Each question builds on the next one. Even if the sharer dismisses the positive news or is evasive, the responder should keep acknowledging.

ACR is one aspect of positive relationships. Partners also need to make time for passions, hobbies, and self-reflection, which may require solitude. It is important that clients do not sacrifice these other important qualities in pursuing this practice.

Today, the technological nature of our current culture makes communication easier but less personal. Less and less of our time is spent in face-to-face interactions. A core quality of a good relationship is personal interaction and connectedness, which is best fostered through face-to-face interaction (refer also to the Core Concepts in Chapter 20, Session 14, for more on this topic). Help clients understand the difference between texting a friend and speaking with him in person.

CULTURAL CONSIDERATIONS

Clients from some cultures may find the *ACR* practice to be ostentatious because good events and experiences are not usually celebrated within their culture. Take Dave, 42, a mental health practitioner from Australia. After completing a day-long PPT training workshop, Dave remarked that he found *ACR* akin to the Australian axiom, "one doesn't pump the bravado." However, a thorough discussion focused on conveying authentic interest by listening and asking questions actively, in a constructive manner, helped Dave overcome hesitation.

As clinicians, we must be aware that cultures differ in self-disclosure of emotions. These differences could be in terms of speaking directly or indirectly, with little eye contact or consistent eye contact, conveying a lot or a little through bodily gestures and postures while responding, requesting or commanding attention while responding, and sharing positive experiences with an animated versus a neutral tone (Gobel, Chen, & Richardson, 2017; Kleinsmith, De Silva, & Bianchi-Berthouze, 2006). An encouraging but not obvious feature of the practice is that *ACR* doesn't only depend on vociferous verbal responses. Body gesturers, postures, listening more, and asking fewer but more relevant questions matter more.

ACR is about offering authentic and positive response. Responders are welcome to adapt it culturally, that is, to use their creativity to find culturally appropriate ways of responding in an active and constructive manner. For example, a clinician from a German cultural background did this exercise during a workshop and remarked, "Rather than using words and expressions, I found it easier to express my active and constructive response nonverbally. During my training in the Gestalt therapy, I learned almost half of communication is conveyed nonverbally by body postures and facial expression."

Accentuating and amplifying good events may be considered hubris and vanity in some cultures. Other cultures may have a practice or norm of minimizing, rather than expanding, the good event. Nevertheless, keep in mind that cultures are dynamic. Offering *ACR* in a culturally sensitive manner may set new and positive precedents. Chris Peterson (2006), one of the pioneers in this field, says that positive psychology has helped him to progress from "mean funny" to "kind funny." Along the same lines, we can offer *ACR* with the good intention that it will strengthen relationships—a goal that is valued across cultures.

Clients from some cultures may wish to express their appreciation for a positive event in culturally adaptive ways. Culturally adaptive ways can be used as long as the spirit and essence of *ACR*—that is, sharing and celebrating a positive experience authentically—remains intact.

MAINTENANCE

Discuss the following tips with your clients so that they can maintain their progress:

- In *ACR*, the authentic inquiry, not the volume of inquiry, matters. It is what is seen, felt, valued, and expanded authentically. These steps need practice in a variety of situations.
- *ACR* is about specificity. Each question builds on the next one. Even if the sharer dismisses or is evasive, the responder should keep acknowledging.
- *ACR* is about attunement, getting to know one another deeply and authentically, in which both parties feel understood, validated, and cared for.
- *ACR* is not only for partners. It can be used when friends or other family members share a good event.
- The impact of *ACR* is most likely to increase if you are able to set aside negative emotions, feeling, and doubts for a while and be with your loved one celebrating and sharing the positive moments. You can discuss negatives, complaints, doubts, or adverse impacts on you later on.
- *ACR* offers a concrete way to enhance the ability to recognize, understand, and respond to positive emotions, feelings, and experiences of loved ones. Ask your partner how this process can help the two of you to enhance your understanding of other issues, situations, events, or experiences that could also benefit from *ACR*.

END-OF-SESSION RELAXATION

We recommend that each session end with the same brief relaxation practice that started the session.

RESOURCES

Readings

- Gable, S. L., Reis, H. T., Impett, E. A., & Asher, E. R. (2004). What do you do when things go right? The intrapersonal and interpersonal benefits of sharing positive events. *Journal of Personality and Social Psychology, 87*, 228–245.

- Gable, S.L., & Reis, H.T. (2010). Good news! Capitalizing on positive events in an interpersonal context. In M. P. Zanna (Ed.), *Advances in Experimental Social Psychology* (Vol. 42, 195–257). San Diego, CA: Elsevier Academic Press.

- Lambert, N. M., Clark, M. S., Durtschi, J., Fincham, F. D., & Graham, S. M. (2010). Benefits of expressing gratitude to a partner changes one's view of the relationship. *Psychological Science, 21*(4), 574–580.

- Stanton, S. C. E., Campbell, L., & Loving, T. J. (2014). Energized by love: Thinking about romantic relationships increases positive affect and blood glucose levels. *Psychophysiology, 51*(10), 990–995. doi:10.1111/psyp.12249

- Woods, S., Lambert, N., Brown, P., Fincham, F., & May, R. (2015). "I'm so excited for you!" How an enthusiastic responding intervention enhances close relationships. *Journal of Social and Personal Relationships, 32*(1), 24–40.

Videos

- YouTube: Active Constructive Responding:
  https://youtu.be/qRORihbXMnA?list=PLLBhiMXTg8qvQ4Ge94wRFYZhk66t_wm1e
- Shelley Gable explains Active Constructive Response (ACR):
  https://youtu.be/OF9kfJmS_0k
- It Is Not About the Nail: a hilarious illustration on the importance of "I just need you to listen":
  https://youtu.be/-4EDhdAHrOg

Websites

- People will like you:
  http://www.pbs.org/thisemotionallife/blogs/happiness-exercise-how-make-people-love-you
- Using positive psychology in your relationships:
  http://health.usnews.com/health-news/family-health/brain-and-behavior/articles/2009/06/24/using-positive-psychology-in-your-relationships
- Paul Ekman: Atlas of Emotions, aims to build vocabulary of emotions:
  http://atlasofemotions.org/#introduction/disgust

## 20

SESSION FOURTEEN: ALTRUISM

IN SESSION FOURTEEN, CLIENTS LEARN HOW BEING altruistic helps both themselves and others. The central positive psychotherapy (PPT) practice covered in this session is the *Gift of Time*.

SESSION FOURTEEN OUTLINE
Core Concepts
    In-Session Activity: Video Capturing The Practice Of The *Gift Of Time*
    Reflection & Discussion
    Vignette
    Fit & Flexibility
    Cultural Considerations
    Maintenance
Resources

CORE CONCEPTS
Altruism is benefitting others, at one's own will, without being asked for it and without any financial reimbursement. In PPT, meaning entails using one's signature strengths to belong to and serve something that one believes is bigger than the self. One wants to make a life that matters to the world and creates a difference for the better. The psychological benefits of altruism are significant:

- Converging lines of evidence show that volunteerism is associated with increased longevity, improved ability to carry out activities of daily living, better health coping behavior, healthier lifestyle habits, improved quality of life, reliable social support, increased positive interaction with others, less chronic pain and hospital admission, and overall decreased psychological distress (Casiday, Kinsman, & Fisher, 2008; Musick & Wilson, 2003; Nedelcu & Michod, 2006; Soosai-Nathan, Negri, & Delle Fave, 2013).
- Evidence has also found that after adjusting for a number of relevant characteristics, people volunteering for the environment maintained higher levels of physical activity and reported better self-rated health and fewer depressive symptoms (Pillemer et al., 2010).
- Volunteerism and giving are strongly linked with happiness and well-being. People purchase and consume products with the goal of becoming happier, but they rarely attain that goal from their purchase behavior (Kasser & Kanner, 2004; Lyubormirsky, 2007). Over time, *products* lose their charm due to hedonic adaptation, but *experiences* get better with time (Kasser & Kanner, 2004; Van Boven & Gilovich, 2003). When people invest money to buy products, they expect clear and uninterrupted satisfaction or pleasure from these products. On the other hand, when people engage in experiences such as volunteering, they tend to reflect at a deeper level such as whether their involvement was worth it or not. Moreover, products are associated with utility, while experiences are linked with emotions. Experiences connect us with people (through interactions), while products and gadgets—especially today's technological devices—pull us away from the people around us. Indeed, we do connect with many people on

Facebook and other social media platforms, but often we are distant from our colleagues in the next office, from our neighbors next door, and from our loved ones in the next room.

- Those who help others incur health benefits themselves. In a randomized study, 106 Canadian Grade 10 students fluent in English and free from a chronic health condition volunteered for two months helping elementary school children. Cardiovascular risk markers including C-reactive protein level, total cholesterol level, and body mass index were monitored. Results showed that those who increased the most in empathy and altruistic behaviors, and who decreased the most in negative mood, also showed the greatest decreases in cardiovascular risk over time (Schreier, Kimberly, Schonert-Reichl, & Chen, 2013). This study offers the first epidemiological evidence for a positive association.

- Robert Putnum (2000), a political scientist from Harvard University who drew empirical evidence from nearly 500,000 interviews conducted over the past quarter century, shows that social capital—built by positive relationships—has become significantly weakened. Compared to the 1950s, active involvement in most organizations has dropped by more than 50%, attendance at places of worship has dropped 25% to 50%, and the rate of entertaining friends in one's home has dropped by 45%, among many other trends. Putnam suggests the grim truth that altruism, volunteering, and philanthropy have been on a steady decline since the 1950s.

In summary, helping others shifts the attentional focus from indulging in one's own thoughts (i.e., brooding over depressive thinking) as attention is allocated from unhealthy thinking to a healthier behavioral endeavor. While the former makes one vulnerable and reinforces one's self-perception as victim, the later fosters self-efficacy. However, as noted, there has been an overall decline in volunteerism and altruistic behavior. How can this unfortunate trend be impacted by PPT? After nurturing close relationships, PPT now enlarges interpersonal well-being by encouraging clients to help others to help themselves.

START-OF-SESSION RELAXATION

At the start of every session, begin with a brief relaxation exercise. Refer to Appendix A: Relaxation & Mindfulness Practices, which can be found at the end of this manual. A copy of this appendix also appears in the client workbook. Continue the session with a review of the client's *Gratitude Journal* as well as a review of the core concepts taught in the previous session.

IN-SESSION ACTIVITY: VIDEO CAPTURING THE PRACTICE OF THE *GIFT OF TIME*

The in-session practice for this session focuses on watching a video that captures the concept of altruism and illustrates the *Gift of Time* practice. Screen this YouTube video, and then ask clients to reflect and discuss, using the Reflection & Discussion questions.

Gift, Singapore Inspiration Drama Short Film (Duration: 7:30)
https://youtu.be/1DUYlHZsZfc?list=PL8m
This short film depicts a son who discovers a big secret about his father, one that changes the son's understanding of his father.

REFLECTION & DISCUSSION

- What stood out for you in this video about altruism?
- Did the material remind you of anything from your own experiences regarding altruism?

- What specific actions, if any, did the video ask you to think about regarding the cultivation of altruism in your daily life?
- Why did the father keep the secret of giving from his son?
- In the video, the father gives a lot, despite not having much. How can his example help people who may think that they have nothing or very little to offer?

Clinician Note

The self-care of clients may already be compromised. Talk with such clients to make sure that their altruistic endeavors don't negatively impact their self-care needs. A detailed discussion of their level of distress and well-being will help clients decide on the scale of their altruistic endeavors as well as reveal their exposure to potential vulnerability.

Clients from marginalized backgrounds with limited resources are less likely to volunteer than their wealthier and healthier counterparts.

Clients already committed to taking care of a family member with chronic health problems, those who often have to take care of a family member due to frequent but unplanned health challenges and those taking care of elderly parents or family members with developmental disabilities may not be able to volunteer. Therefore, it is important to discuss the topic of volunteering with clients, sensitively taking into account their situational challenges.

Homework

After watching the video and discussing the questions in session, ask clients to complete Worksheet 14.1 as homework. Note that this and all worksheets (a) appear within the corresponding session of this manual, (b) are reprinted for the client in the accompanying client workbook, and (c) can be downloaded from our companion website at www.oup.com/ppt. Depending on the clients, this assignment can be done before the next session, or possibly after PPT is over, since clients are being asked to offer time as a gift.

The aim of this practice is for you to give someone you care about the Gift of Time by doing something for them that requires a fair amount of time and involves using one of your signature strengths.

It will make the exercise more gratifying for you if you use your signature strength to deliver the gift. For example:

- *Someone who is creative might write an anniversary note for a best friend.*
- *Someone who is playful and humorous might arrange a roast.*
- *Someone who is kind might prepare a four-course dinner for his or her sick roommate or partner.*

After completing this exercise, write about your experience giving the Gift of Time. Be sure to record exactly what you did and how long it took:

_____

_____

_____

_____

_____

_____

_____

_____

_____

_____

_____

_____

REFLECTION & DISCUSSION

After completing this practice, ask clients to reflect and discuss:

- How did you feel as you were giving your gift?
- How did you feel after giving your gift?
- How did the recipient of your gift react?
- Were there any consequences (positive or negative) resulting from giving your gift?
- Did you use one or more of your signature strengths? If so, which one and how?
- Have you undertaken such an activity in the past? What was it? Did you find that it was different this time around? If so, what differences did you notice?
- Have there been times in the past when you were asked to give the *Gift of Time* and you did not want to?
- Have you been a recipient of someone else's *Gift of Time*? What was it?
- Are you willing to give the *Gift of Time* regularly for a particular cause? What cause might this be?
- Do you anticipate any adaptation? That is, after a while, do you think the *Gift of Time* might not provide as much satisfaction as it did the first time? If so, what steps can you take address this?

VIGNETTE: KISHANA AND HER *GIFT OF TIME*

Kishana is a 47-year-old mother of three and an executive coach. She attended a three-day PPT training, which assigned homework. Kishana chose to complete the *Gift of Time* assignment. Following is her reflection on this practice, written three months after attending the workshop, while she was in the middle of her practice of the *Gift of Time*.

"From a very young age, my mother—my biggest role model—instilled a deep sense in me that we can always give something to others, I mean positive. Initially I didn't understand as we had very little for our own subsistence. But as I recall, my mother would always find time to help others. A single mother on a meager income, she was in sales where her professional worth was gauged in how much she sold—not how much she served. Yet [she believed] in finding time to help others by doing things, such as walking two blocks to put out the garbage cans of an elderly woman who couldn't do it herself or who often forgot, holding the doors as we entered or existed malls and halls, collecting leftover food from restaurants on weekends (when I wanted her to take me to fun places) and bringing it to food banks or shelters, and teaching newly arrived refugees how to navigate complex social systems. I watched my mother doing all of these chores, and she often dragged me along. Begrudgingly, I went along because often she did not have anyone else to look after me. As an adolescent, I became interested in physical exercise. There was a gym next to the food bank where my mother often volunteered, and seeing my mother's dedication, the gym owner offered me a free membership. I loved running, swimming, and building my muscles. I thought that my mother did not have power—so I became powerful in the gym. Mother was loved for her good work, but love doesn't get you power. Instead, I saw people taking advantage of her loving personality. When they needed her love, care, and help, she gave it all. Quietly, I resented her.

"We forged through tough years. I was good at my studies, very good at sports. Good grades won me a scholarship and I moved far away for college. I loved my newfound freedom. I worked at my studies and practiced even harder. From varsity, I was now competing at the state level in swimming.

"On a dreadful fall evening, I was walking back to my dorm from practice, when I stepped on some wet leaves and slipped on the slick marble floor of our dorm hall

. . . falling on my left shoulder and hitting my head on a corner. When I opened my eyes, I was in the hospital, with my shoulder in a cast and my head in a bandage. The next few weeks were steeped in the despair of not being able to compete at the upcoming state championship meet, and the worry that I could lose my scholarship. My mother visited me several times, but she couldn't stay longer.

"Three months later, I dipped into the pool but could barely swim and I got out of the pool. I sat on a bench, wrapped in depression, and began to cry with what I hoped were invisible tears. But someone saw them. This was an elderly gentleman. He gently tapped my shoulder and asked me why I had been away. His face was familiar, and then I remembered: while I trained in the swimmer-designated lanes, he swam in the community-designed lanes. So I told him about my accident, and he then told be about himself—a three-time national swimming champion who had had his share of injuries. He offered to help me with rehabilitation—at no charge—which was above and beyond what my college rehab team could have provided. I couldn't believe this amazing offer and graciously accepted.

"For the next three months, he gave me at least an hour almost every day, working on rehab strategies customized to my body type and injury. He never asked me for a penny. As an astute observer and experienced swimmer, he communicated subtleties of strokes and postures—better than my coach would have done. I recovered and within six months, I was almost back to my previous best. I asked him why he had spent so much time with me. He responded, 'I had a miserable marriage, and after my divorce, even my children don't care for me. However, my mother was a very happy woman. She was poor and a Holocaust survivor. She had very little to give in material terms, but she had a big heart, which allowed her to find ample time to help others. I didn't understand then why she spent so much time helping others, and in fact, I resented it. But now, I understand why she was so happy. And spending this time with you has shown me how happy I can become by helping someone else.' "

FIT & FLEXIBILITY

Some clients who are socially anxious or shy by disposition may have a hard time approaching other people—when the altruistic endeavors involves others—for fear of social judgment. Help these clients to use small steps, such as joining an organization that has a well-developed volunteer program. This will offer them a structure and clear instructions on what to do, thereby lowering their social anxiety. They can also work with a team of volunteers to avoid approaching people one on one.

It is very important to approach the concerns of other people wisely. Altruistic individuals do not impose themselves upon other people or try to help those who do not want to be helped. Remind clients to ensure that their altruistic outreach meets the stated needs of others.

People are best able to help those around them when they have the necessary skills, expertise, experience, and means. Encourage clients to discuss specifics with recipients to ensure that all parties' expectations are realistic. There are many ways that clients can help others.

Evidence shows that active hands-on engagement with nature (e.g., tree thinning, infrastructure improvement, removal of invasive species, footpath repair work, litter removal, and the creation of new habitats or green spaces) is another way to engage in the *Gift of Time*. Also known as environmental volunteerism, this innovative approach has been found to be effective, particularly for individuals from marginalized communities and offenders who want to reintegrate into society. Participants engaged in environmental volunteerism report a sense of place, self-discovery, and feeling part of a whole. This approach also develops a sense of responsibility and enlarges the social networks of participants. Furthermore, it can be used as an adjunct to clinical treatment.

We must always remember that what we perceive as a problem may not be a problem for others. Clients must maintain an open and empathic perspective, allowing them to be guided by the *other person's* needs.

Remind clients that altruistic acts are gifts that can be enjoyed by the giver and do not have to be a burden. Similarly, altruistic acts must be considered from a larger social and moral standpoint.

CULTURAL CONSIDERATIONS

For some clients, altruism may be an important part of their social, religious, or cultural heritage. If such clients are open, explore with them the culturally or religiously embedded altruistic practices that they identify with meaningfully.

Remind clients to consider cultural differences between the giver and the recipient; the client (as the giver) should ensure with the recipient that whatever is being offered (e.g., the *Gift of Time*) is culturally appropriate. For example, one of our Caucasian clients put a lot of effort into collecting gently used items for a newborn and offered them as a gift to an immigrant family. The family's response was lukewarm, disappointing the client. After some exploration, it became clear to her that it is a cultural practice among the immigrant family that newborns be gifted with new clothes. However, older siblings can take gently used clothes.

Also keep in mind that altruistic endeavors are linked to economic and social conditions. Some clients may want to give the *Gift of Time* but, due to long hours at work and responsibilities at home, they may not have time or may lack the expertise or skills to optimally use the available time.

MAINTENANCE

Discuss the following tips with your clients so that they can maintain their progress:

- Imagine a world where individuals are knowledgeable and equipped with skills for life-long engagement in philanthropy as givers of time, talent, and treasure for the common good. In order to be altruistic, we don't have to give big things. We can look for simple opportunities in everyday life to be generous with our time— by helping someone out or by complimenting someone for her positive behavior.
- Learn more about important altruists, who, despite mental health issues, shared their strengths, skills, and kindness with others. Examples include Lady Diana (eating concerns), Martin Luther King (depression), and Mother Theresa (depression). Which one might you most identify with? What prompted those altruists to give to their causes? How did their actions change the world?
- Get involved in local school and community clubs and organizations, which provide opportunities to volunteer and donate time or skills.
- Start an altruistic endeavor on a small scale. Give it time consistently. Over a period of time, this endeavor will likely offer you purpose, meaning, and motivation to continue.
- Providing help to others will likely enable you to further refine your own social and personal intelligence, in terms of understanding subtleties of needs of others.
- Altruistic endeavors often connect us with networks of people who can help us learn skills needed for volunteering. This enlarges our social circles and teaches us about resources and services already present in the community, as well as how to utilize them effectively.

END-OF-SESSION RELAXATION

We recommend that each session end with the same brief relaxation practice that started the session.

RESOURCES

Readings

- Chen, E., & Miller, G. E. (2012). "Shift-and-persist" strategies: Why low socioeconomic status isn't always bad for health. *Perspectives on Psychological Science*, *7*(2), 135–158. doi:10.1177/1745691612436694
- Kranke, D., Weiss, E. L., Heslin, K. C., & Dobalian, A. (2017). We are disaster response experts: A qualitative study on the mental health impact of volunteering in disaster settings among combat veterans. *Social Work in Public Health*, *32*(8), 500.
- Poulin, M. J., Brown, S. L., Dillard, A. J., & Smith, D. M. (2013). Giving to others and the association between stress and mortality. *American Journal of Public Health*, *103*(9), 1649–1655.
- Tabassum, F., Mohan, J., & Smith, P. (2016). Association of volunteering with mental well-being: A lifecourse analysis of a national population-based longitudinal study in the UK. *BMJ Open*, *6*(8), e011327.
- Welp, L. R., & Brown, C. M. (2014). Self-compassion, empathy, and helping intentions. *Journal of Positive Psychology*, *9*(1), 54–65. doi:10.1080/17439760.2013.831465

Videos

- Kindness Boomerang—"One Day":
  https://www.youtube.com/watch?v=nwAYpLVyeFU
- *Gift*, Singapore Inspiration Drama Short Film:
  https://youtu.be/1DUYlHZsZfc?list=PL8m
- The Science of Kindness:
  https://www.youtube.com/watch?v=FA1qgXovaxU

Websites

- The Random Acts of Kindness:
  https://www.kindness.org/
- Compassion Charter:
  https://charterforcompassion.org/
- Me to We:
  https://www.metowe.com/
- *Greater Good* magazine:
  https://greatergood.berkeley.edu/

## 21

SESSION FIFTEEN: MEANING AND PURPOSE

SESSION FIFTEEN FOCUSES ON THE SEARCH AND pursuit of meaningful endeavors for the greater good. The central positive psychotherapy (PPT) practice in this session is *Positive Legacy.* This is the last session in Phase Three of PPT and the last session overall.

SESSION FIFTEEN OUTLINE
Reaching the End of the PPT Journey
Core Concepts
    In-Session Practice: *A Story from Your Past and Envisioning a Future Goal*
    Reflection & Discussion
    In-Session Practice: *Positive Legacy*
    Reflection & Discussion
    Vignettes
    Fit & Flexibility
    Cultural Considerations
    Maintenance
Resources

REACHING THE END OF THE PPT JOURNEY
We close PPT with a session that integrates the three phases:

- The narrative of resilience (positive introduction),
- The hope of cultivating a better version of the self, and
- The aspiration of leaving a positive legacy.

CORE CONCEPTS
There are many ways to achieve a meaningful life: close interpersonal relationships (recent sessions included practices for positive relationships and positive communication), generativity (creation, reproduction), altruism (as covered in the previous session), social activism or service, and careers experienced as callings and spirituality. Feeling that our lives have purpose means that we feel the world is a different place because we are in it. Absence of purpose, on the other hand, makes us perceive the world as a threatening place, which provokes anxiety and depression (Schnell, 2009). The absence of purpose is a partial explanation for the substantial increase in depression rates (Ruckenbauer, Yazdani, & Ravaglia, 2007).

"Meaning" refers to a coherent understanding of the world that promotes the pursuit of long-term goals that provide a sense of purpose and fulfillment. Baumeister (2005) suggests that the pursuit of meaning serves four purposes in our lives:

- Meaning helps us articulate life goals within the timeframe that includes our past, present, and future.
- Meaning provides a sense of efficacy or control. Meaning allows us to believe that we are more than just pawns controlled by the events of the world.

- Meaning helps create ways to justify actions.
- Activities associated with meaning often bond people with a shared sense of community.

Victor Frankl, in his seminal work on meaning (e.g., *The Will to Meaning* [Frankl, 1988]; *Man's Searching for Meaning* [Frankl, 1963]; *The Doctor and the Soul* [Frankl, 1973]), argued that meaning is always possible and that it is a fundamental drive for people. No matter the circumstances, individuals are always free to choose the perspective they will take on their experiences. Building on the work of Freud and Adler, Frankl argued that the pursuit of meaning must be included along with the pursuits of pleasure and power as a core human attribute.

Meaning does not need to be a grand, life-encompassing concept. There is also situational meaning; that is, meaning in relation to smaller scale events. For example, winning a card game, video game, or sports game might provide a great deal of excitement because the game provided short-term purpose and related value. However, this does not necessarily signify that the game had great significance for one's life in general.

Meaning tends to exist in interpersonal settings. Because humans are such social animals, people tend to have goals that promote their group (e.g., "I want to become a doctor to help my community") or goals that are derived from the values of their group (e.g., "I want to become a doctor because that is a prestigious profession").

Evidence shows that having meaning in life is good for our mental health. And there are many ways to achieve meaning. Committing to something larger than oneself—often through altruism and service to others—is important for meaning (Steger, 2012).

The essence of meaning is connection. Meaning can link two things even if they are physically separate entities, such as if they belong to the same category (banana and apple are both fruit), are owned by the same person (Jason has a guitar and a basketball), or are both used for a common goal (collecting warm blankets and food for the local homeless shelter). Unfortunately, this connection—social and communal—has weakened significantly due to the rise of "extreme individualism." Seligman (1991) noted that extreme individualism maximizes the "depressive explanatory style," which prompts people to explain commonplace failures with permanent, pervasive, and personal causes. Seligman also noted that the decline of the larger, benevolent institutions (God, nation, family) no longer matters, since personal failures seem catastrophic and permanent.

START-OF-SESSION RELAXATION

At the start of every session, begin with a brief relaxation exercise. Refer to Appendix A: Relaxation & Mindfulness Practices, which can be found at the end of this manual. A copy of this appendix also appears in the client workbook. Continue the session with a review of the client's *Gratitude Journal* as well as a review of the core concepts taught in the previous session.

IN-SESSION PRACTICE: *A STORY FROM YOUR PAST AND ENVISIONING A FUTURE GOAL*

The *Positive Introduction* practice was introduced in PPT Session One. If at that time you asked clients to write their stories; to put the final story in an envelope; to seal, sign, and date the envelope; and to give the envelopes to you—now is the time to bring out the envelopes and ask clients to read their stories, before introducing Worksheet 15.1: Recalling Your Story and Envisioning a Future Goal. Note that this and all worksheets (a) appear within the corresponding session of this manual, (b) are reprinted for the client in the accompanying client workbook, and (c) can be downloaded from the companion website at www.oup.com/ppt. If you did not collect the stories at that time, allow clients a few minutes to remember what they wrote about.

Recalling your Positive Introduction story from Session One, please answer the following questions. Feel free to draw upon other things you have learned about yourself throughout the course of treatment.

What meaning can you derive from the experience of resilience in your story?

_____

_____

_____

_____

_____

Now that you have a much more sophisticated knowledge of character strengths, which character strengths do you think are most prominent in your story? Do you still use these strengths in your everyday life? If so, how?

_____

_____

_____

_____

_____

_____

Does your story of resilience tell you anything about your life's purpose?

_____

_____

_____

_____

_____

_____

In general, what creative or significant achievement would you like to pursue in the next 10 years?

_____

_____

_____

_____

_____

_____

Specifically, think of one achievement in art, science, relationships (social), or academics that you would like to accomplish that is good, both for you and for others.

_____
_____
_____
_____
_____

What makes this achievement an important goal for you and why?

_____
_____
_____
_____
_____

How does this goal make a difference for others?

_____
_____
_____
_____
_____
_____

What steps do you need to take to accomplish this goal in the next 10 years? What would you need to do, year by year?

_____
_____
_____
_____
_____

Which of your signature strengths will you use most often to accomplish your goal?

_____
_____
_____
_____
_____

REFLECTION & DISCUSSION

After completing this practice, ask clients to reflect and discuss:

- What was the experience of rereading your story of resilience again?
- If you are given an opportunity to rewrite your story of resilience, would you write in the same way you wrote a couple of months ago? If not, what would you change?
- In what ways have last few sessions of PPT influenced your thinking about the purpose and meaning of life?
- What was the process like for you of reflecting on and then writing about your goals for the future?
- What might happen if you accomplish your goals? What might happen if you do not accomplish your goals?

IN-SESSION PRACTICE: *POSITIVE LEGACY*

SUGGESTED SCRIPT FOR THE CLINICIAN

The following script is taken from Peterson (2006):

We each have a bucket list: things we want to do "someday," goals we hope to achieve, and places we'd like to visit when we "have time." However, we may find that we will never have time unless we make time. Worksheet 15.2: Your Positive Legacy forces us to envision our future and really think about how we're going to fulfill our hopes and dreams.

Think ahead to your life as you would like it to be and how you would like to be remembered by those closest to you. What accomplishments and/or personal strengths would they mention about you? In other words, what would you like your legacy to be? Write this down in the space provided. Don't be modest, but be realistic.

_____

_____

_____

_____

_____

_____

_____

_____

_____

_____

_____

Once you are finished, look back over what you wrote and ask yourself if you have a plan to create a legacy that is both realistic and within your power to do so.

After you've finished writing, put this worksheet aside and keep it somewhere safe. Read it again a year from now, or five years from now. Ask yourself whether you have made progress toward achieving your goals, and feel free to revise if new goals have emerged.

REFLECTION & DISCUSSION

Positive psychology has offered valuable scientific insights on makers and markers of our well-being. For example, after meeting basic needs, more money doesn't add much to happiness (Lucas, 2007), whereas more engagement, satisfying relationships, and meaningful endeavors add and maintain our well-being (Peterson, Park, & Seligman, 2005). In the light of this finding, what sort of legacy should we leave behind? After completing the *Positive Legacy* practice, ask clients to reflect and discuss:

*   How was the process of writing your *Positive Legacy*?
*   What was the most difficult part of this practice? Is the notion too abstract? Did it feel immodest to write something noteworthy about your future self? Are you not much concerned with how you will be remembered?
*   Can you think of someone living or deceased who you knew well enough that you feel this person's life is an illustration of how you would like to be remembered? If you have someone in mind, think about what you would write to this person. If you don't have anyone in mind, please use a historical figure.
*   What short- and long-term goals can you set to accomplish your *Positive Legacy*?
*   What concrete actions would you like to undertake in order to accomplish your short- and long-term goals? What is the timeline for completion of these actions?
*   In what ways can you use your signature strengths to do something that would enable you to leave a *Positive Legacy*?

VIGNETTE: BRIAN'S LEGACY

Brian, a 23-year-old client, was seen in individual and group PPT and wrote his *Positive Legacy* in one of the group sessions. This is the original draft, with no editing.

"I would like to be remembered as a person who expressed himself as an individual, pursuing the things that mattered most, with ambition and compassion: a teacher, a healer, a friend, an authentic and liberating person who, above all, was a humble student.

"An accomplishment I would like to be remembered for would be having helped those who asked and those who needed it. A person who changed the outer world by cleansing inner worlds.

"My legacy will be leaving the world and the people I encountered slightly better off than when I found them.

"**What plan do I have to bring about my legacy?** I cannot help others find peace and happiness without first finding my own. Through mindful practice, living, and interacting, I am selfish to be kind. By caring for myself, I am learning to care for others."

VIGNETTE: SAM: I WILL BE REMEMBERED AS A GOOD FATHER

Sam, a 47-year-old business executive, completed the *Positive Legacy* practice as part of a self-development course. Following are his reflections about the process, followed by his *Positive Legacy*.

"**Reflections:** It was not an easy exercise as I have been trying to figure out how I can be a happy person and what happiness means. I am spending a lot of time reflecting on who I am and what I want to be. I have spent most of my time and energy expanding my business over the past six years and I can see, with a sense of pride, that this is giving its dividends handsomely.

"However, writing this positive legacy was difficult when it came to my family. If I look at what positive legacy I want to leave behind, I see that I am doing very little in this important domain of my life. In the past six years, I've done a lot for my business, but only a little for whom I am building this business.

"This exercise helped me to realize that for whom I am doing all of this, they are distant from me—emotionally and often physically. I am scaling heights of monetary achievement but feel every high brings me to a new low. I feel the more I climb, the farther I am from my loved ones. Yet, I cannot find a way to get back to base. This realization depressed me but I used my business strengths—not quitting hope—and was able to focus on what would be good for me and my family. I came up with the following three aspects:

1. I would like to be remembered as a father who was present in the lives of my two sons. As much as I invest in my business, I will invest in my family. Currently, I am going home after a 10- to 12-hour work day. I will go home after 8 hours of work. Rather than working more, I will try to work smarter.

2. When I get home, rather than sitting in front of the television, I will turn all screens off and will engage with my boys, using my strength of curiosity about their day, discussing sports with them, and doing a small home chore together.

3. I will make sure that I will book two, 2-week vacations per year with my family, each within six months apart. I will vow not to take my smart phone on my vacations.

"I think if I do these three things consistently, I will be remembered as a good father."

FIT & FLEXIBILITY

The search and pursuit of meaningful endeavors for the greater good—leaving a *Positive Legacy*—may be challenging for some clients. Due to psychological distress and/or cognitive rigidities, the assumptions of some client worldviews may be unfavorable. For example, a client who has recently lost a close family member under very tragic circumstances or a client experiencing severe depression marked by a significant degree of hopelessness may struggle to search and pursue meaning in life. Severely depressed clients tend to score low on meaningfulness (Peterson, Park, & Seligman, 2005).

Some clients may struggle to find and pursue meaning because the construction of meaning is an active and effortful process. Due to psychological stress, the motivation to find and pursue meaningful experiences may be limited for such clients.

Clients who have experienced a recent trauma or significant loss, those who are grieving, or those who have lost significant assets as a result of an accident or natural disaster may also find it difficult to search for meaning. They may not be denying or minimizing psychiatric stress (Hicks & King, 2009). Similarly, clients with acute anxiety may be challenged to find meaning.

Evidence also shows that threats to belongingness decrease our beliefs that life is meaningful (Stillman & Baumeister, 2009). Therefore, clients with weak social links or feelings of isolation may experience difficulties in searching for meaning. However, don't hesitate to ask your clients about meaning. Being asked about meaning by the clinician can be very important for the client. Irvin Yalom (1980), author of *Existential Psychotherapy*, states that "virtually every patient I have worked with has either gratuitously expressed concern about the lack of meaning in his or her life or has readily responded to inquiries I have made about the issue."

CULTURAL CONSIDERATIONS

Our understanding of the world comes through the lens of culture, so the search and pursuit of meaning is highly culturally sensitive. The way an individual perceives an experience—meaningful or not—is shaped largely by her or his immediate culture. Conceptualization of culture along the individualist-collectivist spectrum may be an oversimplification in our rapidly changing, diverse, urbanizing, digital world. Nonetheless, some notions still hold true. For example, for most clients from individualistic cultural backgrounds (e.g., European and North American), meaning and purpose will entail the pursuit of individualist goals, self-enhancement, and autonomy. Most clients from collectivist cultures may find meaning through efforts and actions that preserve and strengthen positive and adaptive familial and communal harmony (Kitayama & Markus, 2000; Steger et al., 2008).

Similarly, sources of purpose differ from culture to culture. For example, in Chinese Taoism, the meaning of life may be primarily based on living in harmony with nature, instead of struggling against the Tao (Lin, 2001). Buddhism advocates an attitude of acceptance and contentment with adverse situations because suffering—the result of desire and karma—is inevitable (Lin, 2001). Clinically, these cultural differences may manifest in terms of clients from an East Asian cultural background appearing to show acquiescence, whereas clients from a European or North American cultural background may actively work to better a situation. Similarly, for clients from most Asian and African cultural backgrounds, the meaning of life depends, for the most part, on one's ability to forge close relationships with cultural norms, family, and community. In fact, an integrative view of multiple lines of research has suggested that people find meaning in life but little about the meaning of life. Relationships, particularly with family, are reported to be the most important source of meaning in people's lives in all cultures and age groups (Glaw et al., 2017).

For clients from European and North American cultural background, a meaningful life may depend on living an authentic life, and to attain that authenticity, clients may defy entrenched social institutions. Such examples include fighting for LGBTQ rights, supporting marriage equality, or working for environmental or political causes. Finally, for some clients, meaning is pursued through religious and spiritual quests. That is, for some clients, being a good Christian, Muslim, Hindu, Jew, or Buddhist is synonymous with living a meaningful life.

MAINTENANCE
Discuss the following tips with your clients so that they can maintain their progress:

- Meaning gives life coherence and increases self-efficacy. It is also associated with health and better relationships. Meaning can be global or local. To maintain a sense of meaning and purpose, select a global meaning. The global meaning refers to your goals and beliefs regarding issues in the larger world like justice, equality, and fairness. Meaning can also be maintained by working on a local issue that involves pursuing specific goals and objectives in your community or family.

- We can also maintain a sense of meaning and purpose by contemplating and discussing events that had a profound or significant impact on us but that we have not yet had a chance to reflect on. Such reflection can help us understand the meaning and purpose over time.

- Keep in mind that meaning is not constant; it may change with age, circumstances, or significant life events.

- To maintain a sense of purpose, one doesn't always have to do something. Meaning can also be maintained by reducing activities or by learning to say no to activities that do not feel purposeful. This could look like letting go of people, ideas, and things in your life that no longer make you happy. For example, take a look around your home. Are there clothes or books that you don't need anymore? Perhaps consider donating them. Do you have unhelpful or self-defeating thoughts that visit you frequently? Consider replacing those with more helpful ones. Are there people in your life who hurt you and who may be distracting you from your meaning? Can you think of ways to limit their importance in your life?

END-OF-SESSION RELAXATION

We recommend that each session end with the same brief relaxation practice that started the session.

Psychotherapy is not an easy voyage, and, despite its name, positive psychotherapy is no exception. PPT is not necessarily moving on toward something; rather, it is more about moving in—to expand the inner space of clients so that they can better understand the yin and yang of their emotions and experiences. Through structured practices, you have helped your clients to manage their stressors, and you have taught them to deploy their strengths. They oscillate, at times, between stressors and strengths, between hope and skepticism, and between the temptation to give up and the courage to try something new.

The fact that we have arrived at the final session shows that you have persisted, and, with you, your clients have persisted with courage and hope. Clients began the PPT journey by creating a narrative of resilience, and, with your guidance, they have shaped this narrative into a contextualized index of strengths—carefully calibrated and culturally nuanced. Session after session, you facilitated these client practices—some rough, some tough—to create a better version of your client, assuming that we have communicated our intentions through concrete actions.

We don't claim that one round of psychotherapy—PPT or other well-established approaches—is sufficient to lastingly heal and nurture all symptoms and strengths. Growth is continuous, and you might very well be the first (perhaps the only) person in your client's life to shine the light of hope and optimism in ways that no one else has. Feel accomplished and fulfilled, and take pride in yourself for playing your part in celebrating our unique human ability to heal and help one another.

RESOURCES

Readings

- Grundy, A. C., Bee, P., Meade, O., Callaghan, P., Beatty, S., Olleveant, N., & Lovell, K. (2016). Bringing meaning to user involvement in mental health care planning: A qualitative exploration of service user perspectives. *Journal of Psychiatric and Mental Health Nursing, 23*(1), 12–21. doi:10.1111/jpm.12275
- Löffler, S., Knappe, R., Joraschky, P., & Pöhlmann, K. (2010). Meaning in life and mental health: Personal meaning systems of psychotherapists and psychotherapy patients. *Zeitschrift Für Psychosomatische Medizin Und Psychotherapie, 56*(4), 358.
- Wilt, J. A., Stauner, N., Lindberg, M. J., Grubbs, J. B., Exline, J. J., & Pargament, K. I. (2017). Struggle with ultimate meaning: Nuanced associations with search for meaning, presence of meaning, and mental health. *The Journal of Positive Psychology, 13*(3), 240–251.

Videos

- YouTube: The Time You Have:
  https://www.youtube.com/watch?v=BOksW_NabEk
- YouTube: Hugo—Purpose:
  https://www.youtube.com/watch?v=7jzLeNYe46g
- YouTube: Peaceful Warrior—Everything Has a Purpose (Duration 3:20):
  https://youtu.be/w1jaPahTM4o?list=PL8m55Iz0Oco4BRLkwj9KM9yxbCsLC5mjb

Websites

- John Templeton Foundation:
  https://www.templeton.org/about
- Virtue, Happiness and Meaning of Life:
  https://virtue.uchicago.edu/
- The Mind & Life Institute:
  https://www.mindandlife.org/

APPENDIX A

Relaxation & Mindfulness Practices

CORE CONCEPTS

Mindfulness is maintaining a moment-by-moment awareness of our thoughts, feelings, bodily sensations, and surrounding environment, without being judgmental or being less judgmental. Mindfulness allows us to accept what we cannot change and enables us to see what can be changed.

Some specific events, experiences, and interactions stay in our heads. Whenever we think of them, emotions spring up and leave us feeling sad, happy, angry, or unsure. Sometimes we act on these feelings without much awareness. Mindfulness is being aware of this whole process by observing the flow of our thoughts and emotions without acting upon them immediately.

Mindfulness also helps us develop awareness of our actions and reactions in specific situations, especially situations that bother us. We also learn how our actions impact others. Developing awareness without judgment can help us be open and receptive to different perspectives.

For example, being mindful about a negative interaction with a friend can help us see the wider perspective. Perhaps the negative interaction was not caused by something we might have done. Instead, it could be that our friend might be upset about something completely unrelated to us. By being mindful, we break down a complex experience into its parts, allowing us to be open to widening our perspective. Mindfulness can strengthen our openness, self-regulation, and social intelligence.

IN-SESSION MINDFULNESS PRACTICES

Mindfulness can be developed, but it requires regular practice. The following are five mindfulness and relaxation practices that can be incorporated into positive psychotherapy (PPT) sessions or used at home.

PRACTICE ONE: A MINDFUL MINUTE

Instructions

1. Sit in a comfortable position with your hands resting on or close to your thighs and with your head, neck, and chest in a relaxed straight line. Rest your feet flat on the floor.
2. Bring your attention to your breath. Notice how it enters your body and how it leaves your body. Focus as you inhale and exhale, on how your chest expands and contracts.
3. Gently bring your breath deeper into your belly. Continue repeating this breathing cycle. Try to make each inhalation and exhalation last for 6 to 8 seconds. Start over after each breath.
4. Rather than trying to stop any other thoughts, keep your attention focused, and count very quietly or in your head. Your attention will wander, and your job is to gently bring it back and start again. Consider this a practice of not only focusing but also one in which you will make many starts—distraction, start again, distraction, start again. If doing this practice in session, when one minute is up, you will hear a sound.[1]

---

[1] If this practice is done in session, the clinician should gently bring the client out of the exercise with a soothing sound.

PRACTICE TWO: BREATHING

Instructions

1. Make sure you are sitting in a relaxed and comfortable position.
2. Keep your head, neck, and chest in a relaxed (not rigid) upright position.
3. Relax your shoulders. Bring your back toward the back of the chair.
4. Rest your hands softly on your thighs or wherever you feel comfortable.
5. If you feel comfortable, let your eyelids slowly and gently close, just as the curtain in a theatre closes.
6. Take a deep breath through your nose, hold it for a few seconds, and then exhale slowly and gently.
7. Repeat this breathing two more times, each time deepening it, from your chest down into your belly.
8. With every breath in and breath out, try to relax your whole body from head to toe.
9. Breathe smoothly, without pause.
10. Next, shape your breath; a good breath has three qualities (Sovik, 2005):
    * Smooth
    * Even (approximately equal duration of inhalation and exhalation)
    * Without sound
11. Relax the effort to breathe and let it naturally flow, as if your whole body is breathing.
12. Focus on your breath as it enters and exits through your nostrils.
13. Take 10 breaths that are smooth, even, and without sound. Open your eyes.

PRACTICE THREE: STRETCH & RELAX

Instructions

Sit in the Relaxation Position and practice the following stretches.

The Relaxation Position

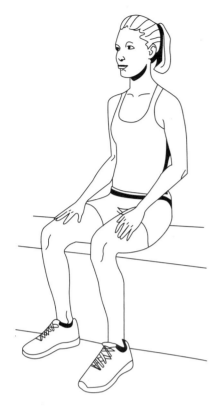

Sit with your head, neck, and chest aligned, legs uncrossed, feet flat on the floor, and hands on or close to knee caps (adapted from Cautela & Gorden, 1978).

Head

- Keeping your shoulders steady, bring your head slowly to the right.[2]
- Take three relaxed breaths, starting with exhaling.
- Repeat on the other side.

[2] Or preferred side; from here on, please include the preferred side in your directions. For the sake of balance, we alternate between sides, from posture to posture.

Ear

- Keeping your shoulders steady, bring your left ear to your left shoulder without moving the shoulder.
- Take three relaxed breaths.
- Repeat the same on the other side.

Neck

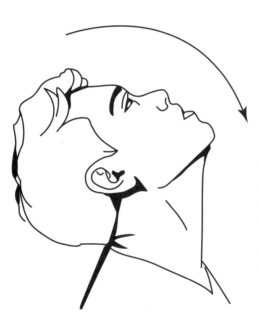

Align your head, neck, and chest, keeping your shoulders balanced. Slowly lift up your face toward the ceiling. Keep lifting until you reach a limit that is not uncomfortable. Holding your head steady, stretch the front part of your neck and hold this stretch for as long as you can comfortably do so. Exhale and slowly bring your face back. Rather than stopping in the neutral position, bring your chin down into your chest. Hold the posture, and feel the stretch in the back of your neck. When you are ready, bring your face back to a neutral position

Face Massage

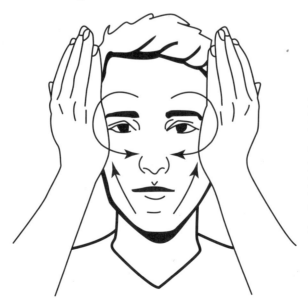

Place the lower parts of your palms on either side of your upper cheek bones, close to your temples. Begin to make small circular movements with your palms, moving downward. Once you reach your jaw bone, move upward, and then follow any bony parts of your face (adapted from Bellentine, 1977).

Eyes and Forehead Massage

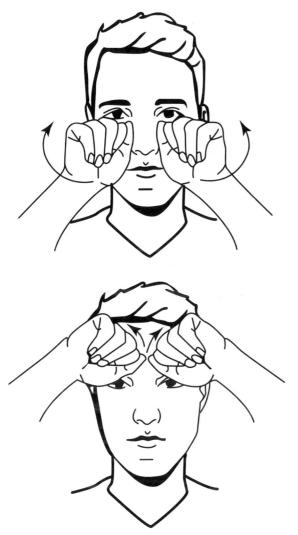

Make loose fists with your hands, placing palm and finger joints (the knuckles) at the bottom of your eye sockets and pressing gently against the socket bones. Move your knuckles slowly toward your temples. From the temples, move slightly up, pressing your eyebrows and forehead. Repeat this routine several times. Carry on pressing with your knuckles on any bony parts of your face.

PRACTICE FOUR: POSITIVE IMAGERY

Instructions

If you are doing this practice in session, your clinician can read the following script. If you are doing this practice at home, record the script so that you can listen to it while doing the practice. To begin, sit comfortably.

Close your eyes and imagine a place in your mind. This place can be indoors or outdoors, but it is a place where you effortlessly feel comfortable. Take a few relaxing breaths to fully feel that you have arrived here. See if you can focus on one sensation at a time. What things do you see? [pause] Look around slowly. [pause] What things do you hear? Notice the sounds—near, far, and perhaps very far away. Next, what do you smell? Natural smells, some artificial smells. [pause]. Now touch something, feel its texture—smooth or rough, hard or soft, heavy or light. Look around, and if there are any materials, colors, stones, features, or other materials, touch them. See if you can use them to make something. It doesn't have to be perfectly sized or symmetrical. Or you don't have to make anything. Feel at complete ease to do something or nothing. Relax. Take a few deep breaths. Try, but not too hard, to memorize details of this place, like a mental picture. This is your place, your place to relax. Gently and slowly trace you steps to leave, the same way you came in.

PRACTICE FIVE: LOVE & KINDNESS MEDITATION

Instructions

The following meditation practice has been adapted from Sharon Salzberg's (1995) book, *Love-Kindness*. This practice recites specific words and phrases evoking a "boundless warm-hearted feeling." The strength of this feeling is not limited to or by family, religion, or social class. The meditation begins with ourselves, and we gradually extend the wish for well-being and happiness to all.

Begin with the following phrases:

May I be happy. May I be well. May I be safe. May I be peaceful and at ease.

While saying these phrases, allow yourself to immerse into the intentions they express. Loving-kindness meditation helps us to connect our noble intentions with the well-being of others. Let feelings of love, kindness, openness, and acceptance embrace you, and let these feelings expand as you repeat these phrases. As you continue the meditation, you can bring in your own image and direct this love and kindness toward yourself.

After directing loving-kindness toward yourself, bring to your attention a friend or someone in your life who has deeply cared for you. Then slowly repeat phrases of loving-kindness toward that person:

May you be happy. May you be well. May you be safe. May you be peaceful and at ease.

As you say these phrases, immerse into their intention or heartfelt or heart full meaning. And, if any feelings of loving-kindness arise, connect the feelings with the phrases so that the feelings may become stronger as you repeat the words.

As you continue the meditation, you can enlarge the circle and bring to mind other friends, family members, neighbors, acquaintances, strangers, animals, and finally people with whom you have difficulty.

ADDITIONAL RESOURCES

The following are additional relaxation resources you may find useful.

Rolf-Solvik, a clinical psychologist, associated with the Himalayan Institute:
Learn Diaphragmatic Breathing for Deep Relaxation:
https://youtu.be/Q82YnmL0Kr8

Jon Kabat-Zinn, one of the most distinguished practitioners in mindfulness, guides a 30-minute body scan meditation practice:
https://youtu.be/_DTmGtznab4

Sharon Salzberg, a distinguished practitioner, teaches love and kindness:
https://youtu.be/buTQP4Geabk

This animated video, based on Martin Boroson's book *One-Moment Meditation*, gives you the tools to find calm quickly and effectively. You can practice One-Moment Meditation at home by following along with this video:
https://www.youtube.com/watch?v=F6eFFCi12v8

APPENDIX B

Gratitude Journal

Please write three blessings[1] (good things) each night before going to bed. Next to each blessing, write at least one sentence about:

- Why did this good thing happen today? What does this mean to you?
- What have you learned from taking the time to name this blessing or good thing?
- In what ways did you or others contribute to this blessing or good thing?

DAILY BLESSING: SUNDAY

Sunday	Date _____
First Blessing Reflection	
Second Blessing Reflection:	
Third Blessing Reflection:	

DAILY BLESSING: MONDAY

Monday	Date _____
First Blessing Reflection	
Second Blessing Reflection:	
Third Blessing Reflection:	

[1] To make additional copies of this *Gratitude Journal*, go to the companion website www.oup. com/ppt. to print them out.

DAILY BLESSING: TUESDAY

Tuesday	Date: _____
First Blessing Reflection	
Second Blessing Reflection:	
Third Blessing Reflection:	

DAILY BLESSING: WEDNESDAY

Wednesday	Date: _____
First Blessing Reflection	
Second Blessing Reflection:	
Third Blessing Reflection:	

DAILY BLESSING: THURSDAY

Thursday	Date: _____
First Blessing Reflection	
Second Blessing Reflection:	
Third Blessing Reflection:	

DAILY BLESSING: FRIDAY

Friday	Date: _____
First Blessing Reflection	
Second Blessing Reflection:	
Third Blessing Reflection:	

DAILY BLESSING: SATURDAY

Saturday	Date: _____
First Blessing Reflection	
Second Blessing Reflection:	
Third Blessing Reflection:	

APPENDIX C

Positive Psychotherapy Inventory

The Positive Psychotherapy Inventory (PPTI) is the primary measure to assess client well-being based on the PERMA theory of well-being, discussed in Chapter 2 of this manual. The PPTI assesses well-being in terms of positive emotions, engagement, relationships, meaning, and accomplishment. The PPTI has been used in several published outcome studies (e.g., Schrank et al., 2014; Seligman, Rashid, & Parks, 2006; Uliaszek et al., 2016), and it has been translated into Turkish (Guney, 2011), Persian (Khanjani et al., 2014), and German (Wammerl et al., 2015). The psychometric properties of PPTI are presented here.

INVENTORY C1

Positive Psychotherapy Inventory

*Please read each of the statements carefully. In the shaded box, rate yourself using the 5-point scale at the top of the form. Please **only mark the shaded box** in each line.*

Some questions are regarding strengths. Strengths are stable traits that manifest through thoughts, feelings, and actions; are morally valued; and are beneficial to self and others. Examples of strengths include optimism, zest, spirituality, fairness, modesty, social intelligence, perseverance, curiosity, creativity, and teamwork.

C.1
STRENGTHS STATEMENTS

5: Very much like me	4: Like me	3: Neutral	2: Not like me	1: Not at all like me				
				P	E	R	M	A
1. I feel joyful.				☐				
2. I know my strengths.					☐			
3. I feel connected to people with whom I interact regularly.						☐		
4. What I do matters to society.							☐	
5. I am an ambitious person.								☐
6. Others say I look happy.				☐				
7. I pursue activities that use my strengths.					☐			
8. I feel close to my loved ones.						☐		
9. I feel that my life has a purpose.							☐	
10. The accomplishments of others inspire me to take actions to achieve my personal goals.								☐
11. I notice good things in my life and feel thankful.				☐				
12. I use my strengths to solve my problems.					☐			
13. During tough times, there is always someone I can turn to for support.						☐		
14. I participate in religious or spiritual activities.							☐	
15. I have done many things well in my life.								☐

5: Very much like me	4: Like me	3: Neutral	2: Not like me	1: Not at all like me				
				P	E	R	M	A
16. I feel relaxed.				☐				
17. My concentration is good during activities that use my strengths.					☐			
18. I have relationships that support me in growing and flourishing.						☐		
19. I do things that contribute to a larger cause.							☐	
20. When I set a goal, I am able to accomplish it.								☐
21. I laugh heartily.				☐				
22. Time passes quickly when I am engaged in activities that use my strengths.					☐			
23. There is at least one person in my life who listens well enough to understand my feelings and me.						☐		
24. I use my strengths to help others.							☐	
25. Achieving my goals motivates me to accomplish new goals.								☐
Total Score								

Please add up the scores from the boxes in each vertical column above, and transfer your scores to the following table. Note that at the start of the statements, there are five columns labeled P, E, R, M, and A. Those letters correlate to the letters in the left-hand column in the table.

Range	Clinical	Nonclinical	Your Score
P = Positive Emotions (5–25)	14	21	
E = Engagement (5–25)	16	21	
R = Relationships (5–25)	14	22	
M = Meaning (5–25)	14	19	
A = Accomplishment (5–25)	18	21	
Total (25–125)	76	104	

C.2

SCORING INSTRUCTIONS

Scale	Scoring—Add Items:	Definition of PERMA Elements
Positive Emotions	1 + 6 + 11 + 16 + 21	Experiencing positive emotions such as contentment, pride, serenity, hope, optimism, trust, confidence, gratitude
Engagement	2 + 7 + 12 + 17 + 22	Immersing oneself deeply in activities that utilize one's strengths to experience an optimal state marked by razor sharp concentration, optimal state of experience with intense focus, and intrinsic motivation to further develop

Scale	Scoring—Add Items:	Definition of PERMA Elements
Relationships	3 + 8 + 13 + 18 + 23	Having positive, secure, and trusting relationships
Meaning	4 + 9 + 14 + 19 + 24	Belonging to and serving something with a sense of purpose and belief that is larger than the self
Accomplishment	5+10+15+20+25	Pursuing success, mastery, and achievement for its own sake

PSYCHOMETRICS

Psychometrics of PPTI have been explored. The largest validation study of PPTI involves a large and culturally diverse sample of young adults ($N = 2501$, age $mean = 22.55$ years; $SD = 2.96$; 68.3% females). These are individuals who participated in a strengths-based program. In addition to PPTI, they completed a number of measures. These included:

- **Psychiatric Distress:** Outcome Questionnaire (OQ-45; Lambert et al., 1996). This 45-item measure assesses overall level of distress, as well as level of distress in three domains: symptomatic distress, interpersonal relations, and social roles.
- **Student Engagement Inventory** (SEI; Rashid & Louden, 2013). This measure assesses students' level of engagement in seven areas: classroom behavior, assignments, examinations, academic motivation, academic resilience, campus engagement, and campus adjustment.
- **Signature Strengths Questionnaire** (SSQ:72; Rashid et al., 2013). These 72 items measure 24 VIA strengths.
- **Grit** (Duckworth et al., 2007). This eight-item self-report scale assesses trait-level perseverance and passion for long-term goals.

The bivariate correlations of the aforementioned measures with clinical sample (determined by clinical range score on OQ-45 score of ≥ 63, and low score) and nonclinical sample (OQ-45 score ≤ 63) are given in Table C1. This table presents the bivariate correlation of PPTI (total score) with measures of psychiatric distress, overall academic engagement, character strengths, and grit. The correlational trend clearly demonstrates that the PPTI well-being measure correlates favorably with positive constructs and negatively with unfavorable constructs.

Structure

PPTI's five scales have shown satisfactory internal consistency. The Cronbach's alphas for the aforementioned sample were: Positive Emotions .77; Engagement .81; Positive Relationships .84; Meaning .71, and Accomplishment .77. Published research has also demonstrated that PPTI has a five-factor underlying structure (Khanjani et al., 2014). Furthermore, the overall score as well as five scales are amendable to change, as results of structured interventions (e.g., Rashid et al., 2017; Schrank et al., 2016; Uliaszek et al., 2016) demonstrate.

Table C1

BIVARIATE CORRELATION OF THE POSITIVE PSYCHOTHERAPY
INVENTORY WITH MEASURES OF STRESS, ACADEMIC ENGAGEMENT,
AND CHARACTER STRENGTHS

	Clinical ($n = 710$)	Well-adjusted ($n = 937$)
Psychiatric Distress (overall)	$-.40^{**}$	$-.38^{**}$
Symptomatic Stress	$-.16^{**}$	$-.12^{**}$
Interpersonal Relationships Difficulties	$-.20^{**}$	$-.16^{**}$
Challenges with Social Roles	$-.23^{**}$	$-.30^{**}$
Academic Engagement (overall)	$.14^{**}$	$.20^{**}$
Classroom & Assignments	$.24^{**}$	$.19^{**}$
Exams & Presentation	$.22^{**}$	$.23^{**}$
Academic Motivation	$.29^{**}$	$.18^{**}$
Campus Involvement	$.24^{**}$	$.22^{**}$
Academic Resilience	$.20^{**}$	$.18^{**}$
Campus Adjustment	$.15^{**}$	$.11^{*}$
Character Strengths (overall)	$.20^{**}$	$.09^{**}$
Appreciation of Beauty	$.07$	$.17^{**}$
Bravery	$.09^{*}$	$.19^{**}$
Citizenship & Teamwork	$.08^{*}$	$.14^{**}$
Creativity	$.04$	$.19^{**}$
Curiosity	$.03$	$.18^{**}$
Fairness	$.03$	$.18^{**}$
Forgiveness	$.07$	$.21^{**}$
Gratitude	$.10^{**}$	$.18^{**}$
Grit	$.16$	$.48^{**}$
Honesty	$.08^{*}$	$.21^{**}$
Hope & Optimism	$.10^{*}$	$.20^{**}$
Humour	$.12^{**}$	$.16^{**}$
Kindness	$.09^{*}$	$.16^{**}$
Leadership	$.10^{**}$	$.21^{**}$
Love	$.16^{**}$	$.20^{**}$
Love of Learning	$.13^{**}$	$.22^{**}$
Humility & Modesty	$-.02$	$.15^{**}$
Open–mindedness	$.04$	$.15^{**}$
Persistence	$.13^{**}$	$.19^{**}$
Perspective	$.08^{*}$	$.18^{**}$
Prudence	$.08^{*}$	$.16^{**}$
Self-regulation	$.01$	$.16^{**}$
Social Intelligence	$.05$	$.17^{**}$
Spirituality	$.06$	$.22^{**}$
Zest	$.13^{**}$	$.17^{**}$

$^{*} = p < .05;$ $^{**} = p < .01.$

Schrank, B., Riches, S., Coggins, T., Rashid, T., Tylee, A., Slade, M. (2014). WELLFOCUS PPT—modified positive psychotherapy to improve well-being: study protocol for pilot randomised controlled. *Trial*, *15*(1), 203.

Seligman, M. E., Rashid, T., & Parks, A. C. (2006). Positive psychotherapy. *American Psychologist*, *61*, 774–788. doi: 10.1037/0003-066X.61.8.774

Rashid, T., Louden, R., Wright, L., Chu, R., Lutchmie-Maharaj A., Hakim, I., Uy, D. A. & Kidd, B. (2017). Flourish: A strengths-based approach to building student resilience. In C. Proctor (Ed.), *Positive Psychology Interventions in Practice* (pp. 29–45). Amsterdam: Springer.

Uliaszek, A. A., Rashid, T., Williams, G. E., & Gulamani, T. (2016). Group therapy for university students: A randomized control trial of dialectical behavior therapy and positive psychotherapy. *Behaviour Research and Therapy*, *77*, 78–85. http://dx.doi.org/10.1016/j.brat.2015.12.003

TRANSLATIONS

Turkish

Guney, S. (2011). The Positive Psychotherapy Inventory (PPTI): Reliability and validity study in Turkish population. *Social and Behavioral Sciences*, *29*, 81–86.

Persian

Khanjani, M., Shahidi, S., FathAbadi, J., Mazaheri, M. A., & Shokri, O. (2014). The factor structure and psychometric properties of the Positive Psychotherapy Inventory (PPTI) in an Iranian sample. *Iranian Journal of Applied Psychology*, *7*(5), 26–47.

German

Wammerl, M., Jaunig, J., Maierunteregger, T., & Streit, P. (2015). The development of a German version of the Positive Psychotherapy Inventory Überschrift (PPTI) and the PERMA-Profiler. Presentation at the World Congress of International Positive Psychology Association, Orlando, FL, June.

Building Your Strengths

Stressors and strengths are part of daily life, although stressors (such as relationship challenges, problems at work or not having a job, work-life balance, being sick, constant traffic, or taxes) may stand out more than strengths (such as curiosity, integrity, kindness, fairness, prudence, and gratitude). This appendix looks at everyday experiences and identifies things you can do to incorporate strengths into your life. It also provides examples of movies, TED Talks, and other online resources that illustrate these strengths. The "therapeutic actions" in this appendix are not a substitute for psychotherapy, should you need that; rather, the material in this resource is meant to raise your awareness that while everyday life includes inevitable hassles, stressors, and problems, it also offers us opportunities to become proficient in learning about and using our strengths toward solving our problems and increasing our well-being.

ORGANIZATION OF THIS APPENDIX

The aim of this appendix is to translate abstract concepts of character strengths into concrete actions and to connect these strengths with relevant multimedia illustrations with which you can easily identify. This appendix is based on the VIA Classification of Character Strengths and Virtues (Peterson & Seligman, 2004). We are grateful to VIA Institute for generously allowing us the classification to devise strengths-based therapeutic resources.

According to Peterson and Seligman (2004), *character strengths* are ubiquitous traits that are valued in their own right and are not necessarily tied to concrete outcomes. Compared to symptoms, for the most part, character strengths do not diminish others; rather, they elevate those who witness the strength, producing admiration rather than jealousy. Clinically, character strengths manifest in many ways. Some are easy to spot and acknowledge in clinical settings (e.g., expressing gratitude or creativity), while other strengths are less visible (e.g., expressing humility or self-regulation; refraining from something that is not apparent). Like character strengths, *virtues* are also valued in every culture and are defined within cultural, religious, and philosophical contexts. In Peterson and Seligman's classification, virtues are clusters of strengths; in other words, virtues are broad routes to a good life.

Table D1 presents 24 character strengths divided into six virtue clusters. Each of these character strengths is discussed in this appendix and includes:

- A *description* of the strength presented
- A discussion of the "*golden mean*," for the strength
- An explanation of which other character strengths *integrate* with the strength under discussion
- Illustrations from *movies*—showing how characters embody the strength
- *Therapeutic actions*—what you can do to enhance your strength
- *Exemplars*—individuals who represent the strength, as presented in TED Talks
- *Books*—to help you delve more deeply into the strength
- *Websites* that expand the concept of the strength

Table D1

CORE VIRTUES AND CORRESPONDING CHARACTER STRENGTHS

	Core Virtues					
	Wisdom & Knowledge	Courage	Humanity	Justice	Temperance	Transcendence
Character Strengths	Creativity Curiosity Open-mindedness Love of learning Perspective	Bravery Persistence Integrity Vitality & Zest	Love Kindness Social intelligence	Citizenship & Teamwork Fairness Leadership	Forgiveness & Mercy Humility & Modesty Prudence Self-regulation	Appreciation of Beauty & Excellence Gratitude Hope & Optimism Humor & Playfulness Spirituality

Table D2, located at the end of this appendix, presents an overview of the character strengths described throughout. This at-a-glance resource summarizes the 24 strengths by presenting their over- and underuse, a brief description of the balanced use of the strength (the golden mean), and how each strength potentially integrates with others.

This appendix is written directly for you (the client), although clinicians can also use it after clients have completed their signature strengths assessment (see Session 2). The resources in this appendix can help clinicians reinforce skills learned in individual sessions, as this appendix applies a strengths-based approach to deal with everyday challenges as well as cultivating more positive emotions, engagement, and positive relationships, helping to create and sustain meaningful goals.

THE GOLDEN MEAN

The "golden mean" is the Aristotelian concept that moral behavior is the mean (middle) between two extremes. In the context of strengths-based positive psychotherapy (PPT), the golden mean implies that a balanced use of strengths is both therapeutic and effective. For example, a balanced use of curiosity would be a mean between excessive use (prying or snooping) and absence (boredom, disinterest, or apathy).

INTEGRATION

Some character strengths share attributes with one another and often work well together. For example:

- To overcome symptoms of depression, you need to understand that not every future event will be negative (hope) and you also need to find practical ways to keep working on them (persistence).
- To deal with impulsive behavior, you need to find ways of regulating how you feel and what you do (self-regulation). In so doing, don't become too hard on yourself for past impulse-control lapses, because you also need self-care (self-forgiveness and self-compassion).
- To deal with relationship challenges, especially when told, "you don't understand me," try to become more aware of other people's feelings and motives, and try different strategies to better grasp the subtleties of complex interpersonal situations (social intelligence). However, you may also benefit from the strengths of playfulness, teamwork, and authenticity to achieve the same ends or to connect with others deeply, especially loved ones.

CORE VIRTUE: WISDOM & KNOWLEDGE

Cognitive strengths that entail the acquisition and use of knowledge

1. CREATIVITY

Description

If this is one of your top strengths, you can use creativity to devise new ways of solving problems that compromise your well-being, such as finding a creative and positive way to respond to on-going stressors or dealing with a difficult person. Most creative expressions that include art (painting, pottery, graphic design), writing (poetry, stories, essays), and performance (singing, acting, playing an instrument) carry tremendous therapeutic potential. These expressions use attentional, cognitive, and emotional resources that might otherwise be spent brooding, wallowing, or blaming.

The Golden Mean

You are not content with doing most things as usual or blindly confirming to norms. Yet, your creative endeavors are not considered to be odd or weird, even by your closest friends. You also don't want to be merely content; rather, you want to be innovative. From a therapeutic standpoint, a balanced use of creativity entails trying new solutions to old problems that cause ongoing stress. Before you try these solutions, however, consider their impact on others. (For example, you can use your creativity to redesign your office—if it is your individual office—or on a project for which only you are responsible. However, redesigning a common space or infusing new and creative ideas into a group project—without involving others—is not a balanced expression of creativity.) When working with others, you will be best served by your own creativity when leading or facilitating a brainstorming session that is inclusive and open to new ideas.

- *Overuse of strength:* oddity, weirdness, eccentricity
- *Underuse of strength*: dullness, banality, conformity

Integration

You can use the strengths of curiosity, persistence, zest, and bravery to refine your creativity. Also, as noted above, if your creative expression impacts others, use the strengths of social intelligence, teamwork, and open-mindedness to include those others in finding co-creative solutions to problems that impact well-being.

Sadness and suffering are often cited as generators of creativity. However, there may be many paths and processes leading to creative expression. Consider when children are playing. They are happy (positive emotions) and often create role plays and imaginary characters and create new scenarios from existing settings. Strengths such as gratitude, appreciation of beauty, playfulness and humor—with relatively more explicit expressions of positive emotions—can facilitate creativity. Creative expression—from conception to fruition—needs support from persistence and self-regulation. Persistence is important to finish what is started, and self-regulation is needed to stay focused or to re-establish focus, if distracted.

Movies

- *Pianist (2002)*—Wladyslaw Szpilman's character is inspiring in this World War II movie. Despite the incredible cruelty of the Nazis, Szpilman relies on his creativity to survive.

- *Gravity (2013)*—This film presents an excellent illustration of creative problem solving as two astronauts work together to survive after an accident that leaves them stranded in space.
- *Julie & Julia (2009)*—Based on the celebrity chef Julia Child, the movie shows many facets of creativity both by Julia Child and another woman, Julie Powell.

Therapeutic Actions

- **Create new solutions for old problems:** Compile an original and practical list of solutions or tips that will address old, ongoing problems faced by you and your peers. Share this list with your friends through social media (or any other way you find appropriate) to elicit feedback.
- **Tackle boring tasks:** Make a list of tasks that you find boring yet have to do. Look for different and creative ways to accomplish these tasks. Find ways to incorporate them into your work or chores to make these times more enjoyable.
- **Offer creative solutions:** Offer at least one creative solution to the challenges of a sibling or friend. Share your relevant experiences, successes, and setbacks from when you tried something similar yourself. Practice being open to their creative ideas as well as to your own.
- **Use leftovers (food, paper, etc.) to make new products:** Consider the artistic or practical uses for items before you throw them away.
- **Collect and organize:** Collect and organize assorted materials (e.g., websites, online videos, sketchbooks, crayons, pastels, or flipcharts) that readily enable you to translate new ideas into concrete form.
- **Improve your attention:** If you experience attentional challenges—such as overlooking important details, getting distracted easily, being unable to keep in mind multiple pieces of information at the same time—pursuing a creative endeavor that engages you, can help you improve your attention.

Exemplars (TED Talks)

Visit https://www.ted.com/talks and search for the following talks to hear from individuals who represent the strength of creativity:

- William Kamkwamba: How I harnessed the wind
- Isaac Mizrahi: Fashion and creativity
- Linda Hill: How to manage for collective creativity
- Kary Mullis: Play! Experiment! Discover!
- Richard Turere: My invention that made peace with lions

Books

- Carlson, S. (2010). *Your Creative Brain: Seven steps to Maximize Imagination, Productivity, and Innovation in Your Life*. San Francisco: Wiley.
- Csikszentmihalyi, M. (1996). *Creativity: Flow and the Psychology of Discovery and Invention*. New York: HarperCollins.
- Edwards, B. (2013). *Drawing on the Right Side of the Brain: A Course in Enhancing Creativity and Artistic Confidence*. London: Souvenir Press.
- Drapeau, P. (2014). *Sparking Student Creativity: Practical Ways to Promote Innovative Thinking and Problem Solving*. Alexandria, VA: ASCD.

Websites

- Inspiring Creativity: A short film about creative thinking and behaviors: http://www.highsnobiety.com/2014/05/16/watch-inspiring-creativity-a-short-film-about-creative-thinking-and-behaviors/
- The Imagination Institute: Focuses on the measurement, growth, and improvement of imagination across all sectors of society: http://imagination-institute.org/
- Shelley Carson's website: Complete a test to explore your creative mindset: http://www.shelleycarson.com/creative-brain-test https://www.authentichappiness.sas.upenn.edu/learn/creativity
- 25 things creative people do differently: http://www.powerofpositivity.com/25-things-creative-people-differently/
- The Artist's Way—tools to enhance your creativity, videos with the author Julia Cameron: www.theartistway.com

2. CURIOSITY

Description

Curiosity involves actively recognizing and pursuing challenging opportunities and seeking out new knowledge. In the therapeutic context, you can use curiosity to be open to experiences you may have been avoiding because these experiences make you feel afraid or anxious, such as riding in a crowded underground train, asking a question at an information desk, or talking to a stranger at a social gathering. Or maybe there are objects that make you uncomfortable, such as needles, germs in public washrooms, or specific foods. Curiosity has tremendous therapeutic potential especially if you have assumed that your fears cannot be changed. Instead of being fixated on these experiences, curiosity will enable you to be flexible. Its components, including being open and embracing uncertainty, the unknown, and the new, will help you understand the nuances and subtleties of your fears, which can facilitate both healing and growth.

The Golden Mean

We habituate to (i.e., get used to) almost all positive experiences and products. A balanced approach to curiosity helps to ward off boredom, apathy, and disinterest. Curiosity helps you seek out new or fresh aspects of an experience, process, or product, especially aspects you have not grasped fully. Also, without becoming anxiously preoccupied, curiosity can change the mundane aspects of your daily routine into engaged, interested, and motivated living. Balanced application of curiosity toward self-understanding is critical for growth. Instead of overanalyzing, being self-absorbed, or self-securitizing excessively, be sufficiently curious to challenge the limits of your knowledge—about yourself and about the world around you.

- *Overuse of strength*: prying, snooping, nosiness
- *Underuse of strength:* boredom, disinterest, apathy

Integration

Curiosity is closely tied with other strengths and attributes, such as creativity, persistence, and open-mindedness. Whenever you find yourself entangled in complex situation, use your curiosity, in concert with other strengths, to extract a balanced, yet optimal, use of your curiosity. At times, your curiosity needs courage to find its adaptive expression, especially when you feel ambivalent (part angry, part sad) and cannot identify a specific cause. It might be that your ambivalence is related to avoiding fears, confronting a person in authority who mistreated you, or emotionally numbing yourself from a traumatic experience. The curiosity to explore the root causes of your distress is a critical first step, before you can look for ways to manage this distress.

Movies

- *October Sky (1999)*—The curiosity of Homer Hickam, inspired by the launch of Sputnik, motivates him and his friends to build their own rockets, and eventually they get a spot in the National Science Awards competition.
- *10 Items or Less (2006)*—A "has-been" actor, in pursuit of a new role, goes to a grocery store in a small industrial town to observe a worker, displaying a high level of curiosity while interacting with a wide range of people.
- *Indiana Jones and The Raiders of the Lost Ark (1981)*—An archaeological adventure—covering a booby-trapped temple in Peru to the search for ancient artefacts—shows numerous aspects of curiosity.

Therapeutic Actions

- **Confront your fears:** Make a list of experiences or things that make you afraid, uncomfortable, or anxious. Make sure you list things that you fear and also *avoid*, either by not doing them (e.g., avoiding certain places, foods, or people) or by doing something else (e.g., taking a detour, eating substitute foods, or not interacting with people). Expand your knowledge about ways to deal with your fear by reading expert opinions, watching recommended videos, and speaking with someone who could help you with useful tips.
- **Deal with boredom through cultural explorations:** If you experience boredom and are tired of routine, try something new. For example, eat food from a different culture or engage in a cultural experience that carries an element of novelty for you. Explore the cultural context of the experience from someone familiar with the culture. Share your impressions with a friend or friends in person or through social media.
- **Cope with the anxiety of uncertainty:** We want to understand, manage, and predict events in our lives. However, it is almost impossible to do so, which often causes anxiety. Instead of coping with this anxiety through unhealthy means (e.g., by "filling in the blanks" with inaccurate information acquired impulsively), use curiosity to embrace uncertainty and be open to new information. This process will help you learn to tolerate uncertainty so that you will better be able to cope with anxiety. Rather than searching for certainty, be curious about the process that leads to certainty.
- **Overcome biases by diversifying social connections:** We often socialize with people who are like us. This helps us identify with them and hurts us by limiting our social exposure. Such limited exposure maintains or reinforces our biases toward people and cultures different from us. Arrange a face-to-face conversation or a coffee date with a person from a different culture, and spend an hour, at least once a month, learning about the person and his or her culture. Be inquisitive, nonjudgmental, and open about your own culture.
- **Develop curiosity about nature:** Nature holds tremendous therapeutic potential. Reallocate an hour that you would spend worrying, doubting, and stressing over your unsolved problems, to exploring nature. For at least one hour a week, explore the processes of nature, by being in the woods, or a park, or by a stream, in the yard, and so on. Write, draw, or paint in order to record your impressions and feelings.

Exemplars (TED Talks)

Visit https://www.ted.com/talks and search for the following talks to hear from individuals who represent the strength of curiosity:

- Kary Mullis: Play! Experiment! Discover!
- Brian Cox: Why we need the explorers
- Taylor Wilson: Yup, I built a nuclear fusion reactor
- Jack Andraka: A promising test for pancreatic cancer . . . from a teenager

Books

- Goldin, I., & Kutarna, C. (2016). *Age of Discovery: Navigating the Risks and Rewards of Our New Renaissance.* Bloomsbury, UK: St Martin's Press.
- Gruwell, E. (1999). *The Freedom Writers Diary: How a Teacher and 150 Teens Used Writing to Change Themselves and the World around Them.* New York: Doubleday.
- Grazer, B., & Fishman, C. (2015). *A Curious Mind: The Secret to a Bigger Life.* Toronto: Simon & Schuster.
- Kashdan, T. (2009). *Curious.* New York: William Morrow.
- Leslie, I. (2014). *Curious: The Desire to Know and Why Your Future Depends on It.* New York: Basic Books.

Websites

- Discover how cultivating an inquiring mind can help you lead a happier, healthier life: https://experiencelife.com/article/the-power-of-curiosity/
- Four reasons why curiosity is important and how it can be developed: http://www.lifehack.org/articles/productivity/4-reasons-why-curiosity-is-important-and-how-to-develop-it.html
- Curiosity prepares the brain for better learning: http://www.scientificamerican.com/article/curiosity-prepares-the-brain-for-better-learning/

3. OPEN-MINDEDNESS

Description

Open-mindedness is our ability to think things through and examine them from all sides. In the therapeutic context, open-mindedness entails a willingness to consider evidence against our own beliefs about ourselves. Psychotherapy is an interpersonal endeavor to evaluate one's beliefs, especially those that maintain symptoms and stress. Using the strength of open-mindedness, especially to grasp a complex personal situation, will encourage you to look at different perspectives not yet considered to solve problems. Open-mindedness will encourage you to maintain the "reality orientation," that is, being unbiased and perceiving problems objectively. You will therefore be better able to counteract the pervasive "my-side bias" that prevents many people from considering views other than their own.

The Golden Mean

For the most part, open-mindedness entails critical inquiry, sifting the quality of information carefully. In solving your everyday problems or tackling big challenges, a lack of open-mindedness prevents you from reflecting, and you likely perceive your problems in black and white. You likely are seen as being rigid, your stance would likely be called stubborn, and this stubbornness can exacerbate symptomatic distress. If you experience symptoms of depression and anxiety, and also face adversity, a setback, or a failure, you are more likely to attribute the challenge to your own shortcomings. You are likely to assume that the challenge will last forever and that it will adversely impact all aspects of your life.

Similarly, an overuse of this strength will make you overanalytical, cynical, and skeptical, and you won't be able to trust people or processes. A balanced use of open-mindedness requires that you exercise critical inquiry but do not discount emotional aspects of the situation that may not be fully explained by facts alone. (For example, after a break up, which you rationally justify is good for you, you may continue to feel sad and bad. It is important to mourn the loss, without being swept away by it.)

- *Overuse of strength:* cynicism, skepticism
- *Underuse of strength:* dogmatism, "unreflectiveness", rigidity, overly simplistic

Integration

Open-mindedness works synergistically with a number of strengths. For example, being open-minded and organically engaged in critical thinking allows you to be open to alternative explanations and innovative solutions—hallmarks of creativity and curiosity. Open-mindedness also entails being open to multiple perspectives and tapping into wisdom. Furthermore, the critical appraisal associated with open-mindedness reinforces fairness and integrity.

Movies

- *The Help (2011)*—Eugenia Skeeter, an open-minded white female writer, strives to tell the stories and perspectives of black maids in a clearly stratified and highly racist society.
- *The Matrix (1999)*—Neo, the protagonist, displays open-mindedness by questioning the meaning of reality.
- *The Social Network (2010)*—This movie tells how Mark Zuckerberg founded Facebook. A scene depicting the first meeting of a difficult college course shows the lack of open-mindedness of the professor, while the movie shows how Zuckerberg, despite experiencing social deficits, exercises his flexible and critical thinking strengths.
- *Apocalypse Now (1979)*—In an adaptation of Joseph Conrad's novel, *Heart of Darkness*, famed film director Francis Ford Coppola depicts a critical inquiry into primal madness, brought on by the Vietnam War.
- *Water (2005)*—This film displays the lives of three widows showing extraordinary judgment to remain open to new experiences confronting injustice and negative societal traditions.

Therapeutic Actions

- **Reflect on and rewrite your challenges:** Monitor and record at least three unhealthy thoughts and beliefs that make you sad, anxious, or ambivalent. (For example, *"My wife constantly leaves a mess everywhere and this really annoys me! I never say anything, but I feel like she doesn't respect me. Why does this always happen to me?"*) Reflect on and write about an alternative way of explaining these problems to yourself, one that includes some of the attributes of open-mindedness.
- **Reflect on and write about decisions that backfired:** Reflect on and write about three recent decisions you made that backfired or did not produce the desired and adaptive outcome. Share your reflections with a trusted and wise friend. Ask your friend to critically appraise your judgment. Commit to yourself that you will listen to this appraisal without getting angry or defensive.

- **Play devil's advocate:** Reflect on and select an issue about which you have strong opinions. Deliberately think through an argument for the other side. Dispassionately review credible sources that may support you to hold this opposing view. This exercise may open your mind to a new perspective you may not have considered before.
- **Mentor someone from a different ethnic or religious background:** Reflect on what skills or expertise you can teach someone from a disadvantaged or marginalized group. Approach this task with the expectation that you want to, and can, learn as much from the mentee as she or he can learn from you.
- **Reappraise causes of your failure**: Identify causes of three recent failures, set-backs, less than optimal results, or disappointments. Review the attributes of open-mindedness, and then appraise the situations again. Find patterns, if any, such as why you always feel bad or anxious or powerless when talking to this person, or if there is a specific cause that you typically endorse. (For example, *"I always miss something important before this meeting."*)

Exemplars (TED Talks)

Visit https://www.ted.com/talks and search for the following talks to hear from individuals who represent the strength of open-mindedness:

- Alia Crum: Change Your mindset, Change the game, TEDxTraverseCity
- Adam Savage: How simple ideas lead to scientific discoveries
- Adam Grant: The surprising habits of original thinkers
- Vernā Myers: How to overcome our biases? Walk boldly toward them
- Dalia Mogahed: What do you think when you look at me?

Books

- Costa, A. (1985). *Developing Minds: A Resource Book for Teaching Thinking.* Alexandria, VA: Association for Supervision and Curriculum Development.
- Hare, W. (1985). *In Defence of Open-Mindedness.* Kingston, UK: McGill-Queen's University Press.
- Markova, D. (1996). *The Open Mind: Exploring the 6 Patterns of Natural Intelligence.* Berkeley, CA: Conari Press.

Websites

- YouTube: Critical Thinking: A look at some of the principles of critical thinking: https://youtu.be/6OLPL5p0fMg
- YouTube: Top 5 Mind Opening and Quality Movies: https://youtu.be/gsjEX91vAgY
- Open-mindedness, its benefits, its role as a "corrective virtue," and its exercises: https://www.authentichappiness.sas.upenn.edu/newsletters/authentichappinesscoaching/open-mindedness

4. LOVE OF LEARNING

Description

Love of learning involves enthusiastically studying new skills, topics, and bodies of knowledge. If this is one of your top strengths, you most likely enjoy learning, and, over time, you build a reservoir of knowledge of specific topics and domains. You don't need external prompts to "study;" rather, you are internally motivated to enhance and accumulate diverse dimensions of data and information to constantly strengthen your knowledge base on specific topics—from computers to culinary arts, from movies to museums, or from Lagos to literature. You create or are drawn to hubs of learning—be it a school, a book club, a discussion group, a lecture, a workshop, or even taking a course. Obstacles, challenges, and setbacks do not dampen your desire for learning.

The Golden Mean

Resisting learning and acquiring new knowledge and understanding most likely impedes one's growth and is often one of the signs of underlying depression. Going deeper into learning most likely brings about numerous benefits. However, knowledge is a concrete resource, and knowledge of statistics, facts, figures, historical events, scientific findings, and concrete evidence, can instill an air of over confidence and, in some cases, arrogance, which can easily create a division between those who know (or the know-it-all) and those who don't know, or don't know enough. Therefore, it is important that in a data-, information-, and knowledge-rich world, you not create or climb on a hierarchy of knowledge and learning and end up treating others (those without your quantity of knowledge) any less. More importantly, don't discount emotions. Having access to your worries, fears, and doubts is critical, as these emotions provide the context for your rationality and knowledge so that you can comprehend the wholeness of a situation to optimally solve your problems.

- *Overuse of strength:* "know it all"-ism
- *Underuse of strength:* complacency, smugness

Integration

Love of learning goes hand in hand with other strengths within the virtue of Knowledge & Wisdom. For example, love of learning accompanies curiosity and persistence. Without persistence, it is difficult to acquire a deeper understanding of any subject. Likewise, love of learning synergistically enhances critical thinking and widens perspective.

Movies

- *Theory of Everything (2014)*—An extraordinary story of one of the world's greatest living minds, the renowned astrophysicist Stephen Hawking displays love of learning despite extraordinary challenges.
- *Akeelah and the Bee (2006)*—The passion of an American adolescent to learn unfolds as she reluctantly participates and eventually wins the National Spelling Bee competition.
- *A Beautiful Mind (2001)*—This is the story of Noble Laurate John Nash and his passion for self-discovery and knowledge despite severe mental health challenges.

Therapeutic Actions

- **Reallocate time to learn about adaptive coping:** We often spend a lot of time thinking and brooding about our problems, and less time thinking about how to cope with them adaptively. Monitor yourself to estimate how much time you spend thinking about your problems. Reallocate that time to learn about how others have successfully coped with similar issues.
- **Share your learning:** Identify topics that you can share with your peers. Share information in a humble, conversational manner. Reflect afterwards. Most likely you will feel satisfied, and this will likely increase your self-efficacy.

- **Follow an ongoing situation:** Follow an ongoing local or global event about which you can personally identify or feel affinity for. Make a list of things you don't know about the event, and find credible sources to enhance your learning.
- **Learn through leisure:** Travel to new places and blend education with leisure. While you are there, take a tour, take a cooking class, or visit a local museum to learn more about the local culture and history.
- **Co-learn:** Learn with a friend with whom you share one or more areas of intellectual interest. Discuss specific areas that you each will study separately. Share your findings over a cup of coffee or tea, preferably in a café. You can also co-learn with a loved one, including your partner, parents, children, or extended family members. This will strengthen your relationships, and you will spend time together in a positive, rather than a potentially negative, way.

Exemplars (TED Talks)

Visit https://www.ted.com/talks and search for the following talks to hear from individuals who represent the strength of love of learning:

- Salman Khan: Let us Use Video to Reinvent Education
- Bunker Roy: Learning from a barefoot movement
- Ramsey Musallam: 3 rules to spark learning

Books

- Yousafzai, M., & Lamb, C. (2013). *I Am Malala: The Girl Who Stood Up for Education and Was Shot by the Taliban.* London: Hachette.
- Watson, J. C., & Watson, J. C. (2011). *Critical Thinking: An Introduction to Reasoning Well.* London: Continuum.
- Markova, D. (1996). *The Open Mind: Exploring the 6 Patterns of Natural Intelligence.* Berkeley, CA: Conari Press.

Websites

- Coursera offers a number of free online courses: https://www.coursera.org/
- Free course from Massachusetts Institute of Technology: http://ocw.mit.edu/index.htm
- Free courses online courses from Yale University: http://oyc.yale.edu/

5. PERSPECTIVE

Description

Perspective, which is often called wisdom, is distinct from intelligence and involves a superior level of knowledge and judgment. This strength allows you to provide wise counsel to others. A number of our psychological problems are characterized by assumptions. For example, we think that we can do many things, especially when it comes to things that require interacting with others. When others fall short of our expectations and don't (or are unable to) do what we desire, we become disappointed and, in some cases, depressed. (For example, "*I was hoping that my family would understand why I am making this difficult decision. . . .*") From a therapeutic standpoint, perspective helps you to evaluate what you can do, what you cannot do, what you can realistically expect, and what may not be realistic.

We experience ambivalence when we are unable to discern conflicting information or unable to balance competing positives (e.g., *"Should I work more to earn more money so that we can go on vacation, or should I use this time to play a board game with my loved ones, so that we can do something together now?"*). The strength of perspective will help you weigh an option for the greater good—be it related to self-care or caring for others. Perspective also allows you to address important and difficult questions about morality and the meaning of life. People with perspective are aware of broad patterns of meaning in their lives, their own strengths and weaknesses, and the necessity of contributing to their society.

The Golden Mean

Perspective, by definition, is the golden mean. That is, if it is one of your top strengths, you know how to strike a balance between your work and personal life. You are good at setting realistic expectations. You are good at separating positives from negatives and weighing them appropriately. With this strength, you can weigh personal factors (e.g., *"I always make a fool of myself"*) versus situational factors (e.g., *"Yesterday, my presentation did not go well because my colleague did not provide the critical data that I needed.*") A balanced use of perspective entails having the ability to see both the forest from the trees and the trees in the forest. It is also about tolerating some short-term pain (e.g., confronting an anxious situation) for long-term gains (e.g., getting rid of your anxiety). However, be mindful that not all aspects of your life need perspective. Appraising and dealing with every mundane situation from the lens of perspective can make your decisions arcane or pedantic.

- *Overuse of strength:* elitism, arcane, pedantic
- *Underuse of strength:* superficiality

Integration

In some ways, perspective encompasses the strengths discussed previously. That is, perspective encompasses learning, curiosity, creativity, and understanding what proportion of your specific strengths best work together toward your satisfaction and well-being (e.g., a proportionate use of kindness and fairness).

Movies

- *Hugo (2011)*—Hugo, a 12-year-old boy living in the Gare Montparnasse train station in Paris, offers perspective on experiences with what really matters in life. The movie is also a brilliant illustration of resilience and social intelligence.
- *Peaceful Warrior (2006)*—Socrates, played by Nick Nolte, teaches Dan, an ambitious teenager, the strength of perspective, humility, and focus through actions and applied scenarios.
- *American Beauty (1999)*—Lester Burnham, a middle-aged businessman trapped in his own misery, undergoes a rapid transformation to realize what is truly important in his life.

Therapeutic Actions

- **Set goals for things that frustrate you:** Set five small goals That address your day-to-day stressors (such as feeling irritable at your partner for not bringing the dishes back into the kitchen from the dinner table, or feeling frustrated at forgetting passwords to important websites). Break down the goals into practical steps, accomplish them on time, and monitor your progress from week to week.

- **Choose a role model for problem-solving:** Select a role model who exemplifies perseverance, and determine how you can follow in her or his footsteps. Try to select a person who has dealt with challenges similar to yours, with whom you can identify. If this person is living and someone you know, speak with him or her about this strength.
- **Broaden your outlook and monitor temporary stressors:** Explain the broad outlook of your life in one or two sentences as a weekly exercise. Monitor whether temporary stressors have an impact on your overall perspective. If you do see this pattern, brainstorm ways that your perspective can remain constant through daily joys and struggles.
- **Volunteer the time you would otherwise spend analyzing your problems:** Pursue endeavors that have a significant impact on the world. Reallocate your time and resources to pursue this endeavor. This reallocation will positively distract your mind from thinking about your problems, some of which need fresh perspective. If you are unable to solve a problem right away, positive distraction allows you to reconsider from a fresh perspective.
- **Connect beliefs with emotions:** Connect your beliefs with your emotions by reading books or watching films of personal experiences on issues that matter to you personally. Put a human face on the issue and recall that when you feel your opinion on the issue is getting too heated.

Exemplars (TED Talks)

Visit https://www.ted.com/talks and search for the following talks to hear from individuals who represent the strength of perspective:

- Barry Schwartz: Using our practical wisdom
- Joshua Prager: Wisdom from great writers on every year of life
- Rory Sutherland: Perspective is everything

Books

- Frankl, V. (2006). *Man's Search for Meaning.* Boston: Beacon Press.
- Hall, Stephen, (2010). *Wisdom: From Philosophy to Neuroscience.* New York: Random House.
- Sternberg, R. J., ed. (1990). *Wisdom: Its Nature, Origins, and Development.* Cambridge: Cambridge University Press.
- Vaillant, G. E. (2003*). Aging Well: Surprising Guideposts to a Happier Life from the Landmark Study of Adult Development.* New York: Little Brown.

Websites

- This website details the work of Thomas D. Gilovich, who studies beliefs, judgment and decision-making. He studies how these factors affect, and are affected by, emotions, behavior and perception:
  http://www.psych.cornell.edu/people/Faculty/tdg1.html
- Barry Schwarz studies practical wisdom and the paradox of choice. He discusses the disadvantages of having infinite choices, which he argues exhausts the society and the human psyche:
  https://www.ted.com/speakers/barry_schwartz

CORE VIRTUE: COURAGE

Exercising the will to accomplish goals in the face of opposition, external or internal

6. BRAVERY

Description

Bravery (courage) is the capacity to take action to aid others in spite of significant risks or dangers. When you are psychologically distressed and *also* face challenges, threats, or adversities—real or perceived—this can become a "double whammy," and the impact can therefore be two-fold. Sometimes our challenges, threats, and adversities themselves are overwhelming enough to cause psychological problems. If bravery is one of your top strengths, it can help you take action to deal with the challenge in an adaptive way. Bravery does not let you avoid or shrink from challenges, and you usually exercise this strength well aware of the risks involved. If bravery is one of your signature strengths, you place a high value on it. That is, when you feel stressed, sad, frightened, angry, or overwhelmed, the strength of bravery will most likely motivate you to take an action. Brave individuals avoid shrinking from the threats, challenges, or pain associated with attempting to do good works. Brave acts are undertaken voluntarily, with full knowledge of the potential adversity involved. Brave individuals place the highest importance on higher purpose and morality, no matter what the consequences.

The Golden Mean

To deal with your problems with the help of bravery, it is important that you not feel coerced or entirely extrinsically motivated. Courageous actions—physical or emotional—ought to be based on your own values. (For example, if you confront a family member who is being emotionally or physically abusive to another family member, or if you take a stand in support of a vulnerable or oppressed person, such action will be authentic if it is guided by your deeply held personal values that this action is the right thing to do.) A balanced use of courage requires the existence of a real threat or risk that can be averted by your courageous action. A balanced use of bravery also entails that you be aware of the consequences of your action or inaction. (For example, you will want to ensure that your use of bravery is not taking undue risk that comes with the cost of comprising your and other's safety.) Note that not using courage can often result in feelings of helplessness. Thus, overuse of bravery (e.g., disclosure, reputation, collective reprisals) and underuse of bravery (e.g., hopelessness, passivity, demotivation) can create problems both for yourself and others.

- *Overuse of strength:* risk-taking, foolishness
- *Underuse of strength:* debilitating fear, cowardice

Integration

Bravery can potentially interact with numerous other strengths. For example, bravery can entail *using* (i.e., committing) strengths such as fairness, authenticity, or perspective, or *not using* (i.e., omitting) strengths such as perspective, prudence, self-regulation, or forgiveness. Bravery also works well with strengths like zest, social and personal intelligence, persistence, and self-regulation.

Examples include wanting to face your fear in spite of accessing uncomfortable emotions and memories, appraising with an open mind (judgment), taking action to halt the cycle of negativity or resisting impulses (self-regulation), and committing to adhere to your goal (persistence).

Movies

- *Milk (2008)*—This movie depicts Harvey Milks' courage to become the first openly gay person to be elected to public office in California.
- *The Kite Runner (2007)*—A moving tale of two friends, Amir and Hassan, whose friendship flourishes in pre-Soviet-invasion Kabul, in the mid to late 1970s. The film shows how Amir musters the courage to rescue Hassan's son from war-ravaged and Taliban-ruled Afghanistan.
- *Schindler's List (1993)*—Oskar Schindler is a German businessman whose bravery saves over a thousand Jews during World War II.
- *The Help (2011)*—Eugenia, also known as "Skeeter," is a courageous white female writer who strives to tell the stories and perspectives of black maids in a clearly stratified and highly racist society.

Therapeutic Actions

- **Resolve interpersonal distress with brave "one-to-ones":** Write about three interpersonal situations that cause you ongoing distress, such as fear or inhibition, especially with people in a position of authority and with whom you interact regularly. Reflect on how a balanced use of bravery can decrease your distress. (For example, *"I want to speak with my professor, alone after class, to bravely express myself."*)
- **Embrace darker and negative experiences with bravery:** Make a list of emotions from which you often run. Turn these into statements such as, *"I will make a complete fool of myself;. I am so afraid of being rejected or being alone; I cannot do anything to stop him acting this way, so I just leave the situation altogether"* and evaluate the cost of not facing such emotions. Then, using bravery, visualize embracing the full range of your emotions, such as what might be the worst and the best scenarios if you were to stay and do something. Bravery can help you embrace the full range of your emotions, especially in distressful situations.
- **Speak the truth that will set you free:** Use bravery to share a truth about yourself with your closest relations. This is a truth that is important enough that it impacts your relationships in a negative way, is an important aspect of your life, and one you are not sharing because of fear of rejection. (For example, *"I am really afraid to tell my parents that I am a lesbian. It is such an important part of me, but how will they take it? But if I don't tell them, then I am not being my authentic self with my family."*)
- **Ask difficult questions or question the status quo:** In group situations, such as at work, with your family, or among friends, use bravery to ask difficult questions or to question the status quo. Examples include questioning why do specific policies or rituals systematically keep specific people or groups on the fringes, not allowing them to assume leadership roles. Propose bold yet realistic solutions.
- **Stand up for someone or for a cause:** Stand up for someone who is unable to stand up for him- or herself, such as a younger sibling, a battered woman, a vulnerable immigrant, or a worker who is unaware of his rights. You can join an organization that courageously stands for those who need the support most.

Exemplars (TED Talks)

Visit https://www.ted.com/talks and search for the following talks to hear from individuals who represent the strength of bravery:

- Ash Beckham: We're all hiding something. Let's find the courage to open up
- Clint Smith: The danger of silence
- Eman Mohammed: The courage to tell a hidden story

Books

- Diener, R. (2012). *The Courage Quotient: How Science Can Make You Braver.* San Francisco: Jossey-Bass.
- Pury, C. (2010). *The Psychology of Courage: Modern Research on an Ancient Virtue.* Washington, DC: American Psychological Association.
- Pausch, R., & Zaslow, J. (2008). *The Last Lecture.* New York: Hyperion.

Websites

- The skill of bravery, its benefits, and the balance between fear and over-confidence: http://www.skillsyouneed.com/ps/courage.html
- Nine teens and their incredible acts of bravery: http://theweek.com/articles/468498/9-heroic-teens-incredible-acts-bravery-updated

7. PERSISTENCE

Description

Persistence is the mental strength necessary to continue striving for our goals in the face of obstacles and setbacks. From the therapeutic perspective, a number of psychological problems adversely impact attention and the ability to concentrate. Persistence (perseverance) is the strength that can help you deal with attentional problems because it enables you to remain goal-directed despite challenges, especially those due to distraction. With this strength, even if you are distracted, persistence brings you back to complete the task. You do your best to finish what you start and find ways to overcome hiccups and hardships. If you become bored and lackadaisical—another common feature of many psychological concerns—finding a task in which you can persist is an organic and therapeutic way to feel self-efficacious, uplifted, and satisfied when you finish the task.

The Golden Mean

The key to a balanced use of persistence is knowing when and where to persist and when to stop and cut your losses. To determine whether to persist or not, ask yourself what might happen if you do not finish this specific task. Equally important is your ability to adapt to changing situations. For example, in pursuing a desired career, you need to adapt to inevitable changes in market conditions, in technology, and in the larger socioeconomic framework. Finally, to optimally use this strength, you need to constantly be aware of your goal. (For example, to persist in successfully obtaining a social media certification that involves taking multiple courses in the evenings and on the weekends, you need to evaluate your goals and "keep your eyes on the prize.")

- *Overuse of strength:* obsessiveness, fixation, pursuit of unattainable goals
- *Underuse of strength:* laziness, apathy

Integration

To evaluate when persistence is adaptive versus when it enters the realm of obsessive and compulsive preoccupation, you need other strengths, such as perspective, social intelligence, judgment (open-mindedness), and prudence. To persist, especially if you experience setbacks, challenges, or obstacles, you need a good dose of hope and optimism. Without hope and optimism, motivation to persist will be sapped. However, you need to keep your hopes and optimism in the realm of what is realistic.

Movies

- *Life of Pi (2010)*—This movie presents the epic journey of a young man who perseveres and survives on the open sea to strike an unlikely connection with a ferocious Bengali Tiger.
- *127 Hours (2010)*—In a remarkable display of persistence and courage, Ralston, a mountain climber, becomes trapped under a boulder while canyoneering alone near Moab, Utah.
- *The King's Speech (2010)*—England's King George VI perseveres to overcome a speech impediment.

Therapeutic Actions

- **Tackle tasks that overwhelm you:** List five big tasks that you have to do, but that often overwhelm you, such as doing your taxes, responding to non-stop email, or preparing a holiday dinner for your partner's large family. Break these tasks into smaller steps, and congratulate yourself or celebrate—in small ways—when you finish each step. Monitor your progress step by step.
- **Find a role model who persisted despite challenges:** Select a role model who exemplifies perseverance and determine how you can follow in this person's footsteps. Try to find someone who has experienced mental health challenges similar to yours. Ideally meet this person face-to-face, or connect with him or her through other ways, to explore how he or she overcame challenges and perseverance.
- **Persist while acquiring new skills:** Your persistence may come to a halt simply because you do not have the next skill level to move forward. (For example, after designing a product, don't hesitate to ask for help in either learning new skills or having someone work with you, so that you can finish the project and produce it.)
- **Incorporate elements of "flow":** If you struggle to persist, explore flow, an intrinsically motivated state of deep immersion. Explore activities that induce flow; you will persist, and, in the process, you will grow.
- **Work with others:** A potentially therapeutic use of persistence is working with other like-minded individuals. The company of others can increase your skills and your motivation to persist.

Exemplars (TED Talks)

Visit https://www.ted.com/talks and search for the following talks to hear from individuals who represent the strength of persistence:

- Angela Lee Duckworth: Grit: The power of passion and perseverance
- Elizabeth Gilbert: Success, failure and the drive to keep creating
- Richard St. John: 8 secrets of success

Books

- Duckworth, A. (2016). *Grit: The Power of Passion and Perseverance.* New York: Simon & Schuster.
- Luthans, F., Youssef, C., & Avolio, B. (2007). *Psychological Capital: Developing the Human Competitive Edge.* New York: Oxford University Press.
- Tough, P. (2012). *How Children Succeed: Grit, Curiosity, and the Hidden Power of Character.* New York: Houghton Mifflin Harcourt.

Websites

- Self-determination theory discusses intrinsic motivation, values and how they affect well-being and goals:
  http://www.selfdeterminationtheory.org/
- Edward L. Deci studies motivation and self-determination and their effects on different facets of life, such as mental health, education, and work:
  http://www.psych.rochester.edu/people/deci_edward/index.html

8. INTEGRITY

Description

The strength of integrity (authenticity) is manifested by speaking the truth and presenting oneself in a genuine way. From a therapeutic standpoint, a number of psychological conditions entail ambivalence, inhibition, fear, embarrassment, and rejection, which keep us from sharing our emotions, thoughts, and, more importantly, needs, in an authentic manner. Integrity helps you to be open and honest about your thoughts and emotions. If integrity and authenticity are your top strengths, you easily take ownership of your actions, which enables you to behave in accordance with your values. In other words, there is little dissonance and alienation, which, in turn, improves your reality testing and social reasoning. An individual high on integrity is less likely to experience cognitive distortions and social fears. She is better able to understand and handle the context of complex dilemmas often posed by psychopathology.

A person of integrity is open and honest about his own thoughts, feelings, and responsibilities, being careful not to mislead others through action or omission. This strength allows you to feel a sense of ownership over your own internal states, regardless of whether those states are popular or socially comfortable, and to experience a sense of authentic wholeness.

The Golden Mean

Living in accordance with your values and taking ownership of your emotions and thoughts in an interpersonally complex world are not easy tasks, given the impact of cultural, religious, political, economic, ecological, and even technological (especially social media) influences. Therefore, a balanced use of integrity depends on the context. (For example, not every situation is amenable to authentic expressions like, "*I am not as good as others;*" "*Often I feel worthless,*" "*I am too embarrassed to ask for help; others will see me as weak.*" Also, sharing whatever you are thinking on Facebook or Twitter may not be the optimal way to represent yourself authentically.) To live an authentic and honest life, courage to withstand external pressures is indeed necessary. An authentic life also entails being credible, being real, and speaking the truth. Note that authenticity and fairness are not applicable in absolute terms; cultures differ vastly in terms of authentic representation of the self. Therefore, a balanced use of authenticity, honesty, and integrity can better be appraised within the cultural context. However, whatever the cultural framework might be, underuse of authenticity could lead to not expressing your emotions, interests, and needs. This in turn could limit your self-efficacy—if you cannot own your needs, how can you meet them? Furthermore, underuse of this strength forces you to adopt different roles in different situations, causing a fragmented personality that is more controlled or influenced by external forces than by yourself.

- *Overuse of strength:* righteousness
- *Underuse of strength:* shallowness, phoniness

Integration

Integrity works well when you are also attuned to your needs and motivations. Zest and vitality nicely complement integrity, and perspective and social intelligence are two key strengths that can help you understand context. In addition, emotional intelligence (as a sub-domain of social intelligence) provides you cues to feel, own, and express your internal states in a way that feels appropriate and authentic to you. Kindness and love are two other attributes that go hand in hand with integrity. Genuine love marked by caring and sharing encourages authenticity and vice-versa.

Movies

- *Separation (2011, Iran)*—During the dissolution of a marriage, this film presents an inspiring display of integrity and honesty by a person who is accused of lying.
- *Erin Brockovich (2000)*—The lead character's deep sense of integrity to bring the truth to light eventually results in one of the biggest class-action lawsuits in U.S. history.
- *The Legend of Bagger Vance (2000)*—Rannulph Junnah, once the best golfer in Savannah, Georgia, overcomes alcoholism to reconstruct both his golf game and his life through the strengths of authenticity and integrity.
- *Dead Poet Society (1989)*—English teacher John Keating, teaches boys about the joys of poetry, but in essence, they learn and eventually show the strengths of honesty and integrity.

Therapeutic Actions

- **Evaluate inhibitions, judgments, and rejection—lack of authenticity:** Reflect on and write about five situations that stressed you. Evaluate each situation as to whether it was partly due to inhibition, fear of judgment, or rejection, especially those caused by social norms and expectations. With a close friend or family member, discuss ways of finding how you can express yourself authentically.
- **Look for situations that facilitate your authenticity:** Reflect on and write about situations that naturally allow you to be yourself. Pay close attention to both internal and external factors that facilitate your authenticity. Discuss with a confidant how you can create more such situations.
- **Foster authentic interaction:** A number of our psychological stressors spring from our inability to authentically relate to others with integrity. Review models of feedback that are both authentic and constructive, and that build—not block—the relationship.
- **Seek authentic roles:** Seek roles with clear structure that allow you to be authentic and honest, especially if you feel inhibited at work. Pursue positions in organizations that foster honest, forthright communication.
- **Clarify moral convictions:** Identify your area of strongest moral conviction. (For example, doing your job optimally and giving it your best.) How can you bring these convictions into other areas of your life where you tend to struggle? (For example, obeying traffic rules, always opting for environmentally friendly options, standing up for some being mistreated.) Set small, measurable goals to improve your behavior that lead to greater integrity.

Visit https://www.ted.com/talks and search for the following talks to hear from individuals who represent the strength of integrity:

- Brené Brown: The power of vulnerability
- Malcolm McLaren: Authentic creativity vs. karaoke culture
- Heather Brooke: My battle to expose government corruption

Books

- Brown, B. (2010). *The Gifts of Imperfection: Let Go of Who You Think You're Supposed To Be and Embrace Who You Are.* Center City, MN: Hazelden.
- Cloud, H. (2006). *Integrity: The Courage to Meet the Demands of Reality.* New York: Harper.
- Simons, T. (2008). *The Integrity Dividend Leading by the Power of Your Word.* San Francisco: Jossey-Bass.

Websites

- Profiling voices, victims and witnesses of corruption and work toward a world free of corruption:
  https://www.transparency.org
- The International Center for Academic Integrity works to identify, promote, and affirm the values of academic integrity among students, faculty, teachers, and administrators:
  http://www.academicintegrity.org/icai/home.php

9. VITALITY & ZEST

Description

Vitality is an approach to life marked by an appreciation of energy, liveliness, excitement, and zest. From a psychological perspective, a lack of vitality breeds depression, passivity, and boredom. Vitality includes positive emotions such as joy, exuberance, and excitement, as well as contentment, satisfaction, and gratification. If vitality and zest are among your top strengths, you approach life whole-heartedly. You have both emotional and physical vigor when pursuing everyday activities. You often feel inspired and turn this feeling into creative projects and initiatives. You give your best to your projects, and this engagement often encourages others. A life of vigor allows you to experience the overlap of the mental and physical realms of experience as stress decreases and health increases.

The Golden Mean

A balanced use of vitality is critical, but it is not easy to distinguish between balance and overuse. Both of these states can easily be viewed as passion. However, when vitality is overused, it can become a passion that is internalized so deeply that it becomes part of your identity. On the other hand, not using vitality would leave you passive and unmotivated. For a balanced use, it is important that zest and vitality become part of your personality, but only a part, among many other parts. A balanced use of vitality means that you pursue many activities with enthusiasm, but you do not neglect your other responsibilities.

- *Overuse of strength:* hyperactivity
- *Underuse of strength:* passivity, inhibition

Integration

Vitality is a strength that works best with strengths from other virtues such as prudence, self-regulation, curiosity, playfulness, and appreciation of beauty, which are also utilized to create experiences that are wholesome. (For example, learning a musical instrument may require you to establish a practice routine [self-regulation], to appreciate music already created [appreciation of beauty and excellence], to enjoy the learning process [curiosity], to improvise and have fun with it [playfulness, creativity], and to learn music as well fulfilling other responsibilities [prudence].)

Movies

- *Hector and the Search for Happiness (2014)*—This movie presents a quirky psychiatrist's quest to feel alive and search for the meaning of life. The film displays a number of character strengths including zest, curiosity, love, perspective, gratitude, and courage.
- *Silver Lining Playbook (2012)*—The main character, Pat, has a motto—*excelsior* (which is a Latin word meaning *forever upward*)—which embodies zest and vitality, as Pat recovers from setbacks and becomes determined, energetic, and more attentive.
- *Up (2009)*—An uplifting story (literally and metaphorically) of 78-year-old Carl, who pursues his lifelong dream of seeing the wilds of South America, along with an unlikely companion.
- *My Left Foot (1993)*—Born a quadriplegic in a poor Irish family, Christy Brown (with the help of his dedicated mother and teacher) learns to write using the only limb he has any control over: his left foot. This character displays vitality, zest, and enthusiasm for life.

Therapeutic Actions

- **Engage in a "have to do" activity:** A number of psychological conditions sap our motivation. Select a "have to do" activity—one that you have to do (such as completing homework, exercising, or washing the dishes) but that you don't feel like doing. Use your strength of creativity to do the activity in a different and exciting way. You can select a partner and do it with him or her.
- **Go outdoors:** For an hour each week, do at least one outdoor activity, such as hiking, biking, mountain climbing, brisk walking, or jogging. Enjoy both the outdoors and your own internal sensations. Nature carries immense therapeutic potential.
- **Get better sleep:** Improve your sleep hygiene by establishing a regular bed time. Don't eat any later than three or four hours before bed time, and avoid doing any work in bed, ingesting caffeine late in the evening, and so on. Notice changes in your energy level.
- **Join a club:** Get involved with a dance club, go to a concert, or join a performing arts group—at least a monthly event. If there is singing or dancing involved, join in. Alternatively, use your smart phone to take pictures that represent your concept of vitality and zest.
- **Socialize more with happy people:** Spend time with friends who like to laugh heartily. Notice how laughter can be infectious. Alternatively, watch a sitcom on television or go to a comedy club with your friends.

Exemplars (TED Talks)

Visit https://www.ted.com/talks and search for the following talks to hear from individuals who represent the strength of vitality & zest:

- Dan Gilbert: The surprising science of happiness
- Ron Gutman: The hidden power of smiling
- Meklit Hadero: The unexpected beauty of everyday sounds
- Matt Cutts: Try something new for 30 days

Books

- Buckingham, M. (2008). *The Truth About You.* Nashville, TN: Thomas Nelson.
- Elfin, P. (2014). *Dig Deep & Fly High: Reclaim Your Zest and Vitality by Loving Yourself from Inside Out.* Mona Vale, NSW: Penelope Ward.
- Peale, V. N. (1967). *Enthusiasm Makes the Difference.* New York: Simon & Schuster.

Websites

- Robert Vallerand explains what passion is and what differentiates obsessive passion from harmonious passion:
  https://vimeo.com/30755287
- Website of self-determination theory, which is concerned with supporting our natural or intrinsic tendencies to behave in effective and healthy ways:
  http://www.selfdeterminationtheory.org
- Four Reasons to Cultivate Zest in Life:
  https://greatergood.berkeley.edu/article/item/four_reasons_to_cultivate_zest_in_life

CORE VIRTUE: HUMANITY

Emotional strengths that show the exercise of will in the face of opposition or internal threat

10. LOVE

Description

Love includes both the capacity to love and be loved. The defining characteristic of this strength is valuing and caring for others, in particular those with whom sharing and caring is reciprocated. If love is among your top strengths, giving and receiving love comes easily to you. You can express your love toward those who you depend on and toward those who you romantically, sexually, and emotionally love. This strength allows you to put trust in others and make them a priority in your decision-making. You experience a sense of deep contentment from the devotion of those you love.

The Golden Mean

Love is arguably the wellspring from which your numerous other strengths flow. That makes striking a balance between love and other strengths challenging, especially when you may be feeling sad, anxious, ambivalent, or upset. If you tend to avoid (likely due to anxiety) instead of confront a repeat offender, you may be exercising your strength of love, possibly overlooking or even forgiving the offender. Likewise, the fear of loss of a relationship (likely due to depression) may compromise your strength of love, and you may tolerate unfair treatment. Relatedly, a skewed and selective expression of love can develop for one specific person—a romantic partner, parent, child, sibling, or friend—hurting others with whom you have to relate. Note that a balanced application of love is quintessentially framed within the cultural context of the individual: In interdependent cultures, this balance is to love the family as a whole, whereas in individualistic cultures, this implies balancing love and work appropriately.

- *Overuse of strength:* emotional promiscuity
- *Underuse of stren*gth: isolation, detachment

Integration

Love, a universal need to forge mutually caring relationships, acts like "super glue" that can integrate almost any number of other strengths. In this book, Session 3: Practical Wisdom, discusses numerous strategies to adaptively integrate strengths. Because of love's all-encompassing and idiosyncratic nature, it is important to be aware of which guiding principles integrate various strengths most adaptively, given the situation or challenge at hand. (For example, if you are experiencing relationship distress, you may integrate love with social intelligence and courage to relieve the distress, whereas someone else with a similar challenge can resolve it by integrating love with playfulness and creativity.)

Movies

- *Doctor Zhivago (1965)*—An epic story showing love—the capacity to love and be loved—of a physician who is torn between love of his wife and love of his life, set amidst the Russian Revolution.
- *The English Patient (1996)*—Set during World War II, this film tells a powerful story of love, when a young nurse cares for a mysterious stranger.
- *The Bridges of Madison County (1995)*—Francesca Johnson, a married mother, falls in love with a traveling photographer; the romance lasts only four days, but it changes her life drastically.
- *Brokeback Mountain (2005)*—This film presents the deep love story between two cowboys who fall in love almost by accident, set in the conservative landscape and social milieu of the 1960s, when gay love was still largely unaccepted.

Therapeutic Actions

- **Love is a learnable skill:** If your love is causing you distress, evaluate the sources and consequences of your distress. Love is an acquired skill that needs practice. Explore specific evidence-based skills, such as looking at the strengths of your loved ones (see the *Tree of Positive Relationships* practice in Session 12: Positive Relationships; and the *Active Constructive Responding* practice in Session 13: Positive Communication).
- **Keep up-to-date with your partner/loved ones:** Stay connected with your loved ones. Take five minutes out of your work day to send a text, or call to ask how their day is going, especially on important days. Regularly ask your loved ones about current stressors, worries, projects, hopes, dreams, friends, and adversaries.
- **Avoid "relationship fatigue":** Most relationships start on a positive note. Over time, however, partners start assuming that they have figured each other out, and the negativity bias tends to minimize the positives and accentuate the negatives. This bias slows the growth of relationships, while anger and resentment accumulate. Use love, together with creativity and curiosity, to explore something new about your partner, and do something the two of you have not tried previously.
- **Share a deep sense of meaning:** Flourishing relationships grow when couples and families play and laugh together, and when they share a deep sense of meaning. Such meaning can be shared in a number of ways, such as having values in common (e.g.,

autonomy, familial harmony, and career success) and understanding the actions that express these values.

- **Spend time together:** Arrange regular family leisure activities, such as walking, hiking, biking, or camping together; taking family yoga or dance classes; or attending sporting events, retreats, concerts, or cultural festivals as a family. These activities will build pleasant, instead of toxic, memories.

Exemplars (TED Talks)

Visit https://www.ted.com/talks and search for the following talks to hear from individuals who represent the strength of love:

- Robert Waldinger: What makes a good life? Lessons from the longest study on happiness
- Helen Fisher: Why we love, why we cheat
- Yann Dall'Aglio: Love—you're doing it wrong
- Mandy Len Catron: Falling in love is the easy part

Books

- Fredrickson, B. L. (2013). *Love 2.0*. New York: Plume.
- Gottman, J. M., & Silver. N. (1999). *The Seven Principles for Making Marriage Work*. New York: Three Rivers Press.
- Pileggi Pawelski, S., & Pawelski, J. (2018). *Happy Together: Using the Science of Positive Psychology to Build Love That Lasts*. New York: TarcherPerigee.
- Vaillant, G. E. (2012). *Triumphs of Experience: The Men of the Harvard Grant Study*. Cambridge, MA: Belknap Press of Harvard University Press.

Websites

- The Gottman Institute offers research-based assessment techniques and intervention strategies as well as information about training in couple's therapy: https://www.gottman.com/
- The Attachment Lab: The Research on attachment focuses on understanding the conscious and unconscious dynamics of the attachment behavioral system: http://psychology.ucdavis.edu/research/research-labs/adult-attachment-lab
- The Centre for Family Research, at the University of Cambridge, has a worldwide reputation for innovative research that increases understanding of children, parents and family relationships: https://www.cfr.cam.ac.uk

11. KINDNESS

Description

Kindness includes numerous attributes such as being considerate, courteous, and caring. If kindness is among your top strengths, you translate these attributes into actions, deeds, and endeavors for others, without being asked and without expecting tangible outcomes. Kindness is not merely what you want to do. You are also aware of your motives, skills, and the likely impact of your efforts. Although the act of kindness is done without the expectation of personal gain, from a psychotherapeutic perspective, the person receiving the act of kindness experiences positive emotions and so does the person doing the act. Thus kindness can act as a buffer for a person in distress, by re-directing attention from oneself to others in adaptive ways. If kindness is your strength, you find joy in helping others. It doesn't matter if you know the other person or not; you are motivated to help unconditionally.

The Golden Mean

Indeed, there is value and importance in undertaking spontaneous and random acts of kindness that address immediate needs. Such acts may include resolving someone's technological glitch, providing an injured person with first aid, listening mindfully to someone who needs to share his or her distress, or cooking a meal for a sick friend. However, some consideration is needed in doing acts of kindness that may require a lot of effort, energy, and time. (Examples include tutoring, helping with a household construction or building project, and assisting with professional expertise such as accounting, legal, or medical.) For all such situations, explain any potential risks and outcomes. Also consider whether the help you are offering is actually needed; is accepted; is offered respectfully; is pragmatic; and is not contingent on any direct, indirect, or secondary gains. Ensure that you consult with the recipient about the process and logistics, as a number of factors may not be obvious. Also make sure that your kindness is not perceived as leniency or does not evolve into dependency. Always connect your acts of kindness with your deeper values. It is very important to understand that kindness also includes being kind to the self. Kindness devoid of self-compassion can be an excuse to avoid or suppress your own harsh inner critic. A balanced use of kindness entails that you are not being unduly critical of yourself.

- *Overuse of strength:* intrusiveness
- *Underuse of strength:* indifference, cruelty, mean-spiritedness

Integration

Kindness works well with a number of other strengths. For example, deploying facets of emotional intelligence can help you appraise the nuances of situations such as: Is kindness relevant to the situation, or could some other strength bring about a better outcome? If, for example, a task requires a very specific skill set that you yourself can only accomplish in part, you can ask someone else to help you (teamwork), or clarify the extent of what you know so that the recipient is aware of what you can and cannot accomplish (authenticity), and then get the rest of the task done elsewhere. If you are eager to help someone and you have the skills to deliver the help but you are afraid of making mistakes, consult and collaborate with the recipient, and utilize other strengths such as prudence, judgment, and open-mindedness to create an optimal experience of expressing your kindness.

Movies

- *Blind Side (2009)*—Based on a true story of kindness and compassion, Michael Oher, a homeless and traumatized boy, is adopted by Sean and Leigh Anne Tuohy—a connection that leads Michael to play in the National Football League.
- *Children of Heaven (1997, Iran)*—This movie shows kindness and compassion, rather than traditional sibling rivalry, between a brother and sister who share a pair of shoes.
- *The Secret Life of Bees (2008)* –A moving story that shows a powerful connection between strangers. A 14-year-old girl escapes a troubled world to find care and love in the home of the Boatwright sisters and their engrossing world of beekeeping.
- *The Cider House Rules (1999)*—Homer, a youth residing in an orphanage in Maine, learns both medicine and the value of kind actions over blind deference to rules.

Therapeutic Actions

- **Build self-efficacy:** Commit to doing at least one act of kindness to help others. When you help others genuinely, you do so without the expectation of any reward or other benefit. However, you are likely to reap psychological benefits as helping others builds your own self-efficacy, which in turn, decreases psychiatric distress.
- **Be kind to yourself:** Psychologically distressed people—especially those battling depression—harshly criticize themselves and think of themselves as the cause of their distress. If you are like this, start to use self-compassion, that is, be kind to yourself. Instead of exclusively focusing on your deficits, affirm your strengths in an authentic manner.
- **Express kindness through communication:** Use kinder and softer words to people when interacting through email, writing letters, talking on the phone, or interacting on social media. Create a list of tips and strategies for being kind on social media. Post this list and elicit responses and suggestions from you friends and family.
- **Expand your kindness and cultural connections:** Select one specific and distinct culture. Using different sources, including a few from within the culture, devise a list of cultural expressions that are often misunderstood by people outside the culture. Share the list with your social circles.
- **Engage in spontaneous acts of kindness:** While driving, give way to others, and be courteous toward pedestrians and bicyclists. When entering or exiting buildings, hold the doors for others. Help fix someone's flat tire, or offer your cell phone to a stranded motorist. Carry jumper cables and flares in your trunk in case you need to help someone on the road.
- **Share belongings and expertise:** Share your belongings with others (e.g., lawn mower, snow blower, or jumper cables). Offer to help them if they don't know how to operate the equipment or to go about accomplishing a task.

Exemplars (TED Talks)

Visit https://www.ted.com/talks and search for the following talks to hear from individuals who represent the strength of kindness:

- Karen Armstrong: Charter of Compassion
- Matthieu Ricard: How to let altruism be your guide
- Robert Thurman: Expanding our circle of compassion
- Hannah Brencher: Love letters to strangers
- Abigail Marsh: Why some people are more altruistic than others

Books

- Keltner, D., & Marsh, J., & Smith, J. A. (Eds.). (2010). *The Compassionate Instinct: The Science of Human Goodness*. New York: W. W. Norton.
- Rifkin, J. (2009). *The Empathic Civilization: The Race to Global Consciousness in a World in Crisis*. New York: Penguin.
- Ferrucci, P. (2007). *The Power of Kindness: The Unexpected Benefits of Leading a Compassionate Life*. Paperback edition. New York: Penguin.

Websites

- A list of 35 little acts of kindness you can do: http://www.oprah.com/spirit/35-Little-Acts-of-Kindness
- The Random Acts of Kindness, an internationally recognized non-profit organization that provides resources and tools that encourage acts of kindness: https://www.randomactsofkindness.org

- The Roots of Empathy and Compassion; Paul Ekman describes some of the necessary components of empathy and compassion:
  https://youtu.be/3AgvKJK-nrk
- Evidence-based article showing the benefits of a compassionate mind
  http://www.psychologicalscience.org/index.php/publications/observer/2013/may-june-13/the-compassionate-mind.html
- How to Increase Your Compassion Bandwidth:
  Bandwidth   http://greatergood.berkeley.edu/article/item/how_to_increase_your_compassion_bandwidth

12. SOCIAL INTELLIGENCE

Description

People with social intelligence (which also includes emotional and personal intelligence) are aware of their own emotions and intentions as well as those of others. If this is one of your top strengths, you are most likely well aware of your own emotions, motives, and reactions (personal intelligence), as well as keenly aware of others (social intelligence). You have an uncanny ability to notice a shift in emotions in others and are able to make necessary adjustments to ensure a cordial milieu is maintained. While working with others, you make sure everyone feels comfortable, included, and valued, especially in endeavors that include a group. From a therapeutic standpoint, social intelligence offers you access to your own feelings as well as to feelings of others. This access can work in fostering, maintaining, and deepening healthy relationships.

The Golden Mean

A balanced use of social intelligence enables you to notice nuanced differences among other people, especially when their mood or motivation changes. This strength lets you respond in ways that are appropriate to the situation. You connect with others almost effortlessly. You react appropriately, and when needed, you express sympathy, empathy, or simply are able to put yourself in another's shoes. (For example, if something triggers sadness in your friend, your social intelligence will notice it, and you will be able to say or do something that doesn't make your friend feel isolated.) You have the ability to know the whole person. Much like love and kindness, social intelligence is one of the key strengths for a healthy life.

Deficit and excess of this strength are associated with psychological problems. A lack of social intelligence doesn't allow you to connect with others on a deeper level. Therefore, you are unable to forge connections that can be therapeutic and supportive, especially when you are stressed, sad, and/or anxious—states that are, by default, isolating and do not easily enable you to open up to others. You may also feel that sharing your psychological distress with others is embarrassing because they may not understand it and you may be burdening them unnecessarily. However, if you have deep and secure relationships due to your social intelligence, it is relatively easy for you to open up to others and seek support. In this way, your social intelligence offers you buffers, especially during difficult times.

There are also severe deficits of social intelligence. These manifest through conditions like autism, Asperger's syndrome, and schizoid personality disorder. These conditions, which have strong biological roots and need specialized, sustained treatment, do benefit from buildable aspects of social intelligence.

An excess of social intelligence can also be problematic. For example, knowing and understanding others, amidst complex social contexts, is time consuming and requires considerable emotional investment. If you invest these resources excessively, you may not have time for yourself. Second, you may garner a flattering reputation of being available for everyone but may very likely set up unrealistic expectations in others who would like to confide in you. You may become the "one pseudo-therapist" for many, and this could, and most likely would, exhaust you emotionally. Your social intelligence may become over-taxed; you might start showing signs of irritability and being less emphatic—having heard the same story from many—and ultimately you may start feeling inadequate. Therefore, a balanced use of social intelligence entails that you are mindful of your own well-being.

- *Overuse of strength:* psycho-babbling, self-deception
- *Underuse of strength*: obtuseness, cluelessness

Integration

To accomplish a balanced use of social intelligence, you will need to use it along with other strengths, such as perspective, which is critical. In deploying social and personal intelligence in any endeavor, always keep the big picture (the meaning and purpose) front and center. Social intelligence works well when you also use your judgment and open-mindedness to examine the situation from all possible angles to catch any potential biases. Vitality and zest can accentuate social intelligence, especially when an event or situation needs motivation and hope. Social intelligence can also resolve many tense situations if you are able to spot a lighter, playful, and humorous aspect of the situation to break the impasse or relieve the tension.

Movies

- *Monsieur Lazhar (2011)*—Bahir Lazhar, an Algerian immigrant and replacement teacher, uses his social intelligence to connect with students in a class that just lost their teacher in a traumatic way.
- *Children of a Lesser God (1986)*—This film beautifully depicts social and personal intelligence as the relationship between a speech therapist and a woman with hearing challenges evolves in understanding one another's emotions, intentions, and actions.
- *K-Pax (2001)*—A mysterious patient in a mental hospital claims to be an alien from a distant planet, demonstrating a remarkable display of social intelligence in relating to the other patients.
- *I am Sam (2002)*—Sam, a man with significant psychological challenges, fights for custody of his young daughter, arguing successfully that it is not brains but love and relationships that count the most.

Therapeutic Actions

- **Tackle uncomfortable situations with emotional intelligence:** Consider tackling a social situation that typically produces feelings of anxiety and depression for you. (Examples may include sharing your thoughts in a work meeting on issues you disagree with, discussing an unresolved issue that continues to bother you with family members, and communicating feedback to a friend about something you disagree with and feel strongly about.) Use your social and personal intelligence and take turns to clarify points not previously clarified. Share your motivation and underlying values, and ask others to do the same. At the very least, this process will help you and others to ascertain values.
- **Listen without interruption:** Listen to your loved ones, especially to those with whom you interact frequently and frankly. Let them know you would like to listen from start to finish, without interrupting or preparing a rebuttal. Make mental notes of points to clarify, and address those when the person is done speaking. Then share your thoughts, and also elicit feedback from the sharer.
- **Unpack offenses**: If someone offends you, attempt to find at least one positive element in his motives. Using notions associated with social intelligence, consider reasons why the offensive behavior may have resulted from temporary, situational factors, rather than from the person's disposition or nature.

- **Elicit feedback:** Ask someone close to you about times when you did not emotionally understand her and also about how she would like to be emotionally understood in the future. Think of a few small, practical steps that you can take when next interacting with this person.
- **Be plain and direct:** In your close relationships, speak plainly and directly about your needs and wishes. Allow others to do the same without judging them or responding with rebuttals.

Exemplars (TED Talks)

Visit https://www.ted.com/talks and search for the following talks to hear from individuals who represent the strength of social intelligence:

- Daniel Goleman: Why aren't we more compassionate?
- Joan Halifax: Compassion and the true meaning of empathy
- David Brooks: The social animal

Books

- Cassady, J. C., & Eissa, M. A. (Eds.) (2008). *Emotional Intelligence: Perspectives on Educational and Positive Psychology.* New York: P. Lang.
- Goleman, D. (2006). *Social Intelligence: The New Science of Human Relationships.* New York: Bantam Books.
- Livermore, D. A. (2009). *Cultural Intelligence: Improving Your CQ to Engage Our Multicultural World.* Grand Rapids, MI: Baker Academic.

Websites

- Yale's Center for Emotional Intelligence:
  http://ei.yale.edu
- Emotional Intelligence Consortium:
  http://www.eiconsortium.org
- Marc Brackett—Yale Center for Emotional Intelligence:
  https://youtu.be/62F9z1OgpRk

CORE VIRTUE: JUSTICE

Interpersonal strengths that involve tending and befriending others

13. CITIZENSHIP & TEAMWORK

Description

The character strength of citizenship, also called teamwork, involves working as a member of a group for the common good. If this is one of your top strengths, you are most likely willing to make sacrifices for the common good of the groups you are involved with, such as your neighborhood, religious community, cohort at school, professional networks, and cultural circles. You feel affinity and closely identify with your neighborhood, city, province or state, and your country, in an adaptive manner, without being xenophobic. These groups and units form sources of identity for you.

If citizenship and teamwork are among your top strengths, you manifest them by fulfilling and/or going over and above your civic responsibilities.

People who participate in activities that build citizenship and teamwork generally have good mental health because these activities connect them with like-minded people, which in turn builds their social trust. Having social trust provides assurance that the world around you is not an unsafe place. Furthermore, participating in community-building activities enhances self-efficacy.

The Golden Mean

A balanced use of citizenship and teamwork entails that you connect with your group or team and find ways of utilizing your strengths, expertise, knowledge, and resources for the welfare of the group. However, citizenship does not mean that you blindly follow the rules and regulations of those in power. A balanced and well-adjusted use of citizenship means that almost every member of the team feels included and is intrinsically motivated to work for the success of the group. Citizenship and teamwork function optimally when team goals take precedence, despite inevitable individual differences. Indeed, each team member maintains his or her own identity, but the collective identity creates group cohesion and solidarity. You may have heard expressions such as, "band of brothers" and "sisterhood," which symbolically represent family.

A balanced use of citizenship also entails that you do not become a spectator. If a few individuals assume a greater role that could diminish your participation, you need to use strengths such as courage and fairness to ensure that the group's harmony is not compromised. A lack of teamwork and citizenship may leave you isolated and deprived of social and community support that can make a significant difference, especially when you experience psychological distress.

- *Overuse of strength:* mindless and automatic obedience
- *Underuse of strength:* selfishness, narcissism

Integration

To optimally use citizenship and teamwork, you will need numerous other strengths, such as knowing yourself and others (emotional and social intelligence). When working with a group of diverse individuals (e.g., in terms of ethnicity, educational background, dispositions, or preferences), you will benefit from open-mindedness, fairness, and being aware and respectful of differences.

Almost every team or group experiences tensions and conflicts. Therefore, you can spark the creativity of group members to brainstorm solutions for the common good and optimal team performance. Well-intentioned humor and playful relieve group tensions, and the task becomes easier if group members share a common purpose (perspective) to increase solidarity. Furthermore, teamwork greatly benefits when the strengths of group members are spotted, acknowledged, and supported.

Movies

- *Field of Dreams (1989)*—An excellent depiction of citizenship and teamwork, this film shows the collaborative efforts of an Iowa farmer who interprets a mysterious message, *if you build it, they will come.*
- *Invictus (2009)*—This is the inspiring true story of a rugby team that wins the World Cup on the field and also unites post-apartheid South Africa off the field.
- *Hotel Rwanda (2004)*—An extraordinary display of social responsibility by Paul Rusesabagina, a hotel manager who, during the Rwanda Genocide, housed over a thousand Tutsi refugees, shielding them from the Hutu militia.
- *Blind Side (2009)*—A homeless and traumatized boy becomes an All American football player and first round NFL draft pick with the help of a caring woman and her family.

Therapeutic Actions

- **Avoid civic alienation:** Many of us disengage from civic participation, assuming that whatever we do, nothing will change. This is a hopeless and pessimistic view—two hallmarks of depression. Get involved in community work and bring your friends along. Indeed, your work will benefit the organization, and, more so, civic engagement will connect you with a noble cause and company, both of which are potent predictors of mental well-being.
- **Build an online community:** Build a web-based community whose members share a noble purpose, such as saving a specific endangered species; raising funds for refugees; or taking civic action against discrimination such as Islamophobia, homophobia, or xenophobia. Share this online hub to build a community.
- **Become involved with a community garden:** Start or join a community garden, which can offer you a supportive, safe, and calming environment. You can interact with others who may (or may not) be struggling with mental health issues. Sharing the space and task (gardening) helps you become part of a community.
- **Join a community mental health support group:** Start or join a community-based mental health organization. Using multimedia resources, you can present illustrations of how others have successfully dealt with mental health challenges. Explore the most effective treatments for specific mental health issues.
- **Decorate a communal place with the art of "lived experiences":** In an available community space, invite individuals with mental health challenges to present their "lived experiences." These would be people who are willing to share their experiences through any number of artistic forms. Individuals can submit their art expression online as well.

Exemplars (TED Talks)

Visit https://www.ted.com/talks and search for the following talks to hear from individuals who represent the strength of citizenship & teamwork:

- Jeremy Rifkin: The empathic civilization
- Douglas Beal: An alternative to GDP that encompasses our wellbeing
- Hugh Evans: What does it mean to be a citizen of the world?
- Bill Strickland: Rebuilding a neighborhood with beauty, dignity, hope

Books

- Putnum, R. (2001). *Bowling Alone: The Collapse and Revival of American Community.* New York: Simon & Schuster.
- Kielburger, C., & Keilburger, M. (2008). *Me to We: Finding Meaning in a Material World.* New York: Simon & Schuster.
- Ricard, M. (2015). *Altruism: The Power of Compassion to Change Yourself and the World.* New York: Little Brown.

Websites

- Me to We, a non-profit organization that advocates connecting with others, building trust, and getting involved in community building initiatives:
  http://www.metowe.com
- Harvard sociologist, Robert Putnum's websites on the decline and rise of community, with resources:
  http://bowlingalone.com
  robertdputnam.com/better-together/

14. FAIRNESS

Description

Fairness involves treating everyone according to universal ideals of equality and justice. If fairness is one of your top strengths, you generally do not let your personal feelings bias your moral or ethical decisions about others, and instead you rely on a broad set of moral values. Your sense of fairness incorporates both a respect for moral guidelines and a compassionate approach to caring for others. This is a strength you can apply across all aspects of your life—personal, professional, leisure, and community—in everyday interactions with social justice issues.

The Golden Mean

A balanced application of fairness entails that you generally abide by the principle of taking the welfare of others into consideration, even if you do not know them. The challenge you may face is the definition of "welfare." You may struggle to decide what is fair and what is right, as the cultural context may pose conflicts between the two and how they represent underlying core values. For example, female attire (a behavioral expression) and modesty (an underlying value) vary vastly from culture to culture and even within the same culture. A woman wearing a bikini in a conservative Muslim country could be considered a sign of immodesty, while such swimwear is perfectly acceptable in a Western country. Likewise, wearing a hijab for Muslim women is expected and admired in Muslim countries, while this veil or headscarf could be perceived by some as a forced choice or a religious or cultural obligation in some Western countries. Therefore, to strike a balance of fairness among competing rights, rituals, and values, interpret fairness in light of each context. Before applying fairness, ask about and understand the sociocultural cues. Seek wise council to interpret them. Fairness, perhaps more than any other strength, is not black and white, and you should therefore be prepared to navigate the grey areas.

Before applying fairness, always explore what the ultimate aim is. For example, look at equity and equality. In the context of fairness, equity is treating everyone in a way in which they are successful or not harmed, while equality is treating everyone the same, even though not everyone needs the same sort or levels of support. Along the same lines, if you treat everyone equally, know that unless you construct a Utopian society, not everyone will be treated fairly. Therefore, rather than applying fairness in absolute terms, use it contextually.

- *Overuse of strength:* impartiality without perspective or empathy, detachment
- *Underuse of strength:* prejudice, partisanship

Integration

For a balanced use of fairness, you will need a number of strengths such as leadership, citizenship, and teamwork, which will enable you to apply fairness easily. Likewise, honesty and authenticity will reinforce a sense of fairness. Kindness should also be considered in applying fairness. (For example, if a teacher keeps punishing a student who exhibits hyperactive behavior due to an underlying attention deficit hyperactivity disorder, punishing this student will likely lose its impact and may leave him more irritable and resentful. But if the teacher uses kindness and offers appropriate modifications to the student, the odds are better that he will improve his behavior.)

Movies

- *The Emperor's Club (2002)*—William Hundert, a principled Classics professor, comes into conflict with a pupil at a prestigious academy, as his attempts to teach the young man to act fairly and morally have mixed results.

- *Philadelphia (1993)*—Andrew Beckett, fired from his law firm for being both gay and HIV-positive, hires homophobic lawyer Joe Miller to act on his behalf. During the legal proceedings, Miller comes to view Beckett as a person worthy of respect and fair treatment, rather than as a stereotype.
- *The Green Zone (2010)*—This is a chilling depiction of fairness and social justice. Roy Miller, a senior CIA officer, unearths evidence of weapons of mass destruction in the Iraq war and realizes that operatives on both sides of the conflict are attempting to spin the story in their favor.
- *Suffragettes (2015)*—This film is an excellent depiction of fairness. It tells a story of ordinary women during the first part of the 20th century who are loving wives, mothers, and daughters. Their main concern is gender inequality. They face sexual harassment in the workplace, domestic violence, and violation of their parental rights, and their salaries are much lower than those of their male colleagues.

Therapeutic Actions

- **Understand biases and preconceptions:** To promote fairness, become aware of the discrimination you witness or experience firsthand. This discrimination may manifest in many ways, including ageism, ableism, gender, sexual orientation, accent, language fluency, religion, and xenophobia. Use your strength of fairness to do something to stop these biases and preconceptions.
- **Increase fairness in everyday life:** Make a list of everyday tasks, interactions, and activities that can use a dose of fairness—things that will increase your stress if they don't become more equitable. (For example, speak with your partner about taking over some of the daily cooking and household tasks.) Find culturally and contextually appropriate ways to apply fairness with the goal of decreasing stress.
- **Identify social issues that bother you:** Make a list of societal issues that upset you the most, focusing on issues that could be resolved by fairness. (For example, does it bother you that females continue to earn significantly less than males for the same work? Does it bother you that indigenous peoples struggle with basic amenities? Or that, despite clear evidence, supermarkets continue to sell harmful, synthetic food products?)
- **Monitor your judgments:** Self-monitor to see whether your judgments are affected by your personal likes and dislikes or if they are based on principles of justice and fairness. Try to minimize the influence of your personal preferences when making future judgments.
- **Speak up for your group:** Be a voice for the rights of others in a manner that respects people from other groups.

Exemplars (TED Talks)

Visit https://www.ted.com/talks and search for the following talks to hear from individuals who represent the strength of fairness:

- Daniel Reisel: The neuroscience of restorative justice
- Paul Zak: Trust, morality—and oxytocin?
- Jonathan Haidt: The moral roots of liberals and conservatives
- Bono: My wish: Three actions for Africa

Books

- Sun, L. (2009). *The Fairness Instinct: The Robin Hood Mentality and Our Biological Nature.* New York: Prometheus Books.
- Harkins, D. (2013). *Beyond the Campus: Building a Sustainable University Community Partnership.* Charlotte, NC: Information Age.

- Last, J. (2014). *Seven Deadly Virtues: 18 Conservative Writers on Why the Virtuous Life Is Funny as Hell*. West Conshohocken, PA: Templeton Press.

Websites

- The difference between equality and equity:
  http://everydayfeminism.com/2014/09/equality-is-not-enough/
- With more than 100 national chapters worldwide, Transparency International works with partners in government, business, and civil society to put effective measures in place to tackle corruption:
  https://www.transparency.org
- Roméo Antonius Dallaire: commandeered the United Nations Assistance Mission for Rwanda in 1993. Since his retirement, he has become an outspoken advocate for human rights, genocide prevention, mental health, and war-affected children:
  http://www.romeodallaire.com

15. LEADERSHIP

Description

Leadership is the process of motivating, directing, and coordinating members of a group to achieve a common goal. If this is one of your top strengths, you assume a dominant role in social interaction; however, effective leadership also requires listening to the opinions and feelings of other group members as much as it involves active direction. As a leader, you are able to help your group achieve goals in a cohesive, efficient, and amiable manner.

The Golden Mean

We see a balanced use of leadership when a person is able to find common ground in a group, despite differences among its members. This common ground is communicated effectively and in different ways, so that group members stay motivated. Some leaders who are remarkable in instilling hope and reinvigorating the spirts of their followers may lack the skills needed to translate their vision into clear, concrete, and tangible tasks and outcomes. Therefore, a balanced use of leadership incorporates the will and motivation plus the concrete steps needed to be successful.

Also, a balanced use of leadership requires following as well as leading. That is, without humility and the ability to listen, a leader can easily evolve into an authoritarian figure. In addition, a balanced use of leadership requires that you be able to build genuine and trusting relationships with the people you lead. Through trust, you have the highest chance of bringing out the best in your group. Relationships based on fear or the abuse of power or authority will induce fear, and, instead of being their best, people in such a group are more likely operate out of fear and mistrust.

- *Overuse of strength:* despotism, bossiness
- *Underuse of strength:* compliance, acquiescence

Integration

Leadership can use any number of strengths to foster well-being and resilience. For example, social intelligence, teamwork, and kindness can build strong ties within your group, and humility and gratitude can make your leadership humane and accessible. Together these strengths can create synergy, which may enable you to stay attuned to your group.

Movies

- *Gandhi (1982)*—The life of Mohandas Gandhi offers the model of leadership based on the ethos of nonviolence, social justice, and humility, ideas that inspired the likes of Martin Luther King Jr.
- *Iron Lady (2011)*—This movie is based on the life of Margaret Thatcher, the British stateswoman and politician who became the first ever female (and longest-serving) prime minister of the United Kingdom in the 20th century.
- *Mandela: Long Walk to Freedom (2013)*—This film chronicles Nelson Mandela's epic leadership journey, starting from his early life, through his coming of age, education, and 27 years in prison, to become the president of post-apartheid South Africa.
- *Lincoln (2012)*—This movie about Abraham Lincoln recounts his extraordinary number of strengths, especially his leadership and courage to go against the current and emancipate slaves despite continuing unrest on the battlefield and strife within his own ranks.

Therapeutic Actions

- **Stand up for someone or champion a cause**: Stand up for someone who is being treated unfairly. Encourage other leaders to emphasize fairness in their group processes. Alternatively, you can champion a cause that you find meaningful. This could involve many issues, such as child labor, underemployment of marginalized groups, school bullying (including cyber-bullying), or the use of environmentally unhealthy chemicals.
- **Read a biography of a leader who struggled with mental health challenges:** Read a biography and/or watch a film about a famous leader who suffered from mental health challenges and who dealt with them through the strength of leadership (e.g., Queen Victoria, Abraham Lincoln, Winston Churchill). What insights can you draw from this leader that may boost your own strength of leadership?
- **Mentor a child:** Mentor a child in your neighborhood or in your circles who could benefit from your skills (e.g., academic, technical, athletic). Assess your mood before and after each mentoring session and also as you see the impact of your efforts.
- **Mediate between two feuding friends:** When two people are in an argument, become a mediator. Invite them to meet with you together, and, after setting some ground rules, which you can enforce, let them share their points of view. Emphasize problem-solving through discussion.
- **Lead a family activity:** Organize and lead a family event that includes both young and old relatives. Use your leadership skills to invite family members to participate in this activity, especially those who may not be on speaking terms or may be holding grudges against one another. Also involve everyone in the conversation, rather than allowing age groups to self-segregate. Draw people's attention to cross-generational similarities.

Exemplars (TED Talks)

Visit https://www.ted.com/talks and search for the following talks to hear from individuals who represent the strength of leadership:

- Roselinde Torres: What it takes to be a great leader
- Simon Sinek: How great leaders inspire action
- Simon Sinek: Why good leaders make you feel safe

Books

- Avolio, B. & Luthans, F. (2006). *The High-Impact Leader.* New York: McGraw-Hill.
- Csikszentmihalyi, M. (2004). *Good Business: Leadership, Flow, and the Making of Meaning.* New York: Penguin.
- Rath, T. & Conchie, B. (2009). *Strengths-Based Leadership.* New York: Gallup Press.

Websites

- The top 10 qualities that make good leaders:
  http://www.forbes.com/sites/tanyaprive/2012/12/19/top-10-qualities-that-make-a-great-leader/
- 20 ways to become a leader right now:
  http://www.inc.com/john-brandon/20-ways-to-become-a-better-leader-right-now.html
- Uma Jogulu's work on leadership, and its cultural influences:
  http://www.buseco.monash.edu.my/about/school/academic/management/uma-jogulu-dr
- Kim Cameron's work revolves around organizational structures and positive leadership:
  http://michiganross.umich.edu/faculty-research/faculty/kim-cameron
- Gilad Chen studies team and leadership effectiveness, as well as work motivation:
  http://www.rhsmith.umd.edu/directory/gilad-chen
- Centre for Health Leadership and Research led by Dr. Ronald R. Lindstrom:
  http://sls.royalroads.ca/centre-health-leadership-and-research

CORE VIRTUE: TEMPERANCE

Strengths that protect against excess

16. FORGIVENESS & MERCY

Description

Forgiveness is a process of gradual change, not a one-time decision and event. In forgiveness, you are willing to forsake your right and desire to take revenge; in fact, you are willing to cease the cycle of revenge, and you will likely be able to find a healthier path toward self-growth. This strength involves forgiving those who have wronged or offended you. Through forgiveness you accept the shortcomings of others; give offenders a second chance; and deliberately put aside the temptation to hold a grudge, ill-feelings, and vindictiveness. Moreover, forgiveness enables you to process the self-destructive negativity that keeps your anger simmering and your other strengths at bay. In order to enact forgiveness, you need mercy. To motivate yourself to go through the process of forgiveness, you need to exercise mercy in terms of accepting the shortcomings of others and making cognitive and emotional space to offer a gift to the transgressor. Mercy is important in initiating the process of forgiveness and holding onto it.

The Golden Mean

To achieve a balanced use of forgiveness, it is also important to thoroughly understand what forgiveness is *not* and what constitutes mercy. In using the strength of forgiveness, you are not absolving, avoiding, overlooking, or ignoring the impact of the offence; nor are you minimizing the need for justice, swapping negative emotions with positive ones, resorting to fate, compromising, opting to resolve unilaterally, or hoping to attain the high moral ground. Forgiveness is not an outcome; rather, it is a process of prosocial change. This often gradual, complex, and difficult process is one in which the person offended willfully decides to stop the cycle of revenge and move beyond the offense, such that the offense—although not expunged from memory—no longer causes ongoing pain.

Attaining forgiveness is exceedingly difficult. However, it is worth pursuing a balanced notion of forgiveness because its lack (being "unforgiving") will likely make you hard-hearted and can leave you embittered by memories of the past. Forgiveness becomes easier when you are able tap into your mercy and kindness. Lack of forgiveness and mercy may impact your relationships as your trust may be tarnished forever. Furthermore, whenever the offence is triggered, this can drain you emotionally and can leave you once again dwelling for days on the negative memories. Too much forgiveness and mercy, on the other hand, can lead to you becoming a non-assertive and vulnerable "doormat." And if you are trying to forgive something that should not be forgiven— such as abuse, gross and repeated violation of other's rights, or offenses that hurt you but the ac- tual victim may be someone else—sometimes the process of forgiveness is not effective.

You most likely need a number of strengths—whether or not these are among your top ones— to optimally use forgiveness. You need courage to overcome internal fear and let go of the anger and revenge. Judgment and open-mindedness can allow you to examine the situation thoroughly from all sides. Kindness can enable you to offer forgiveness, which is an altruistic gift.

- *Overuse of strength:* permissiveness
- *Underuse of strength:* mercilessness, vengefulness

Integration

A regular dose of gratitude—to fill your head and heart with authentic and realistic positive events in your life—can help counteract the bitter memories. Once you decide to forgive, you also need persistence and social support to hold on to forgiveness.

Movies

- *Incendies (2010, France/Canada)*—In a series of flashbacks, twins (a brother and sister) uncover the mystery of their mother's life, which unsettles them, but the strength of forgiveness helps them to reconcile with the past.
- *Pay it Forward (2000)*—Seventh-grader Trevor McKinney undertakes an intriguing assignment—to change the world for the better—which starts a chain of acts of kindness and forgiveness.
- *Dead Man Walking (1995)*—This film tells the tale of a convicted murderer on death row who befriends a nun, who helps him understand that forgiveness is possible even under the worst circumstances.
- *Terms of Endearment (1983)*—Amidst the ups and downs of life, a mother and daughter find ways to see past resentments and transgressions and find joy in their relationship.

Therapeutic Actions

- **Evaluate the effect on you of "unforgiveness":** Explore how not forgiving and resentment torture you emotionally. Do these produce disruptive emotions, such as anger, hatred, fear, worry, sadness, anxiety, or jealousy? Reflect on and write about how these disruptive emotions affect your behavior. Assess their collective impact, especially on your mental health.
- **Let go of negative emotions through forgiveness:** Review Session 6: Forgiveness, which stresses that the process of forgiveness allows you to replace negative emotions with positive ones. Using your strength of perspective, reflect on the benefits of "letting go" of negative emotions through forgiveness.
- **Search your motivation for forgiveness:** You need to feel willing to forgive internally. Mindfully attune yourself to the feelings of holding on to negative emotions related to the offense, and also to emotions that may come from enacting forgiveness.

- **Recall when you were forgiven:** Recall vividly and write about situations in which you offended someone and were forgiven. If the person who forgave you is a loved one, ask what helped him or her to apply forgiveness as a relationship corrective or as a restorative act. Reflect on what it would take for you to apply a similar corrective or restorative action.
- **Plan your response for the next time someone offends you:** Create a plan, and rehearse it if possible. Periodically affirm to yourself, "No matter how he or she offends me, I will respond as I have planned."
- **Move from brooding to empathy:** Are ruminating or brooding getting in the way of your path to forgive? When you brood, then anger, sadness, and ambivalence take over your thinking. Deliberately see if you can replace your thoughts of brooding to empathize with the offender. Try to understand from the offender's perspective why she or he offended you. Then assess whether your reaction is hurting you more than the offender, especially when you slip into brooding.

Exemplars (TED Talks)

Visit https://www.ted.com/talks and search for the following talks to hear from individuals who represent the strength of forgiveness and mercy:

- Aicha el-Wafi and Phyllis Rodriguez: The mothers who found forgiveness, friendship
- Joshua Prager: In search of the man who broke my neck
- Shaka Senghor: Why your worst deeds don't define you

Books

- Enright, R. D., & Fitzgibbons, R. (2001). *Forgiveness Is a Choice: A Step-by-Step Process for Resolving Anger and Restoring Hope.* Washington, DC: APA Books.
- Nussbaum, M. C. (2016). *Anger and Forgiveness: Resentment, Generosity, Justice.* New York: Oxford University Press.
- Tutu, D. (2015). *The Book of Forgiving: The Fourfold Path for Healing Ourselves and Our World.* New York: HarperOne.
- McCullough, M. (2008). *Beyond Revenge: The Evolution of the Forgiveness Instinct.* New York: Wiley.

Websites

- Psychologist Evertt Worthington, a leader in the forgiveness research: http://www.evworthington-forgiveness.com/
- Ten Extraordinary Examples of Forgiveness: http://listverse.com/2013/10/31/10-extraordinary-examples-of-forgiveness/
- Ten Inspiring Stories of Extreme Forgiveness: http://incharacter.org/archives/forgiveness/ten-great-moments-in-forgiveness-history/
- Great Moments in Forgiveness History: http://incharacter.org/archives/forgiveness/ten-great-moments-in-forgiveness-history/

17. HUMILITY & MODESTY

Description

Humility and modesty entail letting your accomplishments and your accolades speak for themselves. You are aware of them but don't feel the need to make others explicitly aware of them. You are also aware of your limitations. If this is one of your top strengths, you do not perceive yourself as being better than others, although your self-esteem is uncompromised. In contemporary culture, which is often blinded by the social media spotlight on one's accomplishments and happiness, you avoid seeking the spotlight. As a humble person, you are honest with yourself, with your fallibility, and with what you cannot do, and you are open to asking for help.

The Golden Mean

A balanced use of humility entails the attributes noted previously, but be aware that an overuse of humility and modesty (being too humble or overly modest) can be hard to spot. To distinguish a balanced versus overuse of humility and modesty, you need to assess the specific situation to determine if you are really fine with it, or if your mental health challenges are leading you to be too unassuming and quiet, while others take advantage of the situation. (For example, you may have been overlooked for a job promotion or leadership role—despite deserving it on the basis of merit—simply because your humility won't allow you to speak up for yourself, or because you have a modest opinion of yourself. It could also be that humility and modesty don't allow you to pursue higher positions that you deserve). To achieve a balance, you need to figure out if you are okay with the status quo, and if you are not, you need to tamp down your humility and assert your rights. If you are unsure about what to do, consult with someone wise and impartial.

On the other hand, if you lack humility and modesty (or if you have been told so), ask a trusted friend to give you honest feedback. Select someone who is not afraid of providing this feedback, and who you are not afraid of hearing it from. Think at length about what this friend has to say, and select a few areas to work on. (For example, resist the need to share your accomplishments with people who are not your closest friends, those to whom you feel the need to prove yourself.) You may also feel a heightened desire to be acknowledged, but this may not be entirely due to a lack of humility. Rather, you might have had experiences of being put down by others, especially older siblings or parents, or being repeatedly told that you, compared to other siblings, may not accomplish much. It is equally plausible that your expression of zest and playfulness may be perceived as a lack of humility and modesty. The golden mean of humility and modesty cannot be appraised and appreciated without understanding all the nuances of the context.

- *Overuse of strength:* self-deprecation
- *Underuse of strength:* foolish self-esteem, arrogance

Integration

Humility, by default, melds well with kindness, social intelligence, self-regulation, and prudence. However, it is important that similar strengths work synergistically to continue the status quo. (For example, if you are known at work to be a humble person, and if kindness, prudence, and humility and modesty are among your top strengths, the combination of these strengths could reinforce nonassertive, unassuming, and down-to-earth tendencies that may not serve you well. You might be better off using strengths such as zest and curiosity, so that you achieve an optimal balance.) As a humble and modest person, you are open to the views of others, so seek opinions about yourself from a trusted friend who will likely highlight your accomplishments. Accept compliments with grace and, of course, humility.

Movies

- *Forest Gump (1994)*—Despite a low IQ, Forest Gump accomplishes a lot: meeting presidents, winning an All American football player award, receiving the Congressional medal of honor, and being featured on magazine covers. Displaying humility, he experiences all of his accomplishments in stride.
- *Peaceful Warrior (2006)*—Dan, brimming with pride for being an elite gymnast, thinks that he has figured out life, until a surprising mentor, Socrates, teaches him humility and wisdom.
- *The Passion of the Christ (2004)*—This film shows the final hours of Jesus Christ and numerous, moving examples of humility.

Therapeutic Actions

- **Cultivate humility through other strengths:** You can deploy your other strengths to cultivate humility. For example, be sensitive (social and emotional intelligence) as to how your inadvertent "showing off" can make others feel. After sharing news of an accomplishment with your family members or close friends, ask a confidant how the news was received. Did it feel like bragging or showing off? Did it draw an inadvertent comparison with someone present, making him or her feel uncomfortable?
- **Listen more, speak less:** If you are aware (or have been told) that you speak more than others in a group situation, concentrate on listening to the words of other people rather than simply waiting for your turn to talk.
- **Acknowledge your mistakes:** Acknowledge your mistakes, especially those that have created a rift between you and your loved ones. Apologize even to those who are younger than you. Be aware of your place as a role model to the next generation.
- **Let others discover your skills, talents, and accomplishments:** Resist showing off your accomplishments, talents, and skills. Allow others to notice them on their own.
- **Compliment sincerely:** Compliment sincerely if you find someone is authentic and better than you in some ways. Accept compliments from others humbly.

Exemplars (TED Talks)

Visit https://www.ted.com/talks and search for the following talks to hear from individuals who represent the strength of humility and modesty:

- Feisal Abdul Rauf: Lose your ego, find your compassion
- Robert Wright: Progress is not a zero-sum game
- Graham Hill: Less stuff, more happiness
- Sam Richards: A radical experiment in empathy

Books

- Hess, E. D., & Ludwig, K. (2017). *Humility Is the New Smart: Rethinking Human Excellence in the Smart Machine Age.* Oakland, CA: Berrett-Koehler.
- Nielsen, R., Marrone, J. A., & Ferraro, H. S. (2014). *Leading with Humility.* New York: Routledge.
- Worthington, E. L. (2007). *Humility: The Quiet Virtue.* West Conshohocken, PA: Templeton Press.

Websites

- How to develop and maintain humility: https://www.bigquestionsonline.com/content/how-do-we-develop-and-maintain-humility
- Best Leaders are Humble Leaders: *Harvard Business Review*: https://hbr.org/2014/05/the-best-leaders-are-humble-leaders
- How we develop and maintain humility: https://www.bigquestionsonline.com/content/how-do-we-develop-and-maintain-humility

18. PRUDENCE

Description

Prudence is a practical orientation toward future goals. If it is your top strength, you are generally quite careful about your choices. You don't take undue risks, and you keep long-term goals in mind when making short-term decisions. Therefore, you are a good planner and also anticipate unexpected outcomes. You generally arrive early or on time. When you are late due to circumstances beyond your control, you find ways to inform those waiting. You drive carefully and follow traffic rules and regulations. When you make a decision or plan, you remove unnecessary distractions. You take your time to clear your mind and gather your thoughts. You monitor and control impulsive behavior and anticipate the consequences of your actions. You refrain from making snap judgments, and you do not yield easily or spontaneously to proposals and ideas.

The Golden Mean

A balanced use of prudence requires making decisions and approaching important tasks with caution and deliberation. However, an overuse of this strength can manifest itself in the form of preoccupation with details and analysis, which may appear like an obsession. Indeed, there are tasks that require meticulous detail—such as performing brain surgery, entering your credit card number on your phone's key pad, and doing a spell check before submitting an editorial to the newspaper. But there are tasks that do not require such meticulous detail—such as perfectly loading the dishwasher, spending more time arranging everything on your desk and far less time on actual the work to be done, and focusing more on the formatting than on the content of a critical report. Utilizing prudence in such situations would be an overuse of the strength. A balanced use of prudence can help you plan well, arrive early or on time, motivate you to follow rules and regulations, and buffer against feeling overwhelmed when unexpected situations surface.

This strength is not synonymous with stinginess or timidity and instead involves an intelligent and efficient perspective toward achieving major goals in life. However, an excessive use of prudence may lead to ambivalence and indecisiveness. You may experience "decision paralysis." On the other hand, a lack of prudence can lead to rushed decisions, overlooking risks, or being lax about rules and regulations. There are always exceptional situations due to extenuating circumstances, but a lack of prudence may not let you adequately assess the situation, and you may make a decision sooner than you should. (For example, if someone asks that you extend the deadline for a grant or job application, a lack of prudence will manifest in you making a decision without fully exploring the ground on which such an exception should be granted, because it may not be fair to those who submitted their applications on time.)

- *Overuse of strength:* prudishness, stuffiness
- *Underuse of strength:* recklessness, sensation-seeking

Integration

You can use any number of strengths to achieve a balanced use of prudence. Social intelligence can help you determine the motives of others. Curiosity can help you explore more to make a prudent decision. Persistence and self-regulation can help you follow through on your prudent decision. Open-mindedness and kindness can help you do a thorough cost-and-benefit analysis and also explore the human dimensions of your decisions.

Movies

- *Shawshank Redemption (1995)*—Andy Dufresne, wrongly convicted of a double murder and serving his sentence at the Shawshank State Prison in Maine, uses his strengths of prudence, social intelligence, and resilience to improve the conditions of the prison, which enhances the dignity of the prisoners.
- *Driving Miss Daisy (1989)*—Daisy Werthan, a wealthy 72-year-old Jewish widow, slowly builds trust and friendship with her African-American chauffer, Hoke Colburn. Their friendship develops through the mutual strength of prudence.
- *The Queen (2006)*—Helen Mirren portrays Queen Elizabeth II and brilliantly captures her strengths, especially her prudence, sense of duty, and stoicism.

Therapeutic Actions

- **Make important decisions when you are relaxed:** Making big decisions when relaxed enables you to consider all the possibilities, rather than making a snap decision that could backfire later on. If you must make a decision under pressure (such as when you are anxious or depressed), take a few seconds to breathe deeply and clear your mind.
- **Remove distractions:** Remove all extraneous distractions before you make your next three important decisions. Take the time to clear your mind and gather your thoughts.
- **Anticipate long-term consequences:** Visualize the consequences of your decisions in 1, 5, and 10 years' time. Take these long-term consequences into account when making short-term choices.
- **Reflect before speaking:** Think twice before saying anything. Do this exercise at least 10 times a week and note its effects.
- **Drive cautiously or follow traffic rules:** Drive cautiously and note that there are fewer time-bound emergencies than you think. Make highway safety a priority, especially during busy times such as rush hour and holiday weekends.

Exemplars (TED Talks)

Visit https://www.ted.com/talks and search for the following talks to hear from individuals who represent the strength of prudence:

- Naomi Klein: Addicted to risk
- Paolo Cardini: Forget multitasking, try monotasking
- Gary Lauder's new traffic sign: Take Turns

Books

- Hariman, R. (2003). *Prudence: Classical Virtue, Postmodern Practice.* University Park: Pennsylvania State University Press.
- McKeown, G. (2014). *Essentialism: The Disciplined Pursuit of Less.* New York: Crown.
- Gracian, J., & Robbins, J. (2011). *The Pocket Oracle and Art of Prudence.* London: Penguin

Websites

- Virtue First Foundation:
  http://virtuefirst.org/virtues/prudence/
- In Praise of Prudence, by Kathryn Britton:
  http://positivepsychologynews.com/news/kathryn-britton/2013031225590

19. SELF-REGULATION

Description

Self-regulation is one's ability to exert control over oneself in order to achieve goals or meet standards. If this is one of your top strengths, you are most likely able to control instinctive responses such as aggression and impulsivity, and instead, you respond according to well-thought-out standards of behavior. In the context of psychological distress, self-regulation allows you to regulate your feelings, thoughts, and actions. When you become overwhelmed, this strength helps you redirect your emotions in a healthy manner. Even when others react strongly, you keep your poise and composure. You do not become incited easily, and you know how to keep your composure.

The Golden Mean

A balanced use of self-regulation depends on the context. You don't underestimate the impact of a serious situation and assume that it will somehow resolve, nor do you overestimate the situation and panic. A balanced use of self-regulation also requires that you are aware of what you are regulating. From a therapeutic perspective, take these three situations: (a) setting concrete goals for losing weight, (b) refraining from spiraling into negativity, and (c) avoiding getting into unhealthy relationships. To lose weight, you need a balanced application of self-regulation to eat healthy foods and to exercise. However, this does not imply becoming overly focused on food labels or, when visiting others, feeling disappointed when they have different eating habits. To counter the negativity spiral, rather than brooding over experiences and events beyond your control, you redirect your thoughts to events and experiences that are within your control, or to positive ones that can provide scaffolding to help prevent negativity. To establish healthy relationships, you look for character and value it, rather than being charmed by looks and other superficial features.

A balanced use of self-regulation also requires you to have a concrete goal, one that can ensure your self-regulation is adaptive, without harming you physically or cognitively. Losing weight in a healthy manner is one thing, but excessive exercising and an extremely controlled diet may make you ill. Excessive emotional control is associated with feelings of isolation. On the other hand, lack of self-regulation is associated with impulsive behavioral patterns, including smoking, drug abuse, and sexual promiscuity. Psychologically, a lack of self-regulation overwhelms us and we tend to make poor choices that often leave us with negative emotions, ruminations, and impulsivity (saying or doing things without thinking) that may offend others and harm our relationships.

- *Overuse of strength:* inhibition, reticence
- *Underuse of strength:* self-indulgence, impulsivity

Integration

A number of strengths work well with self-regulation to produce favorable behaviors and outcomes. Perhaps the most important is persistence, without which self-regulation is hardly possible. Likewise, prudence, fairness, authenticity, perspective, and courage can help you effectively self-regulate. Having the knowledge of a desirable behavior is not sufficient to make it happen; putting this knowledge into concrete action is important. To manage the hurdles in reaching your goal, you will need a healthy dose of optimism, creativity, and courage, along with self-regulation.

Movies

- *Twelve Years a Slave (2013)*—Solomon (Chiwetel Ejiofor), a free black man from upstate New York, is abducted and sold into slavery. He displays extraordinary strength of self-regulation and poise for 12 years, enduring abuse and cruelty, yet retaining his dignity.
- *Black Swan (2010)*—This psychological thriller shows the electrifying, and at times scary, journey of a young ballerina who displays an extreme sense of self-regulation and discipline to give a near-perfect performance.
- *The King's Speech (2010)*—England's Prince Albert ascends the throne as King George VI and has to overcome a severe speech impediment. The movie shows the king's strengths of courage and self-regulation in learning to speak with confidence.

Therapeutic Actions

- **Eliminate objects of temptation:** When dieting, don't keep junk food around; when you want to spend time with others, turn off the television; when abstaining from alcohol, don't socialize in bars or attend events with an open bar; when quitting smoking, replace cigarettes with chewing gum or another adaptive chewing item; or when cutting back on shopping, leave your credit cards or money at home. However, once a month, enjoy a yummy dessert, take a credit card with you, and so on. Otherwise, you may experience burnout. Ask others who you interact with to respect your removal of tempting items and to encourage your positive lifestyle changes.

- **List triggers:** Make a list of situations that trigger intense emotions in you, when you automatically "lose it." Write at least one strategy to neutralize these intense emotions. Keep these strategies accessible for use the next time you feel intense emotions.
- **Try to control your feelings:** The next time you get upset, try to control your emotions and focus on positive attributes of the situation. Become aware of the degree to which you can control your feelings and reactions.
- **Create routines:** Carefully create routines that you can systematically follow. These routines should be therapeutically helpful, such as going to bed at a regular time, exercising three times a week, and so on. Make minor adjustments as needed, but keep the core elements intact.
- **Engage in progressive relaxation when upset:** When you get upset, do a progressive relaxation. Allow your upset thoughts to be interrupted momentarily so that they don't get out of control.
- **Tolerate distress:** List things that regularly upset you. Set a goal to gradually tolerate the distress, and, if you can, completely eliminate it. If you get upset by a certain colleague's behavior, or when the subway is late and then very crowded, or when speaking in public, find ways to decrease this distress. Set specific, measurable goals to lower the distress. (Here are two examples: Avoiding a coworker you don't like could adversely impact your work. So rather than avoiding her, set a goal of not focusing on her personal attributes and instead work with her on a small project you can do together. Or instead of always being annoyed by your teenage son because of the food, music, and attire he currently favors, focus on what you love about him, rather than on the things you don't.)
- **Determine your optimal waking time:** Pay close attention to your biological clock, and do your most important tasks when you are the most alert.

Exemplars (TED Talks)

Visit https://www.ted.com/talks and search for the following talks to hear from individuals who represent the strength of self-regulation:

- Judson Brewer: A simple way to break a bad habit
- Carol Dweck: The power of believing that you can improve
- Michael Merzenich: Growing evidence of brain plasticity
- Arianna Huffington: How to succeed? Get more sleep

Books

- Berger, A. (2011). *Self-Regulation: Brain, Cognition, and Development.* Washington, DC: American Psychological Association.
- Shanker, S. (2012). *Calm, Alert and Learning: Classroom Strategies for Self-Regulation.* Toronto: Pearson.
- Vohs, K. D., & Baumeister, R. F. (Eds.). (2016). *Handbook of Self-Regulation: Research, Theory, and Applications* (3rd ed.). New York: Guilford Press.

Websites

- Canadian Self-Regulation Initiative:
  http://www.self-regulation.ca/about-us/canadian-self-regulation-initiative-csri/
- How to develop focus and feel better:
  https://www.psychologytoday.com/blog/anger-in-the-age-entitlement/201110/self-regulation

- Wilhelm Hofman studies self-regulation in different contexts as well as looking at why people act impulsively in certain contexts:
  http://hofmann.socialpsychology.org/publications
- The MEHRIT Centre presents books, videos, info sheets, and other resources highlighting Dr. Shanker's work in self-regulation:
  www.self-reg.ca/

CORE VIRTUE: TRANSCENDENCE

Strengths that forge connections to the larger universe and provide meaning

20. APPRECIATION OF BEAUTY & EXCELLENCE

Description

Individuals with an appreciation of beauty feel a sense of awe at the scenes and patterns around them. If appreciation of beauty and excellence is one of your top strengths, you take pleasure in observing natural and physical beauty, you admire the skills and talents of other people, and you appreciate the beauty inherent in virtue and morality. You can find beauty in almost every area of life, from nature to the arts to mathematics to science to everyday experience. Observing and admiring natural and physical beauty and experiencing elevated feelings produce positive emotions, which from a therapeutic standpoint, counteract negative emotions. When we observe someone performing an act of courage or self-sacrifice, when a person exhibits composure in a stressful situation or is kind and compassionate, not only do we admire these actions, but sometimes we feel inspired to do the same. Thus, witnessing excellence motivates us to do something similar. This is an organic way of being motivated for positive action—instead of being steeped in the negative feelings associated with a number of psychological disorders.

The Golden Mean

A balanced use of appreciation of beauty and moral excellence requires that we are sensitive and open to noticing, acknowledging, appreciating, and appraising positive experiences. This sensitivity can vary from person to person and can be culturally bound. (For example, you may experience awe while listening to Mozart's opera *Marriage of Figaro* or to Beethoven's *Ninth Symphony,* whereas someone else may experience awe when listing to classical Indian music or Georgian chants, or while watching dancers performing an Argentinian tango or Irish step dance.) Some life-altering events, such as birth and death, a miraculous and unexpected recovery, or a surprising and significant achievement, also have a cultural subtext. To fully appreciate the elevation and awe associated with such events, you need to understand that cultural context—both the macro level (the broader cultural norms, such as practices at Irish funerals) and the micro level (the funeral norms practiced by a specific Irish family). If you see someone moved at a social gathering and you are unable to comprehend it, politely asking the person to explain the importance will help you to understand the awe that is being experienced. Acts of moral courage that involve putting oneself in danger to save others, are more universally understood, even without knowing the language, and can be morally elevating. An artistic expression (e.g., music, dance, acting, painting) can also cultivate elevation as you witness a deeply moving performance. Such elevation can occur when you attend a concert or witness great art in a museum; it can also happen while watching or hearing something on popular media, through programs like *America's* or *Britain's Got Talent, Idol Competitions,* or *Dancing with the Stars*—all can leave us awe struck.

A balanced use of appreciation of beauty and excellence also entails that it is not exercised, expressed, or shared as snobbery, nor is it expressed with the intention of earning external recognition and rewards. A lack of appreciation of beauty and excellence may keep your daily life filled with boredom and lack of motivation, although such lack could be due to a number of factors, such as physical, cultural, or economic barriers.

- *Overuse of strength:* snobbishness, pretentiousness
- *Underuse of strength:* oblivion, unconsciousness

Integration

Appreciation of beauty integrates naturally with numerous strengths, such as creativity and gratitude. You are able to appreciate the creative nature of painting, sculpture, artistic performance, and so on. The very act of appreciation is a hallmark of gratitude. Appreciation almost always connects us with others—in person or virtually—thereby strengthening our social trust and sparking our inspiration, in particular, our moral elevation. This can occur when we see someone going out of her way to save a life, when a first-responder puts his life at risk to save others, or when we witness an exceptional artistic performance by someone unknown or not formally trained. This elevation infuses motivation, zest, and persistence in us to emulate what we have experienced at a deeper level.

Movies

- *Avatar (2009)* –The human/Na'vi hybrids, called Avatars, connect with human minds to explore the beauty of Pandora because the environment is otherwise toxic to humans.
- *Out of Africa (1985)*—Karen Blixen goes to Africa from Denmark in order to start a coffee plantation. Amidst a dysfunctional marriage, she begins to appreciate the beauty of her surroundings.
- *The Color of Paradise (1999, Iran)*—The film centers on a visually impaired boy who explores beauty in nature through his remaining senses, with a dramatic and emotionally powerful ending.

Therapeutic Actions

- **Explore the fullness of your emotions:** Become aware of your negative emotions—when they surface, how they persist, and how they impact your behavior. At the same time, notice at least one instance of natural beauty around you every day (such as the sunrise, sunset, clouds, sunshine, snowfall, rainbows, trees, moving leaves, chirping birds, flowers, fruits, and vegetables). At the end of the day, critically appraise both the negative and positive emotions, and write about ways to increase the positive ones, especially when you feel distress.
- **Start projects that buffer against negativity:** Think about and then select three projects to do that use creativity, persistence, and appreciation of beauty. Spend time on these projects instead of worrying, being anxious, or feeling stressed. Make sure each project really involves you, especially at times or in ways that buffer you from sliding into negativity.
- **Pay attention to expressions:** Notice how other people appreciate beauty and excellence through specific words, expressions, gestures, and actions. See if you notice these individuals admiring aspects of life that you aren't typically aware of. Incorporate that expression in your vocabulary.
- **Catalogue positive behaviors:** Note weekly how the goodness of other people affects your life. Appreciate the beauty of positive human behavior. Catalogue it, review it weekly, and draw motivation to do something similar.
- **Reflect and write:** Reflect on and write about three aspects of natural beauty, three instances of human creativity or artistic expression, and three experiences of seeing someone do something positive that you can identify with and see yourself doing.
- **Apply appreciation of beauty and gratitude to your close relationships:** Applying this appreciation will likely replace negative feelings. In particular, if you have a slightly

biased view or hold a grudge against someone, focusing on positives and genuinely admiring that person will reduce negativity and replace it with trust and intimacy.

Exemplars (TED Talks)

Visit https://www.ted.com/talks and search for the following talks to hear from individuals who represent the strength of appreciation of beauty & excellence:

- Louie Schwartzberg: Nature. Beauty. Gratitude.
- Bernie Krause: The voice of the natural world
- Mac Stone: Stunning photos of the endangered Everglades

Books

- Cold, B. (2001). *Aesthetics, Well-Being, and Health: Essays within Architecture and Environmental Aesthetics.* Aldershot, UK: Ashgate.
- Murray, C. A. (2003). *Human Accomplishment: The Pursuit of Excellence in the Arts and Sciences, 800 B.C. to 1950.* New York: HarperCollins.
- Wariboko, N. (2009). *The Principle of Excellence: A Framework for Social Ethics.* Lanham, MD: Lexington Books.

Websites

- Fringe Benefits of Appreciation of Beauty and Excellence:
  http://positivepsychologynews.com/news/sherri-fisher/2014091529973
- How to appreciate beauty and enjoy its benefits:
  http://feelhappiness.com/how-to-appreciate-beauty/

21. GRATITUDE

Description

Gratitude is an awareness of and thankfulness for the good things in one's life. If gratitude is one of your top strengths, you take time to express thanks and contemplate all that you have been given in life. When you look back on your life, you don't become paralyzed or preoccupied by negative memories; rather, you are likely to re-evaluate and reappraise your negative memories and extract meaning from them. You never take things for granted, and you express your gratitude to a specific person, to divinity, or simply to nature. Therefore, you generally view the world as more positive than negative, and this trust helps you extend the gratitude to others. In fact, gratitude is often "other-oriented." That is, you express gratitude to someone, with someone, or for someone, and this process builds positive relationships. You are more likely to focus on positive aspects when relating with others.

The Golden Mean

A balanced use of gratitude requires that you neither feel entitled to receive a positive outcome nor that you take any positive event or outcome for granted. A balanced and adaptive use of gratitude is generally not compatible with negative emotion. That is, when you are genuinely grateful, you don't feel anger, bitterness, envy, greed, impoverished, or inferior/superior to others. An appropriate use of gratitude, in fact, thwarts such feelings. However, there are situations—such as becoming pregnant after trying for several years, only to learn that the child will likely have significant developmental delays; or the relief experienced at the end of an abusive relationship, the memories of which still bother you; or miraculously surviving an accident but losing mobility—that encapsulate multiple emotions, some positive, some negative.

Also, be mindful that if you effusively express gratitude for every little thing, the receiver of such gratitude may get used to this expression, may take it for granted, and may not acknowledge it appropriately. Others may feel uncomfortable with an elaborate and public expression of thanks. Therefore, it is important to understand the personal disposition and situational dynamics before expressing gratitude. On the other hand, not expressing gratitude when you should can give the impression that you have a sense of entitlement, or that you are too self-absorbed to take notice of positive things around you.

A sensible use of gratitude promotes a balanced self-image. You are happy with what you have and refrain from social comparisons. However, this doesn't imply that you don't strive and instead become complacent—but you don't strive in relation to others or feel resentful at their progress and want to catch up. You find your own inner measures of competence.

- *Overuse of strength:* ingratiation
- *Underuse of strength:* entitlement, privilege

Integration

Gratitude works well with a number of strengths, such as kindness, love, and social and emotional intelligence, to help you be perceptive and sensitive to other's needs and to express your care through actions. Gratitude also fosters savoring of positive experiences. You are able to exercise mindful attention to notice a positive event or experience and share it with others. Using your strength of appreciation of beauty and excellence, you also notice the positive events and attributes of others, and you genuinely share this feedback with them, thereby strengthening social ties. Like most positive emotions, gratitude opens your cognitive and attentional channels, allowing you to incorporate diverse and fresh perspectives in problem-solving and undertaking a creative endeavor. A balanced use of gratitude also inhibits social comparisons.

Gratitude helps us cope with stress and trauma. It fosters positive reinterpreting or reframing. After the initial shock, gratitude helps us evaluate what is most important in our lives. Expressing gratefulness during personal adversity, loss, or trauma might be hard and may seem irrelevant at the time. However, such expression may be the most important thing that you can do, as it may help you to adjust, cope, and grow. Another marker of the balanced application of gratitude is prosocial behavior; that is, gratitude promotes moral behavior. You become sensitive and caring about other's needs and share your resources with them.

Movies

- *The Fault in Our Stars (2014)*—Two teenagers with cancer fall in love, rather miraculously. This movie is a reminder to be grateful for the love and beauty around us, as we may not be around forever to enjoy it.
- *Amélie (2001, France)*—Amélie approaches life with an inquisitive nature and an appreciation for the little things. She befriends a shut-in neighbor, plays pranks, and returns lost items to their owners.
- *Sunshine (1999)*—This epic film follows the lives of three generations of Jewish men living in Hungary. The movie ends with the grandson's ultimate realization of his gratitude toward his family and his heritage, regardless of the pain of the past.

Therapeutic Actions

- **Cultivate gratitude:** Simultaneous expression of gratitude and negative emotions is incompatible. In other words, if you are feeling grateful, it is highly unlikely that you also feel angry, ambivalent, stressed, or sad. Using the strategies that follow (e.g., express thanks, unlearn self-pity), cultivate gratitude on daily basis. The more you experience positive emotions, the less you will feel negative emotions, or the time you are stuck in negative emotions will decrease.

- **Express thanks:** Express thanks to everyone who has contributed to your success, no matter how small such contribution might have been. Be aware of the degree to which your success is a product of others' helpful influence in addition to your own hard work. Express thanks without just saying "thanks"—be more descriptive and specific (e.g., *"I appreciate your prudent advice"*). Closely observe how other people express gratitude.
- **Unlearn self-pity:** Gratitude helps you appreciate what you have, what you have accomplished, and what resources and support you enjoy. This, in turn, makes you more confident and effective. This process can help you unlearn habits like self-pity and feeling victimized.
- **Deal with trauma:** Gratitude also helps you cope with stress and trauma. It enables you to positively reinterpret or reframe events from the past that still bother you.
- **Practice daily gratitude:** Set aside at least 10 minutes a day to savor a pleasant experience. Decide to withhold any conscious decisions during these ten minutes.

Exemplars (TED Talks)

Visit https://www.ted.com/talks and search for the following talks to hear from individuals who represent the strength of gratitude:

- David Steindl-Rast: Want to be happy? Be grateful
- Laura Trice: Remember to say thank you
- Chip Conley: Measuring what makes life worthwhile

Books

- Emmons, R.A. (2007). *THANKS! How the New Science of Gratitude Can Make You Happier.* Boston: Houghton-Mifflin.
- Sacks, O. (2015). *Gratitude* (1st ed.). Toronto: Alfred A. Knopf.
- Watkins, P. C. (2013). *Gratitude and the Good Life: Toward a Psychology of Appreciation.* Dordrecht: Springer.

Websites

- A practical guide to cultivating gratitude:
  http://www.unstuck.com/gratitude.html
- Robert Emmon's lab on Gratitude:
  http://emmons.faculty.ucdavis.edu
- Alex Wood studies the good in other people, as well as himself:
  http://www.alexwoodpsychology.com/
- Adam Grant studies the advantages of give and take in workplace interactions, and for success:
  https://adam-grant.socialpsychology.org/publications

22. HOPE & OPTIMISM

Description

Hope and optimism is the expectation that good things will happen in the future. Although "hope" and "optimism" are sometimes used interchangeably, research has shown subtle differences. From a therapeutic standpoint, depression can develop when an individual explains the causes of failure in pessimistic terms, whereas an optimist looks at failure differently. For example, a person with depression might think that a single failure (a) is likely to ruin her entire life, (b) impacts every area of her life, and (c) persists forever. An optimist, on the other hand, will understand that (a) a single failure doesn't mean that he will fail in every endeavor, (b) failure happens but it doesn't last forever, and (c) failure doesn't ruin everything in life. Likewise, if you are experiencing depressive symptoms, working on hope will help you boost your will and, at the same time, will provide you with specific strategies to harness your will or motivation into action. Hope and optimism can lead you to explore and expect the best from yourself.

The Golden Mean

A balanced use of hope and optimism requires that you don't set unrealistic expectations or goals, especially if you are psychologically distressed. Start with realistic and achievable goals, particularly ones for which you have support.

One of the guiding principles of PPT is fundamentally believing in your own strengths, and your act of seeking help (i.e., engaging in PPT) is an act of hope and optimism. You have the courage to acknowledge that you need help, and you have made a very good start. In many ways, PPT is an effort to set personalized goals. Using your strengths, both you and your clinician can set goals that are meaningful for you, and together you will monitor progress as therapy progresses. The more realistic the goals, the faster your recovery and journey toward well-being will be. Celebrate as you accomplish each goal or part thereof.

For a balanced use of hope and optimism, it is important that you establish goals early in therapy because the odds of change in your symptoms are much higher in the first five weeks or sessions. If you fail to establish goals, or are too spontaneous in goal selection, you may lose your motivation to change, and, over time, your symptoms may worsen. Writing about a positive future version of yourself (see Session Four: A Better Version of Me) will also likely help you set and revise realistic goals. Lastly, hope and optimism should also be viewed within the cultural context.

- *Overuse of strength:* Panglossian outlook
- *Underuse of strength:* pessimism, despair

Integration

A number of strengths can meld with hope and optimism to offer optimal therapeutic benefits. For example, turning hope and optimism into goals is important, and you need strengths like courage and persistence to accomplish these goals. Optimism, in particular, needs a good dose of courage and zest because sometimes we really want to do something but our inner critic and criticism from others derail our progress. We may not believe in our strengths and pay more attention to our deficits.

Movies

- ***The Diving Bell and the Butterfly (2007)***—This is the remarkable tale of Jean-Dominique Bauby, a French editor, who suffered a stroke and became paralyzed; his only way of communicating with the outside world was by blinking one eye. His hope and optimism helped him learn to speak through his seemingly irrelevant gestures, and he began to produce words.
- ***Cinderella Man (2005)***—During the depths of the Great Depression, legendary athlete Jim Braddock—a once-promising light heavyweight boxer—uses his hope and optimism to find his way back into the ring and pull off a surprising third-round win.
- ***Gone with the Wind (1939)***—Scarlett O'Hara is living during the tumultuous years of the Civil War in a society torn by every sort of strife. In addition, she must contend with the trials of unrequited love and romantic frustration. In spite of all these obstacles, Scarlett maintains her sense of hope and continues to strive toward a better future for herself.

- *Good Will Hunting (1997)*—Will Hunting, a janitor at MIT, has a gift for mathematics. To deal with his difficult past and articulate his sense of hope and optimism, he needs the good counsel of a compassionate therapist who believes in him.

Therapeutic Actions

- **Apply optimism and hope:** List three things that deplete your hope and optimism. Using the ideas and strengths discussed earlier, apply hope and optimism to decrease your distress.
- **Cultivate optimistic company:** Surround yourself with optimistic and future-minded friends, particularly when you are facing a setback. Accept their encouragement and help, and let them know that you will be there for them when they face obstacles.
- **Succeed after struggle:** Recall a situation in which you—or someone close to you—successfully overcame a difficult obstacle. Remember this precedent if you are faced with a similar situation in the future.
- **Visualize your life:** Reflect on where and what you want to be in 1, 5, and 10 years. Sketch a pathway that you can follow to get there. Include manageable steps and ways to chart your progress.
- **Tackling adversity:** When facing adversity, focus on how you overcame a similar situation in the past. Let your successes set the precedent for your future endeavors.

Exemplars (TED Talks)

Visit https://www.ted.com/talks and search for the following talks to hear from individuals who represent the strength of hope & optimism:

- Tali Sharot: The optimism bias
- Martin Seligman: The new era of positive psychology
- Douglas Beal: An alternative to GDP that encompasses our well-being
- Laura Carstensen: Older people are happier
- Carlos Morales Finds Hope After Tragedy While Raising Quadruplets on His Own

Books

- Gillham, J. (2000). *The Science of Optimism and Hope*: West Conshohocken, PA, Templeton Press.
- Seligman, M. (2006). *Learned Optimism: How to Change Your Mind and Your Life.* New York: Vintage Books.
- Tali Sharot, T. (2011). *The Optimism Bias: A Tour of the Irrationally Positive Brain.* Toronto: Knopf.
- Snyder, C. R. (1994). *The Psychology of Hope: You Can Get There from Here.* New York: Free Press.
- Seligman, M. (2018). *The Hope Circuit: A Psychologist's Journey from Helplessness to Optimism.* New York: Hachette Book Group.

Websites

- Overview of hope research:
  http://www.thepositivepsychologypeople.com/hope-research/
- Shane J. Lopez, PhD:
  http://www.hopemonger.com/

23. HUMOR & PLAYFULNESS

Description

Humor involves an enjoyment of laughing, friendly teasing, and bringing happiness to others. As an integral part of social play, humor offers us a different perspective. If humor and playfulness is one of your top strengths, you know how to take the edge off a stressful situation while maintaining group cohesion. From a therapeutic standpoint, humor offers a viable way to release negative emotions. With this strength, you are able to see the lighter side of life for many situations, finding things to be cheerful about rather than letting adversity get you down. Humor means more than just telling jokes; rather, humor is a playful and imaginative approach to life.

The Golden Mean

Too much humor can make you look like a fool, whereas a severe lack of this strength can make you too serious and boring. A balanced use of humor and playfulness, although not easy, is very desirable. Without sacrificing empathy and cultural sensitivity, a well-delivered joke, quick retort, observation, or comment can offer a fresh and different perspective, and can expand your thinking and improve your sense of self. Context, however, is crucial in using humor and playfulness. For example, in situations that may benefit from a little burst of humor with a quick shift to serious deliberations, overusing humor can give the impression that you are not being serious, and hence are unreliable. On the other hand, a serious tone and stoic expression that cannot be penetrated by a quick joke or light-hearted comment can isolate you from others and keep them from freely sharing their thoughts and feelings with you.

- *Overuse of strength:* buffoon-like, clown-like
- *Underuse of strength:* cheerlessness, grimness

Integration

A number of strengths can help harness playfulness, such as social intelligence, zest, curiosity, teamwork, kindness, authenticity, and fairness. If a playful remark, joke, or anecdote is shared mindfully, it can amiably relieve a stressful situation without offending others and offer a new perspective. Note that a balanced and adaptive use of humor and playfulness requires that this joke or funny story be relevant, engaging, and culturally sensitive.

Movies

- *Patch Adams (1999)*—Patch Adams commits himself to a psychiatric ward and finds joy in helping his fellow patients. Disturbed by the staff's cold approach to the patients, he vows to change the system and enrolls in medical school. His unorthodox blend of medicine and humor brings him both praise and at times condemnation.
- *Life is Beautiful (1998, Italy)*—Guido, a charming Jewish man, never loses his cleverness, hope, or humor, especially in protecting his young son from the horrors of the Holocaust by pretending the whole affair is a game.
- *Amadeus (1984)*—This film depicts the humor and laughter of young Mozart, who in addition to his creativity and perseverance shows his lighter side when engaging in practical jokes.

Therapeutic Actions

- **Use cognitively distracting humor:** If you feel stressed, depressed, or angry, create a playlist of funny YouTube or other online videos. Make sure the content engages you so that you are disengaged from negative emotions. Keep the list updated.
- **Cheer up a gloomy friend:** Cheer up someone whose likes and dislikes you know well. This will also help you in dealing with your own distresses.
- **Befriend someone who is funny:** Become friends with someone who has a great sense of humor. Watch how he or she uses this strength to deal with difficult situations and bad news.
- **Look for the lighter side of a serious situation:** When something serious happens, try to find a fun and lighter side to the situation. Strike a balance between taking things seriously enough and not taking them too seriously.
- **Engage in outdoor fun:** Go out with your friends at least once a month to run, hike, cross-country ski, bike, and so on. Note how the group dynamic improves when you laugh together.

Exemplars (TED Talks)

Visit https://www.ted.com/talks and search for the following talks to hear from individuals who represent the strength of humor & playfulness:

- Jane McGonigal: The game that can give you 10 extra years of life
- Liza Donnelly: Drawing on humor for change
- John Hunter: Teaching with the World Peace Game
- Cosmin Mihaiu: Physical therapy is boring—play a game instead
- Ze Frank: Nerdcore comedy

Books

- Akhtar, M. C. (2011). *Play and Playfulness: Developmental, Cultural, and Clinical Aspects.* Lanham, MD: Jason Aronson.
- McGonigal, J. (2011). *Reality Is Broken: Why Games Make Us Better and How They Can Change the World.* New York: Penguin Press.
- Schaefer, C. E. (2003). *Play Therapy with Adults.* Hoboken, NJ: Wiley.
- Russ, S. W., & Niec, L. N. (2011). *Play in Clinical Practice: Evidence-Based Approaches.* New York: Guilford Press.

Websites

- Cognitive neuroscientist Scott Weems talks about his book *HA! The Science of When We Laugh and Why*:
http://www.scientificamerican.com/podcast/episode/humor-science-weems/
- Scientists discover the secret of humor:
http://www.telegraph.co.uk/news/science/science-news/7938976/Scientists-discover-the-secret-of-humour.html
- The Science of Humor: This website contains detailed information on humor research:
http://moreintelligentlife.com/story/the-science-of-humour;
- Signs you have a good sense of humor:
http://www.huffingtonpost.com/2014/08/29/good-sense-of-humor_n_5731418.html

24. SPIRITUALITY

Description

Spirituality is a universal part of human experience involving knowledge of one's place within the larger scheme of things. Spirituality can include—but is not limited to—religious belief and practice. With the help of this strength, you become aware of both the sacred and secular in everyday life. This is a strength that offers you a sense of comfort in the face of adversity and the experience of transcending the ordinary to reach something fundamental. You feel the comfort that there is someone or something greater than you, a force to rely on. Having a sense of spirituality offers you emotional support that you can handle adversity. To enhance your sense of spirituality, you take specific actions that generally follow established spiritual or religious norms. While following these actions, you feel that your life has meaning.

The Golden Mean

A balanced sense of spirituality indicates that your life is imbued with meaning and purpose, although the meaning and purpose do not have to be grand and earth-shattering. A balanced use of spirituality, meaning, and purpose can be accomplished through tangible prosocial activities, such as volunteering at a food bank, a center for children with disabilities, or a home for senior citizens. Becoming involved with a religious institution (such as a church, mosque, or temple), professional association, leisure or sports club, non-profit organization, environmental task force, or humanitarian group all offer opportunities to connect with something larger. Regardless of the particular way in which you establish a spiritual and meaningful life, ensure that the aim or meaning is always clear. There are multiple paths to spirituality. Each path could lead you to something greater than yourself—your purpose. Before embarking on any path, reflect on where and to what end this path will bring you. A total lack of spirituality, meaning, and purpose could leave you feeling empty, unfulfilled, and existentially anxious about the aimlessness of your life.

- *Overuse of strength:* fanaticism, radicalism
- *Underuse of strength:* anomie, isolation

Integration

A number of strengths integrate naturally with spirituality, including gratitude, self-regulation, persistence, authenticity, appreciation of beauty, and hope. In addition to specific strengths, a number of strengths-based actions can offer you soothing and satisfying experiences of spirituality. These include mentoring, going on a retreat with your partner or close friend, meditating or praying together or sharing the same space, and periodically reviewing your life to reflect on its meaning and how your actions and habits are congruent with this meaning.

Movies

- *Contact (1997)*—Dr. Eleanor Arroway, a scientist working on the search for extraterrestrial intelligence, discovers a signal from a faraway star. This discovery throws society into turmoil as the age-old conflict erupts between reason and belief.
- *Priest (1994, Britain)*—Fr. Greg Plinkington lives two lives, one as a conservative Catholic priest and the other as a gay man with a lover. When a girl in his confessional tells him about sexual abuse at the hands of her father, his frustration with the laws of the Catholic Church boils over, and he must reconcile his inner beliefs with the tenets of his doctrinal faith.
- *Eat Pray Love (2010)*—Despite having a home and successful career, Liz's divorce leaves her confused and at a crossroads. She ventures out on a quest of self-discovery and travels

to different places in the world, where she steps out of her comfort zone to learn more about herself.

Therapeutic Actions

- **List experiences that make you feel detached and ones that forge connections:** Make a weekly or monthly list of experiences that leave you feeling fragmented, distracted, and detached. Next to each such experience, write about a potential experience that would forge strong connections in your life.
- **Fine-tune your quest**: If you find yourself steeped in negative feelings (such as sadness, stress, or anger), deliberately immerse yourself in nature, art, music, poetry, or literature that instills a sense of awe and wonder in you. Gradually fine-tune your awareness. These experiences can connect you with your spiritual quest.
- **Practice relaxation:** Spend 10 minutes daily breathing deeply, relaxing, and meditating (emptying the mind of thoughts by focusing on breathing). Observe how you feel afterward.
- **Explore different religions:** Take a class, do online research, meet someone from a different religion, or attend a congregation of a different religion. Speak to people who practice this faith, and get to know them as people.
- **Explore your purpose:** If you feel lost, ambivalent, or empty, explore a fundamental purpose of your life, and link your actions to this purpose. Each day, ask yourself if you accomplished anything toward fulfilling this purpose.
- **Write your own eulogy:** Write your eulogy or ask your loved ones how they would like to remember you. Do they mention your signature strengths?

Exemplars (TED Talks)

Visit https://www.ted.com/talks and search for the following talks to hear from individuals who represent the strength of spirituality:

- Lesley Hazleton: On reading the Koran
- Dan Dennett: Let's teach religion—all religion—in schools
- Julia Sweeney: Letting go of God
- Kwame Anthony Appiah: Is religion good or bad? (This is a trick question)

Books

- Aslan, R. (2017). *God: A Human History*. New York: Random House.
- Newberg, A., & Waldman, M. R. (2006). *Why We Believe What We Believe: Uncovering Our Biological Need for Meaning, Spirituality, and Truth*. New York: Free Press.
- Valliant, G. (2008). *Spiritual Evolution: How We Are Wired for Faith, Hope, and Love*. New York: Broadway.

Websites

- How to get in touch with your spiritual side:
  http://www.actionforhappiness.org/take-action/get-in-touch-with-your-spiritual-side
- Research on spirituality by Michael McCullough:
  http://www.psy.miami.edu/faculty/mmccullough/
- Research on spirituality by Kenneth I. Pargament:
  http://www.bgsu.edu/arts-and-sciences/center-for-family-demographic-research/about-cfdr/research-affiliates/kenneth-i-pargament.html

Table D2
BALANCED USE OF CHARACTER STRENGTHS

Strength	Overuse (too much)	Underuse (lack of, or too little)	Golden Mean	Integration (interaction with other strengths)
Wisdom & Knowledge				
Cognitive strengths that entail the acquisition and use of knowledge				
Creativity	Oddity, weirdness, eccentricity	Dullness, banality, conformity	Adaptive, positive, and innovative ways of doing things	Curiosity, open-mindedness, and zest
Curiosity	Prying, snooping, nosiness	Boredom, disinterest, apathy	Exploration and openness that is neither boring nor intrusive	Persistence, open-mindedness, and courage
Open-mindedness	Cynicism, skepticism	Dogmatism, "unreflectiveness," rigidity, overly simplistic	Unbiased critical inquiry toward adaptive change, if needed	Perspective, curiosity, and fairness
Love of learning	"Know-it-all"-ism	Complacency, smugness	Deepening knowledge to better understand self and society	Curiosity, open-mindedness, and persistence
Perspective	Elitism, arcane, pedantic	Superficiality	Synthesis of knowledge to understand context	Social intelligence, integrity, and courage
Courage				
Exercising the will to accomplish goals in the face of opposition, external or internal				
Bravery	Risk-taking, foolishness	Debilitating fear, cowardice	Facing and responding to threats and fear without jeopardizing safety and well-being	Self-regulation, integrity, and persistence
Persistence	Obsessiveness, fixation, pursuit of unattainable goals	Laziness, apathy	Finishing what is started and needs be finished	Courage, perspective, and zest
Integrity	Righteousness	Shallowness, phoniness	Being real and true, without external pressures or rewards	Fairness, courage, and perspective
Vitality & Zest	Hyperactivity	Passivity, inhibition	Enthusiasm that is not obsession or too much inhibition	Self-regulation, hope, and courage
Humanity				
Emotional strengths that show the exercise of will in the face of opposition or internal threat				
Love	Emotional promiscuity	Isolation, detachment	Genuinely loving and caring for others without making extreme sacrifices	Kindness, Social intelligence, and hope
Kindness	Intrusiveness	Indifference, cruelty, mean-spiritedness	Doing actions for others that are needed, are not asked for, and don't carry tangible rewards	Social intelligence, citizenship & teamwork, and perspective
Social Intelligence	Psycho-babbling, self-deception	Obtuseness, cluelessness	Nuanced understanding of emotions, motives, and corresponding changes.	Kindness, love, and self-regulation

Justice
Interpersonal strengths that involve tending and befriending others

Strength				
Citizenship & Teamwork	Mindless and automatic obedience	Selfishness, narcissism	Being inclusive and harmonious for the common good	Social intelligence, leadership, and hope
Fairness	Impartiality without perspective or empathy, detachment	Prejudice, partisanship	Doing the right thing, without being influenced by personal and societal biases	Integrity, courage, and open-mindedness
Leadership	Despotism, bossiness	Compliance, acquiescence	Aspiring and bringing others toward a positive common goal	Zest, teamwork, and social intelligence

Temperance
Strengths that protect against excess

Strength				
Forgiveness & Mercy	Permissiveness	Mercilessness, vengefulness	Willingly ceasing cycle of revenge	Kindness, social intelligence, and integrity
Humility & Modesty	Self-deprecation	Foolish self-esteem, arrogance	Without compromising self-care, not seeking spotlight despite deserving it	Gratitude, integrity, and spirituality
Prudence	Prudishness, stuffiness	Recklessness, sensation-seeking	Being cautious without being preoccupied or nonchalant about potential and realistic risks	Persistence, self-regulation, and curiosity
Self-Regulation	Inhibition, reticence	Self-indulgence, impulsivity	Regulating emotions and actions without feeling stifled or restrained	Perspective, persistence, and hope

Transcendence
Strengths that forge connections to the larger universe and provide meaning

Strength				
Appreciation of Beauty & Excellence	Snobbishness, pretentiousness	Oblivion, unconsciousness	Intrinsically appreciating beauty and excellence without snobbery	Gratitude, zest, and creativity
Gratitude	Ingratiation	Entitlement, privilege	Deep and genuine sense of thankfulness without feeling obligated	Kindness, love, and social intelligence
Hope & Optimism	Panglossian outlook	Pessimism, despair	Being optimistic within realistic bounds	Open-mindedness, courage, and zest
Humor & Playfulness	Buffoon-like, clown-like	Cheerlessness, grimness	Expressing lighter and playful aspects of a situation with good intentions	Zest, social intelligence, and integrity
Spirituality	Fanaticism, radicalism	Anomie, isolation	Pursuing adaptive paths through meaningful actions	Gratitude, humility, and kindness

REFERENCES

Ackerman, S., Zuroff, D. C., & Moskowitz, D. S. (2000). Generativity in midlife and young adults: Links to agency, communion, and subjective well-being. *International Journal of Aging & Human Development, 50,* 17–41.

Adler, J. M., & McAdams, D. P. (2007). Telling stories about therapy: Ego development, well-being, and the therapeutic relationship. In R. Josselson, D. P. McAdams, & A. Lieblich (Eds.), *The meaning of others: Narrative studies of relationships* (pp. 213–236). Washington, DC: American Psychological Association.

Ajzen, I., & Sheikh, S. (2013). Action versus inaction: Anticipated affect in the theory of planned behavior. *Journal of Applied Social Psychology, 43*(1), 155–162. doi:10.1111/j.1559-1816.2012.00989.x

Alarcon, G. M., Bowling, N. A., & Khazon, S. (2013). Great expectations: A meta-analytic examination of optimism and hope. *Personality and Individual Differences, 54*(7), 821–827. doi:10.1016/j.paid.2012.12.004

Aldao, A., Nolen-Hoeksema, S., & Schweizer, S. (2010). Emotion-regulation strategies across psychopathology: A meta-analytic review. *Clinical Psychology Review, 30*(2), 217–237.

Al-Krenawi, A., Elbedour, S., Parsons, J. E., Onwuegbuzie, A. J., Bart, W. M., & Ferguson, A. (2011). Trauma and war: Positive psychology/strengths approach. *Arab Journal of Psychiatry, 22,* 103–112.

Allan, B. A., & Duffy, R. D. (2014). Examining moderators of signature strengths use and well-being: Calling and signature strengths level. *Journal of Happiness Studies, 15*(2), 323–337. doi:10.1007/s10902-013-9424-0

American Psychiatric Association. (2013). *Diagnostic and statistical manual of mental disorders* (5th ed.). Arlington, VA: American Psychiatric Association.

Anderson, A. K., Wais, P. E., & Gabrieli, J. D. (2006). Emotion enhances remembrance of neutral events past. *Proceedings of the National Academy of Sciences of the United States of America, 103*(5),1599–604.

Anderson, C. A., & Bushman, B. J. (2002). Human aggression. *Annual Review of Psychology, 53*(1), 27–51.

Andreassen, T. (2001). From disgust to delight. *Journal of Service Research, 4*(1), 39–49.

Andrewes, H. E., Walker, V., & O'Neill, B. (2014). Exploring the use of positive psychology interventions in brain injury survivors with challenging behaviour. *Brain Injury, 28*(7), 965–971. doi:10.3109/02699052.2014.888764

Asebedo, S. D., & Seay, M. C. (2014). Positive psychological attributes and retirement satisfaction. *Journal of Financial Counseling and Planning, 25*(2), 161–173. Retrieved from http://search.proquest.com/docview/1635267624?accountid=14771

Asgharipoor, N., Farid, A. A., Arshadi, H., & Sahebi, A. (2012). A comparative study on the effectiveness of positive psychotherapy and group cognitive-behavioral therapy for the patients suffering from major depressive disorder. *Iranian Journal of Psychiatry and Behavioral Sciences, 6*(2), 33.

Azañedo, C. M., Fernández-Abascal, E. G., & Barraca, J. (2014). Character strengths in Spain: Validation of the Values in Action Inventory of Strengths (VIA-IS) in a Spanish sample. *Clínica y Salud, 25,* 123–130. doi:10.1016/j.clysa.2014.06.002

Baer, R. A., Smith, G. T., & Allen, K. B. (2004). Assessment of mindfulness by self-report: The Kentucky Inventory of Mindfulness Skills. *Assessment, 11,* 191–206.

Barlow, H. D. (2008). *Handbook of clinical disorders.* New York: Guilford Press.

Bartels, M., Cacioppo, J. T., van Beijsterveldt, Toos, C. E. M., & Boomsma, D. I. (2013). Exploring the association between well-being and psychopathology in adolescents. *Behavior Genetics, 43*(3), 177–190.

Baumeister, R. F. (2005). *The cultural animal: Human nature, meaning, and social life.* New York: Oxford University Press.

Baumeister, R. F., Bratslavsky, E., Finkenauer, C., & Vohs, K. D. (2001). Bad is stronger than good. *Review of General Psychology, 5,* 323–370. doi:10.1037/1089-2680.5.4.323

Baumeister, R. F., & Leary, M. R. (1995). The need to belong: Desire for interpersonal attachment as a fundamental human motivation. *Psychological Bulletin, 117*, 497–529.

Bay, M. (2012). *Comparing positive psychotherapy with cognitive behavioral therapy in treating depression.* Unpublished manuscript. Paris West University Nanterre La Défense (Université Paris Ouest Nanterre La Défense).

Bearse, J. L., McMinn, M. R., Seegobin, W., & Free, K. (2013). Barriers to psychologists seeking mental health care. *Professional Psychology: Research and Practice, 44*(3), 150–157. http://dx.doi.org/10.1037/a0031182

Beck, A. T., Epstein, N., Brown, G., & Steer, R. A (1988). An inventory for measuring clinical anxiety: Psychometric properties. *Journal of Consulting and Clinical Psychology, 56*, 893–897.

Beck, A. T., Steer, R. A., & Brown, G. K. (1996). *BDI-II. Beck Depression Inventory: Manual* (2nd ed). Boston: Harcourt Brace.

Berntson, G. G., Thomas Bigger, J., Eckberg, D. L., Grossman, P., Kaufmann, P. G., Malik, M., . . . Der Molen, M. W. (1997). Heart rate variability: Origins, methods, and interpretive caveats. *Psychophysiology, 34*(6), 623–648.

Berthold, A., & Ruch, W. (2014). Satisfaction with life and character strengths of non-religious and religious people: It's practicing one's religion that makes the difference. *Frontiers in Psychology, 5*, 876. doi:10.3389/fpsyg.2014. 00876

Bertisch, H., Rath, J., Long, C., Ashman, T., & Rashid, T. (2014). Positive psychology in rehabilitation medicine: A brief report. *NeuroRehabilitation, 34*(3), 573–585. doi:10.3233/NRE-141059

Berzoff, J., & Kita, E. (2010). Compassion fatigue and countertransference: Two different concepts. *Clinical Social Work Journal, 38*(3), 341–349. http://dx.doi.org/10.1007/s10615-010-0271-8

Birchwood, M., Smith, J., Cochrane, R., & Wetton, S. (1990). The Social Functioning Scale: The development and validation of a new scale of social adjustment for use in family intervention programmes with schizophrenic patients. *British Journal of Psychiatry, 157*, 853–859.

Biswas-Diener, R., Kashdan, T. K., & Minhas, G. (2011). A dynamic approach to psychological strength development and intervention. *The Journal of Positive Psychology 6*(2), 106–118.

Bjelland, I., Dahl, A. A., Haug, T. T., & Neckelmann, D. (2002). The validity of the Hospital Anxiety and Depression Scale. An updated literature review. *Journal of Psychosomatic Research, 52*, 69–77.

Boisvert, C., & Faust, D. (2002). Iatrogenic symptoms in psychotherapy: A theoretical exploration of the potential impact of labels, language, and belief systems. *American Journal of Psychotherapy, 56*, 244–259.

Bolier, L., Haverman, M., Westerhof, G., Riper, H., Smit, F., & Bohlmeijer, E. (2013). Positive psychology interventions: A meta-analysis of randomized controlled studies. *BMC Public Health, 13*, 119.

Bonanno, G. A., & Mancini, A. D. (2012). Beyond resilience and PTSD: Mapping the heterogeneity of responses to potential trauma. *Psychological Trauma: Theory, Research, Practice, and Policy, 4*(1), 74–83. doi:10.1037/a0017829

Bron, T. I., van Rijen, Elisabeth, H. M., van Abeelen, A. M., & Lambregtse-van, D. B. (2012). Development of regulation disorders into specific psychopathology. *Infant Mental Health Journal, 33*(2), 212–221. http://dx.doi.org/10.1002/imhj.21325

Bryant, F. B. (1989). A four-factor model of perceived control: Avoiding, coping obtaining, and savoring. *Journal of Personality, 57*, 773–797.

Bryant, F. B. (2003). Savoring Beliefs Inventory (SBI): A scale for measuring beliefs about savouring. *Journal of Mental Health, 12*, 175–196.

Bryant, F. B., Smart, C. M., & King, S. P. (2005). Using the past to enhance the present: Boosting happiness through positive reminiscence. *Journal of Happiness Studies, 6*, 227–260.

Bryant, F. B., & Veroff, J. (2007). *Savoring: A new model of positive experience.* Mahwah, NJ: Erlbaum.

Buckingham, M., & Clifton, D.O. (2001). *Now, discover your strengths.* New York: Free Press.

Bureau of Labor Statistics. (2015). American time use survey. Retrieved from http://www.bls.gov/tus/charts/home.htm# on December 1, 2015.

Bureau of Labor Statistics. (2016). American time use survey. Retrieved from https://www.bls.gov/tus/documents.htm on December 31, 2017.

Burton, C. M., & King, L. A. (2004). The health benefits of writing about intensely positive experiences. *Journal of Research in Personality, 38,* 150–163.

Buschor, C., Proyer, R. T., & Ruch, W. (2013). Self and peer rated character strengths: How do they relate to satisfaction with life and orientations to happiness? *Journal of Positive Psychology, 8,* 116–127. doi:10.1080/17439760.2012.758305

Bushman, B. J., Baumeister, R. F., & Phillips, C. M. (2001). Do people aggress to improve their mood? Catharsis beliefs, affect regulation opportunity, and aggressive responding. *Journal of Personality and Social Psychology, 81*(1), 17–32.

Calhoun, L. G., & Tedeschi, R. G. (Eds.). (2006). *Handbook of posttraumatic growth: Research and practice.* Mahwah, NJ: Erlbaum.

Calmes, C. A., & Roberts, J. E. (2008). Rumination in interpersonal relationships: Does co-rumination explain gender differences in emotional distress and relationship satisfaction among college students? *Cognitive Therapy and Research, 32*(4), 577–590. https://doi.org/10.1007/s10608-008-9200-3

Carr, A., Finnegan, L., Griffin, E., Cotter, P., & Hyland, A. (2017). A randomized controlled trial of the Say Yes To Life (SYTL) positive psychology group psychotherapy program for depression: An interim report. *Journal of Contemporary Psychotherapy, 47*(3), 153–161. https://doi.org/10.1007/s10879-016-9343-6

Carrier, L. M., Rosen, L. D., Cheever, N. A., & Lim, A. F. (2015). Causes, effects, and practicalities of everyday multitasking. *Developmental Review, 35,* 64–78. https://doi.org/10.1016/j.dr.2014.12.005

Carver, C. S., Scheier, M. F., & Segerstrom, S. C. (2010). Optimism. *Clinical Psychology Review, 30*(7), 879–889. doi:10.1016/j.cpr.2010.01.006

Casellas-Grau, A., Font, A., & Vives, J. (2014). Positive psychology interventions in breast cancer. A systematic review. *Psycho-Oncology, 23*(1), 9–19. https://doi.org/10.1002/pon.3353

Casiday, R., Kinsman, E., Fisher, C., & Bambra, C. (2008). *Volunteering and health: What impact does it really have?* London: Volunteering England.

Castonguay, L. G. (2013). Psychotherapy outcome: An issue worth re-revisiting 50 years later. *Psychotherapy, 50*(1), 52–67. doi:10.1037/a0030898

Chaves, C., López-Gómez, I., Hervas, G., & Vazquez, C. (2017). A comparative study on the efficacy of a positive psychology intervention and a cognitive behavioral therapy for clinical depression. *Cognitive Therapy and Research, 41*(3), 417–433. doi: 10.1007/s10608-016-9778-9

Cheavens, J. S., Feldman, D., Gum. A., Michael, S. T., & Snyder, C. R. (2006). Hope therapy in a community sample: A pilot investigation. *Social Indicators Research, 77,* 61–78.

Cheavens, J. S., Strunk, D. S., Sophie Lazarus, S. A., Goldstein, L. A. (2012). The compensation and capitalization models: A test of two approaches to individualizing the treatment of depression. *Behaviour Research and Therapy, 50,* 699–706.

Chibnall, J. T., & Tait, R. C. (1994). The short form of the Beck Depression Inventory: Validity issues with chronic pain patients. *The Clinical Journal of Pain, 10,* 261–266.

Chida, Y., & Steptoe, A. (2009). The association of anger and hostility with future coronary heart disease: A meta-analytic review of prospective evidence. *Journal of the American College of Cardiology, 53,* 936–946.

Chowdhury, T. G., Ratneshwar, S., & Mohanty, P. (2009). The time-harried shopper: Exploring the differences between maximizers and satisficers. *Marketeting Letters, 20,* 155–167.

Cooney, R. E., Joormann, J., Atlas, L. Y., Eugène, F., & Gotlib, I. H. (2007). Remembering the good times: Neural correlates of affect regulation. *Neuroreport, 18*(17), 1771–1774.

Cooper, H., & Frattaroli, J. (2006). Experimental disclosure and its moderators: A meta-analysis. *Psychological Bulletin, 132*(6), 823–865. doi:10.1037/0033-2909.132.6.823

Cordaro, D. T., Sun, R., Keltner, D., Kamble, S., Huddar, N., & McNeil, G. (2018). Universals and cultural variations in 22 emotional expressions across five cultures. *Emotion, 18*(1), 75–93. http://dx.doi.org/10.1037/emo0000302

Cornish, M. A., & Wade, N. G. (2015). A therapeutic model of self-forgiveness with intervention strategies for counselors. *Journal of Counseling & Development, 93*(1), 96–104. http://dx.doi.org/10.1037/cou0000080

Corrigan, P. (2004). How stigma interferes with mental health care. *American Psychologist, 59,* 614–625.

Corrigan, P. W., Salzer, M., Ralph, R., Sangster, Y., & Keck, L. (2004). Examining the factor structure of the Recovery Assessment Scale. *Schizophrenia Bulletin, 30,* 1035–1041.

Costa-Requena, G., & Gil, F. (2010). Posttraumatic stress disorder symptoms in cancer: Psychometric analysis of the Spanish Posttraumatic Stress Disorder Checklist–Civilian version. *PsychoOncology, 19,* 500–507. http://dx.doi.org/10.1002/pon

Coyne, J. C., & Tennen, H. (2010). Positive psychology in cancer care: Bad science, exaggerated claims, and unproven medicine. *Annals of Behavioral Medicine, 39,* 16–26. doi:10.1007/s12160-009-9154-z

Crits-Christoph, P., Connolly Gibbons, M. B., Ring-Kurtz, S., Gallop, R., Stirman, S., Present, J., . . . Goldstein, L. (2008). Changes in positive quality of life over the course of psychotherapy. *Psychotherapy, 45*(4), 419–430. doi:10.1037/a0014340

Csikszentmihalyi, M. (1990). *Flow: The psychology of optimal experience.* New York: HarperCollins.

Cuadra-Peralta, A., Veloso-Besio, C., Pérez, M., & Zúñiga, M. (2010). Resultados de la psicoterapia positiva en pacientes con depresión [Positive psychotherapy results in patients with depression.]. *Terapia Psicológica, 28,* 127–134. doi:doi:10.4067/S0718-48082010000100012

D'raven, L. L., & Pasha-Zaidi, N. (2014). Positive psychology interventions: A review for counselling practitioners/interventions de psychologie positive: Une revue à l'intention des conseillers praticiens. *Canadian Journal of Counselling and Psychotherapy, 48*(4), 383–408.

Davidson, L., Shahar, G., Lawless, M. S., Sells, D., & Tondora, J. (2006). Play, pleasure, and other positive life events: "Non-specific" factors in recovery from mental illness? *Psychiatry, 69*(2), 151–163. doi:10.1521/psyc.2006.69.2.151

Davis, D. E., Choe, E., Meyers, J., Wade, N., Varjas, K., Gifford, A., . . . Worthington, E. L. Jr. (2016). Thankful for the little things: A meta-analysis of gratitude interventions. *Journal of Counseling Psychology, 63*(1), 20–31.

Dawda, D., & Hart, S. D. (2000). Assessing emotional intelligence: Reliability and validity of the bar-on emotional quotient inventory (EQ-i) in university students. *Personality and Individual Differences, 28*(4), 797–812.

De Shazer, S., Berg, I. K., Lipchik, E., Nunnally, E., Molnar, A., Gingerich, W., & Weiner-Davis, M. (1986). Brief therapy: Focused solution development. *Family Process, 25*(2), 207–221.

Deacon, B. J. (2013). The biomedical model of mental disorder: A critical analysis of its validity, utility, and effects on psychotherapy research. *Clinical Psychology Review, 33*(7), 846–861.

Deci, E. L., & Ryan, R. M. (2008). Self-determination theory: A macrotheory of human motivation, development and health. *Canadian Psychology, 49,* 182–185. doi:10.1037/a0012801

Deighton, R. M., Gurris, N., & Traue, H. (2007). Factors affecting burnout and compassion fatigue in psychotherapists treating torture survivors: Is the therapist's attitude to working through trauma relevant? *Journal of Traumatic Stress, 20*(1), 63–75. http://dx.doi.org/10.1002/jts.20180

Demir, M. (2010). Close relationships and happiness among emerging adults. *Journal of Happiness Studies, 11*(3), 293–313. doi:10.1007/s10902-009-9141-x

Derogatis, L. R. (1993). *Brief Symptom Inventory (BSI): Administration, scoring, and procedures manual* (3rd ed.). Minneapolis, MN: National Computer Systems.

Dewey, J. (1934). *Art as experience.* New York: Minton, Balch & Company.

Dittmar, H., Bond, R., Hurst, M., & Kasser, T. (2014). The relationship between materialism and personal well-being: A meta-analysis. *Journal of Personality and Social Psychology, 107*(5), 879–924. http://doi.org/10.1037/a0037409

Donaldson, S. I., Csikszentmihalyi, M., & Nakamura, J. (Eds.). (2011). *Applied positive psychology: Improving everyday life, health, schools, work, and society.* London: Routledge Academic.

Donaldson, S. I., Dollwet, M., & Rao, M. A. (2015). Happiness, excellence, and optimal human functioning revisited: Examining the peer-reviewed literature linked to positive psychology. *The Journal of Positive Psychology, 10*(3), 185–195. doi:10.1080/17439760.2014.943801

Douglass, R. P., & Duffy, R. D. (2015). Strengths use and life satisfaction: A moderated mediation approach. *Journal of Happiness Studies, 16*(3), 619–632.

Dowlatabadi, M. M., Ahmadi, S. M., Sorbi, M. H., Beiki, O., Khademeh Razavi, T., & Bidaki, R. (2016). The effectiveness of group positive psychotherapy on depression and happiness in breast cancer patients: A randomized controlled trial. *Electronic Physician*, 8(3), 2175–2180. https://doi.org/10.19082/2175

Drvaric, L., Gerritsen, C., Rashid, T., Bagby, R. M., & Mizrahi, R. (2015). High stress, low resilience in people at clinical high risk for psychosis: Should we consider a strengths-based approach? *Canadian Psychology*, 56(3), 332–347.

Duan, W., Ho, S. M. Y., Tang, X., Li, T., & Zhang, Y. (2014). Character strength-based intervention to promote satisfaction with life in the Chinese university context. *Journal of Happiness Studies*, 15(6), 1347–1361. doi:10.1007/s10902-013-9479-y

Duckworth, A. L., Steen, T. A., & Seligman, M. E. P. (2005). Positive psychology in clinical practice. *Annual Review of Clinical Psychology*, 1(1), 629–651. doi:10.1146/annurev. clinpsy.1.102803.144154

Duckworth, A. L., Peterson, C., Matthews, M. D., & Kelly, D. R. (2007). Grit: Perseverance and passion for long-term goals. *Journal of Personality and Social Psychology*, 92, 1087–1101.

Ehrenreich, B. (2009). *Bright-sided: How positive thinking is undermining America.* New York: Metropolitan Books.

Eichstaedt, J. C., Schwartz, H. A., Kern, M. L., Park, G., Labarthe, D. R., Merchant, R. M., . . . Seligman, M. E. P. (2015). Psychological language on Twitter predicts county-level heart disease mortality. *Psychological Science*, 26(2), 159–169. http://doi.org/10.1177/0956797614557867

Elkins, D. (2009). The medical model in psychotherapy. *Journal of Humanistic Psychology*, 49(1), 66–84.

Emmons, R. A. (2007). Gratitude, subjective well-being, and the brain. In R. J. Larsen & M. Eid (Eds.), *The science of subjective well-being* (pp. 469–492). New York: Guilford Press.

Emmons, R. A., & McCullough, M. E. (2003). Counting blessing versus burdens: An experimental investigation of gratitude and subjective well-being in daily life. *Journal of Personality and Social Psychology*, 84(2), 377–389.

Emmons, R. A., & Mishra, A. (2012). Why gratitude enhances well-being: What we know, what we need to know. In K. Sheldon, T. Kashdan, & M. F. Steger (Eds.), *Designing the future of positive psychology: Taking stock and moving forward.* New York: Oxford University Press.

Enright, R., & Fitzgibbons, R. (2015). *Forgiveness therapy.* Washington, DC: American Psychological Association.

Evans, I. M. (1993). Constructional perspectives in clinical assessment. *Psychological Assessment*, 5, 264–272. http://dx.doi.org/10.1037/1040-3590.5.3.264

Fadla, A. (2014). Self-leadership. *Leadership Excellence*, 31(8), 10–11.

Fava, G. A. (2016). Well-being therapy. In A. M. Wood & J. Johnson (Eds.), *The Wiley handbook of positive clinical psychology* (pp. 395–407). Chichester, UK: John Wiley. http://doi.org/10.1002/9781118468197

Fava, G. A., & Ruini, C. (2003). Development and characteristics of a well-being enhancing psychotherapeutic strategy: Well-being therapy. *Journal of Behavior Therapy and Experimental Psychiatry*, 34(1), 45–63. doi:10.1016/S0005-7916(03)00019-3

Fazio, R. J., Rashid, T., Hayward, H., & Lopez, S. J. (2008). Growth through loss and adversity: A choice worth making. In S. J. Lopez (Ed.), *Positive psychology: Exploring the best in people: Vol. 3, Growing in the face of adversity* (pp. 1–28). Westport, CT: Praeger.

Fehr, R., Gelfand, M. J., & Nag, M. (2010). The road to forgiveness: A meta-analytic synthesis of its situational and dispositional correlates. *Psychological Bulletin*, 136, 894–914. doi:10.1037/a0019993

Feldman, G. C., Joormann, J., & Johnson, S. L. (2008). Responses to positive affect: A self-report measure of rumination and dampening. *Cognitive Therapy and Research*, 32(4), 507–525. doi:10.1007/s10608-006-9083-0

Finlay, W. M. L., & Lyons, E. (2000). Social categorizations, social comparisons and stigma: Presentations of self in people with learning difficulties. *British Journal of Social Psychology*, 39, 129–146.

First, M. B., Spitzer, R. L., Gibbon, M., & Williams, J. (2007). *Structured Clinical Interview for DSM-IV-TR Axis I disorders, Research Version, Patient Edition (SCID-VP).* New York: Biometrics Research, New York State Psychiatric Institute.

Fisher, K., & Robinson, J. (2009). Average weekly time spent in 30 basic activities across 17 countries. *Social Indicators Research*, 93(1), 249–254. doi:10.1007/s11205-008-9372-y

Fitzpatrick, M. R., & Stalikas, A. (2008). Integrating positive emotions into theory, research, and practice: A new challenge for psychotherapy. *Journal of Psychotherapy Integration, 18,* 248–258.

Flinchbaugh, C. L., Moore, E. W. G., Chang, Y. K., & May, D. R. (2012). Student well-being interventions: The effects of stress management techniques and gratitude journaling in the management education classroom. *Journal of Management Education, 36*(2), 191–219. doi:10.1177/1052562911430062

Flückiger, C., Caspar, F., Holtforth, M. G., & Willutzki, U. (2009). Working with patients' strengths: A microprocess approach. *Psychotherapy Research, 19*(2), 213–223. https://doi.org/10.1080/10503300902755300

Flückiger, C., & Grosse Holtforth, M. (2008). Focusing the therapist's attention on the patient's strengths: A preliminary study to foster a mechanism of change in outpatient psychotherapy. *Journal of Clinical Psychology, 64,* 876–890.

Folkman, S., & Moskowitz, J. T. (2000). Positive affect and the other side of coping. *American Psychologist, 55*(6), 647–654.

Fordyce, M. W. (1983). A program to increase happiness: Further studies. *Journal of Consulting Psychology, 30,* 483–498.

Forest, J., Mageau, G. V. A., Crevier-Braud, L., Bergeron, L., Dubreuil, P., & Lavigne, G. V. L. (2012). Harmonious passion as an explanation of the relation between signature strengths' use and well-being at work: Test of an intervention program. *Human Relations, 65*(9), 1233–1252.

Forgeard, M. J. C., & Seligman, M. E. P. (2012). Seeing the glass half full: A review of the causes and consequences of optimism. *Pratiques Psychologiques, 18*(2), 107–120. doi:10.1016/j.prps.2012.02.002

Fowers, B. J. (2005). *Virtue and psychology: Pursuing excellent in ordinary practices.* Washington, DC: American Psychological Association.

Frank, J. D., & Frank, J. B. (1991). *Persuasion and healing: A comparative study of psychotherapy* (3rd ed.). Baltimore: Johns Hopkins University Press.

Frankl, V. E. (1963). *Man's search for meaning: An introduction to Logotherapy.* New York: Washington Square Press.

Frankl, V. E. (1986). *The doctor and the soul: From psychotherapy to Logotherapy.* New York: Penguin Books.

Frankl, V. E. (1988). *The will to meaning: Foundations and applications of Logotherapy.* Expanded Edition. New York: Penguin Books.

Frattaroli, J. (2006). Experimental disclosure and its moderators: A meta-analysis. *Psychological Bulletin, 132*(6), 823–865. http://doi.org/10.1037/0033-2909.132.6.823

Fredrickson, B. (2014). *Love 2.0: Creating happiness and health in moments of connection.* New York: Plume.

Fredrickson, B. L. (2001). The role of positive emotions in positive psychology. *American Psychologist, 56,* 218–226.

Fredrickson, B. L. (2009). *Positivity: Discover the ratio that tips your life toward flourishing.* New York: Crown.

Fredrickson, B. L., & Branigan, C. (2005). Positive emotions broaden the scope of attention and thought-action repertoires. *Cognition and Emotion, 19,* 313–332.

Fredrickson, B. L., Grewen, K. M., Coffey, K. A., Algoe, S. B., Firestine, A. M., Arevalo, J. M. G., . . . Cole, S. W. (2013). A functional genomic perspective on human well-being. *Proceedings of the National Academy of Sciences of the United States of America, 110*(33), 13684–13689. doi:10.1073/pnas.1305419110

Fredrickson, B. L., & Losada, M. F. (2005). Positive affect and the complex dynamics of human flourishing. *American Psychologist, 60*(7), 678–686.

Fredrickson, B. L., Tugade, M. M., Waugh, C. E., & Larkin, G. R. (2003). What good are positive emotions in crisis? A prospective study of resilience and emotions following the terrorist attacks on the United States on September 11th, 2001. *Journal of Personality and Social Psychology, 84,* 365–376.

Freidlin, P., Littman-Ovadia, H., & Niemiec, R. M. (2017). Positive psychopathology: Social anxiety via character strengths underuse and overuse. *Personality and Individual Differences, 108,* 50–54.

Frisch, M. B. (2013). Evidence-based well-being/positive psychology assessment and intervention with quality of life therapy and coaching and the Quality of Life Inventory (QOLI). *Social Indicators Research, 114*(2), 193–227. doi:10.1007/s11205-012-0140-7

Frisch, M. B. (2016). Quality of life therapy. In A. M. Wood, & J. Johnson (Eds.), *The Wiley handbook of positive clinical psychology* (pp. 409–425). Chichester, UK: John Wiley. http://doi.org/10.1002/9781118468197

Froh, J. J., Emmons, R. A., Card, N. A., Bono, G., & Wilson, J. A. (2011). Gratitude and the reduced costs of materialism in adolescents. *Journal of Happiness Studies, 12*(2), 289–302.

Fung, B. K., Ho, S. M., Fung, A. S., Leung, E. Y. P., Chow, S. P., Ip, W. Y., . . . Barlaan, P. I. G. (2011). The development of a strength-focused mutual support group for caretakers of children with cerebral palsy. *East Asian Archives of Psychiatry, 21*(2), 64.

Furchtlehner, L. M., & Laireiter, A.-R. (2016, September). *Comparing positive psychotherapy (PPT) and cognitive behavior therapy (CBT) in the treatment of depression: Preliminary ITT results from a RCT study.* Paper presented at the 1st Conference on Positive Psychology of DACH PP (German-language Association of Positive Psychology), Berlin.

Furnes, B., & Dysvik, E. (2013). Experiences of memory-writing in bereaved people. *Bereavement Care, 32*(2), 65–73. doi:10.1080/02682621.2013.812817

Gable, S. L., Reis, H. T., Impett, E. A., & Asher, E. R. (2004). What do you do when things go right? The intrapersonal and interpersonal benefits of sharing positive events. *Journal of Personality and Social Psychology, 87*, 228–245.

Gander, F., Proyer, R., Ruch, W., & Wyss, T. (2013). Strength-based positive interventions: Further evidence for their potential in enhancing well-being and alleviating depression. *Journal of Happiness Studies, 14*(4), 1241–1259. doi:10.1007/s10902-012-9380-0

Gelso, C. J., Nutt Williams, E., & Fretz, B. R. (2014). Working with strengths: Counseling psychology's calling. In *Counseling psychology* (3rd ed., pp. 157–178). Washington, DC: American Psychological Association. doi:10.1037/14378-007

Gilman, R., Schumm, J. A., & Chard, K. M. (2012). Hope as a change mechanism in the treatment of posttraumatic stress disorder. *Psychological Trauma: Theory, Research, Practice, and Policy, 4*, 270–277. doi:10.1037/a0024252

Glasgow, R. E., Vogt, T. M., & Boles, S. M. (1999). Evaluating the public health impact of health promotion interventions: The RE-AIM framework. *American Journal of Public Health, 89*, 1322–1327.

Glaw, X., Kable, A., Hazelton, M., & Inder, K. (2017). Meaning in life and meaning of life in mental health care: An integrative literature review. *Issues in Mental Health Nursing, 38*(3), 242–252.

Gobel, M. S., Chen, A., & Richardson, D. C. (2017). How different cultures look at faces depends on the interpersonal context. *Canadian Journal of Experimental Psychology, 71*(3), 258–264. http://dx.doi.org.myaccess.library.utoronto.ca/10.1037/cep0000119

Goodwin, E. M. (2010). *Does group positive psychotherapy help improve relationship satisfaction in a stressed and/or anxious population?* (Doctoral dissertation). Retrieved from *ProQuest Dissertations and Theses,* 166 (Order No. 3428275, Palo Alto University).

Govindji, R., & Linley, P. A. (2007). Strengths use, self-concordance and well-being: Implications for strengths coaching and coaching psychologists. *International Coaching Psychology Review, 2*, 143–153.

Grace, J. J., Kinsella, E. L., Muldoon, O. T., & Fortune, D. (2015). Post-traumatic growth following acquired brain injury: A systematic review and meta-analysis. *Frontiers in Psychology, 6*, 1162.

Grafanaki, S., Brennan, M., Holmes, S., Tang, K., & Alvarez, S. (2007). "In search of flow" in counselling and psychotherapy: Identifying the necessary ingredients of peak moments of therapy interaction, person-centered and experiential psychotherapies. *International Journal of Person-Centred and Experiential Psychotherapies, 6*, 239–255.

Graham, J. E., Lobel, M., Glass, P., & Lokshina, I. (2008). Effects of written constructive anger expression in chronic pain patients: Making meaning from pain. *Journal of Behavioral Medicine, 31*, 201–212.

Gratz, K. L., & Roemer, L. (2004). Multidimensional assessment of emotion regulation and dysregulation: Development, factor structure, and initial validation of the difficulties in emotion regulation scale. *Journal of Psychopathology and Behavioral Assessment, 26*, 41–54.

Gresham, F. M., & Elliott, S. N. (1990). *Social skills rating system manual.* Circle Pines, MN: American Guidance Service.

Guney, S. (2011). The Positive Psychotherapy Inventory (PPTI): Reliability and validity study in Turkish population. *Social and Behavioral Sciences, 29,* 81–86.

Güsewell, A., & Ruch, W. (2012). Are there multiple channels by which to connect with beauty and excellence? *Journal of Positive Psychology, 7,* 516–529. doi:10.1080/17439760.2012.726636

Hamilton, M. (1960). A rating scale for depression. *Journal of Neurology, Neurosurgery, and Psychiatry, 23,* 56–62.

Hanna, F. J. (2002). Building hope for change. In F. J. Hanna, *Therapy with difficult clients: Using the precursors model to awaken change* (pp. 265–273). Washington, DC: American Psychological Association.

Hansen, N. B., Lambert, M. J., & Forman, E. V. (2002). The psychotherapy dose-response effect and its implications for treatment delivery services. *Clinical Psychology: Science and Practice, 9,* 329–343.

Harris, A., & Thoresen, C. E. (2006). Extending the influence of positive psychology interventions into health care settings: Lessons from self-efficacy and forgiveness. *The Journal of Positive Psychology, 1,* 27–36.

Harris, A. H. S., Luskin, F., Norman, S. B., Standard, S., Bruning, J., Evans, S., & Thoresen, C. E. (2006). Effects of a group forgiveness intervention on forgiveness, perceived stress, and trait-anger. *Journal of Clinical Psychology, 62,* 715–733. doi:10.1002/jclp.20264

Harris, A. H. S., Thoresen, C. E., & Lopez, S. J. (2007). Integrating positive psychology into counseling: Why and (when appropriate) how. *Journal of Counseling & Development, 85,* 3–13.

Harrison, A., Al-Khairulla, H., & Kikoler, M. (2016). The feasibility, acceptability and possible benefit of a positive psychology intervention group in an adolescent inpatient eating disorder service. *The Journal of Positive Psychology, 11*(5), 449–459.

Harrison, R. L., & Westwood, M. J. (2009). Preventing vicarious traumatization of mental health therapists: Identifying protective practices. *Psychotherapy: Theory, Research, Practice, Training, 46*(2), 203–219. http://dx.doi.org/10.1037/a0016081

Hart, D. S. (2014). Review of lying down in the ever-falling snow: Canadian health professionals' experience of compassion fatigue. *Canadian Journal of Counselling and Psychotherapy, 48*(1), 77–79.

Harvey, A., Watkins, E., Mansell, W., & Shafran, R. (2004). *Cognitive behavioural processes across psychological disorders: A transdiagnostic approach to research and treatment.* New York: Oxford University Press.

Hawkes, D. (2011). Review of solution focused therapy for the helping professions. *Journal of Social Work Practice, 25*(3), 379–380.

Headey, B., Schupp, J., Tucci, I., & Wagner, G. G. (2010). Authentic happiness theory supported by impact of religion on life satisfaction: A longitudinal analysis with data for Germany. *The Journal of Positive Psychology, 5,* 73–82.

Heatherton, T. F., Kozlowski, L. T., Frecker, R. C., & Fagerström, K. (1991). The Fagerström test for nicotine dependence: A revision of the Fagerström tolerance questionnaire. *British Journal of Addiction, 86,* 1119–1127. http://dx.doi.org/10.1111/j.1360-0443.1991.tb01879.x

Hicks, J. A., & King, L. A. (2009). Meaning in life as a subjective judgment and a lived experience. *Social and Personality Psychology Compass, 3*(4), 638–658. doi:10.1111/j.1751-9004.2009.00193.x

Ho, H. C. Y., Yeung, D. Y., & Kwok, S. Y. C. L. (2014). Development and evaluation of the positive psychology intervention for older adults. *The Journal of Positive Psychology, 9*(3), 187–197. doi:10.1080/ 17439760.2014.888577

Holt-Lunstad, J., Smith, T. B., & Layton, J. B. (2010). Social relationships and mortality risk: A meta-analytic review. *PLoS Medicine, 7*(7). doi:10.1371/journal.pmed.1000316

Hone, L. C., Jarden, A., & Schofield, G. M. (2015). An evaluation of positive psychology intervention effectiveness trials using the re-aim framework: A practice-friendly review. *The Journal of Positive Psychology, 10*(4), 303–322. doi:10.1080/17439760.2014.965267

Honoré, C. (2005). *In praise of slowness: Challenging the cult of speed.* New York: HarperCollins.

Hortop, E. G., Wrosch, C., & Gagné, M. (2013). The why and how of goal pursuits: Effects of global autonomous motivation and perceived control on emotional well-being. *Motivation and Emotion, 37*(4), 675–687.

Horvath, A. O., Del Re, A. C., Flückiger, C., Symonds, D., Horvath, A. O., & Del Re, A. C. (2011). Alliance in individual psychotherapy. *Psychotherapy, 48*(1), 9–16.

Houltberg, B. J., Henry, C. S., Merten, M. J., & Robinson, L. C. (2011). Adolescents' perceptions of family connectedness, intrinsic religiosity, and depressed mood. *Journal of Child and Family Studies, 20*(1), 111–119.

Huebner, E. S. (1991). Initial development of the Students' Life Satisfaction Scale. *School Psychology International, 12*, 231–243.

Huffman, J. C., DuBois, C. M., Healy, B. C., Boehm, J. K., Kashdan, T. B., Celano, C. M., & Lyubomirsky, S. (2014). Feasibility and utility of positive psychology exercises for suicidal inpatients. *General Hospital Psychiatry, 36*(1), 88–94.

Huffman, J. C., DuBois, C. M., Millstein, R. A., Celano, C. M., & Wexler, D. (2015). Positive psychological interventions for patients with type 2 diabetes: Rationale, theoretical model, and intervention development. *Journal of Diabetes Research, 2015*, 1–18. doi:10.1155/2015/428349

Huffman, J. C., Mastromauro, C. A., Boehm, J. K., Seabrook, R., Fricchione, G. L., Denninger, J. W., & Lyubomirsky, S. (2011). Development of a positive psychology intervention for patients with acute cardiovascular disease. *Heart International, 6*(2). https://doi.org/10.4081/hi.2011.e14

Hunt, M., Auriemma, J., & Cashaw, A. C. A. (2003). Self-report bias and underreporting of depression on the BDI-II. *Journal of Personality Assessment, 80*, 26–30. doi:10.1207/S15327752JPA8001_10

Huta, V., & Hawley, L. (2008). Psychological strengths and cognitive vulnerabilities: Are they two ends of the same continuum or do they have independent relationships with well-being and ill-being? *Journal of Happiness Studies, 11*(1), 71–93. doi:10.1007/s10902-008-9123-4

Huynh, K. H., Hall, B., Hurst, M. A., & Bikos, L. H. (2015). Evaluation of the positive re-entry in corrections program: A positive psychology intervention with prison inmates. *International Journal of Offender Therapy and Comparative Criminology, 59*(9), 1006.

Hwang, K., Kwon, A., & Hong, C. (2017). A preliminary study of new positive psychology interventions: Neurofeedback-aided meditation therapy and modified positive psychotherapy. *Current Psychology, 36*(3), 683–695. http://doi.org/10.1007/s12144-016-9538-8

Jahoda, M. (1958). *Current concepts of positive mental health*. New York: Basic Books.

Jayawickreme, E., & Blackie, L. E. R. (2014). Post-traumatic growth as positive personality change: Evidence, controversies and future directions. *European Journal of Personality, 28*(4), 312–331.

Jelinek, L., Stockbauer, C., Randjbar, S., Kellner, M., Ehring, T., & Moritz, S. (2010). Characteristics and organization of the worst moment of trauma memories in posttraumatic stress disorder. *Behaviour Research and Therapy, 48*(7), 680–685. https://doi.org/10.1016/j.brat.2010.03.014

Johnson, D. P., Penn, D. L., Fredrickson, B. L., Meyer, P. S., Kring, A. M., & Brantley, M. (2009). Loving-kindness meditation to enhance recovery from negative symptoms of schizophrenia. *Journal of Clinical Psychology, 65*, 499–509. doi:10.1002/jclp.20591

Johnson, J., Gooding, P. A., Wood, A. M., & Tarrier, N. (2010). Resilience as positive coping appraisals: Testing the schematic appraisals model of suicide (SAMS). *Behaviour Research and Therapy, 48*, 179–186.

Johnson, J., Gooding, P. A., Wood, A. M., Taylor, P. J., Pratt, D., & Tarrier, N. (2010). Resilience to suicidal ideation in psychosis: Positive self-appraisals buffer the impact of hopelessness. *Behaviour Research and Therapy, 48*, 883–889.

Johnson, J., & Wood, A. M. (2017). Integrating positive and clinical psychology: Viewing human functioning as continua from positive to negative can benefit clinical assessment, interventions and understandings of resilience. *Cognitive Therapy and Research, 41*(3), 335–349. doi:10.1007/s10608-015-9728-y

Joormann, J., Dkane, M., & Gotlib, I. H. (2006). Adaptive and maladaptive components of rumination? Diagnostic specificity and relation to depressive biases. *Behavior Therapy, 37*, 269–280. doi:10.1016/j.beth.2006.01.002

Joormann, J., & Siemer, M. (2004). Memory accessibility, mood regulation, and dysphoria: Difficulties in repairing sad mood with happy memories? *Journal of Abnormal Psychology, 113*(2), 179–188. doi:10.1037/0021-843X.113.2.179

Joormann, J., Siemer, M., & Gotlib, I. H. (2007). Mood regulation in depression: Differential effects of distraction and recall of happy memories on sad mood. *Journal of Abnormal Psychology, 116*(3), 484–490. doi:10.1037/0021-843X.116.3.484

Joseph, S., & Linley, A. P. (2006). *Positive therapy: A meta-theory for positive psychological practice*. New York: Rutledge.

Kahler, C. W., Spillane, N. S., Day, A. M., Cioe, P. A., Parks, A., Leventhal, A. M., & Brown, R. A. (2015). Positive psychotherapy for smoking cessation: A pilot randomized controlled trial. *Nicotine & Tobacco Research, 17*(11), 1385–1392.

Kahneman, D. (2011). *Thinking fast and slow*. London: Allen Lane.

Kahneman, D., Krueger, A. B., Schkade, D., Schwarz, N., Stone, A. A., Schwartz, N., & Stone, A. A. (2006). Would you be happier if you were richer? A focusing illusion. *Science, 312*(5782), 1908–1910. doi:10.1126/science.1129688

Kaitlin, A. H., Karly, M. M., & Mezulis, A. (2017). Ruminating on the positive: Paths from trait positive emotionality to event-specific gratitude. *Journal of Happiness Studies*, 1–17. https://doi.org/10.1007/s10902-017-9940-4

Kapur, N., Cole, J., Manly, T., Viskontas, I., Ninteman, A., Hasher, L., & Pascual-Leone, A. (2013). Positive clinical neuroscience: Explorations in positive neurology. *The Neuroscientist, 19*(4), 354–369. doi:10.1177/ 1073858412470976

Kashdan, T. B., Julian, T., Merritt, K., & Uswatte, G. (2006). Social anxiety and posttraumatic stress in combat veterans: Relations to well-being and character strengths. *Behaviour Research and Therapy, 44*, 561–583.

Kashdan, T. B., & Rottenberg, J. (2010). Psychological flexibility as a fundamental aspect of health. *Clinical Psychology Review, 30*, 865–878.

Kasser, T. (2002). *The high price of materialism*. Cambridge, MA: MIT Press.

Kasser, T., & Kanner, A. D. (Eds.). (2004). *Psychology and consumer culture: The struggle for a good life in a materialistic world*. Washington, DC: American Psychological Association. http://dx.doi.org/10.1037/10658-000

Kazdin, A. E. (2009). Understanding how and why psychotherapy leads to change. *Psychotherapy Research, 19*(4–5), 418–428.

Kelly, J. R. (1997). Changing issues in leisure-family research—again. *Journal of Leisure Research, 29*(1), 132–134.

Kern, M. L., Waters, L. E., Adler, A., & White, M. A. (2015). A multidimensional approach to measuring well-being in students: Application of the PERMA framework. *The Journal of Positive Psychology, 10*(3), 262–271. https://doi.org/10.1080/17439760.2014.936962

Kerner, E. A., & Fitzpatrick, M. R. (2007). Integrating writing into psychotherapy practice: A matrix of change processes and structural dimensions. *Psychotherapy: Theory, Research, Practice, Training, 44*(3), 333–346.

Kerr, S. L., O'Donovan, A., & Pepping, C. A. (2015). Can gratitude and kindness interventions enhance well-being in a clinical sample? *Journal of Happiness Studies, 16*(1), 17–36. http://dx.doi.org/10.1007/s10902-013-9492-1

Keyes, C. L. M. (2013). *Promotion and protection of positive mental health: Towards complete mental health in human development*. New York: Oxford University Press.

Keyes, C. L M., & Eduardo, J. S. (2012). To flourish or not: Level of positive mental health predicts ten-year all-cause mortality. *American Journal of Public Health 102*, 2164–2172.

Khanjani, M., Shahidi, S., FathAbadi, J., Mazaheri, M. A., & Shokri, O. (2014). The factor structure and psychometric properties of the Positive Psychotherapy Inventory (PPTI) in an Iranian sample. *Iranian Journal of Applied Psychology, 7*(5), 26–47. (In Persian)

Khumalo, I. P.,Wissing, M. P., & Temane, Q. M. (2008). Exploring the validity of the Values-In-Action Inventory of Strengths (VIA-IS) in an African context. *Journal of Psychology in Africa, 18*, 133–142. doi:10.1080/14330237.2008.10820180

King L. A., & Milner, K. N. (2000). Writing about the perceived benefits of traumatic events: Implications for physical health. *Personality and Social Psychology Bulletin. 26*, 220–230.

Kirsch, I., Moore, T. J., Scoboria, A., & Nicholls, S. S. (2002). The emperor's new drugs: An analysis of antidepressant medication data submitted to the U.S. Food and Drug Administration. *Prevention & Treatment, 5,* art. 23.

Kitayama, S., & Markus, H. R. (2000). The pursuit of happiness and the realization of sympathy: Cultural patterns of self, social relations, and well-being. In J. B. P. Sinha (Ed.), *Culture and subjective well-being* (pp. 113–161). Thousand Oaks, CA: SAGE.

Kleinsmith, A., De Silva, P. R., & Bianchi-Berthouze, N. (2006). Cross-cultural differences in recognizing affect from body posture. *Interacting with Computers, 18*(6), 1371–1389.

Ko, Y. S., & Hyun, M. Y. (2015). Effects of a positive psychotherapy program on depression, self-esteem, and hope in patients with major depressive disorders. *Journal of Korean Academy of Psychiatric and Mental Health Nursing, 24*(4), 246. https://doi.org/10.12934/jkpmhn.2015.24.4.246

Kovacs, M. (1992). *Children Depression Inventory: Manual.* New York: Multi Health System.

Kross, E., Ayduk, O., & Mischel, W. (2005). When asking "why" doesn't hurt: Distinguishing reflective processing of negative emotions from rumination. *Psychological Science, 16,* 709–715.

Lai, J. C. L., & Yue, X. (2000). Measuring optimism in Hong Kong and mainland Chinese with the revised life orientation test. *Personality and Individual Differences, 28*(4), 781–796.

Lambert, M. (2007). Presidential address: What we have learned from a decade of research aimed at improving psychotherapy outcome in routine care. *Psychotherapy Research, 17*(1), 1–14. doi:10.1080/10503300601032506

Lambert, M. J. (2013). Outcome in psychotherapy: The past and important advances. *Psychotherapy, 50*(1), 42–51.

Lambert, M. J., Burlingame, G. M., Umphress, V. J., Hansen, N. B., Vermeersch, D., Clouse, G., & Yanchar, S. (1996). The reliability and validity of the Outcome Questionnaire. *Clinical Psychology and Psychotherapy, 3,*106–116.

Lambert, M. J., Hansen, N. B., & Finch, A. E. (2001). Patient-focused research: Using patient outcome data to enhance treatment effects. *Journal of Consulting and Clinical Psychology, 69*(2), 159–172. Retrieved from http://www.ncbi.nlm.nih.gov/pubmed/11393594

Lambert, M. J., Whipple, J. L., Hawkins, E. J., Vermeersch, D. A., Nielsen, S. L., & Smart, D. W. (2003). Is it time for clinicians to routinely track patient outcome? A meta-analysis. *Clinical Psychology: Science and Practice, 10,* 288–301.

Lambert, N. M., Fincham, F. D., & Stillman, T. F. (2012). Gratitude and depressive symptoms: The role of positive reframing and positive emotion. *Cognition and Emotion, 26*(4), 615–633. doi:10.1080 /02699931.2011.595393

Lambert D'raven, L. T., Moliver, N., & Thompson, D. (2015). Happiness intervention decreases pain and depression, boosts happiness among primary care patients. Primary *Health Care Research & Development, 16*(2), 114–126. https://doi.org/10.1017/S146342361300056X

Lambert D'raven, L., & Pasha-Zaidi, N. (2016). Using the PERMA model in the United Arab Emirates. *Social Indicators Research, 125*(3), 905–933.

Lamont, A. (2011). University students' strong experiences of music: Pleasure, engagement, and meaning. *Music and Emotion, 15,* 229–249.

Langston, C. A., & Langston, C. A. (1994). Capitalizing on and coping with daily-life events: Expressive responses to positive events. *Journal of Personality and Social Psychology, 67*(6), 1112–1125. doi:10.1037/0022-3514.67.6.1112

Larsen, D., Edey, W., & Lemay, L. (2007). Understanding the role of hope in counselling: Exploring the intentional uses of hope. *Counselling Psychology Quarterly, 20*(4), 401–416.

Larsen, D. L., Attkisson, C. C., Hargreaves, W. A., & Nguyen, T. D. (1979). Assessment of client/patient satisfaction: Development of a general scale. *Evaluation and Program Planning, 2,* 197–207. http://dx.doi.org/10.1016/0149-7189(79)90094-6

Larsen, D. J., & Stege, R. (2010). Hope-focused practices during early psychotherapy sessions: Part I: Implicit approaches. *Journal of Psychotherapy Integration, 20*(3), 271–292. doi:10.1037/a0020820

Le Boutillier, C., Leamy, M., Bird, V., Davidson, L., Williams, J., & Slade, M. (2011). What does recovery mean in practice? A qualitative analysis of international recovery-oriented practice guidance. *Psychiatric Services, 62,* 1470–1476.

Lemay, E. P. Jr., Clark, M. S., & Feeney, B. C. (2007). Projection of responsiveness to needs and the construction of satisfying communal relationships. *Journal of Personality & Social Psychology*, *92*, 834–853.

Leotti, L. A., Iyengar, S. S., & Ochsner, K. N. (2010). Born to choose: The origins and value of the need for control. *Trends in Cognitive Sciences*, *14*(10), 457–463.

Leykin, Y., & DeRubeis, R. J. (2009). Allegiance in psychotherapy outcome research: Separating association from bias. *Clinical Psychology: Science and Practice*, *16*, 54–65. doi:10.1111/j.1468-2850.2009.01143.x

Lightsey, O. (2006). Resilience, meaning, and well-being. *The Counseling Psychologist*, *34*, 96–107. doi:10.1177/0011000005282369

Lin, A. (2001). *Exploring sources of life meaning among Chinese* (Unpublished master's thesis). Langley: Trinity Western University.

Linley, P. A. (2008). *Average to A+: Realising strengths in yourself and others.* Leicester, UK: CAPP Press.

Linley, P. A., Nielsen, K. M., Wood, A. M., Gillett, R., & Biswas-Diener, R. (2010). Using signature strengths in pursuit of goals: Effects on goal progress, need satisfaction, and well-being, and implications for coaching psychologists. *International Coaching Psychology Review*, *5*, 8–17.

Littman-Ovadia, H., & Lavy, S. (2012). Character strengths in Israel. *European Journal of Psychological Assessment*, *28*, 41–50. doi:10.1027/1015-5759/a000089

Littman-Ovadia, H., & Steger, M. (2010). Character strengths and well-being among volunteers and employees: Toward an integrative model. *The Journal of Positive Psychology*, *5*(6), 419–430. https://doi.org/10.1080/17439760.2010.516765

Long, E. C. J., Angera, J. J., Carter, S. J., Nakamoto, M., & Kalso, M. (1999). Understanding the one you love: A longitudinal assessment of an empathy training program for couples in romantic relationships. *Family Relations*, *48*(3), 235. https://doi.org/10.2307/585632

Lounsbury, J. W., Fisher, L. A., Levy, J. J., & Welsh, D. P. (2009). Investigation of character strengths in relation to the academic success of college students. *Individual Differences Research*, *7*(1), 52–69.

Lü, W., Wang, Z., & Liu, Y. (2013). A pilot study on changes of cardiac vagal tone in individuals with low trait positive affect: The effect of positive psychotherapy. *International Journal of Psychophysiology*, *88*(2), 213–217.

Lucas, R. E. (2007). Adaptation and the set-point model of subjective well-being: Does happiness change after major life events? *Current Directions in Psychological Science*, *16*(2), 75–79. doi:10.1111/j.1467-8721.2007.00479.x

Lyubormirsky, S. (2007). *The how of happiness: A scientific approach to getting the life you want.* New York: Penguin.

Lyubomirsky, S., King, L., & Diener, E. (2005). The benefits of frequent positive affect: Does happiness lead to success? *Psychological Bulletin*, *131*(6), 803–855. doi:10.1037/0033-2909.131.6.803

Lyubomirsky, S., & Layous, K. (2013). How do simple positive activities increase well-being? *Current Directions in Psychological Science*, *22*, 57–62. doi:10.1177/0963721412469809

Macaskill, A. (2016). Review of positive psychology applications in clinical medical populations. *Healthcare*, *4*(3), 66.

Macaskill, A., & Denovan, A. (2014). Assessing psychological health: The contribution of psychological strengths. *British Journal of Guidance & Counselling*, *42*(3), 320–337. doi:10.1080/03069885.2014.898739

Maddux, J. E. (2008). Positive psychology and the illness ideology: Toward a positive clinical psychology. *Applied Psychology*, *57*, 54–70. doi:10.1111/j.1464-0597.2008.00354.x

Maisel, N. C., & Gable, S. L. (2009). The paradox of received support: The importance of responsiveness. *Psychological Science*, *20*, 928–932.

Markus, H., & Nurius, P. (1986). Possible selves. *American Psychologist*, *41*, 954–969.

Marques, S. C., Pais-Ribeiro, J. L., & Lopez, S. J. (2011). The role of positive psychology constructs in predicting mental health and academic achievement in children and adolescents: A two-year longitudinal study. *Journal of Happiness Studies*, *12*(6), 1049–1062. doi:10.1007/s10902-010-9244-4

Martinez-Marti, M. L., & Ruch, W. (2014). Character strengths and well-being across the life span: Data from a representative sample of German-speaking adults living in Switzerland. *Frontiers in Psychology, 5*, 1253. doi: 10.3389/fpsyg.2014.01253

Martínez-Martí, M. L., & Ruch, W. (2017). Character strengths predict resilience over and above positive affect, self-efficacy, optimism, social support, self-esteem, and life satisfaction. *The Journal of Positive Psychology, 12*(2), 110–119.

Maslow, A. H. (1970). *Motivation and personality* (2nd ed.). New York: Harper & Row.

Mazzucchelli, T., Kane, R., & Rees, C. (2009). Behavioral activation treatments for depression in adults: A meta-analysis and review. *Clinical Psychology: Science and Practice, 16*(4), 383–411. http://doi.org/10.1111/j.1468-2850.2009.01178.x

Mazzucchelli, T. G., Kane, R. T., & Rees, C. S. (2010). Behavioral activation interventions for well-being: A meta-analysis. *The Journal of Positive Psychology, 5*(2), 105–121. doi:10.1080/17439760903569154

McAdams, D. P. (2008). Personal narratives and the life story. In O. P. John, R. W. Robins, & L. A. Pervin (Eds.), *Handbook of personality: Theory and research* (3rd ed., pp. 242–262). New York: Guilford Press.

McCormick, B. P., Funderburk, J. A., Lee, Y., & Hale-Fought, M. (2005). Activity characteristics and emotional experience: Predicting boredom and anxiety in the daily life of community mental health clients. *Journal of Leisure Research, 37*, 236–253.

McCullough, M. E. (2008). *Beyond revenge: The evolution of the forgiveness instinct.* San Francisco: Jossey-Bass.

McCullough, M. E., Pedersen, E. J., Tabak, B. A., & Carter, E. C. (2014). Conciliatory gestures promote forgiveness and reduce anger in humans. *Proceedings of the National Academy of Sciences of the United States of America, 111*(30), 12111–12116.

McGrath, R. E. (2015). Integrating psychological and cultural perspectives on virtue: The hierarchical structure of character strengths. *The Journal of Positive Psychology, 10*(5), 407–424.

McKnight, P. E., & Kashdan, T. B. (2009). Purpose in life as a system that creates and sustains health and well-being: An integrative, testable theory. *Review of General Psychology, 13*(3), 242–251. http://doi.org/10.1037/a0017152

McLean, K. C., Pasupathi, M., & Pals. J. L. (2007). Selves creating stories creating selves: A process model of narrative self development in adolescence and adulthood. *Personality and Social Psychology Review, 11*, 262–278.

McLean, K. C., & Pratt, M. W. (2006). Life's little (and big) lessons: Identity statuses and meaning-making in the turning point narratives of emerging adults. *Developmental Psychology, 42*(4), 714–722. doi:10.1037/0012-1649.42.4.714

McNulty, J. K., & Fincham, F. D. (2012). Beyond positive psychology? Toward a contextual view of psychological process and well-being. *American Psychologist, 67*, 101–110.

McWilliams, N. (1994). *Psychoanalytic diagnosis.* New York: Guilford Press.

Messias, E., Saini, A., Sinato, P., & Welch, S. (2010). Bearing grudges and physical health: Relationship to smoking, cardiovascular health and ulcers. *Social Psychiatry and Psychiatric Epidemiology, 45*(2), 183–187.

Meyer, P. S., Johnson, D. P., Parks, A., Iwanski, C., & Penn, D. L. (2012). Positive living: A pilot study of group positive psychotherapy for people with schizophrenia. *The Journal of Positive Psychology, 7*, 239–248. doi:10.1080/17439760.2012.677467

Michalak, J., & Holtforth, M. G. (2006). Where do we go from here? The goal perspective in psychotherapy. *Clinical Psychology: Science and Practice, 13*(4), 346–365. doi:10.1111/j.1468-2850.2006.00048.x

Minear, M., Brasher, F., McCurdy, M., Lewis, J., & Younggren, A. (2013). Working memory, fluid intelligence, and impulsiveness in heavy media multitaskers. *Psychonomic Bulletin & Review, 20*(6), 1274–1281. doi:10.3758/s13423-013-0456-6

Mitchell, J., Stanimirovic, R., Klein, B., & Vella-Brodrick, D. (2009). A randomised controlled trial of a self-guided Internet intervention promoting well-being. *Computers in Human Behavior, 25*, 749–760. doi:10.1016/j.chb.2009.02.003

Mongrain, M., & Anselmo- Matthews, T. (2012). Do positive psychology exercises work? A replication of Seligman et al. (2005). *Journal of Clinical Psychology, 68*, 382–389.

Montgomery S. A., & Asberg, M. (1979). A new depression scale designed to be sensitive to change. *British Journal of Psychiatry, 134*, 382–389.

Morganson, V. J., Litano, M. L., & O'Neill, S. K. (2014). Promoting work–family balance through positive psychology: A practical review of the literature. *The Psychologist-Manager Journal, 17*(4), 221–244. https://doi.org/10.1037/mgr0000023

Müller, R., Gertz, K. J., Molton, I. R., Terrill, A. L., Bombardier, C. H., Ehde, D. M., & Jensen, M. P. (2016). Effects of a tailored positive psychology intervention on well-being and pain in individuals with chronic pain and a physical disability: A feasibility trial. *The Clinical Journal of Pain, 32*(1), 32–44.

Murray, G., & Johnson, S. L. (2010). The clinical significance of creativity in bipolar disorder. *Clinical Psychology Review, 30*, 721–732. doi:10.1016/j.cpr.2010.05.006

Murray, H. A. (1938). *Explorations in personality.* Oxford: Oxford University Press.

Musick, M. A., & Wilson, J. (2003). Volunteering and depression: The role of psychological and social resources in different age groups. *Social Science & Medicine, 56*(2), 259–269.

Nakamura, J., & Csikszentmihalyi, M. (2002). The concept of flow. In C. R. Snyder & S. J. Lopez (Eds.), *Handbook of positive psychology* (pp. 89–105). New York and Oxford: Oxford University Press.

National Collaborating Centre for Methods and Tools. (2008). *Quality assessment tool for quantitative studies: Effective public health practice project.* Hamilton, ON: McMaster University.

Nedelcu, A. M., & Michod, R. E. (2006). The evolutionary origin of an altruistic gene. *Molecular Biology And Evolution, 23*(8), 1460–1464.

Neimeyer, R. A., Burke, L. A., Mackay, M. M., & van Dyke Stringer, J. G. (2010). Grief therapy and the reconstruction of meaning: From principles to practice. *Journal of Contemporary Psychotherapy, 40*, 73–83. doi:10.1007/s10879-009-9135-3

Nelson, C., & Johnston, M. (2008). Adult Needs and Strengths Assessment–abbreviated referral version to specify psychiatric care needed for incoming patients: Exploratory analysis. *Psychological Reports, 102*, 131–143.

Nes, L. S., & Segerstrom, S. C. (2006). Dispositional optimism and coping: A meta-analytic review. *Personality and Social Psychology Review, 10*(3), 235–251. doi:10.1207/s15327957pspr1003_3

Newman, C. F., Leahy, R. L., Beck, A. T., Reilly-Harrington, N. A., & Gyulai, L. (2002). *Bipolar disorder: A cognitive therapy approach.* Washington, DC: American Psychological Association.

Niemiec, R., & Wedding, D. (2013). Positive psychology at the movies: *Using films to build virtues and character strengths* (3rd ed.): Cambridge, MA: Hogrefe & Huber.

Nikrahan, G. R., Laferton, J. A. C., Asgari, K., Kalantari, M., Abedi, M. R., Etesampour, A., . . . Huffman, J. C. (2016). Effects of positive psychology interventions on risk biomarkers in coronary patients: A randomized, wait-list controlled pilot trial. *Psychosomatics, 57*(4), 359–368.

Nisbett, R. E. (2008). Eastern and Western ways of perceiving the world. In Y. Shoda, D. Cervone, & G. Downey (Eds.), *Persons in context: Constructing a science of the individual* (pp. 62–83). New York: Guildford Press.

Nolen-Hoeksema, S., & Davis, C.G. (1999). "Thanks for sharing that": Ruminators and their social support networks. *Journal of Personality and Social Psychology, 77*, 801–814.

Nolen-Hoeksema, S., Wisco, B., & Lyubomirsky, S. (2008). Rethinking rumination. *Perspectives on Psychological Science, 3*(5), 400–424.

Norem, J. K., & Chang, E. C. (2001). A very full glass: Adding complexity to our thinking about the implications and applications of optimism and pessimism research. In E. C. Chang (Ed.), *Optimism and pessimism: Implications for theory, research and practice* (pp. 347–367). Washington, DC: APA Press.

Ochoa, C., Casellas-Grau, A., Vives, J., Font, A., & Borràs, J. (2017). Positive psychotherapy for distressed cancer survivors: Posttraumatic growth facilitation reduces posttraumatic stress. *International Journal of Clinical and Health Psychology, 17*(1), 28–37.

O'Connell, B. H., O'Shea, D., & Gallagher, S. (2016). Enhancing social relationships through positive psychology activities: A randomised controlled trial. *The Journal of Positive Psychology, 11*(2), 149–162.

Odou, N., & Vella-Brodrick, D. A. (2013). The efficacy of positive psychology interventions to increase well-being and the role of mental imagery ability. *Social Indicators Research, 110*(1), 111–129. doi:10.1007/s11205-011-9919-1

Oettingen, G., & Gollwitzer, P. M. (2009). Embodied goal pursuit. *European Journal of Social Psychology, 39*(7), 1210–1213.

Oksanen, T., Kouvonen, A., Vahtera, J., Virtanen, M., & Kivimäki, M. (2010). Prospective study of workplace social capital and depression: Are vertical and horizontal components equally important? *Journal of Epidemiology and Community Health, 64*, 684–689. doi:10.1136/jech.2008.086074

Overall, J. E., & Gorham, D. R. (1962). The Brief Psychiatric Rating Scale. *Psychological Reports, 10*, 790–812.

Park, C. L., & Blumberg, C. J. (2002). Disclosing trauma through writing: Testing the meaning-making hypothesis. *Cognitive Therapy and Research, 26*, 597–616.

Park, N., & Peterson, C. (2006). Values in Action (VIA) inventory of character strengths for youth. *Adolescent & Family Health, 4*, 35–40.

Park, N., Peterson, C., & Seligman, M. E. P. (2004). Strengths of character and well-being. *Journal of Social & Clinical Psychology, 23*, 603–619.

Parks, A. C., & Schueller, S. M. (Eds.). (2014). *The Wiley-Blackwell handbook of positive psychological interventions*. Oxford: Wiley-Blackwell.

Parks, A., Della Porta, M., Pierce, R. S., Zilca, R., & Lyubomirsky, S. (2012). Pursuing happiness in everyday life: The characteristics and behaviors of online happiness seekers. *Emotion, 12*, 1222–1234.

Parks-Sheiner, A. C. (2009). *Positive psychotherapy: Building a model of empirically supported self-help* (Doctoral dissertation). University of Pennsylvania.

Pediaditakis, N. (2014). The association between major mental disorders and geniuses. *Psychiatric Times, 31*(9). 32.

Pedrotti, J. T. (2011). Broadening perspectives: Strategies to infuse multiculturalism into a positive psychology course. *The Journal of Positive Psychology, 6*(6), 506–513. doi:10.1080 /17439760.2011.634817

Peeters, G., & Czapinski, J. (1990). Positive-negative asymmetry in evaluations: The distinction between affective and informational negativity effects. *European Review of Social Psychology, 1*, 33–60.

Pennebaker, J. W. (1997). *Opening up: The healing power of expressing emotions*. New York: Guildford Press.

Pennebaker, J. W., & Evans, J. F. (2014). *Expressive writing: Words that heal*. Enumclaw, WA: Idyll Arbor.

Peseschkian, N. (2000). *Positive psychotherapy*. New Delhi: Sterling.

Peseschkian, N., & Tritt, K. (1998). Positive psychotherapy: Effectiveness study and quality assurance. *The European Journal of Psychotherapy, 1*, 93–104.

Peterson, C. (2006). *Primer in positive psychology*. New York: Oxford University Press.

Peterson, C., Park, N., & Seligman, M. E. P. (2005). Orientations to happiness and life satisfaction: The full life versus the empty life. *Journal of Happiness Studies, 6*, 25–41.

Peterson, C., Ruch, W., Beerman, U., Park, N., & Seligman, M. E. P. (2007). Strengths of character, orientations to happiness, and life satisfaction. *The Journal of Positive Psychology, 2*, 149–156.

Peterson, C., & Seligman, M. E. P. (2004). *Character strengths and virtues: A handbook and classification*. New York and Oxford: Oxford University Press and Washington, DC: American Psychological Association.

Phillips, L., & Rolfe, A. (2016). Words that work? Exploring client writing in therapy. *Counselling and Psychotherapy Research, 16*(3), 193–200.

Pillemer, K., Fuller-Rowell, T. E., Reid, M. C., & Wells, N. M. (2010). Environmental volunteering and health outcomes over a 20-year period. *The Gerontologist, 50*, 594–602. doi:10.1093/geront/gnq007

Pine, A., & Houston, J. (1993). *One door closes, another door opens*. Toronto: Delacorte/Random House Canada.

Pirkis, J. E., Burgess, P. M., Kirk, P. K., Dodson, S., Coombs, T. J., & Williamson, M. K. (2005). A review of the psychometric properties of the Health of the Nation Outcome Scales (HoNOS) family of measures. *Health and Quality of Life Outcomes, 3*(1), 76.

Pratto, F., & John, O. P. (1991). Automatic vigilance: The attention grabbing power of negative social information. *Journal of Personality and Social Psychology, 61*, 380–391.

Proctor, C., Tsukayama, E., Wood, A. M., Maltby, J., Eades, J. F., & Linley, P. A. (2011). Strengths gym: The impact of a character strengths-based intervention on the life satisfaction and well-being of adolescents. *The Journal of Positive Psychology, 6*(5), 377–388. https://doi.org/10.1080/17439760.2011.594079

Proyer, R. T., Gander, F., Wellenzohn, S., & Ruch, W. (2013).What good are character strengths beyond subjective well-being? The contribution of the good character oneself-reported health-oriented behavior, physical fitness, and the subjective health status. *The Journal of Positive Psychology, 8*, 222–232.doi:10.1080/17439760.2013.777767

Putnam, R. (2000). *Bowling alone: The collapse and revival of American community.* New York: Simon & Schuster.

Quinlan, D., Swain, N., & Vella-Brodrick, D. A. (2012). Character strengths interventions: Building on what we know for improved outcomes. *Journal of Happiness Studies, 13*(6), 1145–1163. doi:10.1007/s10902-011-9311-5

Quinlan, D. M., Swain, N., Cameron, C., & Vella-Brodrick, D. A. (2015). How "other people matter" in a classroom-based strengths intervention: Exploring interpersonal strategies and classroom outcomes. *The Journal of Positive Psychology, 10*(1), 77–89.

Quoidbach, J., Mikolajczak, M., & Gross, J. J. (2015). Positive interventions: An emotion regulation perspective. *Psychological Bulletin, 141*(3), 655.

Radloff, L. (1977). The CES-D Scale. *Applied Psychological Measurement, 1*, 385–401. doi:10.1177/014662167700100306

Rapp, C. A., & Goscha, R. J. (2006). *The Strengths Model: Case management with people with psychiatric disabilities* (2nd ed.). New York: Oxford University Press.

Rashid, T. (2004). Enhancing strengths through the teaching of positive psychology. *Dissertation Abstracts International, 64*, 6339.

Rashid, T., & Anjum, A. (2008). Positive psychotherapy for young adults and children. In J. R. Z. Abela & B. L. Hankin (Eds.), *Handbook of depression in children and adolescents* (1st ed., pp. 250–287). New York: Guilford Press.

Rashid, T., Anjum, A., Lennex, C., Quinlin, D., Niemiec, R., Mayerson, D., & Kazemi, F. (2013). In C. Proctor & A. Linley (Eds.), *Research, applications, and interventions for children and adolescents: A positive psychology perspective* (2017). New York: Springer.

Rashid, T., Summers, R., & Seligman, M. E. P. (2015). Positive Psychology; Chapter 30, pp-489-499., In A. Tasman., J. Kay, J. Lieberman, M. First & M. Riba (Eds.), *Psychiatry* (Fourth Edition). Wiley-Blackwell.

Rashid, T., & Howes, R. N. (2016). Positive psychotherapy. In A. M. Wood & J. Johnson (Eds.), *The Wiley handbook of positive clinical psychology* (pp. 321–347). Chichester, UK: John Wiley. http://doi.org/10.1002/9781118468197

Rashid, T., Howes, R., & Louden, R. (2017). Positive psychotherapy. In M. Slad, L. Oades, & A. Jarden (Eds.), *Wellbeing, recovery and mental health* (pp. 112–132). New York: Cambridge University Press.

Rashid, T., & Louden, R. (2013). *Student Engagement Inventory (SEI).* Unpublished data. University of Toronto Scarborough.

Rashid, T., Louden, R., Wright, L., Chu, R., Lutchmie-Maharaj A., Hakim, I., . . . Kidd, B. (2017). Flourish: A strengths-based approach to building student resilience. In C. Proctor (Ed.), *Positive psychology interventions in practice* (pp. 29–45). Amsterdam: Springer.

Rashid, T., & Ostermann, R. F. O. (2009). Strength-based assessment in clinical practice. *Journal of Clinical Psychology, 65*, 488–498.

Rashid, T., & Seligman, M. E. P. (2013). Positive psychotherapy. In D. Wedding & R. J. Corsini (Eds.), *Current psychotherapies* (pp. 461–498). Belmont, CA: Cengage.

Redondo, R. L., Kim, J., Arons, A. L., Ramirez, S., Liu, X., & Tonegawa, S. (2014). Bidirectional switch of the valence associated with a hippocampal contextual memory engram. *Nature, 513*, 426–430. doi:10.1038/nature13725

Reinsch, C. (2014, May). *Adding science to the mix of business and pleasure: An exploratory study of positive psychology interventions with teachers accessing employee assistance counselling.* Paper presented at the Canadian Counselling Psychology's Annual Convention, Manitoba.

Retnowati, S., Ramadiyanti, D. W., Suciati, A. A., Sokang, Y. A., & Viola, H. (2015). Hope intervention against depression in the survivors of cold lava flood from Merapi Mount. *Procedia—Social and Behavioral Sciences, 165*, 170–178. http://doi.org/10.1016/j.sbspro.2014.12.619

Rief, W., Nestoriuc, Y., Weiss, S., Welzel, E., Barsky, A. J., & Hofmann, S. G. (2009). Meta-analysis of the placebo response in antidepressant trials. *Journal of Affective Disorders, 118*(1), 1–8.

Roepke, A. M. (2015). Psychosocial interventions and posttraumatic growth: A meta-analysis. *Journal of Consulting and Clinical Psychology, 83*(1), 129–142.

Ronningstam, E. (2016). Pathological narcissism and narcissistic personality disorder: Recent research and clinical implications. *Current Behavioral Neuroscience Reports, 3*(1), 34–42. doi:10.1007/s40473-016-0060-y

Rozin, P., & Royzman, E. (2001). Negativity bias, negativity dominance, and contagion. *Personality and Social Psychology Review, 5*, 296–320.

Ruch, W., Huber, A., Beermann, U., & Proyer, R. T.(2007). Character strengths as predictors of the "good life" in Austria, Germany and Switzerland. In Romanian Academy, George Barit Institute of History, and Department of Social Research (Eds.), *Studies and researches in social sciences series humanistica* (pp. 123–131). Cluj-Napoca: Argonaut Press. doi:10.5167/uzh-3648

Ruckenbauer, G., Yazdani, F., & Ravaglia, G. (2007). Suicide in old age: Illness or autonomous decision of the will? *Archives of Gerontology and Geriatrics, 44*, 355–358.

Ruini, C., & Fava, G. A. (2009). Well-being therapy for generalized anxiety disorder. *Journal of Clinical Psychology, 65*, 510–519.

Ruini, C., & Vescovelli, F. (2013). The role of gratitude in breast cancer: Its relationships with post-traumatic growth, psychological well-being and distress. *Journal of Happiness Studies, 14*(1), 263–274. doi:10.1007/s10902-012-9330-x

Rust, T., Diessner, R., & Reade, L. (2009). Strengths only or strengths and relative weaknesses? A preliminary study. *The Journal of Psychology, 143*(5), 465–476. Retrieved from http://search.proquest.com/docview/213830202?accountid=14771.

Ryan, R. M., Huta, V., & Deci, E. L. (2008). Living well: A self-determination theory perspective on eudaimonia. *Journal of Happiness Studies, 9*(1), 139–170.

Ryan, R. M., Lynch, M. F., Vansteenkiste, M., & Deci, E. L. (2011). Motivation and autonomy in counseling, psychotherapy, and behavior change: A look at theory and practice 1ψ7. *The Counseling Psychologist, 39*(2), 193–260.

Ryff, C. D. (1989). Happiness is everything, or is it? Explorations on the meaning of psychological well–being. *Journal of Personality and Social Psychology, 57*, 1069–1081.

Ryff, C. D., Heller, A. S., Schaefer, S. M., van Reekum, C., & Davidson, R. J. (2016). Purposeful engagement, healthy aging, and the brain. *Current Behavioral Neuroscience Reports, 3*(4), 318–327.

Ryff, C. D., & Singer. B. (1996). Psychological well-being: Meaning, measurement, and implications for psychotherapy research. *Psychotherapy and Psychosomatics, 65*, 14–23.

Ryff, C. D., Singer, B. H., & Davidson, R. J. (2004). Making a life worth living: Neural correlates of well-being. *Psychological Science, 15*(6), 367–372.

Saleebey, D. (1997). The strengths approach to practice. In D. Saleebey (Ed.), *The strengths perspective in social work practice* (2nd ed., pp. 49–57). New York: Longman.

Sanjuán, P., Montalbetti, T., Pérez-García, A. M., Bermúdez, J., Arranz, H., & Castro, A. (2016). A randomised trial of a positive intervention to promote well-being in cardiac patients. *Applied Psychology: Health and Well-Being, 8*(1), 64–84.

Scheel, M. J., Davis, C. K., & Henderson, J. D. (2012). Therapist use of client strengths: A qualitative study of positive processes. *The Counseling Psychologist, 41*(3), 392–427. doi:10.1177/0011000012439427

Scheier, M. F., Carver, C. S., & Bridges, M. W. (1994). Distinguishing optimism from neuroticism (and trait anxiety, self-mastery, and self-esteem): A reevaluation of the Life Orientation Test. *Journal of Personality and Social Psychology, 67*, 1063–1078. doi:10.1037/0022-3514.67.6.1063

Schmid, K. L., Phelps, E., & Lerner, R. M. (2011). Constructing positive futures: Modeling the relationship between adolescents' hopeful future expectations and intentional self regulation in predicting positive youth development. *Journal of Adolescence, 34*(6), 1127.

Schnell, T. (2009). The Sources of Meaning and Meaning in Life Questionnaire (SoMe): Relations to demographics and well-being, *The Journal of Positive Psychology, 4,* 483–499.

Schotanus-Dijkstra, M., Drossaert, C. H., Pieterse, M. E., Walburg, J. A., & Bohlmeijer, E. T. (2015). Efficacy of a multicomponent positive psychology self-help intervention: Study protocol of a randomized controlled trial. *JMIR Research Protocols, 4*(3), e105. http://doi.org/10.2196/resprot.4162

Schrank, B., Bird, V., Rudnick, A., & Slade, M. (2012). Determinants, self-management strategies and interventions for hope in people with mental disorders: Systematic search and narrative review. *Social Science & Medicine, 74*(4), 554–564.

Schrank, B., Brownell, T., Jakaite, Z., Larkin, C., Pesola, F., Riches, S., . . . Slade, M. (2016). Evaluation of a positive psychotherapy group intervention for people with psychosis: Pilot randomised controlled trial. *Epidemiology and Psychiatric Sciences, 25*(3), 235–246. doi:10.1017/S2045796015000141

Schrank, B., Riches, S., Coggins, T., Rashid, T., Tylee, A., & Slade, M. (2014). WELLFOCUS PPT—modified positive psychotherapy to improve well-being: Study protocol for pilot randomised controlled. *Trial, 15*(1), 203.

Schrank, B., & Slade, M. (2007). Recovery in psychiatry. *Psychiatric Bulletin, 31,* 321–325.

Schrank, B., Stanghellini, G., & Slade, M. (2008). Hope in psychiatry: A review of the literature. *Acta Psychiatrica Scandinavica, 118*(6), 421–433.

Schreier, H. M. C., Schonert-Reichl, K. A., & Chen, E. (2013). Effect of volunteering on risk factors for cardiovascular disease in adolescents. *JAMA Pediatrics, 167*(4), 327. http://doi.org/10.1001/jamapediatrics.2013.1100

Schueller, S. (2010). Preferences for positive psychology exercises. *The Journal of Positive Psychology, 5,* 192–203.

Schueller, S. M., & Parks, A. C. (2012). Disseminating self-help: Positive psychology exercises in an online trial. *Journal of Medicine Internet Research 14*(3), e63. doi:10.2196/jmir.1850

Schueller, S. M., Kashdan, T. B., & Parks, A. C., (2014). Synthesizing positive psychological interventions: Suggestions for conducting and interpreting meta-analyses. *International Journal of Wellbeing, 4*(1), 91–98. doi:10.5502/ijw.v4i1.5

Schueller, S. M., & Seligman, M. E. P. (2010). Pursuit of pleasure, engagement, and meaning: Relationships to subjective and objective measures of well-being. *The Journal of Positive Psychology, 5*(4), 253–263. doi:10.1080/17439761003794130

Schwartz, B. (2004). *The paradox of choice: Why more is less* (1st ed.). New York: ECCO.

Schwartz, B., & Sharpe, K. E. (2010). *Practical wisdom: The right way to do the right thing.* New York: Riverhead Books.

Schwartz, B., Ward, A., Monterosso, J., Lyubomirsky, S., White, K., & Lehman, D. R. (2002). Maximizing versus satisficing: Happiness is a matter of choice. *Journal of Personality and Social Psychology, 83,* 1178–1197. doi:10.1037/0022-3514.83.5.1178

Secker, J., Membrey, H., Grove, B., & Seebohm P. (2002). Recovering from illness or recovering your life? Implications of clinical versus social models of recovery from mental health problems for employment support services. *Disability & Society, 17,* 403–418.

Sedikides, C., & Gregg, A. P. (2008). Self-enhancement: Food for thought. *Perspectives on Psychological Science, 3,* 102–116.

Segerstrom, S. C. (2007). Optimism and resources: Effects on each other and on health over 10 years. *Journal of Research in Personality, 41*(4), 772–786. http://doi.org/10.1016/j.jrp.2006.09.004

Seligman, M. E. P. (1991). *Learned optimism.* New York: Knopf.

Seligman, M. E. P. (1995). The effectiveness of psychotherapy: The Consumer Reports study. *American Psychologist, 50*(12), 965–974. doi:10.1037/0003-066X.50.12.965

Seligman, M. E. P. (2002a). *Authentic happiness: Using the new positive psychology to realize your potential for lasting fulfillment.* New York: Free Press.

Seligman, M. E. P. (2002b). Positive psychology, positive prevention, and positive therapy. In C. R. Snyder & S. J. Lopez (Eds.), *Handbook of positive psychology* (pp. 3–9). New York: Oxford University Press.

Seligman, M. E. P. (2006). Afterword: Breaking the 65 percent barrier. In M. C. I. S. Csikszentmihalyi (Ed.), *A life worth living: Contributions to positive psychology* (pp. 230–236). New York: Oxford University Press.

Seligman, M. E. P. (2012). *Flourish: A visionary new understanding of happiness and well-being.* New York: Simon & Schuster.

Seligman, M. E. P., & Csikszentmihalyi, M. (2000). Positive psychology: An introduction. *American Psychologist, 55*(1), 5–14. doi:10.1037/0003-066X.55.1.5

Seligman, M. E., Rashid, T., & Parks, A. C. (2006). Positive psychotherapy. *American Psychologist, 61*, 774–788. doi: 10.1037/0003-066X.61.8.774

Seligman, M. E., Steen, T. A., Park, N., & Peterson, C. (2005). Positive psychology progress: Empirical validation of interventions. *American Psychologist, 60*, 410–421. doi:10.1037/0003-066X.60.5.410

Shafer, A. B. (2006). Meta-analysis of the factor structures of four depression questionnaires: Beck, CES-D, Hamilton, and Zung. *Journal of Clinical Psychology, 62*, 123–146.

Sheldon, K. M., & Lyubomirsky, S. (2006). How to increase and sustain positive emotion: The effects of expressing gratitude and visualizing best possible selves. *The Journal of Positive Psychology, 1*(2), 73–82. doi:10.1080/17439760500510676

Sheldon, K. M., Ryan, R. M., Deci, E. L., & Kasser, T. (2004). The independent effects of goal contents and motives on well-being: It's both what you pursue and why you pursue it. *Personality and Social Psychology Bulletin, 30*, 475–486.

Sheridan, S. M., Warnes, E. D., Cowan, R. J., Schemm, A. V., & Clarke, B. L. (2004). Family-centered positive psychology: Focusing on strengths to build student success. *Psychology in the Schools, 41*(1), 7–17.

Siddique, J., Chung, J. Y., Brown, H. C., & Miranda, J. (2012). Comparative effectiveness of medication versus cognitive-behavioral therapy in a randomized controlled trial of low-income young minority women with depression. *Journal of Consulting and Clinical Psychology, 80*(6), 995–1006.

Simons, J. S., & Gaher, R. M. (2005). The Distress Tolerance Scale: Development and validation of a self-report measure. *Motivation and Emotion, 29*, 83–102. http://dx.doi.org/10.1007/s11031-005-7955-3

Sin, N. L., & Lyubomirsky, S. (2009). Enhancing well-being and alleviating depressive symptoms with positive psychology interventions: A practice-friendly meta-analysis. *Journal of Clinical Psychology, 65*, 467–487. doi:10.1002/jclp.20593

Sirgy, M. J., & Wu, J. (2009). The pleasant life, the engaged life, and the meaningful life: What about the balanced life? *Journal of Happiness Studies, 10*, 183–196.

Skaggs, B. G., & Barron, C. R. (2006). Searching for meaning in negative events: Concept analysis. *Journal of Advanced Nursing.* doi:10.1111/j.1365-2648.2006.03761.x

Slade, M. (2010). Mental illness and well-being: The central importance of positive psychology and recovery approaches. *BMC Health Services Research, 10*(26).

Smyth, J., & Pennebaker, J. (2008). Exploring the boundary conditions of expressive writing: In search of the right recipe. *British Journal of Health Psychology, 13*, 1–7.

Snyder, C. R. (1994). *The psychology of hope: You can get there from here.* New York: Free Press.

Snyder, C. R., Cheavens, J., & Michael, S. T. (2005). Hope theory: History and elaborated model. In J. A. Eliott (Ed.), *Interdisciplinary perspectives on hope* (pp. 101–118). New York: Nova Science.

Snyder, C. R., Rand, K., & Sigmon, D. (2002). Hope theory: A member of the positive psychology family. In C. R. Snyder & S. J. Lopez (Eds.), *Handbook of positive psychology* (pp. 257–276). New York: Oxford University Press.

Soosai-Nathan, L., Negri, L., & Delle Fave, A. (2013). Beyond pro-social behaviour: An exploration of altruism in two cultures. *Psychological Studies, 58*(2), 103–114.

Spanier, G. B. (1976). Measuring dyadic adjustment: New scales for assessing the quality of marriage and similar dyads. *Journal of Marriage and the Family, 38*, 15–28.

Spielberger, C. D., Gorsuch, R. L., Lushene, R., Vagg, P. R., & Jacobs, G. A. (1983). *Manual for the State-Trait Anxiety Inventory (Form Y).* Palo Alto, CA: Consulting Psychologists Press.

Steger, M. F. (2012). Experiencing meaning in life: Optimal functioning at the nexus of spirituality, psychopathology, and well-being. In P. T. P. Wong & P. S. Fry (Eds.), *The human quest for meaning* (2nd ed, pp. 165–184). New York: Routledge.

Steger, M. F., Kawabata, Y., Shimai, S., & Otake, K. (2008). The meaningful life in Japan and the United States: Levels and correlates of meaning in life. *Journal of Research in Personality, 42*(3), 660–678. doi:10.1016/j.jrp.2007.09.003

Steger, M. F., & Shin, J. Y. (2010). The relevance of the Meaning in Life Questionnaire to therapeutic practice: A look at the initial evidence. *International Forum for Logotherapy, 33,* 95–104.

Stewart, T., & Suldo, S. (2011). Relationships between social support sources and early adolescents' mental health: The moderating effect of student achievement level. *Psychology in the Schools, 48*(10), 1016–1033. doi:10.1002/pits.20607

Stillman, T. F., & Baumeister, R. F. (2009). Uncertainty, belongingness, and four needs for meaning. *Psychological Inquiry, 20,* 249–251.

Stoner, C. R., Orrell, M., & Spector, A. (2015). Review of positive psychology outcome measures for chronic illness, traumatic brain injury and older adults: Adaptability in dementia? *Dementia and Geriatric Cognitive Disorders, 40*(5–6), 340–357.

Substance Abuse and Mental Health Services Administration. (2015). Evidence-based practices. Retrieved from http://store.samhsa.gov/facet/Professional-Research-Topics/term/Evidence-Based-Practices?narrowToAdd=For-Professionals&pageNumber=1 on November 27, 2015.

Suldo, S. M., & Shaffer, E. J. (2008). Looking beyond psychopathology: The dual-factor model of mental health in youth. *School Psychology Review, 37*(1), 52–68.

Szasz, T. S. (1961). *The myth of mental illness: Foundations of a theory of personal conduct.* New York: Hoeber.

Tabassum, F., Mohan, J., & Smith, P. (2016). Association of volunteering with mental well-being: A lifecourse analysis of a national population-based longitudinal study in the UK. *BMJ Open, 6*(8), e011327.

Tedeschi, R. G., & Calhoun, L. G. (1996). The posttraumatic growth inventory: Measuring the positive legacy of trauma. *Journal of Traumatic Stress, 9*(3), 455–472.

Tennant, R., Hiller, L., Fishwick, R., Platt, S., Joseph, S., Weich, S., . . . Stewart-Brown, S. (2007). The Warwick-Edinburgh Mental Well-being Scale (WEMWBS): Development and UK validation. *Health and Quality of Life Outcomes, 5*(1), 63. https://doi.org/10.1186/1477-7525-5-63

Terrill, A., Einerson, J., Reblin, M., MacKenzie, J., Cardell, B., Berg, C., . . . Richards, L. (2016). Promoting resilience in couples after stroke: Testing feasibility of a dyadic positive psychology-based intervention. *Archives of Physical Medicine and Rehabilitation, 97*(10), e62–e63. https://doi.org/http://dx.doi.org/10.1016/j.apmr.2016.08.190

Toepfer, S., & Walker, K. (2009). Letters of gratitude: Improving well-being through expressive writing. *Journal of Writing Research, 1*(3), 181–198. http://dx.doi.org/10.17239/jowr-2009.01.03.1

Tong, E. M. W. (2014). Differentiation of 13 positive emotions by appraisals. *Cognition & Emotion, 29,* 1–20. doi:10.1080/02699931.2014.922056

Toussaint, L., & Webb, J. R. (2005). Theoretical and empirical connections between forgiveness, mental health and well-being. In E. L. Worthington (Ed.), *Handbook of forgiveness* (pp. 349–362). New York: Routledge.

Trampe, D., Quoidbach, J., & Taquet, M. (2015). Emotions in everyday life. *PLoS One, 10*(12), e0145450.

Trompetter, H. R., de Kleine, E., & Bohlmeijer, E. T. (2017). Why does positive mental health buffer against psychopathology? An exploratory study on self-compassion as a resilience mechanism and adaptive emotion regulation strategy. *Cognitive Therapy and Research, 41*(3), 459–468.

Tsang, J. (2006). Gratitude and prosocial behavior: An experimental test of gratitude. *Cognition and Emotion, 20,* 138–148.

Uliaszek, A. A., Rashid, T., Williams, G. E., & Gulamani, T. (2016). Group therapy for university students: A randomized control trial of dialectical behavior therapy and positive psychotherapy. *Behaviour Research and Therapy, 77,* 78–85. http://dx.doi.org/10.1016/j.brat.2015.12.003

Undurraga, J., & Baldessarini, R. J. (2017). Tricyclic and selective serotonin-reuptake-inhibitor antidepressants compared with placebo in randomized trials for acute major depression. *Journal of Psychopharmacology, 31*(12), 1624–1625. doi:10.1177/0269881117731294

Van Boven, L., & Gilovich, T. (2003). To do or to have? That is the question. *Journal of Personality and Social Psychology, 85,* 1193–1202. doi:10.1037/0022-3514.85.6.1193

Van Dillen, L. F., Koole, S. L., Van Dillen, L. F., & Koole, S. L. (2007). Clearing the mind: A working memory model of distraction from negative mood. *Emotion*, 7(4), 715–723.

Van Tongeren, D. R., Burnette, J. L., O'Boyle, E., Worthington, E. L., & Forsyth, D. R. (2014). A meta-analysis of intergroup forgiveness. *The Journal of Positive Psychology*, 9(1), 81–95. doi:10.1080/ 17439760.2013.844268

Vandenberghe, L., & Silvestre, R. L. S. (2013). Therapists' positive emotions in-session: Why they happen and what they are good for. *Counselling and Psychotherapy Research*, April, 1–9. http://doi.org/10.1080/14733145.2013.790455

Vázquez, C. (2015). Beyond resilience: Positive mental health and the nature of cognitive processes involved in positive appraisals. *The Behavioral and Brain Sciences*, 38, e125.

Vazsonyi, A. T., & Belliston, L. M. (2006). The cultural and developmental significance of parenting processes in adolescent anxiety and depression symptoms. *Journal of Youth and Adolescence*, 35(4), 491–505.

Vella-Brodrick, D. A., Park, N., & Peterson, C. (2009). Three ways to be happy: Pleasure, engagement, and meaning: Findings from Australian and U.S. samples. *Social Indicators Research*, 90, 165–179.

Vertilo, V., & Gibson, J. M. (2014). Influence of character strengths on mental health stigma. *The Journal of Positive Psychology*, 9(3), 266–275. doi:10.1080/17439760.2014.891245

Visser, P. L., Loess, P., Jeglic, E. L., & Hirsch, J. K. (2013). Hope as a moderator of negative life events and depressive symptoms in a diverse sample. *Stress and Health*, 29(1), 82–88. doi:10.1002/smi.2433

Wade, N., Worthington, E., & Haake, S. (2009). Comparison of explicit forgiveness interventions with an alternative treatment: A randomized clinical trial. *Journal of Counseling & Development*, 87, 143–151.

Wallace, J. E. (2013). Social relationships, well-being, and career commitment: Exploring cross-domain effects of social relationships. *Canadian Review of Sociology/Revue Canadienne De Sociologie*, 50(2), 135–153.

Walsh, S., Cassidy, M., & Priebe, S. (2017). The application of positive psychotherapy in mental health care: A systematic review. *Journal of Clinical Psychology*, 73(6), 638–651. http://doi.org/10.1002/jclp.22368

Wammerl, M., Jaunig, J., Maierunteregger, T., & Streit, P. (2015, June). *The development of a German Version of the Positive Psychotherapy Inventory Überschrift (PPTI) and the PERMA-Profiler.* Paper presented at the World Congress of International Positive Psychology Association, Orlando, FL.

Wampold, B. E. (2001). *The great psychotherapy debate: Models, methods, and findings.* Mahwah, NJ: Lawrence Erlbaum.

Wampold, B. E. (2007). Psychotherapy: The humanistic (and effective) treatment. *American Psychologist*, 62, 857–873. doi:10.1037/0003-066X.62.8.857

Watkins, C. E. (2010). The hope, promise, and possibility of psychotherapy. *Journal of Contemporary Psychotherapy*, 40, 195–201. doi:10.1007/s10879-010-9149-x

Watkins, P. C., Cruz, L., Holben, H., & Kolts, R. L. (2008). Taking care of business? Grateful processing of unpleasant memories. *The Journal of Positive Psychology*, 3, 87–99.

Watkins, P. C., Grimm, D. L., & Kolts, R. (2004). Counting your blessings: Positive memories among grateful persons. *Current Psychology*, 23, 52–67.

Weber, M. (2002). *The Protestant ethic and the spirit of capitalism.* New York: Penguin. (Original work published 1905)

Weiten, W. (2006). A very critical look at the self-help movement; A review of SHAM: How the self help movement made America helpless. *Psycritiques*, 51, 2.

Wilson, T. D. (2009). Know thyself. *Perspectives on Psychological Science*, 4(4), 384–389. http://dx.doi.org/10.1111/j.1745-6924.2009.01143.x

Wilson, T. D., & Gilbert, D. T. (2003). Affective forecasting. In M. P. Zanna (Ed.), *Advances in experimental social psychology* (Vol. 35, pp. 345–411). San Diego, CA: Academic Press.

Winslow, C. J., Kaplan, S. A., Bradley-Geist, J., Lindsey, A. P., Ahmad, A. S., & Hargrove, A. K. (2016). An examination of two positive organizational interventions: For whom do these interventions work? *Journal of Occupational Health Psychology*, 22(2), 129.

Wong, Y. J., Owen, J., Gabana, N. T., Brown, J. W., Mcinnis, S., Toth, P., & Gilman, L. (2018). Does gratitude writing improve the mental health of psychotherapy clients? Evidence from a randomized controlled trial. *Psychotherapy Research, 28*(2), 192–202. http://doi.org/10.1080/10503307.2016.1169332

Wood, A. M., Froh, J. J., & Geraghty, A. W. A. (2010). Gratitude and well-being: A review and theoretical integration. *Clinical Psychology Review, 30*(7), 890–905. doi:10.1016/j.cpr.2010.03.005

Wood, A. M., & Johnson, J. (Eds.). (2016). *The Wiley handbook of positive clinical psychology.* Chichester, UK: John Wiley. http://doi.org/10.1002/9781118468197

Wood, A. M., & Joseph, S. (2010). The absence of positive psychological (eudemonic) well-being as a risk factor for depression: A ten year cohort study. *Journal of Affective Disorders, 122*(3), 213–217. doi:10.1016/j.jad.2009.06.032

Wood, A. M., Joseph, S., & Linley, P. (2007). Coping style as a psychological resource of grateful people. *Journal of Social and Clinical Psychology, 26*(9). 1076–1093.

Wood, A. M., Joseph, S., Lloyd, J., & Atkins, S. (2009). Gratitude influences sleep through the mechanism of pre-sleep cognitions. *Journal of Psychosomatic Research, 66*(1), 43–48. doi:10.1016/j.jpsychores.2008.09.002

Wood, A. M., Linley, P. A., Maltby, J., Kashdan, T. B., & Hurling, R. (2011). Using personal and psychological strengths leads to increases in well-being over time: A longitudinal study and the development of the Strengths Use Questionnaire. *Personality and Individual Differences, 50*(1), 15–19. doi:10 .1016/j.paid.2010.08.004

Wood, A. M., Maltby, J., Gillett, R., Linley, P. A., & Joseph, S. (2008). The role of gratitude in the development of social support, stress, and depression: Two longitudinal studies. *Journal of Research in Personality, 42*, 854–871.

Wood, A. M., & Tarrier, N. (2010). Positive clinical psychology: A new vision and strategy for integrated research and practice. *Clinical Psychology Review, 30*(7), 819–829. doi:10.1016/j.cpr.2010.06.003

Wood, A. M., Taylor, P. T., & Joseph, S. (2010). Does the CES-D measure a continuum from depression to happiness? Comparing substantive and artifactual models. *Psychiatry Research, 177*, 120–123.

Worthington, E. L. (2006). *Forgiveness and reconciliation: Theory and application.* New York: Routledge.

Worthington, E. L., & Drinkard, D. T. (2000). Promoting reconciliation through psychoeducational and therapeutic interventions. *Journal of Marital and Family Therapy, 26*, 93–101.

Worthington, E. L., Hook, J. N., Davis, D. E., & McDaniel, M. A. (2011). Religion and spirituality. *Journal of Clinical Psychology, 67*(2), 204–214. doi:10.1002/jclp.20760

Worthington, E. L. Jr., & Wade, N.G. (1999). The psychology of unforgiveness and forgiveness and implications for clinical practice. *Journal of Social & Clinical Psychology, 18*, 385–418.

Worthington, E. L., Witvliet, C. V. O., Pietrini, P., & Miller, A. J. (2007). Forgiveness, health, and well-being: A review of evidence for emotional versus decisional forgiveness, dispositional forgivingness, and reduced unforgiveness. *Journal of Behavioral Medicine, 30*(4), 291–302. https://doi.org/10.1007/s10865-007-9105-8

Worthington, E. L. Jr. (Ed.). (2005). *Handbook of forgiveness.* New York: Brunner-Routledge.

Wright, B. A., & Lopez, S. J. (2009). Widening the diagnostic focus: A case for including human strengths and environmental resources. In S. J. Lopez & C. R. Snyder (Eds.), *The handbook of positive psychology* (pp. 71–87). New York: Oxford University Press. doi:10.1093/oxfordhb/9780195187243.013.0008

Wrzesniewski, A., McCauley, C., Rozin, P., & Schwartz, B. (1997). Jobs, careers, and callings: People's relations to their work. *Journal of Research in Personality, 31*, 21–33.

Yalom, I. D. (1980). *Existential psychotherapy.* New York: Basic Books.

Young, K. C., Kashdan, T. B., & Macatee, R. (2015). Strength balance and implicit strength measurement: New considerations for research on strengths of character. *The Journal of Positive Psychology, 10*(1), 17–24. doi:10.1080/17439760.2014.920406

Zalaquett, C. P., Fuerth, K. M., Stein, C., Ivey, A. E., & Ivey, M. B. (2008). Reframing the DSM-IV-TR from a multicultural/social justice perspective. *Journal of Counseling & Development, 86*, 364–371. doi:10.1002/j.1556-6678.2008.tb00521.x

Zung, W. W. K. (1965). A self-rating depression scale. *Archives of General Psychiatry, 12*, 63–70.

INDEX

Tables, figures, boxes, and worksheets are indicated by an italic *t, f, b,* and *w* following the page number.

P

panic disorder, 28*t*, 41, 57
paranoid personality disorder, 30*t*, 57
partner responsiveness, 220
Pasha-Zidi, N., 14, 15*t*, 17
Pennebaker, James, 125, 186
PERMA, 17–20, 56, 69
    accomplishment, 17*t*, 19–20, 262
    elements, 262–263
    engagement, 17*t*, 18–19, 72, 262
    meaning, 4–5, 17*t*, 19, 56, 263
    positive emotions, 17–18, 17*t*, 53–54, 262
    relationships, 17*t*, 19, 263
persistence, 282–284, 322*t*
personality disorders, 30*t*–32*t*
    antisocial personality disorder, 32*t*
    avoidant personality disorder, 31*t*–32*t*
    borderline personality disorder, 30*t*, 43
    dependent personality disorder, 32*t*
    histrionic personality disorder, 31*t*
    narcissistic personality disorder, 30*t*–31*t*
    obsessive-compulsive personality disorder,
        28*t*, 31*t*, 41
    paranoid personality disorder, 30*t*, 57
person-intervention fit, 56–57
perspective, 277–279, 322*t*
Peseschkian, Nosrat, 44n1
pessimism, 182
Peterson, C., 24, 33, 227, 267
phobia
    agoraphobia, 28*t*
    social, 28*t*
    specific, 28*t*
placebo effect, depression, 6–7
Planned Savoring Activity, 200
Plato, 8
Positive Appraisal, 45*t*, 49–50,
    52*b*, 54–55
    Open and Closed Memories, 140, 141*w*
Positive Communication, 218–229
    core concepts: Positive, 218–220, 219*b*
    cultural considerations, 227–228
    fit & flexibility, 226–227
    Four Ways of Responding to a Good Event
        Shared by a Loved One, 219*b*
    homework practice: *Identify Your Partner's
        Strengths,* 222, 223*w*
    in-session practice: *Active Constructive
        Responding,* 220, 221*w*
    maintenance, 228
    reflection & discussion, 222, 223
    resources, 229
positive emotions, 17–18, 17*t*, 262
    cultivation, 53–54
    motivation, 74

Positive Icons at the Movies (Niemiec &
    Wedding), 42
Positive Imagery, 255–256
Positive Introduction, 45*t*, 48, 52, 55, 56, 122
    Meaning and Purpose, 239, 240*b*
Positive Introduction and *Gratitude
    Journal,* 75–88
    clinician note, 81*b*
    core concepts: Positive, 75–76, 81
    cultural considerations, 80, 86
    fit & flexibility, 80, 85–86
    in-session practice: *Gratitude Journal,* 81–82
    in-session practice: *Positive Introduction,* 75,
        76, 77*w*
    maintenance, 81, 86–87
    reflection & discussion, 78, 84
    resources, 88
    vignettes, 78–80, 84–85
Positive Legacy, 46*t*, 52, 55, 243, 244*w*
    Meaning and Purpose, 243, 244*w*
positive meaning-making, 42
positive psychological interventions, 8–17
    clinical settings, 9–14, 10*t*–13*t*
    effectiveness and relevance, 14, 15*t*–16*t*
    empirically validated, 9
    historical view, 8–9
    PERMA, 17–20, 17*t* (*see also* PERMA)
    Positive Psychotherapy, 9–17
    reviews, 14–17, 15*t*–16*t*
    theoretical framework and applied
        implications, 9
    theoretical underpinnings, 14
positive psychology, 3, 9
positive psychotherapy, 44n1
Positive Psychotherapy (PPT). *See also specific
    sessions; specific topics*
    65% barrier, 4, 6–7
    caveats, conducting, 57–58
    change mechanisms, 53–57, 53*f* (*see also*
        change mechanisms)
    clinical application, ix–x
    on clinician, attenuating impact, 6
    definition and overview, 3–4
    end, reaching, 238
    goal, 4
    growth capacity, inherent, 20
    medical model, broadening, 5–6
    navigating, 206
    need, 4–6
    orientation, 69–71
    origins and development, 9
    outcome, 6, 58–59, 60*t*–64*t*, 64–65
    PERMA (theory of well-being), 17–20, 17*t*
    phases, 44
    positives focus, 3